Ranking and Spicer's
Company Law

Ranking and Spicer's Company Law

Thirteenth Edition

JM Gullick, MA, ACIS
Solicitor

London
Butterworths
1987

United Kingdom	Butterworth & Co (Publishers) Ltd, 88 Kingsway, LONDON WC2B 6AB and 61A North Castle Street, EDINBURGH EH2 3LJ
Australia	Butterworths Pty Ltd, SYDNEY, MELBOURNE, BRISBANE, ADELAIDE, PERTH, CANBERRA and HOBART
Canada	Butterworths. A division of Reed Inc., TORONTO and VANCOUVER
New Zealand	Butterworths of New Zealand Ltd, WELLINGTON and AUCKLAND
Singapore	Butterworth & Co (Asia) Pte Ltd, SINGAPORE
South Africa	Butterworth Publishers (Pty) Ltd, DURBAN and PRETORIA
USA	Butterworth Legal Publishers, ST PAUL, Minnesota, SEATTLE, Washington, BOSTON, Massachusetts, AUSTIN, Texas and D & S Publishers, CLEARWATER, Florida

British Library of Cataloguing in Publication Data

Ranking, D.F. de l'Haste
  Ranking & Spicer's company law.—3rd ed.
  1. Corporation law—Great Britain
  I. Title II. Spicer, E.E. III. Gullick, J.M.
  344.106'66   KD2079
ISBN 0 406 67890 1

Typeset by Phoenix Photosetting, Chatham, Kent
Printed and bound in Great Britain by
Mackays of Chatham Ltd, Kent

Preface to Thirteenth Edition

This revised edition brings the text into line with company law as it stands at the end of 1986, following the considerable changes made by the Insolvency Act 1986. Apart from changes of substance in insolvency procedure made in 1985 the Insolvency Act 1986 also consolidates company law, previously found in the Companies Act 1985, on receivership and liquidation.

The inexorable expansion of company law and its continuing development through the medium of case law has led to a rewriting of large parts of other chapters of the book, apart from those which deal with insolvency.

The process of change continues. Chapters 16 and 17 of this book reflect technical changes in connection with insider dealing and take-over bids, enacted by the Financial Services Act 1986. The same Act also contains basic provisions for a wholesale change in the law on the offer of company securities to investors. In place of existing prospectus law, as described in Chapter 6, the Stock Exchange will have legal powers of regulation of documents publicising new listed securities. For unlisted securities, of public or private companies, there will be control through a modified prospectus system. As an incidental consequence, Pt III and other related sections of the Companies Act 1986, and also The Stock Exchange (Listing) Regulations 1984 will be repealed. The new system will apply to the offer of shares for shares in take-over bids and so the Prevention of Fraud (Investments) Act 1958 will be repealed.

The new regime cannot, however, be described in detail at this stage since much of it is yet to appear in the form of listing and prospectus regulations to be made under the 1986 Act, after full discussion with the many financial interests in the City which it will affect. It will be some time before it is all in place and in operation. We are also led to expect legislation to abolish the ultra vires doctrine, whose passing will be unlamented by practitioners, students and law teachers – though not perhaps by examiners for whom it has been such a fertile source of material for questions. There is also the prospect of changes in procedure to remove anomalies in the registration of company charges, as described in Chapter 9. Finally, the cornucopia of EC Directives will continue to discharge its abundance into the English legislative process. In writing a textbook at any moment in time one must deal with the law we have and defer the still uncertain remainder for a later edition.

As with previous editions, the aim of this book is to provide an exposition of company law to meet the needs both of the student, in preparing for a professional examination, and of the practitioner or company administrator, who is obliged to have conveniently at hand on his office bookshelf, a book of moderate length for reference.

There is no inherent conflict in addressing oneself both to the student and to the professional or business man. The gateway to the understanding and use of company law is a grasp of the principles, with their many exceptions, applications and procedures, which must be made intelligible and coherent. Yet company law, more than most branches of the law, exists in a practical context. It is what it is because over a century or so, the registered company has become the key element of business life. It has been shaped in response to the needs of commerce, as company lawyers (of whom I was one) well understand. I hope that in writing this book I shall have provided something useful to those who may read it.

November 1986   J M Gullick

Contents

Table of statutes

xviii   *Table of statutes*

Table of cases

List of abbreviations

BNA	Business Names Act 1985
CDDA	Company Directors Disqualification Act 1986
CA	Companies Act (of the year indicated)
Cohen Report	Report of the Committee on Company Law Amendment 1945 (Cmd 6659)
Cork Report	Insolvency Law and Practice – Report of the Review Committee 1982 (Cmnd 8558)
CSIDA	Company Securities (Insider Dealing) Act 1985
DTI	Department of Trade and Industry
FA	Finance Act (of the year indicated)
FSA	Financial Services Act 1986
IA	Insolvency Act 1986
Jenkins Report	Report of the Company Law Committee 1962 (Cmnd 1749)
Table A	Table A (Model articles) of The Companies (Tables A to F) Regulations 1985, SI 1985/805

(*Note*: where a section is cited without an abbreviated statute title, it is a section of the CA 1985)

Chapter 1

Nature and types of company

A THE NATURE OF A COMPANY

1.1 The development of company law

Modern company law has its origins in the mid-19th century, when the Limited Liability Act 1855 and the Joint Stock Companies Act 1856 introduced a simpler method of incorporating corporate bodies for commercial purposes, with the possibility of limited liability of members for the company's debts.

Previously it had been possible, and it still is, to form a corporate body by obtaining a Royal Charter (for a 'chartered company') or by promoting a private Act of Parliament to form a 'statutory company'. These procedures, and corporate bodies of these types, still exist for appropriate purposes. But their inherent drawbacks are heavy expense and long delay. By contrast a company may be formed by registration under the Companies Act speedily and at comparatively low cost.

The first Companies Act, the Companies Act 1862, has been followed, and replaced, by a sequence of statutes passed to provide a framework of company law. The principal statute now in force is the Companies Act 1985, which replaced the much amended Companies Act 1948 and the amending statutes. In this book it is also necessary to refer frequently to the Insolvency Act 1986, which repealed parts of the 1985 Act dealing with receivership and liquidation, and consolidated them with new provisions on company insolvency introduced by the Insolvency Act 1985 (which has also been replaced by the similarly named 1986 Act).

In addition it is necessary to refer in the appropriate contexts to the Companies Securities (Insider Dealing) Act 1985, the Business Names Act 1985, the Company Directors Disqualification Act 1986, and other less important statutes containing rules affecting companies. The Financial Services Act 1986, when in full operation, will also modify company law in certain respects.

If a section number is cited in this book without any prefix, it denotes a section of the Companies Act 1985 (and any reference to 'the Companies Act', unless otherwise stated, is a reference to the 1985 Act). Other citations have identifying prefixes. The purpose of these citations is to enable the reader to find the statutory authority for the statement made at that point. Case law is an important element of company law, since judicial decisions both supplement the statutes and establish their meaning. Case summaries are therefore an integral part of the text.

Since the UK became a member of the European Community ('EC') at the beginning of 1973, much of the changes made in company law have been in compliance with EC directives.

The sheer bulk of company law makes it difficult to master. Unfortunately the trend towards still more detailed regulation by statutes seems likely to continue unabated.

1.2 The nature of a company

A company is one type of corporation or corporate body. It is a 'corporation aggregate', ie it must have a plurality of members; the statutory minimum is now two for all companies: s 1(1). In this it differs from a 'corporation sole' which is usually a public office held at any one time by a single individual but constituting a legal entity distinct from the office-holder. In this book 'company' means (unless otherwise stated) a company incorporated by registration under the Companies Acts of Great Britain. A registered company is thus distinguished from other bodies corporate formed either by grant of Royal Charter from the Crown under its prerogative powers or formed as statutory corporations by special statute. The Institute of Chartered Accountants in England and Wales is an example of a chartered corporation; many local authorities are statutory corporations. The word 'company' is also used (but not in this book) to denote an unincorporated association such as a partnership; a firm may, for example, be called 'Smith and Company'. The word 'firm' is properly applicable only to unincorporated bodies such as partnerships but in newspapers and elsewhere it is sometimes applied colloquially to corporations. The word 'limited' in the name of a business enterprise such as a company, has a particular legal meaning (1.3(a) below) and is reserved to companies registered with limited liability: s 34.

The essential characteristic of a registered company, from which many principles of company law are derived, is that 'the company is at law a different person from the subscribers to the memorandum' (ie from the original members and also their successors). This proposition, laid down in the House of Lords in *Salomon's Case* in 1897, had been rejected in the lower courts. The facts and issues of this celebrated case are as follows. Salomon had traded profitably on his own account for many years carrying on the business of a leather merchant and wholesale boot manufacturer. He formed a company with an authorised share capital of £40,000 in £1 shares. At the outset the minimum membership (then seven members) was provided by Salomon, his wife, daughter and four sons, each of whom signed the memorandum as a subscriber for one share. But his six relatives held their shares as nominees for Salomon who was thus the beneficial owner of all seven shares. He then sold his business to the company at a rather optimistic price which was satisfied partly in cash, partly by the issue to Salomon of 20,000 shares and finally by the issue to him of a debenture for the amount of £10,000 secured by a charge on the company's assets. Salomon was thus the sole proprietor of his company and also, by reason of the debenture, a creditor with a priority claim to its assets. The company became insolvent and was wound up a year later. There was no question of fraud; it failed because it lost valuable contracts. If the secured debenture, which Salomon had meanwhile transferred to Broderip for £5,000 (which Salomon lent to the company), was valid then Broderip as successor to Salomon could claim the remaining assets and nothing would be left for the other creditors. The latter, therefore, challenged the validity of the debenture arguing in effect that a man cannot be a debtor to himself.

The High Court held that on these facts the company was a mere agent of Salomon and entitled to an indemnity which would offset any claim against it by him, as its creditor. The Court of Appeal decided in favour of the unsecured creditors on other grounds, ie that the company had not been properly incorporated since it did not have seven members 'independent and unconnected' with each other. The House of Lords overruled both arguments and held that the company was properly incorporated and was a person separate from Salomon with the result that his claim to be a secured creditor of his own company was valid: *Salomon v Salomon & Co* [1897] AC 22.

In a more recent case it has been held that a company owned and managed by one man can be liable to him as his employer under a contract of service.

Lee owned all the shares but one of his company and was its governing director. In the course of its business of aerial crop spraying, etc, Lee was killed in a flying accident while he himself was acting as pilot. It was held that his widow was entitled to recover compensation from the company for his estate: *Lee v Lee's Air Farming Ltd* [1960] 3 All ER 420.

1.3 The characteristics of a company

The status of a company as a person separate from its members is the basis of its main characteristics, ie:

(a) *Limited liability*. A company is always liable without limit for its debts. If, however, it is a company formed with liability of members limited by shares or by guarantee their obligation to contribute to its assets available to meet its debts is limited (1.19 and 1.20 below): IA s 74(2). Where liability is thus limited this fact is stated in the memorandum. A company may, however, also be formed with unlimited liability of members (1.21).

(b) *Perpetual succession*. Changes of membership of a company in no way affect its continued existence as a separate person.

(c) *Transferable shares*. The proprietary interest (and any liability) of a member in a company which has a share capital (as most companies do) is measured in units called 'shares' (or less often as units of 'stock'). 'Member' and 'shareholder' are interchangeable terms in such cases. Shares are a form of intangible property which is transferable. The transfer must be in writing. The right of transfer may be restricted by the articles: ss 182–183.

(d) *Memorandum and articles*. As an abstract person the company needs to have a written constitution both to define what the company is, eg its name, objects and share capital, and to regulate the internal and external conduct of the company's affairs. For historical reasons there are two documents, ie the memorandum of association (in this book called 'the memorandum') and the articles of association ('the articles'). A company limited by shares may adopt all or part of statutory model articles '(Table A)' in lieu of special articles of its own. The memorandum and articles are open to public inspection at the registry and so any person dealing with a company is deemed to know (ie has 'constructive notice' of) their contents except where that rule is excluded by statute, ie by s 35 (Chapter 3: 3.17).

(e) *Directors and secretary*. A company cannot manage itself and so it must have at least one, in the case of a public company at least two, directors appointed under the articles, usually by the members: s 282. It must also have a secretary: s 283. The directors may also be members. But the members as such have no inherent powers as managers nor as agents; ultimate control, however, rests with the members voting at general meetings. These are the 'organs' of the company, ie the board of directors and the general meeting.

(f) *Capital.* The shares issued to members of a limited company must have a fixed nominal ('par') value: s 2(5). When the shares are issued the company must obtain in exchange for them consideration in money or money's worth at least equal to the par value. The capital subscribed for shares may not (except in the case of an unlimited company) be returned to members as dividend. There are various procedures (explained in Chapter 5 and elsewhere) by which a limited company may lawfully return capital to its members. In effect a limited company must retain its capital as a fund from which to pay its debts. The assets in which the capital is invested are the property of the company in which its members as proprietors of the company have no insurable interest.

The company's principal asset was felled timber lying on land owned by M who also owned the entire issued share capital of the company. He insured the timber in his own name. It was destroyed by fire. The insurers repudiated liability on the grounds that he had no insurable interest in the property insured since the company, not M, was its owner: *Macaura v Northern Assurance Co Ltd* [1925] AC 619.

In all these respects a company differs from a partnership. Partners have unlimited liability for the firm's debts (except in the rare case of limited partners of a registered limited partnership). A change among the partners terminates the partnership; even if they agree that the firm shall nonetheless continue it is no longer the original firm. No partner can assign his interest so as to make his assignee a partner in his place unless the other partners agree. A partnership may exist without any written agreement. The partners manage the business as proprietors and make contracts as agents of the firm. The assets of the firm are owned directly by them and they may by mutual agreement withdraw capital without formality.

In deciding whether to carry on business as a partnership or through a company, tax considerations are often very important factors. Limited liability is an obvious advantage of a limited company. But if a company has only a small capital in relation to its commitments the creditors often insist that the directors and/or members shall give up limited liability by becoming personal guarantors of the company's debts. Unlike a partnership a company can borrow on the security of a floating charge covering current as well as fixed assets. The number of members of a company (now even a private company) is not restricted by a maximum. But the normal maximum number of partners for a commercial partnership is 20: s 716. In the professions there is often no choice as a partnership is the only permitted form of association: in this case, however, the limit on numbers of partners is lifted. A company (unless unlimited) must always deliver annual accounts to the registrar for filing and also an annual return which is a summary of current information. Companies are thus subject to disclosure requirements about their affairs and to much detailed regulation. A partnership, however, is free of these requirements.

1.4 Lifting the veil of incorporation

The distinction between a company and its members is called 'the veil of incorporation'. It is an inappropriate term since the identity of the members can be discovered by exercising the right, given to the public, of inspecting the register of members: s 356. But there are exceptions to the general rule which are collectively referred to as 'lifting the veil of incorporation'. The effect of lifting the veil is either to render other persons, usually members or directors, jointly liable with the company for its debts or to identify them with the company as a single person. There is no single reason for the various exceptions described below (1.5 to 1.13). Their general purpose, however, is to prevent abuses or to recognise the reality of a particular situation.

1.5 Minimum membership

Every company must have at least two members: s 1(1). If a member dies he ceases to be a member; he might also in his lifetime transfer his shares to the only other existing member. Thus the number of members can be reduced to one. If the following conditions are met, ie:

(a) the number of members falls to one; and
(b) the company carries on business in that situation for a period of at least six months; and
(c) the one remaining member becomes aware of the situation

then he becomes jointly and severally liable with the company for its debts contracted after the six months period and after he becomes aware of being the sole member: s 24.

The member's liability is confined to 'debts' and arguably (there is no case on the point) he is not liable for unliquidated claims such as damages for breach of contract. The company is still jointly and severally liable with him and if he has to pay its debts he is entitled to claim contribution from the company.

In practice the surviving member is usually able within the first six months 'no liability' period to arrange that someone else shall become the second member. If all else fails he can transfer one of his own shares to a nominee. The personal representatives of a deceased member who have obtained a grant of representation to his estate may transfer his shares to someone else (or be registered as holders themselves) but are not members unless registered as such: s 183(3). When one company is the wholly-owned subsidiary of another it is usual to register one share of the subsidiary in the name of a nominee of the holding company as sole or as joint holder with the latter.

1.6 Fraudulent or wrongful trading

If it appears to the court that the business of a company then in liquidation has been carried on in such a manner as to defraud its creditors or even to cause them avoidable loss by reason of the negligence or incompetence of the directors, the court may order that the directors (or other persons at fault) shall contribute to the assets of the company as a penalty for fraudulent or wrongful trading. This is a deterrent against continuing to carry on the business of the company when it no longer has reasonable prospects of paying its debts: IA ss 213–14. It is a form of lifting the veil of incorporation by imposing on those who manage a company's business dishonestly or irresponsibly liability for its debts. However, there are a number of detailed rules to be considered (Chapter 20: 20.18–19).

1.7 Failure to use the correct company name

The name of a company is an essential means of identifying it and distinguishing it from others. Every company (with one minor excepted category – Chapter 3: 3.2) is required by law to display its name outside every place of business, on its seal, and on its business letters and other documents mentioned below (Chapter 3: 3.7). To enforce this rule and discourage misleading inaccuracy in the use of the company name it is provided that if the company seal is used or if a letter, notice, bill of exchange, order for goods or money, etc, is issued on behalf of a company and it does not bear the correct name of the company, the officer or agent who took or authorised this action (even if in authorising another person he intended him to use the correct name) becomes liable to the holder of the document bearing an incorrect name *unless* the company makes due payment on it. He is also liable to a fine: s 349.

The most obvious case of liability is where the word 'limited' is omitted from the name of a limited company.

The secretary accepted a bill drawn on the company. The word 'limited' had been omitted from the name on the bill. The secretary was personally liable on the bill: *Penrose v Martyr* (1858) EB & E 499.

If, however, the error in the name was introduced by the creditor who claims on the document, he cannot rely on his own mistake to make another person liable.

The drawer of the bill made the error, ie 'M' instead of 'Michael' in full (see the title of the case below). The director of the drawee company who accepted the bill on its behalf was not personally liable since he had not introduced the error into the bill: *Durham Fancy Goods Ltd v Michael Jackson (Fancy Goods) Ltd* [1968] 2 All ER 987.

The word 'limited' may be abbreviated to 'Ltd' and the words 'public limited company' to 'plc' (or 'PLC') without liability and a Welsh company may use equivalent Welsh terms: ss 25, 27.

Where there is liability under this rule the officer at fault is in the same position as a guarantor of the company's debt. However, his liability is imposed by statute and so he does not obtain a discharge from it under the law of guarantees if the creditor varies the terms of the debt without his consent.

A director signed a company cheque but failed to write the word 'limited' at the end of the company name. The cheque was dishonoured and the payee agreed with the company that it should pay him the amount by instalments. This variation would have discharged a guarantee but it was held that it did not relieve the director of his statutory liability: *British Airways Board v Parish* [1979] 2 Lloyd's Rep 361 (CA).

1.8 Other statutory exceptions

A company which has one or more subsidiaries must usually prepare group accounts in which the assets and liabilities, profits or losses of the subsidiaries are combined with those of the holding company: s 229 (Chapter 14: 14.5). In tax law there are special rules (group relief, exemption from capital gains and other taxes) for transactions within groups of companies. The undistributed profits or the transfers of value of close companies may sometimes be attributed to or treated as if they were profits or assets of 'participators', ie members. In the statutory employment protection code an employee who is transferred from one company to the service of another may retain his continuity of service despite the change of employer.

1.9 Groups of companies

Apart from statutory rules (1.8) the courts have in some circumstances treated a parent company and its subsidiaries as an entity if they carry on a single business. This result does not follow automatically from the relationship of holding and subsidiary company. There must be evidence that there is a single or combined business. At one time this approach was based on the relationship of principal and agent between the two companies. But more recently the courts have been inclined to look for evidence of 'economic entity' in the degree of shared management, capital, etc, of the companies. There is some doubt, however, as to how far the doctrine extends.

A company acquired a business and also the premises on which the previous owners had traded. For convenience the newly acquired business was distinguished from the existing business of the company and it was carried on in the name of a wholly-owned subsidiary. But the profits of the business were treated in the accounts as profits of the holding company which also provided the staff to run the business and which took all the commercial policy decisions which arose from it. The local authority of the area acquired the premises used in the business. These premises were directly owned by the holding company. The latter claimed compensation (as an addition to the market value of the premises) for disturbance of the business. The local authority, however, rejected the claim and argued that the owner of the premises (the holding company) did not carry on the business on those premises since the business belonged, it was said, to the subsidiary. The court, however, upheld the claim of the holding company that it was the owner of the business ousted from the premises by the acquisition. In this decision the court treated the subsidiary as merely the agent of the holding company for carrying on its business. A number of criteria were laid down to determine whether a subsidiary should (in particular cases only) be treated as the agent of the holding company (or vice versa) – who appoints the managers, who determines trading policy, who allocates resources and who takes the profits? They are all really facets of 'control'. This artificial use of the agency principle conflicts with the House of Lords decision in *Salomon's Case* where it was considered and rejected (admittedly the facts were distinctly different). *Smith, Stone & Knight Ltd v Birmingham Corp* [1939] 4 All ER 116.

Under the terms of his service agreement a managing director of a holding company was to have such duties and powers in relation to the business of the holding company and its subsidiaries as might be assigned to him by the board of directors. The board became dissatisfied and resolved that he should confine his activities to the business of one subsidiary. It was held that this decision to exclude him from management of the business of the holding company was not a breach of his contract since the business of the group was a single entity and the board might assign to him duties in connection with any part of it. The basis of the decision was recognition of the unity of the group as an 'economic reality': *Harold Holdsworth & Co (Wakefield) Ltd v Caddies* [1955] 1 WLR 352.

The facts were similar in essentials to those of the case above except that the premises acquired by the local authority belonged to the subsidiary and the business was carried on by the holding company. Applying the economic entity test the court held that 'the three companies should for present purposes be treated as that one': *DHN Food Distributors Ltd v London Borough of Tower Hamlets* [1976] 3 All ER 462.

1.10 Evasion of legal obligations

Since a shareholder and a company are different persons a controlling shareholder might use his company to do what he is restricted from doing and so evade his obligations. But in such a case the court may restrain him by holding the company equally bound.

Horne was a former employee of the plaintiff and subject to a valid restriction imposed by his service agreement against soliciting customers of the plaintiff after leaving its service. Horne established a company of which his wife and an employee were the sole shareholders and directors so that the company might do what he himself could not, by issuing circulars to customers of his former employer. An injunction was granted against both Horne and the company. *Re Bugle Press Ltd* (Chapter 16: 16.4) offers another example of lifting the veil of incorporation to restrain misuse of a company to do what the members themselves could not do: *Gilford Motor Co Ltd v Horne* [1933] Ch 935.

1.11 Members' decisions binding on the company

A company is bound by resolutions passed at general meetings duly convened. The need to hold a meeting gives to a dissenting minority the opportunity both to express its views and to record its disagreement. The decision taken at the meeting is a decision of the company. If, however, *all* the members entitled to attend and vote are agreed their unanimous decision may be treated as a binding decision even though no general meeting or no meeting at all of the company has been held. Although the assent of all members is required, it may be inferred from the passive acquiescence of members who, being aware of the transaction, raise no objection to it.

A debenture had been irregularly issued and the two directors concerned had not been validly appointed. All four shareholders had discussed and agreed upon the transaction. But no general meeting had been held. This agreement of members as individuals was sufficient to make the debenture valid against the liquidator: *Parker and Cooper Ltd v Reading* [1926] Ch 975.

1.12 Residence and nationality

A company is resident for tax purposes in the country in which its central management and control is located, ie where its board of directors meets. In time of war a company may be treated as an enemy alien by reference to the status of its members.

The defendant company was incorporated in England but all its shares except one were held by persons resident in Germany and all the directors resided in Germany. The secretary who held the one remaining share was a British subject resident in England. It was held that the company acquired 'an enemy character' from its members since as an artificial person it must be controlled by others who were in this case enemy aliens: *Daimler Co Ltd v Continental Tyre and Rubber Co (GB) Ltd* [1916] 2 AC 307.

1.13 Torts and crimes

As an employer a company can have a normal vicarious liability for the acts of its employees done in the course of their duties. A company may also have attributed to it and so become liable for the tortious or even criminal acts of any person who is the 'directing mind and will' of the company. Such a person is treated as the company's other self (alter ego). To apply this doctrine it must be shown that the other self had sufficient authority and control. But it is not confined to the decisions of directors: it may be extended to acts of senior employees. A company cannot, however, be a party to a conspiracy with its own directors since a conspiracy requires a mental element on the part of the conspirators, ie intentional combination, and a company cannot have attributed to it the intentions of others so as to conspire with them.

The directors caused the company to give financial assistance to the purchase of its own shares contrary to s 151 by the purchase of assets at a gross overvalue from persons who used the money to purchase the shares. In subsequent proceedings against the directors it was argued that the company was party to the conspiracy (through the knowledge of its directors) and so could not sue its fellow conspirators. The Court of Appeal held, however, that as the victim of the conspiracy the company should not have attributed to it the knowledge of the directors so as to make it a conspirator with them: *Belmont Finance Corp Ltd v Williams Furniture Ltd* [1979] 1 All ER 118.

It has been argued that a company has no legal capacity (under its objects clause) to commit a tort or a crime, ie that any such act must by its nature be ultra vires the company. But the ultra vires doctrine is better regarded as a limitation on the company's capacity to enter into binding contracts, ie it has no relation to its non-contractual liabilities. The cases indicate that a company can be liable for a wrongful act if it is expressly authorised by its management. But an ordinary employee has no implied authority to commit an ultra vires act and in this case it is simply not the act of the company at all.

B TYPES OF COMPANY

1.14 Public and private companies
Until 1907 all registered companies were subject to the same rules of law. This practice was found to be inappropriate since there are significant differences in the safeguards required for large companies which raise share and loan capital from numerous investors with whom they have no other connection and small companies whose members and directors are often drawn from the same small group of persons. In the latter case the managing proprietors might have decided to trade in partnership but probably preferred to form a company mainly to secure the protection of limited liability.

By the Companies Act 1907 a new category of 'private company' was created, ie one which by its articles:

(a) imposed a restriction on the right to transfer its shares;
(b) limited the number of its members to a maximum of 50 (exclusive of members who were or previously had been company employees); and
(c) was prohibited from inviting the public to subscribe for its shares or debentures.

Any other company was a public company.

The EC Second Directive made it necessary to abolish this classification of public and private companies. Instead a public company (to which alone the EC Second Directive rules apply) is defined primarily by reference to authorised share capital which for a public company is set at a minimum of £50,000. If a company satisfies this requirement and some other conditions it may register as a public company. But it does not become a public company, whatever the size of its capital, unless it is registered as such: s 1(3).

Any company which is not a public company is a private company. Private companies have, therefore, become the residual category and are no longer required to include in their articles restrictions which identify them as private companies (though the prohibition against offer of securities of a private company to the public is maintained as a statutory rule: s 81).

A company whose authorised share capital is £50,000 or more is not compelled to register as a public company but may continue as a private company. The subsidiaries of a public company may be, as they usually are, private companies.

A private company may by the prescribed procedure reregister as public (1.17) and a public company may reregister as private (1.18).

When the new classification of public and private companies took effect in 1980, existing public companies, if they wished to retain that status, re-registered under the new category. Existing private companies however automatically retained their status unless they took steps to alter it (1.17).

1.15 Public companies
The new classification of public companies briefly referred to above requires that a public company shall be:

(a) a limited company: s 1(3). An unlimited company must be a private company;
(b) a company with a share capital: s 1(3). A company limited by guarantee must be a private company unless it also has a share capital. This combination is rare and no new companies of that dual type may now be formed: s 1(4);
(c) a company whose memorandum states that it is to be a public company: s 1(3);
(d) a company whose registered name ends with the words 'public limited company' or the permitted abbreviation 'plc' (or the Welsh equivalents if it is a Welsh company as described below (1.25)): ss 25, 27;
(e) a company whose authorized share capital is at least £50,000 or such other 'authorized amount' as may later be fixed by statutory instrument: s 11;
(f) a company which has obtained a certificate of incorporation or of re-registration as a public company: ss 13(6) or 47(1).

A public company is no longer required to have a minimum of seven members. The minimum is now two for public and private companies alike: s 1.

Statutory rules differentiate between public companies and private companies in a number of respects. These differences are in the main a reflection of the larger size of public companies. They need to raise capital from a wide circle of investors by offering securities to the public. The directors who control the business and resources of a large public company are less amenable to control by the numerous and dispersed body of shareholders although an increasing proportion of their shares is concentrated in the hands of institutional shareholders, such as pension funds and unit trusts which are better able to keep in touch with and to assess their current situation. But the trend of company law is towards ever stricter statutory control of directors especially of public companies. Since many public companies carry on their business through subsidiaries which are private companies it is necessary in some cases to extend rules designed for public companies to their subsidiaries to prevent evasion.

The more important statutory rules applicable to public companies are as follows:

(i) a public company must have at least two directors: s 282. For a private company the statutory minimum is one. In either case the minimum may be set at a higher figure by the articles;

(ii) the statutory rules on procedure at general meetings, ie proxies, and on resolutions for the appointment of directors are either applicable only to public companies or differ from those applicable to private companies: ss 372, 292;

(iii) a public company (unlike a private company) may offer its shares or debentures to the public for subscription or purchase: s 81. But the offer is a prospectus to which elaborate rules are applied: ss 56–71 (Chapter 6);

(iv) a company registered as a public company *on its original incorporation* may not do business nor exercise any borrowing powers until it has obtained from the registrar a certificate relating to its allotted share capital and other matters. But such a company may opt to reregister as a private company and if it does it need not obtain a certificate before commencing to do business: s 117;

(v) on allotment the shares of a public company must be paid up as to at least one-quarter of their nominal value plus the whole of any premium. Any non-cash consideration must be valued and received within a maximum of 5 years: ss 101–103;

(vi) a public company is expected to maintain its net assets at a value which is at least half the amount of its called-up share capital. If the net asset value falls below that level the directors must within 28 days of becoming aware of the situation call an extraordinary general meeting to consider whether and if so what measures should be taken to deal with it: s 142;

(vii) a limit is set on dividends of a public company by a requirement that net assets shall at least equal the aggregate of called-up share capital and undistributable reserves. If the amount of net assets is below that figure no dividend may be paid. In any other case the dividend is restricted to the amount which will leave net assets at that figure at least: s 264;

(viii) when a group of companies includes a public company the rules on loans to directors are extended (in relation to all companies of the group) so as to prohibit or to restrict transactions in the nature of or in substitution for loans: ss 330–331.

There are a number of additional rules, on such matters as 'insider dealing' (Chapter 17), disclosure of interests in large shareholdings held by nominees (Chapter 8:8 12–13) and company accounts (Chapter 14), which differentiate between public and private companies by imposing stricter rules on public companies.

To sum up, the decisive advantage of a public company over a private company is its right to raise capital from the public (and the access which it obtains to the general market in securities of the Stock Exchange). If it is a large enough company those advantages are likely to be decisive. It must pay the price in tighter regulation of its affairs.

1.16 Private companies
As the new residual class private companies now have few specific characteristics. Many have only a small authorised and issued share capital

but some, especially wholly-owned subsidiaries of public companies, have a share capital well in excess of £50,000. There is no limit.

The more typical private company, for which private company privileges were designed, is a small concern in which the same individuals combine the role of shareholders and directors. But there is no requirement that they should do so. It is characteristic of this type of private company that the articles give to members a right of pre-emption over each others' shares (Chapter 7: 7.15).

Another special type of private company is the quasi-partnership established by individuals or by companies as the means to carrying on a joint venture. Private companies of this type often include in their articles safeguards to preserve the agreed balance of participation, eg the right to nominate directors or to veto proposals at board meetings (*Salmon's Case* in Chapter 13: 13.4).

Of the three former restrictions which a private company had to include in its articles, two no longer apply. A private company need no longer:

(a) impose restrictions on the transfer of its shares; nor
(b) limit the number of its members to 50.

It is, however, now prohibited by statute from offering its shares or debentures to the public: s 81. This need not appear in the articles. Many private companies which had all three restrictions in their articles are likely – if only by inaction – to retain them. The general restrictions on transfer of shares given to the directors plus the shareholders' pre-emption rights mentioned above reflect the preference of all concerned for keeping the ownership and control of their company within their own circle (and recent remissions of the inheritance tax and capital gains tax rules on business property help them to do so).

1.17 Reregistration of private companies as public companies

A private company may in time expand its business to the point at which its shareholders decide to 'float' it by obtaining a full Stock Exchange listing for its shares or, as an intermediate step, admission to the Unlisted Securities Market (USM), which is a sort of 'junior league' of the Stock Exchange. In either case the company must be converted from private to public to satisfy market requirements for its shares.

Even if the intention in forming a company is to create a public company from the beginning, it is normal practice to register it as a private company and then convert it to a public company shortly afterwards under the procedure described below. By this means the company avoids having to obtain a certificate from the registrar under s 117 in order to commence business (see 1.15(iv) above).

In order to reregister as a public company a private company is required by s 43 to follow a set procedure, ie:

(a) the company must pass a *special resolution* resolving to be reregistered as a public company and making certain alterations to the memorandum and possibly to the articles;
(b) *application* must be made to the registrar together with certain documents; and

(c) the company must *satisfy conditions* with respect to its authorised and issued share *capital*: s 43.

The detailed requirements under each of these heads are set out below.
   The special resolution must:

(i) alter the memorandum so that the memorandum states that the company
     is to be a public company; and
(ii) make whatever other alterations are necessary to bring the memorandum
     in substance and in form into conformity with statutory requirements for a
     memorandum of a public company.

With regard to (ii) it will always be necessary to alter the name of the company
which appears in the memorandum. The word 'limited' (for a private limited
company) is omitted and replaced by 'public limited company' (or 'plc'). It is
also permissible to omit 'company' or 'and company' if that is required: s 43.
For example, a private company with the name 'John Brown and Company
Limited' would thus become 'John Brown plc'. It appears that this change of
name does not require the consent of the registrar under the standard change
of name procedure (Chapter 3: 3.4).
   Finally the special resolution must also make such alterations to the articles
as are requisite in the circumstances. There is no obvious or universal
alteration to be made but the articles might, for example, make some reference
to the status of the company as a private company which would have to be
deleted.
   The other substantive requirement is that the authorised and issued share
capital of the company must conform to public company rules (s 117), ie:

(1) the nominal value of the company's allotted share capital must be at least
    £50,000 to conform with general public company rules. It will be
    remembered that a public company registered as such ab initio must have
    an authorised share capital of at least £50,000 on incorporation and an
    allotted share capital of at least that amount in order to obtain the
    registrar's certificate entitling it to do business: s 117. On becoming a
    public company, a former private company is not required to obtain the
    registrar's certificate that it is entitled to do business but it must comply
    with conditions similar to those for the issue of such a certificate;
(2) in respect of *all* the allotted shares the following conditions must be
    satisfied:
    (A) each share must be paid up at least as to one-quarter of its nominal
        value and the whole of any premium. If, for example, £1 (nominal)
        shares have been allotted at an issue price of £1.20, consideration
        must have been received to a total of at least 45p per share ($\frac{1}{4} \times £1$
        plus 20p premium);
    (B) if any part of the consideration for shares is an undertaking to do
        work or perform services for the company or a third party (eg for a
        subsidiary of the company) the undertaking must have been
        performed or otherwise discharged (eg by payment of cash in lieu);
    (C) if any part of the consideration is an undertaking, eg to transfer an
        asset, the undertaking must have been performed or otherwise
        discharged or there must be a contract under which it is to be
        performed within a period of not more than five years (from the date

of passing the special resolution to reregister as a public company): s 45.

Shares allotted under an employees share scheme however are exempt from these requirements (Chapter 5: 5.12).

The application for reregistration to be made to the registrar must be signed by a director or by the secretary of the company and be supported by the following documents:

(a) a printed copy of the memorandum and articles as altered by the special resolution referred to above. The word 'printed', however, does not mean literally what it says (Chapter 3: 3.23);

(b) a balance sheet ('the relevant balance sheet') made up as at a date not more than seven months before the application;

(c) an unqualified report by the auditors in relation to the balance sheet. 'Unqualified report' is elaborately defined. In brief, the report must be to the effect (without material qualification) that the balance sheet has been properly prepared in accordance with the requirements of the Companies Act and gives a true and fair view of the state of the company's affairs as at the balance sheet date: s 46;

(d) a copy of a written statement by the auditors that in their opinion the relevant balance sheet shows that at the balance sheet date the amount of the net assets was not less than the aggregate of the company's called-up capital and undistributable reserves. Both 'called-up share capital' and 'undistributable reserves' are basic defined terms explained later (Chapter 5: 5.1 and 5.23 respectively);

(e) if between the date of the relevant balance sheet and the passing of the special resolution for reregistration the company has allotted shares for a non-cash consideration, a valuer's report (made within the previous six months) must be attached to the application. It must comply with the rules (Chapter 5: 5.9) which apply when a public company allots shares for a non-cash consideration. This requirement is to prevent a private company from evading public company rules by allotting shares for a non-cash consideration which is over-valued and then reregistering as a public company shortly afterwards;

(f) a statutory declaration in the prescribed form by a director or the secretary of the company that the relevant conditions have been satisfied.

If the registrar is satisfied on receipt of the application and supporting documents he retains them for filing and issues a certificate of incorporation which states that the company is a public company. The issue of the certificate converts the company to the status of a public company and makes effective the alterations of the memorandum and articles. The certificate is conclusive, ie cannot later be set aside, on two points, ie:

(i) that the company is a public company; and

(ii) that the relevant statutory rules of reregistration have been complied with: s 47.

It is also possible to reregister a private unlimited company as a public limited company. The procedure is similar in essentials to that described above: s 48.

1.18 Reregistration of a public company as a private company (s 53)

The company must pass a special resolution resolving to reregister as a private company. The resolution must also:

(a) remove from the memorandum the statement that the company is a public company; and

(b) make such other alterations to the memorandum and articles as are requisite. It will always be necessary to change the name of the company to omit the public company designation ('plc', etc).

The company must then wait 28 days before making application to the registrar for reregistration as this is the period in which members may apply to the court for cancellation of the resolution.

Application to the court may be made by members who:

(i) hold in aggregate not less than 5 per cent in nominal value of the company's issued capital or of any class thereof; or

(ii) are not less than 50 in number; or

(iii) are 5 per cent of its membership if it has no share capital;

and who have not consented to or voted for the resolution which they wish to have cancelled. The company is required to give notice forthwith to the registrar that a members' application has been made to the court. On hearing the members' application the court may make an order either cancelling or confirming the resolution, with or without conditions such as a requirement that some person shall purchase the shares of the dissentient members. The company itself may be required to purchase the shares and thereby reduce its capital. The court may also order that particular alterations be made (or shall not thereafter be made) to the memorandum or articles. No further alteration of the relevant provisions may then be made by the company except by leave of the court. An office copy of any order of the court must be delivered to the registrar by the company within 15 days (or such longer period as the court may direct).

If no members apply to the court within the 28-day period or if they withdraw their application or the court makes an order confirming the special resolution and this has been delivered to the registrar, the company may then submit to the registrar an application in the prescribed form signed by a director or by the secretary of the company together with a printed copy of the memorandum and articles as altered by the resolution.

If the registrar is satisfied he issues a certificate of incorporation as a company which is not a public company. The certificate is conclusive and the alterations to the memorandum and articles then take effect: ss 53–55.

Reregistration as a private company is generally a voluntary act of the company. If, however, a public company obtains a court order for the reduction of share capital (under s 138 – Chapter 5: 5.28) and the reduction will bring its allotted share capital to less than £50,000 the court may order that the company shall first be reregistered as a private company and in its order may specify the alterations to be made in the memorandum and articles: s 139. It is not then necessary for the company to pass a special resolution to reregister. The company simply applies to the registrar for reregistration as a private company in pursuance of the court order before the reduction takes effect. Cancellation of shares (Chapter 5: 5.21) may also entail compulsory reregistration of a public company as private (s 147) if the capital is reduced to less than £50,000.

1.19 Companies limited by shares
The members of a company may have their liability to contribute to the assets of the company either limited by shares or limited by guarantee or it may be unlimited. Companies with liability limited by shares, which may be either public or private, are by far the most numerous and important of the three types.

A member of a company limited by shares is liable to pay to the company the amount (if any) which is due on the shares and which has not already been paid in respect of the shares either by a previous holder or by him. If, for example, a £1 share has been allotted and issued at a price of, say, £1.50 then the amount of £1 is due in respect of the nominal or par value of the share; a premium of 50p is also due because the allottee has agreed to subscribe that extra amount as a condition of the allotment of the share. The liability to pay for shares may be satisfied by payment in cash or (if so agreed) by some non-cash consideration of equivalent value. It is not necessary, however, that all the consideration should be paid or transferred to the company at once. If it is deferred the shares are partly-paid shares on which the balance due must be provided at some time not later than the liquidation of the company. There are special rules on the time at which a public company must receive consideration for its shares and the valuation of a non-cash consideration (Chapter 5 Part A).

1.20 Companies limited by guarantee
If a company limited by guarantee also has a share capital the members have the same liability (if any) in respect of their shares as exists in the case of a company with liability limited only by shares. But no new companies of this dual type can now be incorporated: s 1(4). In the more common case of a company limited by guarantee which has no share capital each member is liable, *when the company is wound up*, to contribute to the company's assets for the purpose of discharging its debts, an amount not exceeding the sum specified in the memorandum.

The member's contingent liability to the company under the guarantee is not an asset of the company. Accordingly while the company continues as a going concern, ie before it is wound up, the company may not mortgage or charge to a third party its potential claim on its members when in liquidation.

A guarantee company which has no share capital can only be a private company. The few existing guarantee companies with share capital (there were said to be 71 in 1979) may possibly include some public companies but the majority are private. A company limited by guarantee is appropriate to the needs of a professional, research or trade association which exists to provide services to its members. It obtains income to meet its expenses by charging fees for its services but does not usually aim to make a profit. The members' guarantee serves as a form of reserve upon which the company can call to meet its terminal expenses in winding up. A company limited by guarantee must include the word 'limited' at the end of its name unless authorised to omit it under s 30 (Chapter 3: 3.2).

Unlike a company limited by shares a guarantee company must on incorporation always register special articles together with its memorandum.

These follow the model of Table C (or Table D if it has a share capital) now found in regulations (SI 1985/805) made under s 8. Table C is a modified version of the Table A articles (Chapter 4: 4.2) for a company limited by shares: Table D is the same as Table A in this respect.

A guarantee company without a share capital may not give to persons who are not members a right to a share of its profits nor allocate to members an entitlement to a specific share of its profits: s 15. The purpose of this restriction is to prevent evasion of the rule which requires that shares, when they exist must have a specified monetary value. If there was a right to profits unrelated to shares the result would be the creation in effect of shares of 'no par value' which is not allowed (although permitted in many foreign systems of company law).

The annual return of a guarantee company with no share capital differs slightly from that of companies which have share capital: s 364.

1.21 Unlimited private companies

As with a guarantee company the liability of a member of an unlimited company arises only when the company goes into liquidation. In that event each member is liable without limit to provide money for the payment of the company's debts.

As long as the company is a going concern it cannot charge or mortgage its potential claims on its members to a third party as security since those claims are not assets of the company. An unpaid creditor of the company cannot sue its members direct to recover from them what the company owes him. His proper remedy is to petition the court for an order for the compulsory winding up of the company so that its liquidator may call on the members to contribute whatever is required to pay the company's debts. In a liquidation of an unlimited company each member is first required to pay whatever amount (if any) is due and unpaid in respect of his shares. If that does not suffice the liquidator then calls for further contributions in proportion to members' shareholdings until he has enough funds to discharge the company's debts. If any member defaults the liquidator may require other members to contribute the amount due from the defaulting (usually insolvent) member.

If the members at the time when liquidation commences are unable between them to contribute the full amount required the liquidator may make calls on former members who ceased to be members within one year of the commencement of winding up. But they are liable only in respect of sums needed to discharge debts incurred before they ceased to be members.

An unlimited company can only be a private company and it must adopt articles which are substantially in accord with the statutory model articles. Its shares, however, need not have a defined monetary ('par') value.

The two main advantages of an unlimited over a limited company are that:

(a) it is not usually (but see below) required to deliver to the registrar a copy of its annual accounts; and
(b) it may return capital to members, if its memorandum and articles authorise it to do so, without having to comply with the statutory rules applicable to limited companies (Chapter 5 Part B).

To prevent evasion an unlimited company must deliver a copy of its accounts to the registrar if, during the period covered by the accounts, it was either the holding company or the subsidiary of a limited company, or if two or more limited companies had shares or powers over the unlimited company, which if combined in one of the limited companies would have made the unlimited company its subsidiary. An unlimited company must also deliver a copy of its accounts to the registrar if it has carried on business as a promoter of a trading stamp scheme within the meaning of the Trading Stamps Act 1964: s 241.

1.22 Reregistration of a private limited company as unlimited
This change increases the liability of members and so their unanimous consent is required. The procedure is as follows (ss 49–50):

(a) application is made to the registrar in the prescribed form and signed by a director or by the secretary;
(b) the application must set out the requisite alterations to be made to the memorandum and articles (or if there are no existing articles new articles in suitable form must be attached);
(c) with the application there must be delivered:
    (i) the written assent to the change of all members of the company; and
    (ii) a statutory declaration made by the directors that the persons whose assents are delivered are the whole membership of the company (or if any consents have been signed by agents that the directors have satisfied themselves by reasonable enquiries that these agents were duly authorised to sign on behalf of the members whose agents they purport to be); and
    (iii) a printed copy of the memorandum incorporating the proposed alterations set out in the application and a printed copy of the articles similarly altered (or, if necessary, new articles – see (b) above).

The registrar retains these documents for filing and issues a certificate of incorporation of the company as unlimited. The certificate is conclusive that the procedure has been properly completed and that the company is (from the date of the certificate) an unlimited company with memorandum and articles in the altered form (ie there is no need for the company to pass a special resolution to make those alterations).

The members of the company at the date of reregistration are then liable without limit for its existing debts and for future debts incurred while they are members. A past member at the date of reregistration is not affected, ie he has the same liability (if any) as he had before the change: IA s 78.

A company can only change its status in this way once. A company which was originally incorporated as unlimited and later reregistered as limited cannot revert to being unlimited. A public company cannot be reregistered as unlimited: s 49(3).

1.23 Reregistration of an unlimited company as limited
In this case the change reduces the liability of members. A majority decision of the members by special resolution therefore suffices.

The company must (ss 51–52) pass a special resolution which:

(a) states whether the liability of members is to be limited by shares or by guarantee; and
(b) alters the memorandum and, if necessary, the articles so as to bring them in form and substance into conformity with the statutory requirements for a company limited by shares or by guarantee as the case may be.

Application is then made to the registrar in the prescribed form and signed by a director or by the secretary. With the application there must be delivered a printed copy of the memorandum and articles as altered. The registrar retains the documents for filing and issues a certificate of incorporation as a limited company appropriate to the form of limitation adopted. The certificate is conclusive that procedural requirements have been satisfied and that the company is from that date a limited company.

Reregistration of an unlimited company as limited might take place when the company was on the verge of going into insolvent liquidation – so that the members might escape liability for its debts beyond the amount (if any) unpaid on their shares. There are special rules, however, which extend their liability if insolvent liquidation occurs within three years of reregistration (Chapter 20: 20.4).

1.24 Holding and subsidiary companies

A company may only own shares of another company if, as is usual, its objects clause gives it an express power to do so.

If one company has a major shareholding in another they may stand in the relationship of holding company and subsidiary. In that event they are both subject to a number of statutory rules. It is, therefore, necessary to have a statutory definition of the circumstances which make one company (Company A) the holding company of another company (Company B): s 736.

There are three alternative tests of the holding company/subsidiary company relationship.

First, A is the holding company of B if A is a member, ie the registered holder of at least one share, of B and also controls the composition of the board of directors of B. The simplest basis of such control of the board is that A's shareholding gives it more than half the voting power exercisable at a general meeting of B. Alternatively A may have control because the memorandum or articles or a contract between A and B give to A the right to appoint directors of B. For the purposes of this test of control it suffices if A can (without obtaining the consent of another person) appoint or remove all or even a majority of the directors of B. The power to appoint and remove directors is deemed to exist so far as a director of B can only be appointed with the support of A, or if any person appointed a director of A automatically becomes a director of B also, or if A itself (or any other subsidiary of A) is also a director of B. This condition applies a test of management control of B by A. It is immaterial that A does not (but it usually does) also have voting control of B.

The second alternative test of holding/subsidiary status is that A holds more than half (in nominal value) of the equity share capital of B. Issued shares are equity share capital unless their right to participate in *both* dividends and return of capital is restricted to specified amounts. In a typical case ordinary shares are equity share capital and preference shares are not. But participating preference shares or preference shares carrying the right to participate in surplus assets on return of capital are equity share capital because their rights in respect of dividends in the first case and return of capital in the second are unrestricted. But equity share capital need not carry any right to vote at general meetings. The test here is ownership of more than half the equity of the subsidiary and not control.

For the purpose of either of these two tests of the holding company/subsidiary company relationship:

(a) shares held or powers exercisable in a fiduciary capacity, eg as trustee for another person, are disregarded;
(b) shares held or powers exercisable by a nominee or another subsidiary of A are unless held as in (a) above attributed to A.

The effect of principle (b) is that under the equity share capital test A need not be a majority shareholder of B if A's nominees or subsidiaries own sufficient equity share capital of B. The entire holding of equity share capital of B held by a subsidiary (X) of A is attributed to A even if X has only a minority holding and X is only a partly-owned subsidiary of A.

For example, suppose that A is the registered holder of 30 per cent of the equity share capital of B and also owns through a nominee (Y) 51 per cent of the equity share capital of X which in turn owns 21 per cent of the equity share capital of B. B is then the subsidiary of A because A, directly and through X, is deemed to hold 51 per cent of the equity share capital of B. By the use of arrangements of this kind it is possible to construct a pyramid of partly-owned subsidiaries through which the ultimate holding company controls (since equity share capital does usually carry the right to vote) a much larger group enterprise than it owns.

Since either test can be applied separately it follows that a subsidiary may have two holding companies. If, for example, B has issued 100 ordinary shares carrying votes to A and 900 non-voting ordinary shares to C, B is the subsidiary of A because A's votes enable it to appoint and remove the directors of B. B is also the subsidiary of C because C holds more than half its equity share capital. It has long been recognised that this situation is unsatisfactory and should be altered to apply a single test of control to establish that one company is the holding company of the other. Something on these lines is likely to be enacted in implementing the EC Seventh Directive (on Group Accounts) which is scheduled for 1987.

The third alternative test of holding/subsidiary company status is consequential to the other two. If B is the subsidiary of X and X is the subsidiary of A, B is also a subsidiary of A.

The holding/subsidiary company relationship is of much commercial importance since large business enterprises find it convenient to operate through a structure of a holding or 'parent' company and subsidiaries, wholly or less often partly owned. The subsidiaries may have been acquired by purchase or take-overs in the past (and are preserved because, eg, business goodwill attaches to them as entities) or they may have been formed by the holding company to carry on part of the group business or to perform a special function, such as holding property or providing transport, for the group companies. As has been explained (1.9 above) the common law is tentatively disposed to recognise the 'economic entity' of a group of companies. Statute law imposes a number of rules designed to prevent the use of subsidiaries in order to evade restrictions on the holding company, for example the prohibition of loans to directors (Chapter 12: 12.11) or the use of company funds to finance purchase of shares (Chapter 5: 5.19). The most extensive statutory aggregation of holding company and subsidiaries is the rule which requires a holding company to produce 'group accounts' as if the assets and liabilities, profits or losses of its subsidiaries were its own (Chapter 14: 14.5). But a holding company has no liability for the debts of a subsidiary (if it is a limited company) though it might severely damage its own commercial credit if it allowed the latter to default.

1.25 Welsh companies

A company may by its memorandum (in its original or altered form) state that its registered office is to be in Wales: s 2. Such a company may use the word 'cyfyngedig' instead of 'limited' in its name (with appropriate equivalents for 'public limited company' and for 'company'): s 25. It may also deliver to the registrar a memorandum and articles (and any other document which it is required to deliver) in Welsh but if it does so the Welsh document must be accompanied by a certified translation in English: s 21. If the Welsh equivalent of 'limited' is used the fact that the company is a limited company must also be stated in English on its prospectuses, letterheads and other documents and outside its places of business (as required by s 351(3) in relation to companies generally).

1.26 Other corporate bodies

The Companies Acts recognise and make reference to corporate bodies which are not companies registered under the Acts. These include bodies incorporated in Great Britain by other means (see 1.1 above) and companies, such as overseas subsidiaries or parent companies incorporated under the company law of other countries. References to a 'body corporate' or 'corporation' in the Acts denote bodies in these categories (but do not include a corporation sole). References to a 'company' are always to a company registered under the Companies Acts of Great Britain only: ss 735 and 740.

1.27 Oversea companies

A company incorporated outside Great Britain which has a place of business in Great Britain is an 'oversea company' subject to ss 691–703 but not to the other provisions of the Companies Act. However, an oversea company incorporated in the Channel Islands or the Isle of Man is subject to the same full requirements as a British company: s 699.

An oversea company must within one month of establishing a place of business in Great Britain deliver to the registrar a copy of its memorandum and articles (or the documents which correspond to them), standard particulars of its directors and secretary (Chapter 12: 12.9) and the name and address of one or more persons resident in Great Britain authorised to accept service of legal process and notices on behalf of the company: s 691(1)(b). Notice must be given of any changes in these particulars within 21 days of the date on which the documents can reasonably be expected to reach Great Britain.

An oversea company is required (with only minor modifications) to deliver each year to the registry accounts which comply with English requirements (Chapter 14 Part A). An English translation must be supplied if the accounts are not in English. The accounts need not be audited: ss 700–703.

There are suitable legal provisions to bring an oversea company within the ambit of English law in respect of registrable charges on its English property, the issue of a prospectus and the use of a company name. The court has jurisdiction to order the compulsory liquidation of a foreign company (not necessarily an oversea company in the technical sense) if it has assets and/or liabilities in this country.

21

Chapter 2

Company formation

A FORMATION AND COMMENCEMENT OF BUSINESS

2.1 Procedure for incorporation of a company
The documents to be delivered to the registrar for the incorporation of a new company must bear the name of the company. As a precaution it is usual, before preparing the documents, to search the index of names of existing companies kept at the registry under s 714, and to refer to the regulations on company names in case there are objections to the name selected for the company (Chapter 3: 3.3). Professional agents will undertake this service for a fee.

To obtain registration of a company, public or private, the documents listed below must be delivered to the registrar and the relevant fees and duties paid:

(a) a memorandum of association (Chapter 3) signed by at least two subscribers each of whom agrees to take at least one share; it must be dated and witnessed and stamped with the registration fee of £50: s 10;

(b) articles of association (Chapter 4) signed by the same subscribers, dated and witnessed. Alternatively a company limited by shares (but no other type of company) may adopt the statutory model articles ('Table A'). The memorandum should then be indorsed 'registered without articles of association'. The common practice for private companies, however, is to register short special articles which adopt Table A with only brief modifications. A company limited by guarantee or an unlimited company must register its own articles: s 7;

(c) a statement in the prescribed form of the names and particulars of the first directors and of the secretary of the company, each of whom must sign the form to record his consent to appointment in that capacity. The statement must also include the intended address of the registered office of the company. When the company is incorporated the directors and secretary named in the statement are automatically appointed to their offices: the purported appointment of any other person, eg by the articles, is void. The statement must be signed by, or on behalf of, the subscribers to the memorandum: s 10;

(d) a statutory declaration by a solicitor engaged in the formation of the company or by a person named in the statement (see (c) above) as director or secretary of compliance with the requirements of the Companies Act in respect of registration: s 12;

(e) a statement of capital unless the company is to have no share capital. The statement bears capital duty at the rate of £1 per £100 (or part thereof) on whichever is the greater of:
  (i) the nominal value of the shares which the subscribers have agreed to take; and
  (ii) the consideration given for the shares: Finance Act 1973 ss 47–49. In the normal cases where two subscribers' shares of £1 each are to be issued at par the minimum duty of £1 (on the first £100) is paid.

Documents (c), (d) and (e) are printed forms of prescribed size and content: s 706.

The registrar examines the documents to satisfy himself that they are formally in order and that the objects specified in the memorandum are lawful. He may have to give final consideration to the choice of name for the new company. If he is satisfied on these points he issues a certificate of incorporation and later publishes a notice in the *London Gazette* that it has been issued: s 711. The company is incorporated with effect from the date of the certificate. It is possible on giving reasonable notice to arrange for the certificate of incorporation to be issued on a prearranged date such as 1 January.

2.2 The certificate of incorporation
The certificate of incorporation is conclusive evidence that all the requirements of the Companies Act in respect to registration have been complied with and that the company is a company authorised to be registered and is duly registered under the Acts and if the certificate states that the company is a public company that it is such a company: s 13(7). The legality and validity of its incorporation cannot thereafter be challenged even if some irregularity is later discovered. If, for example, the certificate of incorporation bears a date earlier than the actual date of its issue transactions of the company between the two dates are valid although they in fact preceded the issue of the certificate.

The certificate of incorporation was dated 6 January 1920 although it was not signed or issued until 8 January 1920. It was held that the issue of shares and debentures on 6 January 1920 was valid. *Jubilee Cotton Mills Ltd v Lewis* [1924] AC 958 HL.

A trade union cannot, however, be registered as a company under the Companies Acts and any such registration is declared to be void: Trade Union and Labour Relations Act 1974 s 2(2) and (4). The certificate is conclusive only as to valid incorporation under company law. The registrar may refuse to permit the registration of companies whose objects appear to him to be of doubtful legality. But his certificate does not prevent a subsequent challenge to the legality of a company's objects.

The registrar declined to register a company whose objects were to deal in tickets in the Irish sweepstake, an illegal activity in the UK. The court upheld the registrar's decision: *R v Registrar of Joint Stock Companies* [1931] 2 KB 197 CA.

The House of Lords rejected a challenge to the legality of the objects of a company established to promote rationalism against religion but in doing so stated that the conclusiveness of the certificate of incorporation did not prevent the challenge from being made: *Bowman v Secular Society Ltd* [1917] AC 406 HL.

It is thought, however, that the proper method of disposing of a company whose objects are illegal is to have it wound up rather than to revoke its incorporation.

2.3 The Companies Registry

For every company on the register the registrar maintains a separate file bearing the company's registration number. For companies incorporated in England or Wales the registry is at Cardiff (with search facilities at the former London registry). For companies incorporated in Scotland (under the same Companies Acts) the registry is in Edinburgh. English company law does not extend beyond Great Britain. Hence a company incorporated in Northern Ireland under its local law has to register as an oversea company if it establishes a place of business in Great Britain (Chapter 1: 1.27).

A member of the public may search the file of a company at the appropriate registry. From this fact derives a doctrine of constructive notice of the existence and contents of documents on the file. Because it is possible for a person dealing with a company to inspect the file he is treated as if he had done so, subject to one major exception mentioned below. It is not clear whether the doctrine of constructive notice covers all documents on the company file but it certainly applies to the memorandum and articles, special and extraordinary resolutions, particulars of registered charges and possibly to particulars of the directors. The major exception referred to above is that a person dealing with a company in circumstances covered by s 35 (Chapter 3: 3.17) is not deemed to have constructive notice of limitations on the capacity of the company or the authority of its directors imposed by its memorandum or articles.

2.4 Commencement of business

A private company may commence business and exercise borrowing powers as soon as it is incorporated. But the power to make contracts is normally vested in the directors. There must, therefore, be at least one meeting of the directors (or a general meeting of members if the transaction is reserved by the memorandum or articles for a general meeting). It is customary (but not enjoined by law) for the directors at their first meeting as a board to appoint one of their number to be chairman, to adopt a common seal for use by the company, to make arrangements to open a company bank account (with authorised cheque signatories) and to allot and issue shares in addition to the subscribers' shares. These are internal and optional matters but a necessary preparation for commencement of business.

A public company incorporated as such may not do business nor exercise any borrowing powers until the registrar has issued a certificate under s 117. Alternatively the company may reregister as a private company to which these rules do not apply.

To obtain the certificate the company submits to the registrar an application in the prescribed form together with a statutory declaration. The registrar must be satisfied that the company's allotted share capital is not less than £50,000 but he may accept the statutory declaration as sufficient evidence on this point.

The statutory declaration is in the prescribed form and signed by a director or secretary of the company. It states the nominal value of the allotted share capital, which must be not less than £50,000, the amount paid up on the shares, the preliminary expenses of forming the company and who is to pay them, and the amount paid or payable (if any) to any promoter (see Part B below). However, shares allotted under an employees share scheme, unless paid up to the same extent as the rest, are not included.

Of the minimum of £50,000 (nominal value) of shares to be allotted the company must receive, in money or money's worth, consideration of at least £12,500, ie one quarter of the nominal value: s 101. This is a minute sum in relation to the initial requirements of a public company. But the point is not significant since, as is explained below, there is a better alternative to s 117 procedure.

The registrar publishes a notice in the *London Gazette* of the receipt of the statutory declaration. If it appears to be in order, therefore, he issues a certificate which is conclusive evidence that the company is entitled to do business and to exercise its borrowing powers: s 117(6).

If a public company does commence business or borrow money before obtaining a s 117 certificate the transaction is valid. However the other party may call on the directors to regularise the position by obtaining the certificate. If they fail to do so within 21 days they must indemnify him against any loss caused by their default – in addition to their liability to a default fine.

If a public company fails to obtain its certificate within a year of incorporation a petition may on that ground be presented to the court for an order for compulsory winding up of the company: IA s 122(1)(b).

It may still be possible, as it was under the previous law, for a public company before obtaining its trading certificate to enter into provisional contracts which would become binding only if and when that certificate is issued. This procedure may, however, be inconvenient if the company plans to enter into transactions with the public, eg by offering to acquire shares of an existing company or companies under a take-over or amalgamation scheme (for which express purpose the new public company may have been formed). In such a case the new public company could allot shares to its promoters to a nominal value of at least £50,000 and obtain £12,500 in cash as part payment in order to qualify immediately for the issue of a trading certificate so obtaining the right to make binding contracts without penalty.

As already stated (Chapter 1: 1.17) it is possible, and much more convenient, to avoid s 117 procedure by forming a private company and then converting it to a public company. Section 117 is one of those company law topics which should be learnt, but it has no practical significance.

2.5 Form of company contracts

The legal capacity of a company to make contracts is much restricted by the ultra vires doctrine (Chapter 3: 3.15). But if the contract is within its contractual capacity it may make it in whatever form would be appropriate to a similar contract made by an individual, ie by deed, by signed agreement in writing or orally or by conduct: s 36. In any such case the contract of the company will be made on its behalf by its representative(s) and they must have authority to do so (Chapter 13).

In signing company documents as agent the signatory should ensure that the name of the company is correctly written (Chapter 1: 1.7) and should sign 'for and on behalf of' the company to make it plain that he signs as agent and without intending to assume personal liability, eg on a bill of exchange: s 37. He may nonetheless make himself personally liable if he adds an unnecessary indorsement.

A company accepted a bill of exchange in the ordinary way and on the back a director and the secretary added their signatures 'for and on behalf of the company' indicating that they signed merely as agents. They were held to be personally liable since no other purpose could be assigned to their indorsement: *Rolfe Lubell & Co v Keith* [1979] 1 All ER 860.

All companies are required to have a common seal for use in executing deeds, etc. The seal must bear the name of the company (and usually nothing more): s 350. The articles (e g Table A, Art 101) provide for safe-keeping of the seal and authorisation of its use by the directors. It is usual either to authorise the sealing of documents by resolution of the board of directors or to appoint a committee of the board with that power. In either case a separate record (the 'sealing book') of the use of the seal should be maintained.

A share certificate if it bears the impress of the common seal is prima facie evidence of title to the shares: s 186. But company documents generally may be authenticated by a simple signature of a director, the secretary or other authorised officer and need not be sealed: s 41.

B PROMOTERS AND PRE-INCORPORATION CONTRACTS

2.6 Promoters

A promoter has been described as 'one who undertakes to form a company with reference to a given project and to set it going, and who takes the necessary steps to accomplish that purpose'. This definition (*Twycross v Grant* (1877) 2 CPD 469) of a promoter includes those who cause a company to be incorporated (unless acting in a professional capacity for clients) and also those who may later find persons to act as its directors, arrange for its shares to be offered to the public or sell assets to it, provided always that in these activities they are generally involved in launching the company.

Salomon (Chapter 1: 1.2) was the promoter of his company, and so is an existing company which simply decides to form a new subsidiary. No legal problems usually arise in cases such as these where the promoter retains the ownership of the new company which he has promoted. But if the promoter arranges that all or part of the share capital of the company shall be offered to the public two issues arise – first, is the offer document accurate and complete? This is a question of prospectus law (Chapter 6). Secondly, has the promoter secured some benefit to himself from the promotion for which the public as investors in the company are directly or indirectly paying the bill? In the late nineteenth and early twentieth century there was a class of 'professional' company promoters to whom these questions were very pertinent and so rules of law were evolved to expose and restrain malpractices. The topic is no longer of much current importance, however, since in modern practice a company flotation is always in the hands of merchant banks or other institutions whose rigorous preliminary investigations and concern for their own reputations effectually eliminates dishonest practices of this particular type. But the rules are still part of current company law.

2.7 Duties of promoters

A promoter stands in a fiduciary relationship to the company which he forms. The primary consequence of that relationship is that he has a duty to disclose to the company any profit which he may secure from acting as promoter.

The promoter may discharge his duty by disclosure either to an independent board of directors or to those who are or may become members of the company.

The promoters sold property to the company at a profit to themselves. Of the five original directors two were at the time absent from the country, one was the nominal vendor (as undisclosed agent for the promoters), one was their 'mere instrument' and the fifth was the Lord Mayor of London 'too much occupied with other duties to be able to give attention to this'. The same solicitor acted both for the vendors and for the company. The facts were not disclosed in a prospectus. Held not to be a case of disclosure to a board of directors independent of the promoters. The company could rescind and recover the price which it had paid: *Erlanger v New Sombrero Phosphate Co* (1878) 3 App Cas 1218.

The alternative mode of disclosure to existing or prospective members is more usual nowadays, since a company prospectus must contain this information: Sch 3 paras 7 and 10. In the case of a private company the promoter is often in close touch with the shareholders. In *Salomon's Case* it was held that he had sufficiently disclosed his interest, as vendor of his business to the company, in his dealings with the six relatives who were the other shareholders.

It must be a proper disclosure of all the transactions from which the promoter secures any benefit from the promotion.

The prospectus disclosed that the promoters had purchased property and resold it to the company at a profit. The property was subject to charges which the promoters had bought at a discount of about £20,000 below their nominal amount. The charges were later discharged by the company by full payment out of moneys raised by the flotation of the company and the promoters thereby obtained an additional and undisclosed profit of £20,000. It was held that they had a duty to disclose this profit also since it was obtained from the promotion. They were made to account for it; *Gluckstein v Barnes* [1900] AC 240.

All which the law requires of a promoter is that he shall properly disclose that he is making a profit while acting as promoter. The company, through its directors or members, can then take an informed decision whether to proceed with the deal with the promoter or decline it.

The promoter is not generally accountable to the company for his profit made on a resale of property to the company. If, however, he has purchased property during the promotion *as agent* for the company then the company as principal may hold the promoter as agent accountable for his profit even if he had disclosed it. It is often difficult to establish that the promoter was acting as agent for the company in purchasing the property. If he bought it before the promotion began he can hardly have done so as agent. If after the promotion has begun he buys property with the object of reselling it to the company, it is possible that he was buying on his own account rather than as agent.

The promoter negotiated for the grant of a lease with the declared intention of assigning it to the company. It was held that he was not the company's agent or trustee in relation to the lease; *Omnium Electric Palaces Ltd v Baines* [1914] 1 Ch 332.

2.8 Remedies against a promoter

Rescission, as illustrated in *Erlanger's Case* above (2.7), is the primary – and often the only – remedy against a promoter who fails to disclose his profit. If rescission is no longer possible and the contract stands, the company cannot generally recover the profit from the promoter in any other way.

The right to rescind (and to recover the purchase price) is lost if:

(a) after gaining knowledge of the true facts the company shows an intention to ratify the contract; or
(b) restitutio in integrum is no longer possible (although in the case of fraud the court may order restitution with some financial adjustment for subsequent irrevocable changes); or
(c) an innocent third party has meanwhile acquired rights to the property.

If the right to rescind is lost, the company is generally without an effective remedy against a promoter, but in some exceptional circumstances it has been permitted to do so.

The facts do not often enable the company to argue that the promoter is accountable as agent (see the *Omnium Case* above). But it is a possible legal basis of claim.

In *Gluckstein's Case* the profit did not arise directly from the promoter's transaction with the company and so rescission was not the appropriate remedy. The court was disposed to penalise a dishonest promoter.

If there has been active deception, damages may be awarded for fraud or negligence.

The promoter purchased property for £24,000 and had it conveyed to its nominee. It then promoted the company, ie the fiduciary relationship began after the promoter acquired the property and so it was not the company's agent at the time. When the company had been formed the promoter's nominee sold the property to the company for £75,000 without disclosure that the promoter was the real vendor. The board of directors was not independent of the promoter and the prospectus did not disclose that the promoter was the vendor. The promoter was held liable to pay the profit to the company as damages; *Re Leeds and Hanley Theatres of Varieties Ltd* [1902] 2 Ch 809.

Apart from claims by the company, a promoter is at risk in two other respects. An individual shareholder who has taken shares in reliance on a misleading prospectus may recover compensation from those who issued it: s 67 (Chapter 6: 6.18).

A person convicted on indictment of an offence in connection with the promotion or formation of a company may be disqualified by court order from being a director, liquidator, receiver or promoter of a company and from being concerned in the management of a company. The disqualification may be for a period of up to 15 years. This is a sanction directed mainly against directors (Chapter 12: 12.3) but it does apply to promoters also.

2.9 Remuneration of promoters

A promoter who has incurred expense in the formation of a company has no right to recover his expenditure (nor remuneration for his services) unless there exists a valid contract with the company to that effect. But the company cannot enter into a contract with him before it is incorporated (2.10 below). However, the promoter is in control of the situation and may also be one of the original directors. So he can generally arrange that the company after incorporation shall pay him what he reasonably requires. If any prospectus is issued within two years the payment must be disclosed: Sch 3 para 10.

If there is more than one promoter their activities do not amount to a partnership through which one could ordinarily recover contribution to his expenses from another.

2.10 Pre-incorporation contracts

A company can only enter into contracts from the time of its incorporation. It may then either authorise in advance or ratify afterwards contracts made by agents on its behalf. But it cannot ratify a contract made on its behalf *before* it was incorporated because ratification is retrospective to the time when the agent purports to make the contract. If the principal did not then exist there is no contract with him by retrospective effect. Acceptance of the benefit of such a contract does not make the company liable in equity to pay for it nor can the company enforce the contract.

Three persons made a contract to purchase goods 'on behalf of the proposed Gravesend Royal Alexandra Hotel Company'. The goods were supplied and used by the company (incorporated subsequently) in its business. The supplier could not recover the price from the company since there can be no contract with a non-existent company but he could recover from the three agents since in these circumstances they had assumed personal liability: *Kelner v Baxter* (1866) LR2 CP174.

The liability of anyone who makes a contract for a company which does not exist is now statutory:

'Where a contract *purports* to be made by a company, or by a person as agent for a company, at a *time* when the company has not been formed, then subject to any *agreement* to the contrary the contract has effect as one entered into by the person purporting to act for the company or as agent for it, and he is personally liable on the contract accordingly'. (s 36(4)).

The implication of these words is that the agent, since he is deemed to have made the contract with himself as a party, may also enforce it against the other party. There is, however, no case on that particular point so far.

The significance of the words in italics was examined by the Court of Appeal in *Phonogram Ltd v Lane* [1982] QB 938. First, the agent does not escape liability by acting in the name of the company without any representation that he is its agent. It is still a contract which 'purports' to be made by the company and he is liable on it.

Secondly, although s 36(4) is based on an EC directive which refers to a contract made for a company 'in formation', the English statute is not limited in scope to cases where the formation of the company has begun but has not yet been completed. In the *Phonogram Case* nothing had been done to form the company and the defendant argued unsuccessfully that s 36(4) did not yet apply. Section 36(4) does apply whenever a person makes a contract for a company which does not then exist.

Thirdly, any agreement to exempt the agent from liability must be express. It will not be implied merely from the understanding of the parties.

Although the company is not bound by a contract made before its incorporation it may by novation enter into a new contract after incorporation (and the pre-incorporation contract is then discharged). The making of a new contract may be inferred from the acts of the parties, but there is no new contract to be inferred from the mere performance of the pre-incorporation contract under the mistaken impression that it is a binding contract.

A pre-incorporation contract was made for the grant of a building lease. After incorporation the company took possession of the land and expended a large sum in erecting buildings on it. There was no evidence of intention to make a fresh agreement. It was held that the acts of the company merely reflected a continuing mistake as to the validity of the earlier agreement which was void: *Re Northumberland Avenue Hotel Co Ltd* (1886) 33 ChD 16 CA.

The normal modern procedure is to prepare a draft contract before incorporation and to include in the objects clause of the memorandum, as the first object, the making and performing of this contract. When the company has been incorporated, the directors may if they see fit – but they are not bound to do so – execute the contract as a post-incorporation contract. Alternatively it is possible to appoint a trustee for the proposed company, acting explicitly as such, who enters into the contract before incorporation. But he and the other party assume personal liability which is only discharged if the company later makes a new contract or their agreement provides for discharge if the company fails to do so. This alternative is not a satisfactory arrangement and is not common in modern practice.

2.11 Contracts with subscribers to the memorandum

Section 104 introduces into English company law rules, embodied in the EC Second Directive, on contracts made between a *public* company (if registered as such since 1980) and:

(a) the *subscribers to its memorandum* of association who formed it as a public company. As already stated, however, this method of forming a public company is very rarely found; or
(b) its *shareholders* at the time of reregistration as a public company if it was previously a private company (Chapter 1: 1.17).

The rules only apply to contracts (made within a period of two years from incorporation or reregistration, as the case may be) under which the company acquires non-cash assets, eg land or patents, which are also assets of a value equal to, or more than one tenth of, the issued share capital of the company at the time.

Section 104 renders any such contract void unless one of three conditions is satisfied:

(1) the assets are acquired in the ordinary course of business – this is unlikely however since the assets must be of substantial minimum value in relation to the company's capital; or
(2) the contract is made under court supervision; or
(3) (i) an independent professional valuer is employed (under the procedure described later (Chapter 5: 5.9)) to value the consideration to be received by the company and also any non-cash consideration to be given by the company; *and*
    (ii) the members of the company pass an ordinary resolution in general meeting to approve the contract.

Where a newly formed public company is involved the intending vendors may readily sidestep s 104 by arranging that someone else shall perform the formal function of being subscribers to the memorandum.

Section 104 might have more practical importance in a situation in which a private company proposes to reregister as public with a view to flotation by a prospectus issue. In such a case the company would probably decide to acquire from shareholders any important assets used in the business but owned by the shareholders. But if the vendor shareholders first subscribe in cash for new shares and the company purchases the assets from them for cash *before* reregistering no valuation or resolution should be necessary (though the tax consequences of this procedure may have to be weighed with the rest).

2.12 Information from the Companies Registry
The company file held by the registry (2.3 above) contains every document which the company delivers to the registry for that purpose. It also contains copies of certificates of registration issued to the company by the registrar.

When a company is incorporated, the file contains a copy of the certificate of incorporation and the original formation documents (2.1 above). Each year's annual accounts (Chapter 14: 14.4) and annual return (Chapter 8: 8.15) will be enclosed as they are received. If there is a change of directors or secretary (Chapter 12: 12.9) or of the address of the company's registered office (Chapter 3: 3.9), the company is required to give formal notice to the registrar and the notice is put on the file. All special and extraordinary and some ordinary resolutions passed in general meeting (Chapter 11: 11.15) are delivered to the registrar in the form of a signed copy for filing. If the memorandum or articles of association are altered a copy of the revised text must similarly be delivered for filing at the registry (Chapter 3: 3.22 and Chapter 4: 4.3).

Charges on company property (Chapter 9: 9.16) generally require registration in the sense that they must be produced to the registrar. But in this case he returns the charge and merely retains for his file brief particulars of the charge. A copy of the charge itself may, however, be inspected at the company's registered office (Chapter 3: 3.10). A public company which issues a prospectus must deliver a copy, before publication, to the registry (Chapter 6: 6.6).

Some registers and other documents which a company is required to maintain may be held either at the registered office or at some other address (in England or Wales) of which notice must be given to the registrar (Chapter 3: 3.10).

The above summary is not exhaustive but indicates the more important documents which may be found on the company's file at the registry. For up-to-date information of the membership of the company it is necessary to inspect (or demand a copy of) the register of members, which is held at the registered office or other disclosed address (Chapter 8: 8.8). But the annual return on file at the registry gives membership particulars as at the date of the return (Chapter 8: 8.15). The annual return also contains a summary of the issued share capital. A return of allotments is required in respect of each allotment (Chapter 5: 5.13).

2.13 Notification in the *London Gazette*
The registrar is required by s 711 to give notice in the *London Gazette* of the issue or receipt of documents of various types relating to companies. He does not of course publish the documents themselves. The gazette notification merely states, with reference to a named company, that a document of a particular category has been received, or issued, as the case may be.

2.14 The effect of failure to give notice in the *Gazette*

If the company fails to deliver a prescribed document to the registrar the company and its officers in default are generally liable to be fined. An indirect consequence is that the registrar will obviously not give notice in the *London Gazette* since he will not have received the document. If there is a failure to deliver any of the following documents the company will be unable to rely on the event to which they relate in its dealings with a person who is unaware of it: s 42. These categories are:

(a) an order for compulsory winding up or the appointment of a liquidator in a voluntary liquidation;
(b) any alteration of the memorandum or articles;
(c) any change among the company's directors;
(d) any change of address of the registered office, insofar as it affects service of a document at that address.

It is also provided that if the document is received and a notice of its receipt is gazetted the company may not during the ensuing 15 days (after gazetting) rely on the relevant event against any person if he was unaware of the event because he was unavoidably prevented from knowing of it during that period.

To give a simple example suppose that X Ltd changes the address of its registered office and fails to give notice within 14 days (s 287) to the registrar who accordingly does not give notice in the *London Gazette* of receipt of a notice from the company. Y Ltd issues a writ to commence proceedings against X Ltd and sends the writ by post to the old address of X Ltd's registered office: s 725 (Chapter 3: 3.9). X Ltd cannot (as a technical defence) rely on the failure to serve the writ by delivery to its current registered office address unless it can show that at the time of posting the writ Y Ltd was actually aware of the change of address, eg by receipt of a letter from X Ltd on which the new address was shown as its registered office. If X Ltd does later give notice of the change of address to the registrar who notifies in the *London Gazette* that he has received it and Z Ltd in the ensuing 15 days posts a writ to the old address X Ltd could now rely on the point that the writ had not been correctly served on it (even if it had been forwarded) unless Z Ltd can show that it was unaware of the change of address and was 'unavoidably prevented' from knowing it. As Z Ltd could always make a search at the registry before issuing its writ and so discover the new address it is not clear how it could possibly be *unavoidably* prevented from that discovery (Chapter 3: 3.9).

Chapter 3

The memorandum of association

3.1 Contents of the memorandum

Every company must have a memorandum of association ('the memorandum') the main purpose of which is to declare the essential elements of its constitution. The minimum contents of a memorandum are defined by statute and model forms of memorandum for every type of company are provided: The Companies (Tables A to F) Regulations 1985, SI 1985/805.

The prescribed contents of a memorandum are:

(a) the name of the company;
(b) if it is to be a public company, a statement to that effect;
(c) whether the registered office is to be situated in England and Wales (or Wales only) or in Scotland;
(d) the objects of the company;
(e) that the liability of members is limited if it is a company limited either by shares or by guarantee. In the latter case there is an additional clause which states the amount which each member undertakes to contribute in a winding up, ie the maximum amount of the guarantee;
(f) if the company is a limited company with a share capital the amount of its authorised share capital divided into shares of fixed amount.

The memorandum ends with a declaration that the subscribers wish to form the company pursuant to the memorandum and agree to take the number of shares (by convention always one share each) set opposite their names. For all companies, public as well as private, it is now only necessary to have two subscribers (s 1) each of whom signs the memorandum; against his signature is written by convention 'one share'. The subscribers' signatures are witnessed, usually by a single witness who signs as such. The memorandum is dated and is treated as deed executed under seal. (It bears no deed stamp but is stamped with the companies registration fee of £50.)

It is possible to include in the memorandum additional clauses if that is desired. The reason for doing so is that a clause which is included in the memorandum may be expressed to be unalterable or, even if not so 'entrenched', may only be altered by procedures which give to a dissenting minority a right of appeal to the court subject to prescribed conditions: s 17. By contrast the provisions of the articles are always alterable (Chapter 4: 4.6) though special procedures and safeguards protect the holders of a class of shares in respect of an alteration of their rights (Chapter 7: 7.12).

3.2 Name: formal requirements

There are two legal rules about the use of the word 'limited'.

First, every company which has limited liability (of its members for its debts), whether limited by shares or by guarantee, must – with one exception (below) – disclose that fact in its company name. The name of a public company must end with the words 'public limited company' or the authorised abbreviation 'plc' (or the Welsh equivalent if it is a Welsh company): ss 25–26. The name of a private limited company ends with the word 'limited' unless it is permitted under s 30 to omit the word: s 25(2).

In examination questions the words 'plc' or 'limited' may be the only clue as to whether the company is public or private. In practice the same information can be obtained from the company's memorandum or its certificate of incorporation. Unless the company is there described as public, it is a private company (see also 3.6 below).

Secondly, the use of the word 'limited' is restricted in business names to the names of registered limited companies. It is an offence to carry on business under a name which includes 'limited' unless it is done through a limited company: s 34. The purpose of this rule is to enable persons who deal with a limited company to recognise it as such as soon as they know its name.

Two types of company incorporated under the Companies Acts do not include 'limited' in their names. One is the obvious category of unlimited company, for which the word 'limited' is inappropriate and misleading.

Secondly, a private company limited by guarantee (and any company limited by shares to which a licence for this purpose was granted under the law in force before 1982) may omit the word 'limited' from its name if it complies with s 30. For this exemption s 30 requires of the company (usually limited by guarantee) that:

(a) its object must be the promotion of commerce, art, science, education, religion, charity or any profession and everything incidental or conducive to any of those objects; and
(b) its memorandum or articles must require that its profits or other income are applied in promoting its objects; must also prohibit payment of dividends to its members; and must require that in liquidation assets otherwise available for distribution to members shall be transferred either to another body with similar objects or to a charitable body (but any such recipient body may be a member of the company in liquidation).

The company (or its promoters) deliver to the registrar a statutory declaration (made by a director or by the secretary or others) and the registrar may accept the declaration as sufficient evidence of entitlement to the exemption and register the name without 'limited'.

The company may not alter the relevant restrictions of its memorandum or articles. If without altering them it acts in breach of those restrictions the DTI may require it to change its name to include 'limited'.

The company must nonetheless state on its letterheads and order forms (3.8 below) that it is a limited company. But it need not publish its name in specified places (3.7 below) nor send a list of its members to the registrar with its annual return (Chapter 8: 8.15).

The system is useful to educational institutions incorporated as companies (the London School of Economics and Political Science for example) and to bodies such as Chambers of Commerce. The prohibition of any payment of dividends deprives it of any usefulness to commercial and trading concerns of the normal type.

3.3 Choice of name

The new system of regulating the choice of company names which was introduced in 1981 has the same objectives as the system which it replaced i e:

(a) the name of a registered company should be distinctive so that it can readily be identified and will not be confused with any other company on the index at the registry. Accordingly the name may not be the same or 'too like' the name of another company. For the same reason every company is given a distinguishing serial number which it must use on its letterheads and on all documents delivered to the registrar;

(b) no company should have a name which is likely to mislead the public as to its real status or activities or have offensive or criminal connotations.

The new system differs from the old in permitting the preliminary scrutiny of proposed names at the registry to be done by use of a suitably programmed computer. Only a small proportion of the names need then be examined individually by registry staff – a laborious method which had begun to break down under the burden of the increasing number of companies on the register.

A company may not (under s 26) be registered by a name:

(a) which includes 'limited', 'plc' etc otherwise than at the end of the name; or

(b) which is the same as any company name on the index of names which the registrar is formally required to maintain by s 714; or

(c) which is considered (by the DTI) to be offensive or to constitute a criminal offence; or

(d) which is likely to give the impression that the company is connected with a government department or a local authority (without official permission); or

(e) which includes any word or expression on the regulated list (3.5 below) of 'sensitive' words unless it has been individually approved by the DTI.

The computer will pick up names which fall into categories (a), (b) or – possibly – (c) and will refer for further examination anything in category (d) or (e).

Under rule (b) a name is treated as 'the same' as another name if there are only minor differences. Eg 'John Smith Limited' is treated as the same as 'John Smith & Company Limited'.

3.4 Change of name

A company may change its name of its own initiative and must do so if the DTI so directs s 28. In either case the company passes a special resolution to change its name but the change does not take effect until the registrar issues a certificate of incorporation under the new name (after processing the change of name under the rules described at 3.3 above). If the registrar withdraws from a company the privilege of omitting 'limited' from its name (3.2 above) it complies merely by a resolution of the board of directors to restore 'limited' to the name.

The statutory power to enforce a change of name is given to restrain abuse or end confusion. Accordingly it is exercisable only in certain circumstances:

(a) within 12 months of registration of a company name the registrar may direct the company to change it if he considers that it is the same or too like the name of another company which was or should have been on the register at the time; and

(b) within five years the registrar may enforce a change of name if the company provided misleading information to obtain its registered name or gave undertakings or assurances which it has not fulfilled.

It is the registrar's practice (the law does not require it) to invite the company or other interested party to put its case to him by letter before he takes a decision on a disputed name. In issuing his direction for a change of name he fixes a period within which the company must comply. Failure to do so is a criminal offence (punishable by fine) on the part of the company and its officers.

Finally, there is also a statutory power (s 32), to which there is no time limit, to compel a company to change its name if it is considered that the existing name gives so misleading an indication of the company's activities as to be likely to cause harm to the public. In this case the company must comply within six weeks of receiving a direction but it has a right of appeal (within three weeks) to the court which may either confirm the direction or set it aside.

This power is rarely used since, among other factors, it is not easy to prove that an unsuitable name is actually causing harm to anyone. In particular a company which changes its business and makes a corresponding change in its objects (3.18 below) is not usually required to change its name also – though it will often prefer to do this of its own initiative. But if a company has been allowed to include a 'sensitive' word such as 'charity' in its name because its original circumstances justified this and it later changes the entire nature of its activities, eg to operating a petrol filling station, it might well be required to make an appropriate change.

3.5 Business names

Most companies carry on a commercial activity. Hence the law on company names may give rise to business identity problems of two kinds.

First, a business or professional activity if carried on successfully soon acquires 'goodwill'. Customers or clients who have dealt with the business in the past return to it again. Others, hearing of the good reputation of the concern, choose it in preference to others equally unknown to them by past contact. 'Goodwill' is a valuable asset and the owner of the business may, if necessary, protect it by a common law 'passing off' action against any attempt to filch it from him. He demonstrates that some other business, by reason of the name of the business or of its products, is causing confusion so that the competitor is drawing away his customers because they believe that the competitor's business and his own are the same enterprise.

As illustrated by the *Buttercup Margarine Case* below, a 'passing off' action is outside the ambit of company law. Either or both of plaintiff and defendant may be, but need not be, registered companies.

A company may thus be restricted from using its company name as its business name by any other trader who asserts successfully that the name or part of it is so much associated with him or his business and their products are so much alike in general nature that confusion results.

The plaintiff, a sole trader, had a network of retail shops in Scotland and the north of England, through which he sold margarine and tea. He traded as 'the Buttercup Dairy Co'. The company was formed to carry on a business of wholesale margarine distributors in the London area but the company's objects included a power to trade as retailers. The plaintiff obtained an injunction to prevent the company from trading *under its own name* on the grounds that there might be confusion especially as the plaintiff planned to extend his business to the south of England using his established trade name: *Ewing v Buttercup Margarine Co Ltd* [1917] 2 Ch 1.

The plaintiff company manufactured a small aerator for use in syphons. The defendants were subscribers to the memorandum of a company to be registered under the name 'Automatic Aerator Patents Ltd' to supply large installations for aerating beer in public houses. There was insufficient evidence that confusion between them was likely; the plaintiffs had no exclusive right to the use of the common word 'aerator': *Aerators Ltd v Tollitt* [1902] 2 Ch 319.

The second problem is that of 'business names' which are subject to regulation under the Business Names Act 1985 ('BNA'). Most companies carry on business under their registered company names. As will be seen (3.7 below) they must display their names and other particulars so that persons dealing with them can identify and locate their legal address (registered office) without difficulty. However a company, like a sole trader or a partnership, has the right if it wishes to do so, to trade under some other name. If it does so it is subject to the BNA rules in addition to company law rules on display of names etc.

A company is subject to BNA rules if it carries on business in Great Britain under a name which does not consist of its corporate name without any addition (other than a statement that the business is carried on in succession to a former owner). It must then:

(a) state its company name in legible characters on all business letters, written orders for goods or services, invoices, receipts or written demands for payment of debts (connected with the business); and
(b) display its company name in a prominent position so that it may easily be read at all premises where the business is carried on and to which customers or suppliers have access.

In addition to its name the company must in all such contexts give an address in Great Britain (which would normally be its registered office – see 3.9 below) at which a document relating to the business may effectively be served on it.

If a representative of such a company does or discusses business with some other person, such as a customer or supplier, the latter has a right to demand particulars of the company's name and legal address. If such demand is made written particulars must be given immediately. This rule might, for example, compel a doorstep salesman to identify the company which he represents.

To prevent the use of pretentious or otherwise misleading names for business purposes, there is a list of 'sensitive' words which may not be included in the registered name of a company or in a business name used by a company (or any other trader) without official permission. Permission is only given if it is considered that the applicant is justified in the use of the word.

In some cases the applicant first approaches a professional body or government department to obtain the consent which he then produces to the registrar. For regulated words not specific to one profession or occupation he must apply direct to the registrar.

Thus a company which wishes to include a regulated word in its company or its business name must obtain approval. For 'Royal' it would apply to the Home Office; for 'Dental' the General Dental Council; for 'International' it would apply direct to the registrar.

3.6 Public company names

A public company must have a distinctive name ending with 'public limited company' (or the abbreviation 'plc' or the Welsh equivalent if it is a Welsh company): ss 25–26.

This principle is buttressed by rules which:

(a) prohibit any person who is not a public company from carrying on trade, profession or business under a name which includes the public company designation: s 33(1); and

(b) a public company is guilty of an offence if, in circumstances in which the fact that it is a public company is likely to be material to any person, it uses a name which may reasonably be expected to give the impression that it is a private company: s 33(2).

3.7 Publication of the company name

A company (unless exempt under s 30 – see 3.2) is required:

(a) to paint or affix its name in a conspicuous position outside every office or place at which its business is carried on;

(b) to have its name engraven on its seal; and

(c) to have its name mentioned in all business letters, notices and official publications, bills of exchange and orders for money or goods, invoices, receipts, etc, issued by the company: ss 348–350.

In each case the name must be in legible letters. Outside an office or place of business the name must be 'easily legible', ie in lettering appropriate to a display for quick reading. Any officer or agent who uses or authorises the use of a seal or document which fails to comply with this requirement is personally liable (as explained in Chapter 1: 1.7) and the company and its officers in default may be fined.

3.8 Publication of other particulars

To comply with EC requirements a company must on all its business letters and order forms mention in legible characters:

(a) the place of registration, ie whether in England or Wales or Scotland;

(b) the number with which it is registered;

(c) the address of its registered office (which must be identified as such);

(d) in the case of a limited private company which is permitted to omit the word 'limited' from its name the fact that it is limited company: s 351. If it is an investment company that fact must be stated (Chapter 5: 5.23).

The DTI considers (but this is doubtful) that 'order forms' include forms, such as coupons in newspaper advertisements, on which customers can order goods or services *from the company*. The narrower interpretation is that it means only forms issued by the company to obtain goods or services from suppliers.

The effect of these rules and those in 3.7, which apply to all companies (with one exception – 3.7 above), and the business name rules, which apply only if the company trades under some name which is not its company name, may be summarised as follows:

(1) *letterheads* should give the company name and the particulars listed above. This requirement also applies to *order forms*;
(2) *other business stationery* and *company cheque forms* should bear the company name. If the company trades under another name its business stationery should also show its registered office address as the address to which legal notices should be delivered;
(3) the *company seal* should show the company name. It does not usually have anything else on it – unless it is a duplicate seal used for issuing share certificates (Chapter 7: 7.2) when it is distinguished by the addition of 'Securities': s 40;
(4) the *business premises* should display a notice giving the company name. If the company trades under another name the notice should also show the registered office address.

Wherever the company name is required it must be given in its correct form. When there are business name requirements (items (2) and (4) above) the company may give some other address (for the receipt of legal notices) but the registered office is the obvious choice.

3.9 Registered office
The particulars delivered to secure incorporation of a company include the intended address of the registered office. The company therefore begins its existence with a registered office and is required at all times to have a registered office: s 10(6).

In exercise of their powers of management the directors may at any time change the address of the registered office but only so that the new address like the old is within the country specified for that purpose in the memorandum. Whenever there is a change of address of the registered office notice of the change must within 14 days be delivered to the registrar: s 287. The registrar then gives notice of change of address: s 711.

The address of the registered office must also be shown on letters and order forms (3.8 above) and on the company's annual return. The address is not shown in the memorandum which merely states the country in which the registered office is to be situate. The effect of this clause of the memorandum, which cannot be altered, is to fix the nationality and domicile of the company and to indicate (by inference only) that the register's file on the company is held and may be inspected at the registry within the country where the registered office is situated. If, for example, the memorandum states that the registered office is to be in England (which in this context includes Wales unless Wales is explicitly mentioned so as to make the company a Welsh company) then the original file is held at the registry at Cardiff (though a microfiche copy is also available at Companies House in London). If the memorandum states that the registered office will be in Scotland the file is held at the registry in Edinburgh.

The registered office provides a known address of the company for two purposes. First, any document, such as a formal notice or legal process, may be effectually served on the company either by leaving it at the registered office or by sending it by post addressed to the company at the registered office: s 725. For that reason it is a routine preliminary in litigation to search the file at the registry to ensure that the writ or summons is posted to the address notified on the file as the registered office. Due service cannot then be disputed. The second purpose of the registered office is to provide premises at which (unless notice has been given to the registrar of a different address) the registers and certain other documents of the company are held (3.10 below).

3.10 Registers and other documents held at the registered office (or alternative address)

The following registers, etc, may, and in some cases must, be held at the registered office:

(a) the register of members and, when it is required, the alphabetical index to that register: ss 353–354 (Chapter 8: 8.8);
(b) the register of directors and secretary: s 288 (Chapter 12: 12.9);
(c) the register of directors' interests in shares or debentures of the company together with the index, if any: s 325 (Chapter 12: 12.10);
(d) the register (if any) of shareholders' interests in a public company carrying unrestricted voting rights in those cases where the interests exceed 5 per cent: s 211 (Chapter 8: 8.13);
(e) the register (if any) of debenture holders: s 190 (Chapter 9: 9.9);
(f) the register (if any) of charges on the property of the company: s 407 (Chapter 9: 9.22);
(g) a copy of every instrument creating a registrable charge or in the case of a series of uniform debentures a specimen debenture: s 406 (Chapter 9: 9.22);
(h) the minute books of general meetings: s 383 (Chapter 11: 11.15);
(i) a copy of each director's contract of service or a memorandum of its terms if there is no written agreement: s 318 (Chapter 12: 12.8);
(j) a copy of any contract for the purchase of shares of the company made within the previous ten years: s 169 (Chapter 5: 5.15).

The register of directors and secretary, the company's register of charges (and copies of the charges) and the minute book of general meetings *must* be kept at the registered office. It may not be held elsewhere.

The register of members may be held at some other office of the company if it is made up there or at the office of an agent employed to do that work. Many large public companies now entrust the maintenance of their register of members to specialist registrars who use computers and other mechanical aids to provide share registration services to a number of client companies. The companies' registers are then held by them at their premises.

If the register of members is held elsewhere than at the registered office the register of directors' interests in shares and debentures must be held with it at the same place. Any register of interests in shares must be held at the same place as the register of directors' interests.

Copies of directors' service agreements, if not held at the registered office, may be held elsewhere either with the register of members or at the company's principal place of business.

A register of debenture holders may be held at any office of the company where it is made up or at the office of an agent employed to do the work. But it need not be held at the same place as the register of members since the recording of issue and transfer of debentures may be in the hands of different registrars.

If these registers or documents are held elsewhere than at the registered office, the place at which they are held must be in the same country as the registered office, i e if the registered office is in England any alternative place selected for holding registers and documents must also be in England. The company must send to the registrar notice of the address (if it is not the registered office) at which registers and documents are kept (and of any change of such address).

The register of members must be open for inspection by the public for at least two hours of each working day (except when the register is closed, e g for making up a dividend list): s 356. There is also a statutory right to obtain from the company within ten days of request a copy of the register of members or any part of it such as a select list of members holding, e g 100 or more shares.

The public has a statutory right to inspect the register of directors and secretary, the register of directors' and the shareholders' interests, the register of debenture holders and the register of charges (Chapter 9: 9.22). An inspection fee of 5p is payable (though not usually demanded) except by members, debenture holders (as regards their own register) and creditors (as regards the register of charges). There is a statutory right to copies of the register of directors and of shareholders' interests and of the register of debenture holders on payment of a fee of 10p per hundred words. The register, etc, must be available for inspection for at least two hours on each working day.

The register of directors' interests must be available for inspection by all persons present at the annual general meeting: Sch 13 paras 25, 29. The Stock Exchange Listing Agreement requires companies whose shares are listed to make available for public inspection in the three weeks up to the annual general meeting copies of directors' service agreements if they have more than one year unexpired.

Even members have no right to inspect the minutes of directors' meetings nor are the minutes required to be kept at any specified place.

3.11 The objects clause
The memorandum must state 'the objects of the company' i e the business or other activity which it is to carry on: s 2. The statutory model forms of memorandum to which companies should conform 'as near as circumstances permit' simply specify a business with a dozen words of description followed by reference to things 'incidental and conducive' to the specified object: Table D (model memorandum of a public company). But the model form gives rise to so much difficulty and uncertainty that in practice no memorandum of a company is ever as brief or concise as this.

The assumption which underlies the statutory model is that a company formed to carry on one type of business will confine itself to that business. In so far as the company needs power to engage in transactions, such as obtaining premises or employing staff to carry on its designated business, the statutory model *implies* that it has specific powers 'incidental and conducive' etc. But in the real world of business a company may branch out into additional and perhaps different types of business. The cycle repair shop at Cowley established by the future Lord Nuffield became in time Morris Motors. The history of Unilever is another example of remarkable growth and diversification. Apart from the diversification factor, the doctrine of implied powers is too vague and uncertain in its legal limits to be safely relied upon. The doctrine of implied powers does not for example automatically enable a company to hold shares of another company (if it had no express power to do so).

To obviate these difficulties it has become standard practice (as exemplified in the model forms of memorandum produced by law stationers for use by the professions and the public):

(a) to specify more than one object. It is usual to begin with the original business envisaged by the promoters of the company and to follow the opening paragraph with alternative or supplementary activities described either in less specific or sometimes in completely unspecific terms (3.12 below); and

(b) to add 20 or 30 paragraphs conferring the express power to engage in many types of transaction. But these powers are not distinguished in the wording of the objects clause from objects in the proper sense. They are expressed as additional objects and the question may arise as to whether a power, e g to acquire business premises, can be treated as an object in itself (3.13 below).

The reason for this elaboration, with all the confusion which may result from it, is the doctrine of ultra vires. This doctrine is that a registered company cannot make a valid and binding contract if that contract is neither within the scope of its express objects (and powers) nor reasonably incidental to accomplishing those objects. A contract outside the company's powers (ultra vires in Latin) is void and is unenforceable unless s 35 (3.17) renders it enforceable against, but never by, the company. Hence the search for the widest and most flexible form of objects clause in order by use of express words to avoid the pitfalls of ultra vires transactions.

At the end of 1985 the DTI set in train a process of consultation with interested parties and experts on the implications of abolishing the ultra vires rule in relation to registered companies. The weight of professional opinion is strongly in favour of making this change in the law. It seems likely that, with some safeguards against collusion and abuse, the objects clause will be reduced to a mere definition of the powers of the company delegated to the directors in managing the business. It will no longer fetter the company's contractual capacity in its dealings with third parties, if the latter are unaware that the directors may be exceeding their powers. However, no decision to make such a fundamental change has yet been made. Although it may be uncontentious, the change may entail some complicated legislation, for which parliamentary time will have to be found.

The term intra vires is used to express the fact that a company is acting within its defined powers. It is best to reserve ultra vires/intra vires for the contractual capacity of the company and not to apply these terms to the acts of directors within or outside their delegated powers of management.

The Court of Appeal recently restated the existing law on ultra vires transactions in the *Rolled Steel Products Case* (of which the facts are given below). It seems that this latest analysis is essentially based on the law of agency related to the persons involved, ie:

(1) the *company* as principal must have legal capacity to enter into the

contracts made on its behalf. The limits of its capacity are determined by interpreting its objects clause;

(2) the *directors* as agents of the company have actual and ostensible authority to make contracts for the company:

    (i) their ostensible authority is to make any contract which is within the company's legal capacity unless the other party (see below) has notice that this authority is restricted or is being exceeded;

    (ii) their actual authority is limited to making contracts for proper purposes related to the company's objects.

If the directors make a contract binding on the company but in excess of their actual authority they are in breach of their fiduciary duty (Chapter 12: 12.18) to the company. But the members of the company may give authority to enter into a transaction within the company's capacity;

(3) the *other party* to the contract is entitled to assume, unless he knows or should know the opposite, that the directors have authority to make the contract with him: *Re David Payne & Co Ltd* [1904] 2 Ch 608. There are two situations in which he has notice that the directors lack the requisite authority:

    (i) if the company's objects clause does not give it capacity to enter into the contract the other party is deemed to know this unless, by reason of s 35 (3.17 below), he has neither constructive notice nor actual knowledge of that fact; and

    (ii) if he knows that in making the contract the directors are exceeding their actual authority or exercising their powers for an improper purpose, the contract, even if it is within the company's legal capacity, is one which the directors have no actual authority to make. In view of what he knows they have no greater ostensible authority than their actual authority in their dealings with him.

If in the course of such a transaction he obtains money, property or benefit from the company he holds it as a constructive trustee for the company, ie must return it, since he obtains it with knowledge of the directors' breach of their fiduciary duty.

In any such situation the other party is in practice concerned mainly with two specific points – what is the capacity of the company ascertained from its objects clause and what did he know or have the means of discovering about the purposes for which the directors made the contract? However, on what he did not actually know or realise but might have known (the principle of constructive notice) his position may be improved by s 35.

The facts of the case below, from which the above analysis has been derived, also help to illustrate how the relevant points may apply in practice.

In a complicated transaction the plaintiff company (RSP) borrowed money and gave a guarantee of another company's liability. The objects clause gave power to enter into these transactions but the express power to give guarantees was limited to such purposes 'as may seem expedient'. The guarantee would benefit one of the directors (S) of RSP. He failed to declare his interest in the transaction at the RSP board meeting (as required by s 317). These facts disqualified him from voting. Without him the board lacked the necessary quorum for a valid decision to give the guarantee. The other party (BSC) through its solicitors obtained a copy of the minutes of the board meeting. From the minutes, and from its part in negotiations leading to the transaction, BSC knew or could have known that the board had no power to give the guarantee.

The Court of Appeal held that the words 'as may seem expedient' restricted the company's capacity to give guarantees to those which benefited the company. Any assumption by BSC that the guarantee was intra vires and for the benefit of the company was negatived by its knowledge that the guarantee was actually for the benefit of S. Secondly BSC was or should have been aware of the invalidity of the proceedings at the board meeting of RSP. The guarantee was therefore void: *Rolled Steel Products (Holdings) Ltd v British Steel Corp* [1985] 2 WLR 908 CA.

The next three sections of this chapter consider the principles developed in earlier cases for determining the legal effect of an objects clause. The rules applicable to directors are explained in a later chapter (Chapter 12).

3.12 Multiple main objects

Three drafting devices may be used to give flexibility and wider scope to an objects clause. These are (1) multiple alternative objects, (2) a declaration that each object is independent of the others and (3) a provision for adopting additional objects at the directors' discretion. Each device is considered and illustrated below.

It is usual to begin an objects clause with a first paragraph which specifies the immediate purpose for which the company is formed. But this is followed by alternative objects and/or more general words spread over three or four additional paragraphs. A transaction is generally intra vires if any part of these multiple objects covers it or if it is incidental to them.

The first three paragraphs of the original objects clause provided for (1) the acquisition of a specified engineering business and (2) the carrying on of various types of engineering and metalworking. After 46 years the company sold its original business but planned to acquire another within the terms of (2) above. A petition was presented for the compulsory liquidation of the company on the ground that its substratum had gone, i e it could no longer carry on business under the terms of its objects clause (see Chapter 18: 18.4 below).

The Court of Appeal dismissed the petition and held that 'the main and paramount object . . . was to carry on an engineering business of a general kind'.

This decision effectively overrode an earlier one (*Stephens v Mysore Reefs (Kangundy) Mining Co Ltd* [1902] 1 Ch 745) in which it was held that the second object was limited in its scope to enterprises which would contribute to the more effective operation of the first and specific business: *Re Kitson & Co Ltd* [1946] 1 All ER 435.

Multiple objects are only an effective device in enlarging the objects clause if the further objects add something to the opening paragraph. Mere repetition of the same thing in different words is 'pure tautology' which adds nothing (see the *German Date Coffee Case* in Chapter 18: 18.4).

The court is always concerned to extract from the words used the apparent intention in using them. One principle of interpretation (illustrated by the *Mysore Reefs Case* above) is the eiusdem generis rule, i e if general words follow specific words in the same context, the general words are to be limited to things 'of the same kind'. As an example 'groceries and other goods' might be construed so as to limit 'other goods' to things normally sold in a grocer's shop. However, this is merely a rule of presumed intention which may be excluded by evidence to the contrary effect.

Hence the second device available for widening an objects clause is to include in it, usually at the end, a declaration that no object 'shall be in any way limited by reference to or inference from the terms of any other paragraph' nor 'shall it be deemed subsidiary or auxiliary to the objects mentioned in the first paragraph'. This 'independent objects declaration' is often called a 'Cotman and Brougham clause' from the case below in which the House of

Lords – reluctantly – upheld it as valid and confirmed its effect.

The first and specific object was to carry on the business of a rubber plantation company. This object was followed by 'a vast variety of objects' and the clause ended with the declaration in the text above. The alternative objects included dealing in shares of other companies. The issue before the court was whether the company's underwriting (Chapter 6: 6.8) of the prospectus of another company was intra vires or not. The House of Lords held that, by reason of the declaration, dealing in shares was an independent object and covered underwriting: *Cotman v Brougham* [1918] AC 514.

The first paragraph of the objects clause specified import and export of various types of goods. A subsequent object, however, included the acquisition of 'any concessions, contracts, rights . . .' and there was an independent objects declaration. The company employed architects and estate agents to secure a building lease. It was held that the words quoted covered this transaction which was therefore intra vires: *Anglo-Overseas Agencies Ltd v Green* [1960] 3 All ER 244.

This form of declaration applies to every part of the objects clause, including the paragraphs which confer 'powers' rather than create 'objects' in the strict sense (3.13). However the essential nature of a power may give it a more limited effect in that context, as explained later.

The third device is the addition to the sequence of objects of a paragraph which authorises the company 'to carry on any trade or business whatsoever which can in the opinion of the directors be advantageously carried on in connection with or as ancillary to any of the above businesses'. This formula, which is less common than the others, also takes its name from the case in which it was first tested and upheld. It is often called a 'Bell Houses clause'.

On theoretical grounds one can object to it as completely unspecific, ie it does not describe any type of business even in general words, and as 'subjective', ie the test is not whether it is in fact advantageous to the company to combine the new business with the existing businesses specified in the objects clause. It merely requires that the directors shall form the (subjective) view that it is advantageous to the company to do so.

The first and specific object of the plaintiff company was to develop land by building houses – and this in fact was the company's main business. In raising loan capital for building projects the company established useful contacts with Swiss financial institutions. Another development company wished to have an introduction to these lenders and the plaintiff company gave that service in return for a commission of £20,000. When the company sued to recover the commission, which had not been paid, the defendant company argued that the contract was void since the plaintiff company's objects clause did not permit it to carry on the business of mortgage brokers. However the Court of Appeal, relying partly, but not entirely, on the 'advantage' clause above, held that the company had been acting intra vires in introducing the defendants to lenders in return for a commission: *Bell Houses Ltd v City Wall Properties Ltd* [1966] 2 All ER 674.

The decision in this case was related to various relevant facts. The company was able to earn a commission by mortgage broking because in the course of its primary business of building it had tapped useful sources of long-term loans. The connection with the lenders was 'incidental' to the building operations and the objects clause expressly provided for activities 'incidental' to the main business. The 'subjective' point was not really an objection in this case because objectively it was to the company's advantage to earn a £20,000 commission as it did.

The company still carried on its building business and so was combining mortgage broking with a specific object. If, as in the *Kitson Case*, it had already abandoned its original and specific object and branched out into something else, the latter activity would not be 'connected with' or 'ancillary to' an existing business and the Bell Houses clause would hardly cover it. There is also authority for the view that a company could not adopt the Bell Houses formula as its *first* object in the opening paragraph: *Re Crown Bank* (1890) 44 Ch D 634. In that situation the registrar would probably refuse to register the company, arguing that it had no 'objects' as required by law.

3.13 Powers express and implied

When a company is incorporated with express objects, specific or general, the law implies powers in favour of the company to enter into whatever transactions are reasonably incidental or conducive to the attainment of its objects. Thus a trading company has implied power to acquire and occupy premises, to employ staff, to sell assets – but not its entire undertaking, to operate a bank account, to borrow money and to mortgage its property as security. In addition to these general powers, applicable to any commercial enterprise, there is an implied power related to the particular nature of the business to do what is incidental to it.

The company was formed with the object of manufacturing coal gas and an additional power to process and sell by-products. It was held that it had an implied power to buy materials which it needed to process the by-products for sale: *Deuchar v Gas Light & Coke Co* [1925] AC 691.

However, the doctrine of implied powers is limited to powers which have some connection with the objects. The reason why there is no implied power to sell the company's undertaking is that such a sale is at variance with the object of carrying on the business.

The company's objects were to build an hotel and to carry on a hotel business. There was also an express power 'to do things incidental to the attainment of the objects'. The directors proposed to let the building temporarily for use as offices. A member objected that there was neither an express nor an implied power to dispose of the undertaking in this way. The court upheld him on that legal point but decided on the facts that a temporary letting of the hotel building was a transaction 'incidental' to the objects and so intra vires: *Simpson v Westminster Palace Hotel Co* (1860) 8 HL Cas 712.

It has also been held in other cases that there is no *implied* power to invest in the shares of another company nor to acquire its undertaking.

There are two objections to relying on implied powers. First, there is some uncertainty as to what is implied. Secondly, the directors as businessmen find it much more convenient to have a list of express powers to refer to in case of need.

As express powers, set out at length in the objects clause, cover every foreseeable contingency – and may be added to (3.18) if something unforeseen arises, it is not often necessary to rely on implied powers. But if some transaction has already been completed, for which the express powers make no provision, it may then be necessary to consider what else is implied by reference to the test of what is (1) incidental and (2) beneficial to the company's business.

An express power, if supported by a Cotman and Brougham declaration, ranks almost as an independent object unconstrained by the objects in the proper sense.

The objects clause included an express power to establish pension schemes for the benefit of past and present directors. After W had retired from his directorship (and had transferred his shares to his son) the company took out a pension policy for the benefit of W. Although there was no formal decision on this transaction at a board meeting, the only two shareholders approved it at the time when the policy was issued. Later when the company was in liquidation the liquidator asserted that the purchase of the pension policy was ultra vires and an act of misfeasance by the directors.

The Court of Appeal held that the power to grant pensions was a substantive object, not limited to transactions incidental and beneficial to the company's business. The shareholders had approved the transaction and so the directors were not liable to make good the cost of the policy to the company: *Re Horsley & Weight Ltd* [1982] 3 WLR 431.

There are, however, some limitations on express powers. First, even an express power will not validate something unlawful. An excessive payment by an insolvent company of 'director's remuneration' without receiving any services from the director may be treated as an unlawful payment of capital to the director as shareholder (the *Halt Garage Case* in Chapter 12: 12.8).

Secondly, the express power may be so worded that it is limited to transactions incidental to the company's business. This was the effect of the words 'as may be expedient' in relation to a power to give guarantees (the *Rolled Steel Products Case* in 3.11 above).

Finally, the very nature of an express power may limit its scope so that it cannot be independent of the main objects.

The company's objects were to provide services to foreign tourists. It was accepted that at the relevant time the company's current activity i e pig-breeding was ultra vires. The company had an express power to borrow and to charge its assets as security and there was an 'independent objects declaration'. In granting a loan for pig-breeding the bank, which had inspected the objects clause, took it to mean that the power to borrow covered borrowing for any purpose whatever.

The Court of Appeal held that a power to borrow is by its nature limited to the purposes defined by the main objects; it is not 'something in the air'. As the loan had been obtained for an ultra vires purpose, of which the bank was aware, the loan itself was ultra vires and irrecoverable: *Re Introductions Ltd* [1970] Ch 199.

Borrowing is the main instance of a power which by its nature is limited. The grant of a pension is not necessarily so restricted (the *Horsley & Weight Case* above).

3.14 The power to make gifts
At one time there was some uncertainty and confusion as to whether a company could make gifts. In this context 'gifts' include all transactions of a gratuitous nature in which a company transfers assets or assumes liabilities without obtaining anything in return.

What is in form a gift may be made to secure some advantage to the company which, however difficult to quantify, makes the 'gift' a transaction for the company's benefit. A power to enter into transactions of that kind may be implied, if not expressed, as incidental to the company's business. .

A chemical manufacturing company made grants of £100,000 to finance scientific research and also training schemes at universities. No *direct* benefit to the company would result from those endowments. It was held, however, that there was sufficient connection between the purpose of the gifts, i e to advance the progress of science in a relevant field, and the commercial activities of the company, to make them incidental to the company's business and intra vires: *Evans v Brunner, Mond & Co Ltd* [1921] 1 Ch 359.

The objects clause included an express power to guarantee the obligations of any other person with whom the company had dealings or which carried on a business in which the company had an interest, direct or indirect. The company gave a guarantee of the indebtedness of another company controlled by the same shareholder as itself. The court upheld the guarantee as intra vires and expressed the opinion that where there is an express power it is unnecessary to consider whether the directors in exercising the power intended to obtain a benefit to the company. On the facts, however, the court concluded that the directors might reasonably have decided that it was in the company's interest to support an associated company: *Charterbridge Corp Ltd v Lloyds Bank Ltd* [1969] 2 All ER 1185.

The decision in the *Charterbridge Case* has been followed in later cases such as *Horsley & Weight* and has recently been approved by the Court of Appeal in the *Rolled Steel Products Case*. It marked a dissent from earlier case law (*Re Lee, Behrens & Co Ltd* [1932] 2 Ch 46). It is only necessary to look for a benefit to the company in making a gift if either the express power is limited to such cases ('as may seem expedient' in the *Rolled Steel Products Case*) or there is no express power and so it is appropriate to consider whether one can be implied.

The issue of company gifts arises when the directors make contributions to the funds of a political party. The long-established and general justification for this practice, increasingly criticised, is that the directors can reasonably conclude that it is indirectly beneficial to the company that a political party shall flourish and be in power – the *Brunner Mond* situation extended to a different field. But his view seems to be in doubt as a result of a recent decision.

The League against Cruel Sports, a limited company, had an express power to subscribe to any institution with objects similar to the main objects of the League. The League gave £30,000 to the Labour Party to be used to promote the aims of the League and also £50,000 to the Party's election fund. The £30,000 gift was not in dispute. It was held, however, that the £50,000 gift, not made for any specific purpose, was not covered by the express power. No power could be implied to make contributions to the general funds of a political party unless the gift is made 'in pursuit of . . . an express authorised object' of the League. Hence the £50,000 gift was ultra vires: *Simmonds v Heffer* [1984] BCLC 298.

It is safer for the company which intends to make such contributions to include in its objects clause an express power (not limited as it was in the above case) and an independent objects declaration.

A company which makes political contributions above a prescribed minimum is required to disclose this gift in its annual accounts: s 235 and Sch 7 para 3. But this recognition of the practice does not automatically make it intra vires for the company.

As long as a company carries on its business, a power to make voluntary payments, such as an ex-gratia lump sum given to a long-service employee on his retirement, is probably implied, if not expressed in the objects clause. It is beneficial to the business to treat employees in this manner. But for 'gifts' to directors, past directors or their dependants, such as a pension to which there is no contractual entitlement, an express power is required (as in the *Horsley & Weight Case* in 3.13 above). Although the *Lee Behrens* decision no longer carries much authority, it would presumably operate to exclude any implication of a power to benefit directors and their dependants. In any of these situations the directors have a duty (Chapter 12: 12.18) to exercise their powers in the interests of the company. If they made a gift for a purpose which the recipient knew was in breach of this duty, it might be void (the *Rolled Steel Products Case* in 3.12 above).

A company which has closed down or sold its business now has a statutory power under s 719 to make voluntary redundancy payments and the like (in excess of its legal obligations under the Employment Protection (Consolidation) Act 1978 s 81) to its employees. This reverses the decision of principle in *Parke v Daily News Ltd* [1962] 2 All ER 929. The power may be exercised as follows:

(a) the directors may make redundancy payments if authorised to do so by the memorandum or articles;
(b) a general meeting may do so by passing an ordinary resolution unless the memorandum or articles require some other kind of resolution;
(c) a liquidator may implement a previous decision of a general meeting to make such payments, but he must first pay the company's debts in full: IA s 187.

In cases (a) or (b) the power is limited, before the company is in liquidation, to payments made out of profits otherwise available for distribution as dividend: s 719(4).

3.15 The effect on the company of an ultra vires transaction

This section deals with the effects of an ultra vires transaction on the company itself, its members and directors. The position of the other party to an ultra vires transaction, who is often the main loser, is discussed in the next two sections.

The company cannot enforce an unperformed ultra vires contract and if it seeks to do so the other party may rely on the fact that it is ultra vires as grounds for repudiating his obligations (as in the *Bell Houses Case* – though in the event the contract was held to be intra vires). If the company has received money or property under the transaction the other party has limited rights to recover it (3.16). It seems – though the position is not entirely clear – that if the company has parted with its money or property under an ultra vires transaction it may recover it. Where there is a right of recovery it is based on the proposition that an ultra vires transaction is void and does not confer title.

The members cannot authorise or ratify a transaction which is ultra vires:

The company's main object was railway construction and its objects clause did not cover the making of a loan to Riche to finance the construction of a railway. The articles provided, however, that the objects might be extended by special resolution passed in general meeting. The House of Lords ruled that even the unanimous consent of the members could not authorise a transaction which was beyond the limits of the objects clause: *Ashbury Rly Carriage and Iron Co Ltd v Riche* (1875) LR 7 HL 653.

At the time of this decision there was no power to alter the original objects clause. Since 1948 the members may, without resort to the court, alter the objects under s 4 (3.18). But such alteration is only effective in respect of subsequent transactions. Even now there can be no retrospective ratification of an ultra vires transaction. There are also situations in which the directors may exceed their delegated powers (limited to the purpose of the company) but the transaction is within the legal capacity of the company. In these cases ratification is possible (Chapter 12: 12.18). Dicta in the *Rolled Steel Products Case* on members' consent to invalid acts of the directors are better understood – though there is some doubt – in this sense.

Members of the company can restrain the company and the directors from entering into or carrying out an ultra vires transaction. For this purpose they apply to the court for a declaration or injunction (as in *Simpson's Case* in 3.13 above).

The directors are liable to make good to the company any loss resulting from an ultra vires transaction since they are in breach of their duty to exercise their powers of management for the proper purposes of the company. They are not generally liable to the other party for his loss – but this is considered in the next section.

3.16 The remedies of the other party

If the conditions set by s 35 are satisfied (see 3.17 below) the other party to an ultra vires contract may enforce it against the company. But he may still have to consider his position under other rules of law which continue in force except insofar as s 35 excludes them. This section deals with those other and earlier rules.

Even under s 35 it is always necessary to consider how much the other party knew at the time of the transaction. The principle of constructive notice (which is excluded by s 35) where it applies means that the other party is deemed both to know and to understand the contents of the objects clause of the company. In the *Introductions Case* (3.13) the bank was aware of the terms of the objects clause but misunderstood their effect. In the case below the other party had not looked at the objects clause at all. But he could have inspected it at the Companies Registry.

The company's main object was the manufacture of women's clothes but it had changed its business entirely and placed an order for coke, for its factory, using a letterhead on which was printed 'Veneered Panel Manufacturers'. The company became insolvent and did not pay for the coke. The supplier's claim failed because he actually knew of the purpose (furniture making) for which the coke was supplied and he was deemed to know (constructive notice) that furniture making was ultra vires the company: *Re Jon Beauforte (London) Ltd* [1953] Ch 131.

In this case the court noted that if the supplier had not been informed of the purpose for which his coke was supplied, that knowledge would not have been imputed to him. In the *Rolled Steel Products Case* the Court of Appeal confirmed that if the transaction *could* be for the purpose of the company (and so intra vires) the other party is entitled to assume that it is until he knows that it is not, and the court cited the *David Payne Case* of 1904 to that effect. But it is unusual to lend money or supply goods to a company in ignorance of the nature of its current business, which is the situation postulated in the *David Payne Case*.

Unless he can rely on s 35 a lender should consider whether he can recover his loan by subrogation or by tracing. If his money has been used to pay a debt of the company which was intra vires, the lender steps into the shoes (subrogation) of the creditor who has been repaid and may recover his money from the company to the extent that it has been so applied. But in this the lender cannot take over any security for the debt given to the other creditor.

If the company still has his loan in identifiable form, eg in a separate bank account, or if he can 'trace' it into an asset which the company has purchased with his money, he may recover the money or claim the asset. There are often practical difficulties. If the loan was paid into a running account with a bank, the lender can only trace it by the rule in *Clayton's Case* (first in first out) and he cannot trace it beyond the point at which the company has something of value into which it was converted. If, for example, the money was used to buy material which has been used in manufacture he cannot trace it into the product.

If the company gave him security for his loan, the security is void if the loan was ultra vires. If he realises the security he must account to the company for the proceeds. If, however, he obtained a guarantee of the loan from a third party, he may enforce the guarantee although the debt is irrecoverable, unless the loan was unlawful as well as ultra vires.

If goods are supplied or property transferred in an ultra vires transaction it appears that the company acquires title to these assets and the other party cannot recover them – but the case law is scanty and uncertain.

As the other party has constructive notice that the transaction is ultra vires he cannot claim against the directors for misleading him on that point. But if they have deceived him on material facts he may have an action in tort for deceit.

3.17 Rights given by s 35
Section 35 (formerly the European Communities Act 1972 s 9(1)) reads:

'In favour of a person dealing with a company in good faith, any transaction decided on by the directors shall be deemed to be one which it is within the capacity of the company to enter into, and the power of the directors to bind the company shall be deemed to be free of any limitation under the memorandum or articles of association. A party to a transaction so decided on shall not be bound to enquiry as to the capacity of the company to enter into it or as to any limitation on the powers of the directors and shall be presumed to have acted in good faith until the contrary is proved'.

Two effects of s 35 are clear. First, it does not render an ultra vires contract intra vires the company but simply enables a person dealing with a company to enforce an ultra vires contract. Any other consequences of the contract being ultra vires continue; eg the company cannot enforce or ratify it, a member can obtain an injunction to restrain the making of it, and the directors are liable to the company for any loss arising from it.

Secondly, s 35, where it applies, abrogates the doctrine of constructive notice of the content and legal effect of the memorandum and articles. Notice will not be imputed and there is no duty to obtain actual notice by inspecting the documents.

On three other points the effect of s 35 will remain uncertain unless the doubts are removed by judicial pronouncement or statutory amendment. These points are the meaning of the phrases (1) a person dealing with a company; (2) in good faith; and (3) any transaction decided on by the directors. The interpretations suggested below are therefore deductions unsupported by actual case law, except as regards point (3).

It is only a person dealing with the company who is protected. 'Dealing' (and 'transaction') imply the making of a contract. If that is so the person who merely receives a gift (3.14) may not be covered. A person who is connected with the company as a director or shareholder would be protected if his transaction were an ordinary commercial contract. But if he is asserting a right given to him as director or shareholder by the articles it is probable that he is not covered by s 35.

The EC First Directive, from which s 35 is derived, refers to 'knowledge' and not to 'good faith'. If the person dealing with the company knows that a transaction is ultra vires he cannot be in good faith. If he suspects, without actually knowing, that it is ultra vires and refuses to examine the memorandum (or articles) and perhaps refuses also to seek advice on their legal effect, after doubts have been raised, he might well be regarded as no longer dealing in good faith. If, as in the *Introductions Case* (decided before s 35 was enacted), he inspected the memorandum and made an innocent mistake as to its legal effect, he might still be in food faith. But if he then failed to seek legal advice on what is now a well-known pitfall, it might cast doubt on his good faith.

It is the standard practice of banks to refer to the memorandum and articles of a customer company before agreeing to make a loan. They do not consider that it is safe to rely on s 35 in respect of a point in the objects clause which may be overlooked or misunderstood.

When this safeguard was introduced into English law in 1973 the general opinion was that the words 'decided on by the directors' (in the plural) limited its scope to decisions taken collectively by the board (as explained in Chapter 13). It follows that a contract negotiated on behalf of the company by a single director, even if duly appointed or held out to be a managing director, is not covered unless either the board of directors gives prior approval to a draft contract subject only to minor technical alterations (if any) made later or ratifies the contract which a single director has previously negotiated. If of course a private company has only one director he is the 'board' and so the plural ('directors') must include the singular in such a case.

The case below casts some doubt on the above view that a contract made by a single director, without reference to the board, does not fall under s 35 but the case was decided on other grounds and so the remark made was merely an obiter dictum.

There was 'a sole effective director to whom all actual authority to act for the board had been delegated'. This director made a payment of company money in settlement of the debt of a third party which the recipient well knew was not a payment for company purposes but amounted to a breach of fiduciary duty to the company by the director who made it. The company sued to recover the money. The court ordered repayment on the grounds that the payee was not 'in good faith' as s 35 requires and, being aware of the director's breach of duty, held the money as constructive trustee for the company. The court expressed the opinion, however, that as the director was the only effective director the payment was a 'transaction decided on by the directors': *International Sales & Agencies Ltd v Marcus* [1982] 3 All ER 551.

3.18 Alteration of the objects
The statutory power to alter the objects clause is the normal safeguard for all concerned if it is realised in advance that a contract is or may be ultra vires or a change is otherwise desirable.

The objects clause may be altered by special resolution but for certain purposes only and subject to the right of a minority to carry their objection to the court for review: s 4.

Of the seven permitted types of alteration only four are important, i e:

(a) to carry on the business more economically or more efficiently;
(b) to attain the main purpose by new or improved means;
(c) to enlarge the local area of operations; and
(d) to carry on some business which under existing circumstances may conveniently or advantageously be combined with the business of the company.

The other three permitted purposes of alteration comprise restricting, abandoning, selling off the business or part of it or amalgamating with others. Of the other purposes listed above, the first three relate to carrying on the existing business in some other way. The fourth is of the greater importance since it permits a company to carry on some new business.

The power to alter the objects so as to cover a new business is widely construed.

The main object of the company was manufacturing but it had in the past confined its activities to holding shares of manufacturing subsidiaries. It proposed to alter its objects clause to permit it (i) to carry on the business of finance, banking and underwriting – which had some relevance to the group manufacturing activities and (ii) to deal in land and other property. Under the legal procedure then (but no longer) in force the company had to obtain the approval of the court for an alteration of its objects clause. The court approved (i) but vetoed (ii): *Re Parent Tyre Co* [1923] 2 Ch 222.

The decision on what new business it is convenient or advantageous to carry on rests with the members who are required for this purpose to approve the change by a three-quarters majority of votes cast, i e by special resolution. In the case referred to above it was said that the additional business must not be destructive of or inconsistent with the existing business, must leave the existing business substantially as before but subject to that the new business may be completely different from the original business. In practice, however, the company is not required to retain and continue its existing business in conjunction with the old. Companies commonly entirely abandon their original business in order to carry on a different one and alter their object to reflect that change by omitting the paragraph which specifies the original business as the main object (or they may even delete the entire objects clause of the original memorandum and adopt a new clause complete with suitable powers in the latest legal drafting form). As there is power in s 4 to abandon objects as well as to adopt new ones it is arguable that such drastic changes are permissible under those statutory provisions as a whole. It is no longer necessary to obtain approval of the alteration by the court (unless objection is raised) and so there is comparatively little modern case law on the subject.

A company was formed with the object of protecting cyclists (by implication – against motorists). It proposed to enlarge its objects to take in the protection of users of vehicles of all kinds. The court, however, disallowed this change on the grounds that it would be destructive of the original object of protecting cyclists against motorists to add the latter: *Re Cyclists Touring Club* [1907] 1 Ch 269.

When the special resolution to alter the objects clause has been passed the company should wait for 21 days in case application is made to the court by members who object to the alteration. When the 21 days has expired or the court has made an order confirming the alteration, the company must within the next 15 days deliver to the registrar a printed copy of the memorandum as altered.

Application by objectors must be made to the court within 21 days of the passing of the special resolution to alter the objects. The application must be made by or on behalf of the holders of not less than 15 per cent of the issued share capital or of a class of shares (or holders of debentures secured by a floating charge issued before 1 December 1947 who are also entitled to notice of the resolution). No member who voted in favour of the special resolution may apply to the court for its cancellation.

The court may confirm the alteration wholly or in part (as in the *Parent Tyre Case*) and on such terms or conditions as it thinks fit, or adjourn the proceedings so that a compromise may be negotiated and then make an order to give effect to it. In particular the court now has power to order the company to purchase the shares of members (as a reduction of capital) and to order an alteration of the memorandum or articles resulting from it. An order for alteration of memorandum or articles takes immediate effect and the company may not thereafter make any further alteration (nor alter the memorandum or articles contrary to an order of the court) except by leave of the court: s 5.

Any member, regardless of the size of his shareholding may object to the court that the alteration is outside the limits permitted by s 4, i e is not any of the seven permitted kinds of alteration. But the right to object is limited to the same 21-day period as applies to objections to alterations of the permitted kinds. The limit of 21 days for a challenge is imposed so that a company which has altered its objects may engage in new activities without the risk of having its transactions in that field declared ultra vires at some later time.

3.19 Limited liability

There is a clause which states (if that be the case) that the liability of members is limited. If members' liability is limited by guarantee there is an additional clause stating the maximum amount which each member undertakes to contribute in a winding up. A company incorporated with limited liability may be reregistered as unlimited (Chapter 1: 1.22 above): ss 49–50.

3.20 Authorised capital

A limited company which has a share capital is required to state the amount of the share capital with which it proposes to be registered and its division into shares of a fixed amount, e g 'The share capital of the company is £100 divided into one hundred shares of £1 each'. This sets a limit on the amount and number of shares which may be issued. If the articles so provide the authorised capital may be increased by the creation of new shares. It is usual for the articles to provide for an increase to be sanctioned by passing an ordinary resolution in general meeting: s 121: Table A Art 32. The issued and authorised capital may also be reduced: Chapter 5 Part C.

3.21 Additional clauses

The memorandum may include additional clauses (3.1 above) on such matters as the rights attached to class of shares or restriction on payment of dividends and return of capital. The memorandum ends with the subscribers' declaration of association, etc (3.1).

3.22 Alteration of the memorandum

The name and objects of the company, its status as a public or private or limited or unlimited company and its authorised capital may all be altered in the manner described in earlier paragraphs of this chapter. Whenever the memorandum has been altered all copies must include the alteration: s 20. A copy of the memorandum as altered must be delivered to the registrar within 15 days: s 18. Within the same period a copy of the resolution by which the alteration was made must be delivered to the registrar who advertises the filing of this resolution in the *London Gazette*: s 711. Until the advertisement is published the alteration is not effective against persons who at the material time are unaware that it has been made: s 42.

The clause which states the country in which the registered office is to be situate fixes the company's domicile permanently. It cannot be altered by any procedure of company law. It can be altered by passing a private Act of Parliament (and usually a second Act in the new country of domicile, e g Australia) but this is a very rare occurrence. The company is then treated as if it has been incorporated by registration in its new country of domicile and is subject to the company law of that country.

If the memorandum includes additional clauses (3.1) which could have been included in the articles the statutory rules on alteration are as follows: s 17:

(a) a clause which is declared to be unalterable cannot be altered except by a scheme of arrangement (Chapter 16: 16.3);
(b) a clause which is stated to be alterable by a specified procedure can only be altered by that procedure;
(c) the provisions of s 17 do not permit the alteration of a clause which has been included by order of the court under s 5 or s 461 (minority protection) nor may any clause be altered so as to require a member without his consent in writing to subscribe for additional shares or to subscribe additional money for his existing shares: s 16;
(d) any clause which varies or abrogates the special rights of any class of shares may not be altered under s 17 (since alteration of these rights is regulated by other rules – Chapter 7: 7.12).

Subject to these limitations and exclusions additional clauses of the memorandum may be altered by special resolution but subject to the same rights of application to the court by objecting members as are provided on an alteration of the objects (see 3.18 above).

3.23 Printed copies

The Companies Act in many contexts prescribes printed copies of the memorandum and/or articles. In practice the registrar accepts photographic or xerox copies and the like provided that they are clear and permanent. Manuscript or typewritten material is not acceptable however.

Chapter 4

The articles of association

4.1 The content of the articles
The articles serve as regulations for the internal management of the company. They deal with such matters as the allotment and issue of shares, the rights attaching to shares, transfer and transmission of shares, the convening and conduct of general meetings and the right to receive notice and to attend and vote, the appointment and powers of directors, the accounts and the payment of dividends.

4.2 Table A
Successive Companies Acts since the first Act of 1862 have provided model forms of articles ('Table A') which apply to companies limited by shares which are incorporated while the Act is in force unless the company has its own special articles which totally or partially exclude Table A. A company limited by guarantee or an unlimited company must be registered with special articles but there are model articles for the use of such companies.

The advantages of statutory model articles are that legal drafting of special articles is reduced to a minimum since even special articles usually incorporate much of the text of the model. There is thus a considerable degree of standardisation with the advantage that the legal effect of common form phrases is well established. Yet there is flexibility since any company can adopt the model selectively or with modifications and include in its articles special articles adapted to its needs.

The general practice of public companies is to adopt full length special articles which expressly exclude the whole of Table A. But the special articles nonetheless follow the wording of Table A where appropriate. Private companies more often adopt short special articles which expressly adopt Table A with only such modifications as are specified in the special articles. It is convenient (but not legally necessary) in such a case to print the complete text of Table A as an appendix differentiating the excluded or modified passages by printing them in italics.

A company incorporated before 1985 when the current Table A took effect is subject to Table A of the Companies Act which was in force at the time of its incorporation unless it excludes it. But it may exclude the Table A of the earlier Act and adopt the Table A of the 1985 Act, with or without modification.

The 1985 Table A now in force applies only to companies incorporated on or after 1 July 1985 and to companies formed before that date which have by special resolution adopted the 1985 Table A as their articles. Unlike previous versions the 1985 Table A is not contained in the Act itself but (with other model articles for guarantee and unlimited companies) is found in a separate statutory instrument (SI 1985/805) made under s 8. It differs from the previous (1948) Table A both in substance and in wording. In general it is simpler and shorter.

Many companies formed before 1 July 1985 will retain their existing articles, usually based on the 1948 model, for some time until they have occasion to adopt new articles. The drawback to doing this is that a number of changes in company law made in 1980–81 override the 1948 Table A or require different articles not found in the 1948 model for certain purposes such as the purchase of their own shares (Chapter 5: 5.15). When a company does adopt the 1985 Table A, or articles based on it, the company may well exercise its option to reproduce some elements of the 1948 model such as restrictions on directors' borrowing powers (Chapter 9: 9.2) or a power to refuse to register a transfer of fully paid shares of a private company (Chapter 7: 7.14) which are in the 1948 but not the 1985 Table A model.

In this book references to articles of Table A indicate the 1985 Table regulations unless otherwise stated.

4.3 Form of the articles
The articles must by s 7(3):

(a) be printed (see Chapter 3: 3.23);
(b) be divided into paragraphs numbered consecutively (Table A has 118 paragraphs);
(c) the first articles with which the company is registered must be signed by the subscribers to the memorandum whose signatures must be attested by a witness and they must be dated: s 7(3)(c). If the company later adopts new articles or delivers altered articles for filing they may be signed for identification but are not executed by signature at the end.

A member is entitled on payment of a fee of 5p to be supplied by the company with a copy of the memorandum and articles which must include all alterations so far made: s 19.

4.4 The memorandum and articles as a contract
The memorandum and articles bind the company and its members to the same extent as if they respectively had been signed and sealed by each member: s 14(1). Although s 14 does not say so, its scope is restricted to rights and obligations of membership and does not extend to members in some other capacity such as directors.

The articles provided that disputes between the company and its members should be submitted to arbitration. However H, who had been expelled from the company, began proceedings in court. His action was dismissed since the articles were a binding contract for arbitration: *Hickman v Kent or Romney Marsh Sheepbreeders Association* [1915] 1 Ch 881. By contrast in *Beattie v E & F Beattie Ltd* [1938] Ch 708 CA a similar provision in the articles for arbitration on disputes was held not to apply to a court action in which the dispute was over the conduct of a member in his capacity of director.

The articles provided that the company should always use the services of E as its solicitor. E was also a member and he sued to enforce his claim to do the company's legal work. His action was dismissed for various reasons including the fact that the articles gave him no enforceable rights in his capacity of solicitor: *Eley v Positive Government Security Life Assurance Co Ltd* (1875) 1 Ex D 88 CA.

The second point to note on s 14 is that it relates only to *personal* rights and obligations of a member.

The articles provided for dividends 'to be paid' which was interpreted to mean paid in money. A member was able to rely on this article in challenging a distribution in non-cash form viz bonus debentures in lieu of cash dividend: *Wood v Odessa Waterworks Co* (1889) 42 Ch D 636.

There are conflicting decisions on members' efforts to compel the company to conduct its affairs in conformity with the articles, which is not an issue which affects the personal rights of members. An action to enforce a managing director's veto succeeded (*Salmon's Case* in Chapter 13: 13.4) but the court declined to overrule a chairman's decision, contrary to the articles, to refuse a demand for a poll (*Macdougall's Case* in Chapter 15: 15.2). The right of a member to vote in accordance with the articles is enforceable (*Pender's Case* in Chapters 15: 15.4).

As s 14 equates the memorandum and articles with a contract made by each member by deed, the period of limitation for an action by the company against a member is 12 years. But the wording of s 14 merely creates a simple contractual obligation on the part of the company with the result that an action by a member against the company, eg to recover an unpaid dividend (*Re Compania de Electricidad Case* in Chapter 5: 5.25), must be brought within 6 years of the dividend falling due.

The articles may impose obligations on members which benefit other members, eg a right of first refusal over or, less often, a duty to purchase shares of a member who wishes to transfer his shares. It is normal legal practice to draft articles so that in these cases the company is the intermediary between members and operates the procedure. Where that is the position a member has no right to sue another member direct. However, exceptionally, as in the case below, the articles may expressly confer on members rights against other members to which s 14 will apply.

The articles, 'very inartistically drawn' by a non-lawyer, provided explicitly that a member who wished to transfer shares should give notice to the directors, who would then be required to buy them at a fair value. The directors were also required to hold at least one qualification share and so they were necessarily also members. The court interpreted these articles as creating rights which members (the transferors) might enforce direct against other members identified as the directors: *Rayfield v Hands* [1958] 2 All ER 194.

It is possible to explain this decision on a different basis. It is suggested that in accepting appointment to their office the directors, in accordance with the articles, must be deemed to have made a standing offer to buy any shares which members might wish to sell. Notice to the directors was acceptance of the offer, creating a separate contract distinct from the articles but incorporating terms from the articles (see 4.5 below). This is not, however, the reason given by the court for its decision.

4.5 Articles as terms of a separate contract

Contracts are often made by reference to some other document, e g a sale of goods may be subject to the seller's standard conditions of sale. In the same way a company contract may incorporate provisions from the articles.

The articles provided that the remuneration of the directors should be £1,000 p a. In accepting appointment as directors, without agreeing any express terms on remuneration, the directors could refer to the articles to determine the amount: *Re New British Iron Co, ex p Beckwith* [1898] 1 Ch 324. This principle works both ways. In other cases it has been held that if the articles require directors to subscribe for qualification shares, they are deemed on accepting appointment to have agreed to do so.

The articles can only be treated as implied terms insofar as they are not overridden by any express terms of the separate contract.

The articles provided for the appointment of a managing director and for the termination of any such appointment if the company in general meeting so resolved. R was appointed managing director at a salary of £7 per week for an indefinite period without any express terms as to notice. In these circumstances the company was entitled to terminate his appointment without notice in accordance with the articles, which were terms of the contract of his employment: *Read v Astoria Garage (Streatham) Ltd* [1952] Ch 637. But in another case the articles provided for the appointment of a managing director for such term as the board might determine and he was appointed to hold office in that capacity so long as he should be a director. That express term was binding on the company: *Nelson v James Nelson & Sons Ltd* [1914] 2 KB 770.

The effect on such a contract of an alteration of the articles is considered in the next section (4.6).

4.6 Alteration of the articles

A company has statutory power (s 9) to alter its articles. But this general power is subject to a number of restrictions, i e:

(a) the articles may not be altered so as to conflict with the Companies Act 1985 or with the memorandum, which is the overriding document: s 9;
(b) a member cannot by an alteration of the articles be compelled without his consent to subscribe for additional shares or to pay an increased amount for the shares which he has: s 16;
(c) the rights attached to a class of shares may only be varied by the prescribed procedure and with a right of appeal to the court: s 127 (Chapter 7: 7.12);
(d) if the court has ordered, e g in connection with an alteration of the objects under s 5 or in minority protection proceedings under s 461, that an alteration shall be made or alternatively that an article shall not be altered, no change may then be made without the leave of the court (Chapter 3: 3.18 and Chapter 15: 15.6).

In addition to these statutory restrictions on the power to alter the articles, the effect of any relevant contract must be considered.

There may be a contract which the company would breach by the alteration of the articles. In such a case the company cannot be restrained from the exercise of its statutory power of alteration of its articles, merely because the alteration would be or even would facilitate a breach of the contract. But inasmuch as there is a breach of contract, the other party may recover damages.

A shareholder who had recently acquired control of the company used his votes to alter the articles so that he had power to remove any director from office. He then used his power to remove Shirlaw from the board. On ceasing to be a director Shirlaw ceased to be managing director. This was a breach of his service agreement. The House of Lords approved the award of damages for breach of contract but also ruled (thus resolving some conflict between earlier cases) that he could not have an injunction to prevent the company from altering its articles to facilitate the breach: *Southern Foundries (1926) Ltd v Shirlaw* [1940] AC 701.

It follows from this decision that a contract by which the company agrees expressly not to alter its articles is unenforceable. Indirect means are generally invalid. If the articles state that the articles are not to be altered, or if they require a larger majority of votes than the three-quarters required to carry a special resolution, these provisions will be void.

There are, however, two possible methods of blocking an alteration of the articles. The articles may provide that on a vote to alter the articles, a shareholder's shares are to carry at least 26 per cent of the total votes. By this means he gains a veto on a special resolution to alter the articles. This is an analogy drawn from the decision of the Court of Appeal in *Bushell v Faith* (Chapter 12: 12.7) that weighted voting is effective to block a resolution to remove a director from office under s 303. Secondly, it would seem that the articles may provide that there shall be no quorum at a general meeting unless a named shareholder is present (Chapter 11: 11.8). He can then prevent the meeting from transacting business by absenting himself from it. However, there are no reported decisions expressly approving these devices as a means of denying to a company the use of its statutory power to alter its articles. The court, if it saw fit, could always direct that a meeting be held with a different quorum under s 371(2) (Chapter 11: 11.3).

Unless the alteration is void under the rules considered in the next section (4.7) a member must accept its effect upon his individual position. In becoming a member of the company he accepted the risk of such a change. But if he has acquired vested rights against the company under the articles, as they then were, the company cannot by altering the articles deprive him of that entitlement. To that limited extent an alteration may not be retrospective; apart from that it may alter the existing position.

The original article gave the company a lien on partly paid shares to secure debts owing to the company by its members. A deceased insolvent shareholder held shares some of which were fully paid and others partly paid with calls on them already overdue and unpaid. The company altered its articles so as to extend the lien to fully paid as well as partly paid shares. His executors objected but it was held that the company could alter its articles so as to create a lien over shares already issued in order to secure an existing debt: *Allen v Gold Reefs of West Africa Ltd* [1900] 1 Ch 656.

Swabey had been a director for some time. The articles provided for directors' fees at the rate of £200 p a. In mid-year the company altered its articles so as to reduce the fees to £5 p m from the start of the year. It was held that Swabey could not be deprived of accrued and unpaid fees at the old rate earned by service as director before the alteration was made: *Swabey v Port Darwin Gold Mining Co* (1889) 1 Meg 385.

4.7 Alterations to be bona fide for the benefit of the company as a whole
An alteration of the articles may be invalid because it has not been made bona fide for the benefit of the company as a whole. The test is whether the majority whose votes carried the special resolution to make the alteration held the

honest opinion that the alteration was capable of benefiting the general body of members of the company. If that is so the alteration is valid although it may be to the advantage of the majority and contrary to the interests of the minority who vote against it. It is a single test but it includes two elements, ie good faith and presumed benefit to members generally. As regards the first element, if the majority were prompted entirely by malice against the minority they would not be acting bona fide even if the alteration was beneficial. The difficulty is to establish that the majority was motivated by pure malice.

After many years of bitter dispute and several lawsuits the majority shareholders decided to sell their shares to an outsider. However the articles gave to their opponent, the minority shareholder (G) a right of first refusal (Chapter 7: 7.15) of any shares which another member might wish to transfer. The majority carried a special resolution to remove this provision from the articles. G challenged the alteration as in the interests of the majority not of the company as a whole. In dismissing his action the Court of Appeal held that the removal of the restriction on transfer was in the interests of the company as a whole since it enabled every shareholder to dispose of his shares free of the restriction: *Greenhalgh v Arderne Cinemas Ltd* [1951] Ch 286.

In this case, as in *Allen's Case* (4.6), the minority assertion that the alteration was damaging to the minority was not a sufficient objection since the concept of 'the company as a whole' (as explained in *Greenhalgh's Case*) includes all members of the company, now or at some future time. On some future occasion a different minority shareholder might benefit from the change. Although Greenhalgh could point to the long-standing feud between him and the majority, that fact did not suffice to establish 'malice' since the majority could reasonably believe that the alteration would be beneficial in the sense explained above. In *Allen's Case* the company itself would clearly benefit.

Most of the other cases on this topic are concerned with alteration of the articles to enable a majority to expel a member by compulsory acquisition of his shares or, in *Shuttleworth's Case* below, to remove a director from a life-long directorship conferred upon him by the original articles. In these cases the power of expulsion is by its nature a means of discriminating against a minority; there is no possible advantage to any minority shareholder at any time in introducing such a power into the constitution of the company. Hence such an alteration is likely to be void unless it is so worded as to limit its use to occasions when some benefit to the company as an entity will result. If the alteration is not restricted in this fashion it will not be validated by showing that in making the alteration the majority had in view some unspecified advantage to the company.

The majority who held 98 per cent of the issued shares were willing to provide additional capital which the company needed provided that they could acquire the shares of the minority. The alteration which gave power to purchase members' shares at a fair value was held to be discriminatory and invalid: *Brown v British Abrasive Wheel Co* [1919] 1 Ch 290.

The alteration conferring power of expulsion was unrestricted in its application. It was held to be invalid although the purpose of the majority was to enforce an informal understanding that only customers of the company should be members (and the objecting minority shareholder had begun to obtain its supplies elsewhere): *Dafen Tinplate Co Ltd v Llanelly Steel Co (1907) Ltd* [1920] 2 Ch 124.

The alteration provided that the directors might require any member who carried on a business competing with the company to transfer his shares to them. The court was satisfied that a competitor might use information obtained as a member to the company's detriment and upheld the alteration: *Sidebotham v Kershaw, Leese & Co* [1920] 1 Ch 154.

The articles provided that certain named individuals should hold office as 'permanent directors' unless disqualified (in circumstances which had not arisen). S, who was one of the directors, failed on 22 occasions within a year to account to the company for money which he had received. The other directors then carried an alteration of the articles by which any permanent director was to vacate office at the request of the other directors – and under this power they removed S. The alteration was held valid: *Shuttleworth v Cox Bros & Co (Maidenhead) Ltd* [1927] 2 KB 9.

At first sight *Shuttleworth's Case,* in which the power of a removal was unrestricted, is at variance with the others. But it can be reconciled on the basis that the alteration conferred a power on the directors which (Chapter 12: 12.18) they could only properly use for the benefit of the company. The case also illustrates the point that insofar as the articles afford terms of a contract the person concerned accepts the risk that the articles may be altered to his detriment.

Although an alteration to permit compulsory acquisition of a member's shares is the main instance of the application of these principles, the same issue, i e benefit to the company, may have to be considered in other contexts.

The original issued capital comprised 400,000 management shares with 8 votes each and 3,600,000 ordinary shares with one vote each. An additional 8,400,000 ordinary shares were issued as consideration for the acquisition of the shares of another company. To restore (in some degree) the voting strength of the management shares the articles were altered to raise the number of votes attached to those shares to 16 per share. The holders of the management shares did not vote on the special resolution to make the alteration. It was held that in voting for the resolution the majority of ordinary shareholders were honestly seeking to secure a benefit to the company, i e continuation of the existing management. They were not discriminating in favour of themselves: *Rights and Issues Investment Trust Ltd v Stylo Shoes Ltd* [1964] 3 All ER 628.

The *Smith & Fawcett Case* (Chapter 7: 7.16) is another example (unconnected with alteration of articles) of continuity of management regarded as a benefit to the company.

Chapter 5

Share capital

A RAISING CAPITAL

5.1 Types of capital

This chapter and the next deal with the rules under which companies raise share capital from investors who are or become members and shareholders of the company. The next chapter is concerned with the offer of shares (or debentures) by general offers to the public known as prospectuses for which there are special procedures. Chapter 7 deals with the rights and liabilities of shareholders in respect of their shares in the company and Chapter 8 with the related questions of rights and liabilities incidental to membership. Chapter 9 explains the rules and procedures by which a company may raise capital through the issue of debentures to investors who thereby have a continuing relationship with the company, sometimes for a long period of years, but who remain creditors and not members of the company.

A number of terms, some defined by statute, are used in connection with share capital. The memorandum of association presented to the registrar to secure the formation of a company must (unless the company is unlimited or is a company limited by guarantee and without a share capital) state 'the amount of share capital with which the company proposes to be registered and the division thereof into shares of a fixed amount': s 2(5). The aggregate amount so stated is the *authorised share capital* which is the maximum amount of share capital which the company may allot and issue. It may, however, increase this amount under the procedure laid down in its articles: s 121. A company may not be registered as a public company unless its authorised capital is at least 'the authorised minimum' which has been fixed at £50,000 but which may be varied by statutory instrument: s 118 (Chapter 1: 1.14). The requirement that the authorised share capital shall be divided into shares of a fixed amount, e g '£100 divided into 100 shares of £1 each', means that every share must have a *nominal value*, i e £1 in the example just given. This is significant since it fixes the minimum value of the consideration in money or money's worth which a company must be entitled to receive under the terms of allotment of its shares: s 100. For this reason the nominal value is also referred to as 'par value' (in Latin par means equal). The allotment of shares 'at par' means that the consideration has been fixed at an amount equal to the nominal value of the shares. Shares may also be allotted 'at a premium'.

Allotted share capital is the total nominal value of shares to which persons are unconditionally entitled with the right to have their names entered in the register of members as the holders of those shares. Allotment is explained later (5.2 below).

Although a company may not allot shares at a discount, ie for a consideration of lesser value than the nominal value of the shares it may allot them on terms that all or part of the consideration is to be received by the company at a later date. (But shares of a public company must usually be paid up to a minimum amount before allotment: s 101).

The next important technical term is *called-up share capital* which is defined as the amount called up on its shares, whether or not actually paid, together with any share capital paid up without being called (eg sums paid on application for the shares) plus any share capital to be paid on a future specified date (whether fixed by the articles, the terms of allotment or by other arrangements); s 737. The balance (if any) is uncalled share capital. The aggregate amount paid to the company on its issued shares is *paid-up share capital*; any amount made payable by the terms of issue and not yet paid is *unpaid capital*. Shares are also classified as *fully paid* or *partly paid shares*. *Paid up in cash* is a term which is explained later (5.7).

A company may by special resolution determine that all or part of its uncalled capital shall be *reserve capital* which may not be called up except in the course of winding up: s 120.

If a company states its share capital on its letterheads or order forms it must be a reference to the paid-up share capital: s 351(2).

The share capital of a company may be divided into classes, such as preference and ordinary shares, so that the holders of shares of any class have different rights from those of another class (Chapter 7 Part B).

5.2 The allotment of shares
The standard procedure is that a person who wishes to subscribe for shares of a company applies to the company (letter of application) which is an offer. If the directors have shares available and authority to issue them to the applicant they formally resolve to allot them to him and the shares are issued to him by the despatch of a letter of allotment which is an acceptance of his offer. A contract is thereby made to which general principles of contract apply, eg a right to rescind for misrepresentation. If the company first publishes a prospectus (Chapter 6) that, although defined as an offer to the public (s 744), is strictly a mere invitation to the public to apply. In the affairs of small private companies the procedure adopted is often informal. But in every case there should be an agreement, since a person can only become a member with his agreement (s 22(2)), and the procedure for allotment of shares should be observed by a formal decision of the company on its side to allot them.

Shares are allotted when a person acquires the unconditional right to be included in the company's register of members in respect of those shares: s 738. The subscribers to the memorandum should be entered in the register as holders of their shares without the formality of allotment (Chapter 8: 8.2) but their shares are then in the technical sense part of the allotted share capital. 'Issued' is not a defined term but is usually taken as the stage at which evidence of title, such as a letter of allotment or share certificate, is issued to the holder.

5.3 The power to allot shares
Any allotment of shares must satisfy three basic conditions:
(a) the limit set by the authorised share capital may not be exceeded. If it is

proposed to allot more shares than remain unallotted the authorised share capital must first be increased (5.27 below);
(b) the directors must have been granted authority to allot the shares. In the exercise of that authority they must also act in good faith and for a proper purpose (Chapter 12: 12.18);
(c) as stated above the consideration for the shares must be at least equal to their nominal value.

The next section deals with the formal authorisation of directors to allot referred to in (b) above.

5.4 Authorisation of the issue of shares

Directors may not exercise any power of the company to allot 'relevant securities' unless they have been authorised to do so by resolution (which may be an ordinary resolution) passed in general meeting or by the articles of the company: s 80.

Relevant securities are:

(i) all shares other than the shares which subscribers to the memorandum (in that document) have agreed to take and shares allotted pursuant to an employees' share scheme (5.12 below); and also
(ii) any right, e g an option, to subscribe for shares and any right to convert any security into shares, e g a convertible debenture since that is an indirect means of obtaining shares.

The authority given to directors may relate to a specified allotment of relevant securities or be a general power. It may be conditional or unconditional.

The authority must, however, be limited in two ways, i e

(1) it must specify the maximum amount of relevant securities which may be allotted thereunder; and
(2) it must specify a date on which the authority will expire. That date may not extend the authority beyond a maximum period of five years at one time. If it is contained in the original articles of the company the period runs from the date of incorporation. In any other case, e g passing a resolution or the adoption of new articles, it runs from the date when the authority is given.

The company in general meeting may renew, revoke or vary the authority given. Any renewal of authority must conform to the principles (1) and (2) above. The resolution passed in general meeting may be an ordinary resolution but a signed copy of it must be delivered to the registrar within 15 days: ss 80 and 380(4)(f).

It is also possible at any time to give authority to the directors to enter into an agreement or to make an offer before their authority expires and to allot the shares pursuant to the agreement or offer after the expiry of their authority.

A company may in its original articles confer authority to allot for the initial period of five years from incorporation and then renew the authority by ordinary resolution. Some companies give authority for a year at a time as part of the routine business of an annual general meeting; it is then less likely that the expiry of a previous authority given more than five years before will be overlooked.

However, either an existing company or a new company may, if its members prefer it, give no authority in advance and thus compel the directors to seek a specific authority by resolution passed in general meeting as and when the occasion arises. Any authority given in advance may be revoked or varied in the same way as it is given (an ordinary resolution overrides the articles in this respect). If the directors allot shares up to the limit of their existing authority or their authority does not cover the proposed allotment or if their authority expires they may seek additional or renewed authority (subject to the limits described above).

If the directors allot relevant securities without having authority to do so, the allotment will be valid. But a director who knowingly and wilfully contravenes or permits or authorises a contravention of the rules commits an offence and is liable on conviction to be fined: s 80(9).

5.5 Shareholders' pre-emption rights

The general intention and effect of ss 89–94 is that if a company proposes to allot ordinary shares (or certain other securities) *for cash* it must first offer the shares or other securities to existing holders of ordinary shares in proportion to their holdings and on the same or more favourable terms. But these rights of pre-emption may be excluded (5.6 below) and there are a number of exceptions and special provisions.

The right of first refusal is given to holders of 'relevant shares' (including shares held in an employees' share scheme as described in 5.12 below). Relevant shares are ordinary shares and any participating preference shares of the company (Chapter 7: 7.9).

The right of first refusal extends to relevant shares issued for cash, other than (1) shares issued through an employees' share scheme (ii) bonus issues (5.11 below) and (iii) shares which the subscribers to the memorandum have agreed to take (Chapter 8: 8.2). A right of first refusal would frustrate the purpose of those arrangements. On the other hand the right does extend to options to subscribe for relevant shares, including convertible debentures (Chapter 9: 9.6). The shares to which the right of refusal extends are called *equity securities* and are defined in s 94(2) and (3).

An offer is made for cash if the consideration is to be paid in money or by cheque to the company or any other person (such as its holding company) or the shares are issued in payment of a debt, as is the case when convertible debentures are converted into shares: s 738(3) and (4).

There are elaborate rules of procedure to implement the right of first refusal. In a normal case a written offer is sent to each member by posting it to the address to which the company sends his notice of a general meeting; alternatively it suffices to hand it to him personally. Holders of share warrants (Chapter 7: 7.4) and members who have no registered address in the UK (Chapter 11: 11.4) are given notice of the offer by notification in the *London Gazette*.

The offer must state a period of not less than 21 days during which it may be accepted and it may not be withdrawn within that period. If an offeree neither accepts nor refuses the offer the company is then free to allot the shares offered to him to some other person. Other shareholders have no further statutory right to be offered shares which other members have not accepted (though the articles may give it to them).

In cases where all the members are minded to decline the offer they may give immediate notice of their decision to the company which need not then wait for the expiry of 21 days before offering the shares to an outsider. It is also possible to express the offer to each shareholder so that he can renounce it in favour of another person (5.11 below).

If the company allots shares without proper compliance with the statutory rules the company and its officers responsible for the default are liable to compensate the members who have been denied their rights. But any proceedings to obtain compensation must be instituted within two years from the date of the return of allotments (5.13) of shares to the outsider or the grant to him of an option to subscribe: s 92.

5.6 Exclusion or disapplication of pre-emption rights

A *private* company may by its memorandum or articles permanently exclude the statutory rights of pre-emption either wholly or in relation to particular kinds of issue. An exclusion is effective only if made in sufficiently explicit terms. It would not suffice to give to the directors a general right to allot shares at their discretion, such as was often found in articles adopted before 1980 when the statutory rules took effect.

If the memorandum or articles give pre-emption rights to a particular class of holders of relevant shares the company should first make the offer to them, following the statutory procedure of 21 days' notice, and allot the shares to those who accept. It must then offer the shares which they have not accepted in accordance with the statutory entitlement to shareholders of every class: s 89(2).

If the company is prohibited, for example by the law of another country, from offering or allotting shares to certain shareholders (resident in the other country) the shares to which those shareholders would have been entitled are added to the shares offered to the general body of shareholders.

Every company, public or private, may by special resolution 'disapply' shareholders' statutory pre-emption rights, either in relation to a particular issue of shares or as part of the authorisation given to the directors (for a period not exceeding five years) to allot shares (5.4). In the latter case the authorisation to allot must be made by special resolution to comply with the disapplication procedure of s 95. In proposing a special resolution for disapplication of pre-emption rights the directors must issue a circular, with the notice convening the meeting, stating the amount which the outsiders will pay for the shares, if the disapplication of members' rights takes effect, the justification for that issue price and the directors' reasons for seeking approval of the disapplication. There are penalties for knowingly or recklessly making misleading statements in that circular.

A signed copy of the special resolution by which the members' rights are disapplied must be delivered to the registrar within 15 days: s 380. As with a simple resolution authorising the directors to allot shares, the registrar is required on receiving a resolution of this type passed by a *public* company, to give notice in the *London Gazette*: s 711(1)(d) and (e).

5.7 Consideration for the allotment of shares

The consideration for the allotment of shares may be provided in money or in money's worth, ie non-cash assets, but it must be at least equal in value to the nominal value of the shares and any premium fixed as part of the issue price.

The whole consideration need not be received at the time of allotment but *public* companies are subject to special rules in this respect (5.8).

Statutory rules, which were introduced in 1980 to comply with an EC directive on *public* companies, lay down time limits for the receipt of any non-cash consideration and also generally require valuation by an independent valuer (5.8 and 5.9 below). Private companies continue to be subject to common law rules on these topics as illustrated below (5.9).

5.8 Time limits on consideration for the shares of public companies

The first and most important rule applies both to cash and to non-cash consideration for shares issued by *public* companies. Such companies may not allot shares unless paid up as to at least one-quarter of the nominal value of the shares and the whole of any premium: s 101(1). Two types of share issue are however exempt from this requirement:

(a) bonus shares (5.11) unless the allottee was or should have been aware of the infringement. This is of little practical importance since bonus shares are usually fully paid at the time of issue; and

(b) shares allotted under an employees' share scheme (5.12). It is often an essential feature of these schemes that the employees are given time to pay for their shares, which may therefore be issued even nil paid in the first instance.

If there is an infringement of s 101 the allottee and possibly a transferee of the shares is liable to pay the required minimum.

The second rule under this head applies to shares of *public* companies which are allotted for a consideration which includes an undertaking to transfer property to the company at a future date: s 102 ('payment by long-term undertaking'). The undertaking must be expressed to require transfer of the property to the company within a period not exceeding five years. If it does not include that condition or if the property is not transferred at the prescribed date, the allottee and possibly a subsequent transferee of the shares is liable to pay the equivalent value of the undertaking in cash.

To prevent collusion in evading these rules the liability (on shares allotted in contravention of them) generally follows the shares into the hands of any person to whom they are transferred. But a person who purchases the shares for value and without notice of the contravention, and any holder of the shares after him, is not liable in the manner described: s 112.

5.9 Valuation of consideration for the shares of public companies

A public company may not (subject to the exceptions mentioned later) allot shares as fully or as partly paid up (as to their nominal value or as to any premium payable on them) for a non-cash consideration unless:

(a) the consideration has been valued; and

(b) a valuation report has been made to the company within the six months before the allotment; and

(c) a copy of the valuation report has been sent to the proposed allottee of the shares: s 103.

The valuation and report are to be made or obtained by a person who is independent of the company and qualified to be appointed or to continue as the auditor of the company. For brevity he is referred to below as 'the auditor' but the company is free to select some other qualified accountant if it wishes. The auditor either values the consideration for the shares himself or if it appears to him to be reasonable, he may have the valuation made or accept an existing valuation from some valuer (for convenience here called 'the sub-valuer') who appears to the auditor to have the requisite knowledge and experience and who is not an officer or servant of the company (or of another company of the same group) nor a partner or employer of such an officer or servant.

The contents of the auditor's valuation report are elaborately defined in detail by ss 108–9 with a view to full disclosure of relevant information and prevention of concealment or fraud. In particular the auditor or sub-valuer is entitled to obtain from officers of the company whatever information or explanation he thinks necessary and it is a criminal offence to supply misleading or false information: s 110.

When the valuation report has been received the company must deliver copies to the allottee, so that he may be aware of its contents and his potential liability, and to the registrar, when the company files the return of allotments, so that the report is on file at the registry and open for public inspection: s 111. The registrar gives notice in the *London Gazette* of the delivery to him of the report: s 711.

There is, however, an important exception. No valuation report is required in a 'take-over' where public company A allots its shares to acquire all the shares of company B. In such a case company A need not procure a valuation of the shares of company B under this procedure: s 103(3). It would be very difficult to fault the judgment of the directors of company A as to the value to their company of acquiring company B. Moreover a take-over is usually exposed to expert comment in the financial press, which is very ready to point out any perceived errors of the directors in framing the terms of their bid for company B.

The same exemption applies to a 'merger', eg when company A allots its shares to acquire not the shares but *all* the assets of company B. This essentially is an acceptance by statute law of the *Wragg Case* below.

Valuation of consideration for the shares of a public company is also required in certain cases, if the company during the 'initial period' acquires assets above a specified value (one-tenth of the nominal value of the company's issued shares) from existing shareholders. This type of transaction has been described above (Chapter 2: 2.11). The procedure, which is of little practical importance is prescribed by s 104.

Finally, a subscriber to the memorandum of a public company must always pay for his subscriber's share in cash: s 106.

An allottee of shares (and a transferee from him up to the point when the shares are acquired by purchase in ignorance of the infringement) must pay cash (with 5 per cent interest) on shares allotted in breach of these rules.

An allotment is made for cash, and so falls outside these rules, if payment is received in the form of a cheque which the company receives in the expectation that it will be honoured. 'Cash consideration' also includes discharge of a debt owed by the company, payment in foreign currency and an undertaking to pay cash at a future date: ss 738–9. A bonus issue (5.11 below) is also treated as an allotment of shares for cash.

In general any asset is capable of being non-cash consideration for shares. However, a *public* company is prohibited from accepting an undertaking to do

69

work or perform services for any person, as consideration for its shares: s 99(2). A contract for services is still valid as a contract but it does not count as consideration.

Private companies are still subject to common law rules, which prohibit allotment of shares for a cash consideration which is less than the nominal value of the shares (the *Ooregum Case*) or for a non-cash consideration which blatantly infringes the general principle (the *Eddystone Case*). But the apparently honest and reasonable judgment of directors that a non-cash asset is worth £x to the company will not be overruled.

The company issued £1 preference shares credited at 15s paid, ie requiring only the remaining 5s to be paid in cash. The allottees were held to be liable to pay the full £1 on their shares:*Ooregum Gold Mining Co of India v Roper* [1892] AC 125.

The company acquired a business at a price of £46,300 partly satisfied by the allotment of 20,000 £1 shares fully paid. There was evidence that the stock-in-trade (among other assets) had been overvalued and it was included in the company's books at £11,000 less than the value put on it in the sale agreement. But the court held that 'it has, however, never been decided that a limited company cannot buy property . . . at any price it thinks proper and pay for them in fully paid shares, provided a limited company does so honestly and not colourably . . .': *Re Wragg Ltd* [1897] 1 Ch 796.

A company allotted shares as fully paid in consideration of past services rendered and expenses incurred. As past consideration is no consideration the allottees, who had accepted and retained their shares, were liable to pay for them in cash: *Re Eddystone Marine Insurance Co* [1893] 3 Ch 9.

5.10 Issue of shares at a premium
A company may be able to obtain consideration for its shares of greater value than the nominal value of the shares allotted. This commonly happens when the market price of the shares of an established company stands above the nominal value of the shares. The company may allot shares at a premium without having any express power in the articles to do so. It is implied. But there is no obligation in company law to obtain a premium because it is possible to do so.

The original shareholders were granted options to take up further shares at par. One of them exercised his option at a time when the shares were worth much more than par. The company could not be restrained from allotting extra shares to him at par: *Hilder v Dexter* [1902] AC 474.

It is arguable that in the exercise of their power to allot shares directors have a duty to obtain the maximum price reasonably obtainable for them. But it is probably safer to conclude that the directors are not in breach of any such duty unless they act dishonestly to benefit themselves or their associates. When a company allots shares for cash it must now usually offer them first to existing shareholders (5.5 above) unless there are provisions to exclude the members' pre-emption rights. In offering shares to existing shareholders there is certainly no duty to obtain the highest possible price. Indeed it is normal practice in a rights issue (5.11 below) to fix the issue price well below the market price of existing issued shares.

A company may also obtain a premium if it allots shares in exchange for a non-cash consideration which is of greater value than the nominal value of the shares. In such a case the element of surplus over nominal value must be treated as a premium to which the statutory rules apply.

The company acquired all the shares of two other companies by allotting its own shares on the basis of one of its shares for each of the shares of the other two companies. It thus allotted its shares of a nominal value of £1.75 m in exchange for shares of companies whose assets were valued at almost £7 m. It was held that the surplus of almost £5 m was properly credited to share premium account since s 130 so requires when shares are issued at a premium 'whether for cash or otherwise': *Henry Head & Co Ltd v Ropner Holdings Ltd* [1952] Ch 124.

If a premium is obtained it must be credited to a share premium account in the books of the company: s 130. Any balance on share premium account may only be returned to members of the company under the procedure for reduction of share capital (5.28 below). Except to the following extent a premium obtained is treated like paid-up share capital:

(a) share premium account may be applied in paying up unissued shares for allotment to members as a bonus issue;
(b) it may be used to write off preliminary expenses of the company or the expenses (including commission paid or discount allowed) of an issue of shares or debentures; or
(c) it may be used to provide the premium payable on redemption of redeemable preference shares or of debentures.

The purpose of these rules is to prevent premium obtained on the issue of shares being used to pay dividends. The members who pay premium to obtain shares have no claim to it on the basis that they provided it. If it is returned on a reduction of share capital all holders of shares entitled to participate in the repayment share equally.

However, the principle illustrated by the *Ropner Case* is in conflict with 'merger accounting' where, in a take-over by share exchange, the surplus value of the company acquired represents accumulated but distributable profits of that company. If the equivalent value has to be placed in a fixed share premium account of the acquiring company the profits are in effect 'frozen' and can no longer be distributed (by the new holding company). It is therefore provided that where the acquiring company secures not less than 90 per cent of the equity capital of the company acquired, any premium obtained need not be credited to share premium account: s 131. There are other analogous reliefs for certain types of group reconstruction entailing the issue of shares in circumstances where there is a theoretical premium: s 132.

5.11 Bonus and rights issues

A company may invite its members to subscribe for additional shares. As a general rule it is now required (5.5 above) to give them the opportunity of subscribing on advantageous terms before any shares are offered for cash to other persons. If existing members avail themselves of this favourable opportunity the shares allotted to them are a *rights issue* since the right to subscribe is given in ratio to existing shareholdings, e g one new share for every four shares already held. Such an offer made to members of a public company may also be a prospectus.

A company, if its articles provide for it (e g Table A Art 110) may apply its undistributed profits to paying up unissued shares so that they can then be allotted as a bonus issue to shareholders (usually only the holders of ordinary shares are so entitled under the articles). Although the company receives no money it is using shareholders' funds and so there is consideration provided by the transfer of an amount from reserves to share capital account. If the individual shareholder retains his bonus shares (he can sell them if he wishes to do so) he owns the same proportion of the issued shares (of the relevant class) as before. But the market value of each share in his holding is proportionately reduced and thereby it becomes more marketable. The purpose of a bonus issue is usually to bring the total issued share capital more into line with the real value of the company by converting reserves into share capital. Reserves which are not available for distribution as dividend may be capitalised in this way.

When a rights issue or a bonus issue is made, the company may simply allot the new shares to the members entitled to them. It is the usual practice, however, for public companies to issue the shares by *renounceable allotment letter*. The allottee may then within a limited period transfer his rights to the shares by signing a form of renunciation. The 'renuncee' applies to the company for registration as the holder of the new shares (for which, in case of a rights issue, he usually pays the subscription moneys).

One of the main inducements to the use of renounceable allotment letters for the issue of new shares of public companies used to be that no stamp duty was paid on dealings in them. However, the Finance Act 1986 has removed that advantage. They still offer the advantage of facilitating rapid dealings in the shares until the market settles down. An existing shareholder may for example decide not to increase his investment in a company by subscribing for the shares allotted to him under a rights issue. By the simple procedure of renunciation he can sell his right to shares – nil paid at that point – at a price which reflects the approximate difference between the offer price and the market price of the shares.

Dealings in renounceable allotment letters are also part of the procedure for allotment of shares or debentures in a prospectus issue (Chapter 6).

5.12 Employees' share schemes

In spite of a sequence of changes of relevant tax law some companies have continued to develop *employees' share schemes*. In their general nature such schemes offer employees of the company (or of all the companies of a group) the opportunity of acquiring shares of the parent company on advantageous terms (as regards the price or the deferred payment of it or the grant of options to subscribe). For the purposes of the new statutory rules on the allotment of shares (5.4 and 5.5 above) and the prospectus rules (Chapter 6: 6.3) it is necessary to distinguish shares issued under these schemes from other issued share capital. 'Employees' share scheme' is defined as meaning a scheme for encouraging or facilitating the holding of shares or debentures of a company by or for the benefit of bona fide employees of the company or of other companies of the same group or the spouses (including widows and widowers) and minor children of such employees: s 743.

The definition of employees' share scheme does not require that the shares shall be allotted direct to the employee shareholders. The shares are often held by trustees usually in trust for individual employees (this form of participation suffices to 'encourage' employee shareholding). 'Bona fide employee' would permit working directors who are employed under service agreements to be members of such schemes.

5.13 Return of allotments

Whenever a limited company has allotted shares it is required within one month of allotment to deliver to the registrar a return of allotments stating the number of shares allotted, their nominal value, the names, addresses and particulars of the allottees, and the amount paid or due and payable on each share: s 88. When the shares are issued by renounceable allotment letter (5.11 above) the company is allowed, by concession, to deliver its return after the period for renunciation has expired so that the names of the persons, whether original allottees or renouncees, who are entered on the register as holders of the shares at the end of the period are shown in the return.

If shares are allotted as fully or partly paid up for a non-cash consideration there must be attached to the return the contract by which the allottees became entitled to their shares. If, for example, the shares have been allotted to satisfy the purchase price of property purchased by the company the contract (signed by the parties) should be attached to the return. If there is no written contract a written summary of its terms may be delivered instead. The contract or the summary of its terms must be stamped with the stamp duty (if any) due on the transfer of the property. Capital duty is also payable on whichever is the greater of the nominal value of the shares issued and the value of the consideration received by the company: FA 1973 Sch 19 paras 4 and 7.

As stated above, when a public company makes an allotment of shares for a non-cash consideration and is required to obtain a valuation report a copy of the report must be delivered to the registrar with the return of allotments: s 111.

B THE MAINTENANCE OF CAPITAL

5.14 The maintenance of capital: The general principle

The protection enjoyed by members of a limited company against the consequences of its insolvency is balanced by rules on the maintenance of capital. The main purpose of those rules is to prevent the return of capital to shareholders (except in strictly regulated circumstances) so that the company's capital shall be available for the payment of its debts. There are a number of subsidiary rules. As an introduction here is a list of the more important topics covered in later sections of this chapter or elsewhere:

(a) redemption of redeemable shares (5.15);
(b) purchase by a company of its own shares (5.15);
(c) financial assistance given by a company for the acquisition of its own shares or the shares of its holding company (5.19);
(d) prohibition against a subsidiary becoming a member of its holding company (5.20);
(e) share premium account (5.10);
(f) forfeiture, surrender or disclaimer of shares (5.21);
(g) disposal or cancellation of shares (5.21);
(h) profits available for distribution as dividend (5.22–24);
(i) reduction of share capital (5.28);
(j) return of capital to members by a company in liquidation (20.11);
(k) loss of capital of a public company (5.26).

5.15 Redemption or purchase by a limited company of its own shares

The Companies Act 1981 introduced a procedure, with suitable safeguards, by which a company may purchase its own shares: s 162. Before coming to the details, the new system needs to be seen in the general context of company law on this subject:

(a) there is still a general prohibition against purchase by a limited company of its own shares unless one of the permitted exceptions applies: s 143. This rule was first established in *Trevor v Whitworth* (1887) 12 App Cas 409 to protect the interests of creditors;

(b) the court has a discretionary power – to permit a fair result – to order a company to purchase its shares in any of the following circumstances:
  (i) alteration of objects (Chapter 3: 3.18);
  (ii) conversion of a public to a private company (Chapter 1: 1.18);
  (iii) protection of a minority (Chapter 15: 15.6);

(c) a company may acquire its own shares as a gift but the shares must be registered in the name of a nominee since a company cannot be a member of itself. Acquisition by gift is permitted because it does not diminish the company's resources available to pay its debts: *Re Castiglione's Will Trusts* [1958] Ch 549;

(d) a company may acquire its own shares in the course of a reduction of capital duly made (5.28) but this method is uncommon;

(e) a company may, if authorised by its articles, forfeit its shares or accept a surrender in lieu (5.21);

(f) an unlimited company may, if authorised by its articles, purchase its own shares – since its members remain liable to contribute whatever is required to enable it to pay its debts. If such a purchase is undertaken to make it difficult for creditors to recover payment, the purchase may be set aside as fraudulent.

The procedure for purchase by a limited company of its own shares is adapted from the procedure for redemption. A private but not a public company is permitted to resort to capital to finance the redemption or purchase of its shares. The next three sections deal with these three related topics.

5.16 Redemption from profits or from proceeds of a new share issue: s 160

A company which is limited by shares or is limited by guarantee and has a share capital may, if authorised to do so by its articles, issue shares which are to be redeemed at a fixed date or at the option of either the company or the holders of the shares. Apart from the requirement that there shall be authority in the articles, there are two limits:

(a) only part, not the whole, of the issued share capital may be in this form; and

(b) only fully paid shares may be redeemed: s 159.

Until 1981 the power to issue redeemable shares was limited to preference shares. Many companies formed before 1981 still have articles which cover the issue of redeemable preference shares only. If such a company now wishes to issue redeemable ordinary shares it must first make a suitable alteration to its articles, eg on the model of the 1985 Table A Art 3.

The articles must specify the terms of redemption, ie the time of redemption and the price to be paid. There may be an option to the company or to the shareholder to redeem or call for redemption at a time of their choice (or within the limits of a period). The shares must be issued as redeemable; they cannot be made so after they have been issued as irredeemable. They must be fully paid at the time of redemption. At the time of issue and of redemption the company must always have other shares in issue which are not redeemable.

The shares must be redeemed by a payment of money. Any amount paid which does not exceed the nominal value of the shares redeemed may be provided either out of distributable profits or out of the proceeds of a new issue of shares. But if a premium is paid, ie more than the nominal value of the shares, it must generally be provided out of distributable profits.

If, however, the shares to be redeemed were issued at a premium and are to be redeemed out of the proceeds of a new issue of shares, a premium payable on redemption may be provided out of those proceeds up to a maximum of the premium obtained on the issue of the shares which are to be redeemed or the balance on share premium account (including any premium obtained on the new issue) whichever is less.

The shares redeemed are cancelled, ie they cannot be reissued, but the authorised share capital is not reduced. If new shares are issued to raise money to redeem shares, then the new are treated (in terms of nominal value) as a replacement for the old so that there is no temporary increase of issued share capital. If the replacement by this means occurs within a month there is exemption from capital duty on the new shares issued: s 161.

The most important safeguard of the system is the capital redemption reserve to which transfers must be made as follows:

(a) an amount equal to the nominal value of shares redeemed is transferred when redemption is out of distributable profits;
(b) an amount equal to the difference between that nominal value and the proceeds of a new share issue when the proceeds are less than the nominal value.

The capital redemption reserve is equivalent to share capital except that it may be used to pay up bonus shares (5.11): s 170(4).

Within one month the company must give notice to the registrar of any redemption of its shares: s 122. He in turn gives notice in the *London Gazette*.

5.17 Purchase of own shares out of profits or proceeds of new issue

A general power is given to a limited company to purchase its own shares (both redeemable and irredeemable) subject to the same rules as apply to redemption except that the terms of purchase need not be set by the articles. It is necessary, however, that the articles should give authority for purchase of shares. Many companies will have to alter their articles to this effect before making a purchase: s 162.

There are three prescribed procedures for the purchase of shares by a company, ie off-market purchase, contingent purchase contract and market purchase. A market purchase is purchase through the marketing arrangements of a recognised stock exchange; off-market purchase is purchase by other means; contingent purchase contracts are a variety of off-market purchase. The salient features of each procedure are briefly described below.

(a) The essential safeguard of an off-market purchase is that a written contract of purchase, which discloses the name(s) of the vendor(s) must be approved by special resolution before the purchase may be made. The contract must be available for inspection by members for 15 days before the meeting and at the meeting at which it is approved. On a vote by show of hands any vote given by a vendor is to be disregarded; on a poll any votes attached to the shares to be sold are similarly to be disregarded in determining the result: s 164. In the case of a public company the approval must be limited to purchases within a period which may not exceed 18 months.

(b) A contingent purchase contract requires the same method of approval as an off-market purchase. Its special feature is that instead of a binding commitment it creates an option for the company or the shareholder to buy or sell his shares, usually at a future date, eg when he retires from employment with the company in the case of an employee shareholder: s 165.

(c) Market purchase through the arrangements of a stock exchange is likely to be restricted in practice to public companies whose shares are listed (or dealt with on the ancillary Unlisted Securities Market of the Stock Exchange). It must be approved by ordinary resolution and give authority limited to a period of not more than 18 months. There is no contract nor any identified vendors (on whom voting restrictions can be imposed). The resolution must specify the maximum number of shares which may be purchased and fix a maximum and minimum price to be paid. But the price may be fixed in terms of a lump sum or a formula. A copy of the resolution must be delivered to the registrar within 15 days and a return made of purchases within 28 days: s 166.

Off-market purchase and contingent purchase contracts are means by which any company, public or private, may arrange to acquire a shareholding (possibly a large one) from a shareholder. It is likely to be particularly useful to private companies with a small number of shareholders. One dies or retires or leaves the service of the company. The other shareholders are unable or do not wish to purchase his shares themselves but can arrange that the company will do so. Purchase is more flexible than redemption since it can apply to shares which were not issued as redeemable or it may be at a negotiated price (unlike redeemable shares for which the terms must be specified in the articles at the outset). The capital redemption reserve safeguard ensures that the amount of fixed capital is not reduced.

A return of shares purchased must be delivered to the registrar within 28 days of the purchase: s 169. Where there is a contract for off-market purchase or contingent purchase a copy of it must be held at the registered office for ten years from the purchase of the shares. A member (and any person in the case of a public company) has the right to inspect it.

5.18 Redemption or purchase of shares out of capital

A private (but not a public) company may, if authorised by its articles, also purchase or redeem its shares out of capital: s 171. This alternative is limited however to situations where the company has insufficient profits (or proceeds of a new issue of shares) and wishes to augment those primary resources by recourse to capital, such as share premium account. There are elaborate safeguards both for members and for creditors of the company.

Any available profits or the proceeds of a new share issue must be fully used before there may be resort to capital. If the nominal value of the shares redeemed or purchased exceeds the permissible capital payment (plus any proceeds of a share issue made for the same purpose) the amount of the excess must be transferred to capital redemption reserve.

The main safeguards for members are that the purchase must be approved by special resolution (with voting restrictions – as for an off-market purchase – on intending vendors) and secondly there is a standstill period of five weeks during which any member of the company who did not vote for the resolution may apply to the court to set it aside: s 176.

The main safeguards for creditors are that the directors must within the week before the resolution is passed make a statutory declaration of solvency supported by a report of the auditors. The directors declare not only that they consider that the company could pay its debts in full after the capital payment is made but also that they anticipate that the company will be able to continue its business, paying its debts as it goes, over the next 12 months. The auditors report that having made enquiry they are not aware of anything which indicates that the directors' declaration is unreasonable and that the amount of the proposed capital payment has been correctly calculated.

A creditor will become aware of what is proposed by advertisement or notice during the standstill period and has a right, like a member, to apply to the court to set aside the resolution.

Finally if the company goes into insolvent liquidation within a year of making the payment out of capital it may be recovered either from the person to whom it was paid or from the directors who made the statutory declaration: IA s 76.

There are a number of supplementary rules to prevent abuse and to provide for special situations which may arise. In planning any form of purchase or redemption of shares those concerned will obviously have to give careful attention to the tax consequences.

5.19 Financial assistance by a company for the purchase of its own shares

The main objection to financial assistance given by a company to enable a third party to acquire its shares is that it may thereby reduce its resources available to pay its debts. Secondly, the person to whom the assistance is given may well become the controlling shareholder and then by use of the company's resources he can exploit the company to the prejudice of minority shareholders. In a simple form what could happen is that X borrows money from a third party to finance the purchase of all the shares or a controlling shareholding of Y Ltd and then uses his control of Y Ltd to divert its resources to the repayment (or guarantee) of the original loan to him.

Earlier attempts to hold this abuse in check were both ineffectual and also risky for innocent lenders, such as the banks, who might find that unknowingly they had financed an unlawful transaction (the *Belmont Case* in Chapter 1: 1.13 caused widespread alarm among banks because of its implications for them).

When Parliament enacted the rules now in force, which are explained below, the opportunity was taken to clarify the law and to provide a procedure by which a private company was permitted, subject to safeguards, to give financial assistance of this kind.

The basic prohibition is retained, ie it is not lawful for a company or its subsidiaries to give financial assistance, directly or indirectly, for the purchase of its shares: s 151. But this is followed by elaborate definitions and by the exception, for private companies, mentioned above.

The definition of financial assistance includes a gift, guarantee, security, indemnity, loan, assumption of liability of another person or anything by which the net assets of the company (if any) are reduced. The prohibition applies to assistance given before or after the purchase of the shares, eg by discharging or reducing the liability of the person by whom the shares are acquired.

In all such cases the main test is – what was the purpose or the main purpose of the company's transaction? If that purpose was to give financial assistance for the acquisition of the shares it is unlawful. The form which the transaction may take is immaterial. It can, for example, be unlawful if it takes the form of buying an asset from a person in order to provide him with the money which he needs and later uses to buy the shares of the company.

If, on the other hand, the main purpose of a transaction is not to assist in the purchase of the company's shares and the directors approve it in good faith in the interests of the company, then it does not infringe the prohibition even though it may incidentally give some assistance to a purchase of shares.

For the removal of doubt it is expressly declared that certain types of transaction do not infringe the prohibition. Thus if a shareholder receives a lawful dividend on his shares and uses the money to pay off a loan obtained to finance the purchase of the shares, that is not unlawful assistance by the company for this purpose. Two other examples of transactions in which the money is used to pay for shares but the rule is not broken are a loan by a bank to a customer who invests some of it in shares of the bank and loans to employees (other than directors) or to the trustees of an employees' share scheme to provide funds with which employees scheme shares are purchased.

However, there remains much doubt, eg if the managers of a company borrow money to finance a 'management buy-out' of the company's shares, it would be difficult to assert that this was not money provided for the purpose of buying the shares.

In the case of a private company a transaction which is or could be financial assistance for the purchase of its shares is made lawful by following a special procedure: ss 155–8. The proposed financial assistance must first be approved by special resolution. Even so a minority of members holding at least ten per cent of the share capital, who did not vote for the resolution, may apply to the court to have it set aside. The main safeguards to creditors are that:

(a) insofar as the financial assistance reduces the company's net assets it must be covered by distributable profits; and
(b) the directors are required to make a statutory declaration of solvency, and ability to continue trading for at least 12 months after the transaction, and this must be supported by an auditors' report.

These safeguards are very like those given to creditors when a private company resorts to capital to buy in its own shares (5.18) but in this case the creditors have no right to take their objections to the court.

If unlawful financial assistance is given, incidental and related transactions are likely to be void as effected for an unlawful purpose.

The company gave a debenture, secured by a floating charge, in support of a loan to finance the purchase of its shares. A third party guaranteed the company's obligations.

The debenture, the floating charge and the guarantee were void: *Heald v O'Connor* [1971] 1 WLR 497.

5.20 Subsidiary a member of its holding company

A company may not (subject to exceptions) be a member of its own holding company and any allotment or transfer of shares of the holding company to its subsidiary is void: s 23.

The rule does not apply where the subsidiary holds shares of its holding company as personal representative or as trustee and neither company is beneficially interested under the trust. There is no beneficial interest where the company concerned has made a loan in the ordinary course of a business which includes the lending of money and the loan is secured by a charge on the shares. As an example a bank executor and trustee company may in that capacity hold shares of the parent banking company for the estate or trust which it administers. It might continue to do so even though as executor it borrowed from its parent company money to pay tax giving a charge over the bank company's shares as security.

There are transitional exemptions covering holdings existing in 1948. A problem can also arise if company A which holds shares of company B later becomes a subsidiary of company B. B is no longer a member of company A, since s 23 so provides, but it still owns the shares. If company A makes a bonus issue it cannot allot bonus shares to company B since that also is expressly forbidden. The practical solution which is usually adopted is that company B sells its shares of company A to a third party.

5.21 Forfeiture, surrender and disclaimer of shares

A company is not permitted to hold its own shares. If it acquires them by redemption or purchase (5.16 and 5.17) the shares are automatically cancelled when acquired: ss 159(4) and 162(2). However, the authorised capital is not thereby reduced.

If the court orders a company to acquire its own shares (see 5.15(b) above) it will give consequential directions for reduction of capital etc.

The other main contingency is that the member to whom shares are allotted may fail to pay for them. In that case the company, if authorised by its articles, may forfeit the shares or accept their surrender and cancel them: s 121(2)(e).

To bring into operation its powers of forfeiture the company must first formally require the allottee to pay all or a specified part of the amount unpaid on his shares (Chapter 7: 7.24). The exact procedure must be followed throughout – otherwise the call and the consequent forfeiture is invalid. If a shareholder is bankrupt his trustee may disclaim shares to which a liability attaches. Disclaimer does not, however, prevent the company from claiming in his bankruptcy for the amount due and unpaid on his shares.

When shares of a public company are forfeited or surrendered very complicated rules (enacted to comply with the EC Second Directive) require that the shares be disposed of or cancelled. Similar principles apply to shares acquired by a public company in which it has a beneficial interest, whether or not it has given financial assistance to its nominee who holds the shares or to some other person: s 146.

If a public company fails to dispose of its own shares within three years it must cancel them (and may do so at any time within that period). The period is only one year if the public company gave financial assistance for the acquisition of its shares by a nominee and has a beneficial interest in them.

If cancellation of shares reduces the total issued capital of a public company to less than £50,000 it must reregister as a private company (Chapter 1: 1.18).

5.22 Profits available for payment of dividends

A company may not make a distribution except out of profits available for the purpose: s 263(1). This rule primarily controls the payment of dividends but distribution is defined to cover any distribution of assets other than:

(a) the issue of shares as fully or partly paid bonus shares (5.11 above);
(b) payments on redemption or purchase of the company's shares (5.15);
(c) a reduction of share capital by extinguishing or reducing liability in respect of unpaid share capital or by repaying paid-up share capital (5.28 below);
(d) a distribution of assets to members in winding up (Chapter 20; 20.11).

The profits available for distribution are the accumulated, realised profits, so far as not previously utilised by distribution or capitalisation less accumulated realised losses so far as not previously written off by a reduction or reorganisation of capital duly made: s 263. This rule has been enacted to implement the EC Second Directive but it applies to all companies because the law on dividends, as it was previously, was very unsatisfactory. The effect of the new formula on distributable profits is best illustrated by reference to the loopholes in the previous law which it closes.

Both profits and losses must be 'accumulated', i e the profit and loss account must be maintained as a continuous record of the company's financial results since incorporation. It is no longer possible to pay a dividend out of current profits without setting off against those profits the losses of previous periods.

At the start of the current year, in which it made a profit, the company had accumulated losses brought forward from previous years. The directors revalued the fixed assets at a higher figure and carried the surplus to a reserve account to which they charged the debit balance on profit and loss account. They then declared a dividend out of the current year's profit. The revaluation was made honestly but without obtaining a professional valuation. It was argued that the losses of previous years were losses of capital caused mainly by making provision for depreciation and that there was no legal obligation to make good such losses out of profits. It was held that the dividend was properly paid out of profits. *Ammonia Soda Co Ltd v Chamberlain* [1918] 1 Ch 266.

The essential objections to *Chamberlain's Case* are that the profit was 'unrealised' and that it was not 'accumulated' by bringing in the losses (and any profits if there had been any) of previous years. The s 263 rule vetoes distributions of that kind.

For some companies there are practical difficulties, arising from their past history, in meeting the tests of s 263. But these are more problems of accountancy practice than of company law.

Whenever any question arises of a 'capital profit', i e a gain on an increase in value of fixed assets, even if realised by sale, it is necessary to pay due regard to the value of all such assets, not merely those which have risen in value.

A company purchased the undertakings and assets of another company. Certain assets were regarded as worthless but later yielded a realised profit. It was held that 'what is profit available for dividend depends upon the result of the whole accounts fairly taken for the year, capital as well as profit and loss'. A windfall profit from one item could not be dealt with in isolation: *Foster v New Trinidad Lake Asphalt Co Ltd* [1901] 1 Ch 208.

Another loophole in the law has been closed by a statutory rule on company accounts which in general requires that depreciation shall be charged in respect of all assets which have a limited life: Sch 4 para 19. A depreciation charge is treated as a 'realised' loss: s 275. There are, however, adjustments to be made when depreciation is raised against a revalued asset on the basis of its revised value.

5.23 Profits available for dividend: public companies
In addition to compliance with the rules applicable to all companies (5.22), a *public* company may only make a distribution if:

(a) the amount of its net assets is at the time not less than the aggregate of its called-up share capital and undistributable reserves; and
(b) the amount of the distribution is such that condition (a) will still be satisfied after the distribution has been made: s 264.

Undistributable reserves are share premium account, capital redemption reserve fund, any surplus of accumulated unrealised profits over accumulated unrealised losses and any other reserve which the company is prohibited from distributing by statute or by its memorandum.

This 'net worth' test imposed on public companies to comply with the EC Second Directive prevents those companies from paying dividends regardless of a loss of capital. The general formula applied to all companies (5.22) requires that realised losses (including provision for depreciation) shall be brought into account in determining whether there is a profit available for dividend. The additional rule of s 264 for public companies brings into the calculation unrealised losses, eg a fall in value of retained fixed assets, but permits such losses to be set off against unrealised profits.

For 'investment companies' there is an alternative formula (s 265) on distributable profits. An investment company must in practice have a Stock Exchange listing for its shares since it may only pay dividends under the alternative formula if it has a listing. It must also declare itself as an investment company on its letterheads, etc: s 351. The alternative formula is intended to relieve investment companies of the difficulty which they might otherwise encounter in connection with the standard 'net worth' test for public companies. The principal assets of investment (trust) companies are listed securities which are subject to considerable fluctuations in value which might bring the net worth of the investment companies below the prescribed level. Yet even in periods when the value of listed securities has fallen they continue to yield fairly steady income as dividends.

Investment companies are permitted to pay dividends out of accumulated, realised profits less accumulated realised losses (regardless of the net worth test) provided that the ratio of assets to liabilities is maintained at a ratio of 3:2 or better.

The detailed requirements for obtaining recognition as an investment company are too complicated for examination in a general book on company law. Broadly the same companies are eligible to qualify (s 266) as are recognized for corporation tax purposes under the Income and Corporation Taxes Act 1970 s 359.

There are also special rules for determining how an insurance company which carries on long-term business may calculate its profits. The basic principle is that any surplus from which a transfer may be made to profit and loss account should be determined by actuarial investigation: s 268.

5.24 Determination of profits available for dividend

The amount of a company's profits available for distribution is determined by reference to its 'relevant accounts': s 270. In normal circumstances the most recent audited annual accounts are the relevant accounts.

The accounts must have been 'properly prepared', ie comply with the accounting requirements of the Companies Act and give a true and fair view of the state of affairs at the end of the period and of the profit or loss for the period covered by the accounts.

If the auditors' report on the accounts is qualified, the company is required to obtain from the auditors a written statement whether the matter referred to as the subject of their qualification is material for determining whether the proposed distribution would contravene the rules on profits available for dividend. But a distinction is drawn between qualifications relating to statutory rules on the preparation of accounts and other qualifications, eg relating to observance of standard accounting practice. It is only the former type of qualified report which then requires a written statement by the auditors. The general result of these rules is that the measure of profits available for dividend is the most recent audited accounts unless the auditors have made a qualified report with reference to statutory accounting matters. If, for example, the auditors stated that they had been unable to satisfy themselves that there had been a proper end-of-year valuation of the company's stocks the profit balance shown in the accounts could hardly be treated as available for dividend since the reliability of the profit figure would be suspect.

If the latest audited annual accounts do not disclose a profit sufficient to cover the proposed dividend *interim* accounts may be produced. In the case of any company these accounts must enable a proper judgment to be made and they must (in the case of a public company) be properly prepared in the sense explained above. They need not be audited but a copy must (in the case of a public company) be delivered to the registrar for filing: s 272.

If a distribution is to be made during a company's first accounting reference period or before any accounts have been laid before a general meeting or delivered to the registrar *initial* accounts may be prepared on similar lines to determine whether there is a profit available for dividend. In this case also there is no requirement that the accounts shall be audited but in the case of a public company an auditors' report is required as to whether the initial accounts have been properly prepared. A copy of the initial accounts must be delivered to the registrar: s 273.

5.25 Dividends: other rules

The statutory rules designed to prevent the payment of dividends out of capital replace earlier inadequate case law in the same field. But they leave substantially unaltered the old rules on liability and on the procedural aspects of dividend payments.

It is provided, however, that if a distribution is made which wholly or in part infringes the statutory rules any member who, at the time of the distribution, knows or has reasonable grounds for believing that it does infringe the rules is liable to repay to the company such part of the distribution as infringes the rules. This is without prejudice to any other obligation which a member may have to repay an unlawful dividend.

Under common law rules a shareholder may obtain an injunction to restrain the payment of a dividend out of capital. The directors who cause such a dividend to be paid may be made personally liable to refund to the company the amount so paid if either they acted in the knowledge that the dividend was paid out of capital or if they did so without having proper accounts prepared showing that sufficient profits were available. But the directors are not liable if they relied on a bona fide valuation of assets which later proves to be unjustified.

For a number of years the directors laid before the company in general meeting balance sheets which showed as assets debts owing to the company which to their knowledge were irrecoverable. By this means an unprofitable business was made to appear profitable. The general meetings approved these accounts and the payment of dividends. It was held that if the directors 'improperly pay away the assets to the shareholders they are liable to replace them'. It was immaterial that the members had approved what was done since it was illegal and ultra vires (Chapter 15: 15.2): *Re Exchange Banking Co, Flitcroft's Case* (1882) 21 Ch D 519.

The company's business was with the southern Confederate States during the American civil war of the 1860s. The accounts valued various assets in confederate territory at their full value. The defeat of the southern states caused a total loss of these assets. Stringer, who as managing director had recommended the dividend, was not liable to make it good to the company since on the basis of the accounts, which were reasonable at the time, the dividend was covered by profits. As there appeared to be profits it was legal to borrow money, not exceeding the profits, to provide cash for the payment of the dividend: *Re Mercantile Trading Co, Stringer's Case* (1869) 4 Ch App 475.

The directors simply declared dividends without having any proper accounts prepared, to determine whether there were sufficient profits. The directors were held liable to make good to the company the unlawful payment of dividends out of capital: *Re Oxford Benefit Building and Investment Society* (1886) 35 Ch D 502.

If the articles provide that dividends are payable in proportion to shares, every share carries the same entitlement regardless of differences in the amount paid up on different shares. But the articles (eg Table A Art 104) often provide that the amount of the dividend shall be related to the amounts paid up on the shares.

A public company with a large number of members will inevitably accumulate unclaimed dividends over a period of years as dividend warrants sent to members are orders to pay which they must present to the company's bank. If they fail to notify the company of a change of address, their warrants may not reach them. The articles (eg Table A Art 108) may provide that the company's liability shall be extinguished after a period of years. It may also become statute-barred under general law. The law on unclaimed dividends was reviewed in the case below.

The company incorporated in 1911 had issued bearer securities and had made reductions of capital and entered into schemes of arrangement as well as declaring dividends. Some holders of bearer securities entitled to money in respect of these transactions could not be traced. The company was in voluntary liquidation. The court held that the untraced holders of bearer securities were creditors for the purpose of company liquidation rules (Chapter 20 Part B), that the limitation period in respect of their claims was six years and that an entry in the balance sheet could be an acknowledgement (as previously held in *Re Gee & Co (Woolwich) Ltd* [1975] 1 Ch 52) which revived the company's liability but only 'if made to the person . . . whose title or claim is being acknowledged'; Limitation Act 1939 s 24(2). Moreover as creditors of a company in liquidation even persons who are entitled to sums owed to them as members must prove their debts. If they do not do so the liquidator may distribute the assets without regard to their claims (Chapter 20: 20.7): *Re Compania de Electricidad de la Provincia de Buenos Aires Ltd* [1978] 3 All ER 668.

The practical difficulty which confronts the shareholder who asserts that his right to arrears of dividends has been kept alive by each year's issue of the accounts is that if the company did not have his up-to-date address, at which to deliver his dividend warrant, he will not have received his copy of the accounts sent to the same address.

Since knowledge is the test of liability of directors (at common law) or of shareholders (under s 277) the company which has paid an unlawful dividend out of capital is likely to claim against the directors in the first instance. Section 277 may, however, be useful if the shareholders have greater resources than the directors.

In most cases a shareholder would argue successfully that he was misled by the accounts and did not know the true position – so that he is not liable under s 277. But s 277 may be useful in case of collusion between directors and wealthy shareholders. If the directors are required to pay back the dividend they have a right of indemnity against shareholders if the latter knew the true position.

Apart from general rules of company law the payment of dividends may be further restricted by the articles. The articles (e g Table A Arts 102–8) usually provide that:

(a) dividend shall only be paid out of profits available for distribution under the Companies Acts. This permits the payment of dividends out of capital as well as trading profits. An alternative formula is to provide for payment of dividends out of trading profits only;

(b) the company in general meeting may declare dividends but not in excess of the amount recommended by the directors;

(c) the directors may pay interim dividends if they consider that the profits justify them in doing so. In practice directors would probably consider interim accounts before declaring a dividend.

Creditors have no power to restrain the payment of dividends. Their only remedy is to petition for an order for compulsory winding up.

Dividends do not become a debt until they have been declared and the date for payment has arrived. A declaration of an interim dividend by the directors may later be rescinded or varied. Until a dividend has been declared a member, even if he holds preference shares on which dividends are payable at fixed dates, has no right to a dividend (see the *Barrow Haematite Steel Case* in Chapter 7: 7.10).

The 1985 Table A, unlike earlier editions, does not confer on the directors an express power to transfer profits to reserve. But such a power is implicit in their general powers of management (and so need not be specified in Table A).

Modern articles (and Table A Art 105) provide expressly that dividends may be paid in specie, e g by distribution of the company's investments in other companies. Unless this is made clear, 'pay' implies payment only in cash (the *Odessa Waterworks Case* in Chapter 4: 4.4). In practice distribution of (taxable) dividends otherwise than in cash is very uncommon.

5.26 Loss of capital of a public company

When the net assets of a *public* company are half or less of the amount of the company's called-up share capital, the directors are required to call an extraordinary general meeting of the company. The notice convening the meeting must be issued not later than 28 days after the earliest day on which a director of the company becomes aware of the financial situation described above. The meeting must be convened for a date not later than 56 days from that day. If the meeting is not convened when it should be, every director who is knowingly and wilfully in default is guilty of an offence punishable by a fine: s 142.

This rule, arising from the EC Second Directive, introduces into English company law an unfamiliar procedure though it is well established in some codes of European law. The purpose of holding the meeting is to permit members to consider whether any and if so what measures should be taken to deal with the situation. The directors are, however, under no obligation to make recommendations to the general meeting nor to implement its decisions. In practice the directors would no doubt lay before the meeting a report on the reasons for the loss of half the capital, the prospects of the immediate future and their recommendations, e g to close down part of the business to reduce losses or to wind up the company.

This procedure presents a number of problems. How should assets be valued if the company is going downhill? On a going concern or a break-up basis? If the directors call such a meeting they are publicising the company's losses to its creditors in a disturbing fashion. This information may well precipitate the immediate collapse which s 142 procedure is intended to avoid.

It seems unlikely that this method will in practice be used. The directors might prefer for example to invite a secured creditor to appoint a receiver or apply to the court under the new procedure introduced by the Insolvency Act 1985 for the appointment of an administrator. They would of course have to take action on these lines before the company's financial situation had become so acute as to bring s 142 into operation. Once the circumstances of s 142 exist the directors must follow that procedure.

C REORGANISATION OF SHARE CAPITAL

5.27 Types of capital reorganisation

A company limited by shares or limited by guarantee and having a share capital may if so authorised by its articles:

(a) increase its authorised share capital by the creation of new shares;
(b) consolidate its shares into shares of larger amount;
(c) subdivide its shares into shares of smaller amount but only so that the proportion of amounts paid and unpaid shall be the same in respect of all divided shares;
(d) convert its paid-up shares into stock or reconvert stock into paid-up shares (Chapter 7: 7.6);

(e) cancel its unissued shares and so reduce the amount of its authorised capital.

Any such change must be effected by resolution passed in general meeting in accordance with the articles: s 121. If the articles do not already give the required authorisation they may be altered by special resolution before the new power is exercised. The articles usually provide that an ordinary resolution shall be passed in any such case to alter the capital.

Notice of any alteration of capital must be given to the registrar within a month (15 days in the case of an increase of authorised share capital): ss 122–3. A copy of the resolution by which any increase of capital was made and a copy of the memorandum containing the altered capital clause must also be delivered to the registrar.

Capital may also be altered by variation of the rights attached to a class of shares (Chapter 7: 7.12), by a reconstruction effected by a scheme of arrangement (Chapter 16: 16.3) or by a reduction of issued, and incidentally of authorised, capital (5.28 below).

5.28 Reduction of share capital

A company limited by shares or a company limited by guarantee having a share capital may if so authorised by its articles and subject to confirmation by the court by special resolution reduce its share capital in any way: s 135.

Three particular methods of reduction of capital are specified but a company is not restricted to these alone. They are:

(a) to extinguish or reduce liability in respect of share capital not paid up. Eg a company has an authorised and issued capital of 100 £1 shares on which 75p per share is paid up. It may reduce the nominal value of each £1 share to 75p (or some intermediate figure) by cancelling up to 25p per share of unpaid capital;

(b) to cancel paid-up capital which is lost or unrepresented by available assets. Eg a company has an authorised issued and fully paid capital of £100 in £1 shares. But its net assets are worth only £75 and there is a debit balance on profit and loss account due to trading losses. The company may cancel up to 25p per share, thereby reducing each share to 75p fully paid and write off the debit balance on profit and loss account;

(c) to pay off paid-up share capital which the company no longer needs. Eg a company has an authorised issued and fully paid capital of £100 in £1 shares. It may repay, say, 25p per share in cash to members, reducing the amount paid up on each share to 75p.

Where the shares were partly paid before any reduction took effect, method (a) may be combined with either of the others. In method (b) and (c) it is usual but not essential to reduce the nominal value of the shares by a corresponding amount. Thus in the examples given in (b) and (c) above the shares would be reduced to 75p (nominal) shares fully paid. The alternative, which is possible but less common, is to leave the nominal value of the shares unaltered so that (in methods (b) and (c) above) they are £1 (nominal) shares as before but now only 75p paid with the result that holders are still liable to pay an additional 25p per share at some later time.

If the company has statutory capital reserves (share premium account or capital redemption reserve fund) all or part of those reserves may be cancelled (method (b)) or repaid (method (c)) under an authorised reduction of share capital. The nominal value of the shares and the amount paid is then unaltered.

Under method (c) repayment may be effected by a distribution of assets other than cash or the company may borrow money to finance the repayment.

The sequence of procedure is as follows:

(i) if there is no existing power to reduce capital in the articles (eg Table A Art 34) a special resolution may be passed to create that power. This may be done first at the meeting convened to reduce the capital;

(ii) a special resolution setting out the details of the proposed reduction of capital is passed;

(iii) application is made to the court by petition with supporting affidavits, minute book, financial statements and possibly guarantees (see below);

(iv) the court considers the proposed reduction, the reasons for and effect of it, and how it may affect the interests of creditors or of each class of shareholder if there is more than one class. The court may order that a notice be published inviting creditors to appear and raise objections if they wish to do so: s 136;

(v) if the court sanctions the reduction it makes an order to that effect and issues a minute showing the particulars of the capital as reduced. The order and minute are delivered to the registrar and notice of registration is published as the court may direct. The reduction takes effect when the order and minute are delivered to the registrar, who issues a certificate of registration which is conclusive that the reduction has been effected in accordance with the Companies Act and that the capital of the company is now as shown in the minute: ss 137–8;

(vi) all copies of the memorandum which may be issued in future must include a copy of the minute which takes effect as an alteration of the capital clause.

The court may direct that the company shall add the words 'and reduced' to its name or that it shall publish a statement of the causes or reasons for the reduction. But it is very rare for such directions to be given.

In the case of a public company if the reduction reduces the nominal value of the issued share capital to less than the authorised minimum (£50,000) the company must be reregistered as a private company before the reduction is registered unless the court otherwise directs: s 139.

If the reduction takes the form of method (a) or method (c) above, the effect will be to reduce the resources available to the company for the payment of its debts. Even method (b) may indirectly affect the interests of creditors since by eliminating accumulated losses the company is thereafter able to pay dividends out of future profits without retaining profits to make good past losses. Section 136 provides that the court may settle a list of creditors and their claims and cause notices to be published giving them the opportunity to appear and object to the reduction. But this procedure may be waived, even in the case of methods (a) or (c), if there are in the court's opinion special circumstances which justify dispensing with it.

The company could not obtain the court's confirmation of the reduction unless it could show that the creditors would nonetheless be paid in full. Mere solvency of the company is not a sufficient circumstance. But it usually enables the company to obtain a guarantee from its bank that existing debts will be paid. Alternatively the company may discharge all the debts or set aside cash sufficient to do so. If by one or more such means the court is satisfied that the interests of creditors will not be prejudiced by the reduction it will not require publication of notices to creditors. This alternative 'special circumstance' procedure is in fact normal modern practice. Apart from other considerations it could damage the company's credit if legal notices inviting creditors to object, which might be misunderstood, were published.

Apart from its consideration of the interests of creditors the court has also to review the possible effect of the reduction on the public interest or on the interests of a class of shareholders. Public interest is rarely a significant factor in the financial relationship between a company and its members. In particular a reduction is likely to be approved even though its purpose is to avoid or reduce tax liability or to escape impending nationalisation.

The reduction should be fair between members holding shares of the same class and between different classes if there is more than one. The first principle will usually require that all shares of the same class should be reduced by the same proportion but exceptions can be made where there is justification. The test of fairness within the class also requires that a majority who give any necessary consent binding on the class as a whole shall act in the interests of the class as a whole and not to secure an advantage to themselves.

The company proposed to reduce its capital by cancelling its redeemable preference shares and issuing an equivalent amount of unsecured loan stock to the holders of those shares. The necessary consent of the preference shareholders as a class was given by extraordinary resolutions passed at a class meeting. At the class meeting 90 per cent of the votes cast to approve the resolution were given by trustee shareholders who also held 52 per cent of the ordinary shares. The trustees had been advised that as ordinary shareholders they would gain more than they would lose as preference shareholders. It was held that a majority vote is only binding if the majority vote in the interests of the class, which was not the case here. It was also held that when the issue of fairness is raised, the burden of proof is on those who assert that the reduction is fair, not on those who assert that it is unfair: *Re Holders Investment Trust Ltd* [1971] 2 All ER 289.

In considering the effect of the reduction on different classes of shareholders the first issue is whether or not the reduction is a variation of class rights (Chapter 7: 7.12). If there are preference shares which carry a right to repayment of capital in priority to ordinary shares (and no express right to participate in surplus assets remaining after the ordinary share capital has been repaid) it is in accordance with the rights of preference shareholders and not a variation of their rights to effect a reduction of share capital by which the preference shares are repaid, leaving only issued ordinary shares outstanding.

The company's assets had been nationalised and the compensation money was used in a repayment (by reduction of capital) of the preference shares. The objections of the preference shareholders to losing an investment which they wished to retain were overruled. There is the same result if the preference shares carry a right to participate in any dividends paid in excess of a specified rate of dividend on ordinary shares. But if they have been given an express right to participate in surplus assets on liquidation or if the company has agreed not to reduce its capital without the consent of the holders of the shares they may object. See also *Scottish Insurance Corp v Wilsons & Clyde Coal Co* (Chapter 7: 7.9) on unsuccessful objections based on loss of income from the investment: *Prudential Assurance Co Ltd v Chatterley-Whitfield Collieries Ltd* [1949] AC 512.

The rights of the preference shareholders may be strengthened if by the terms of issue they are entitled on repayment to a premium over nominal value of the shares equal to the excess of their market price over that value (the Spens formula) but in recent times preference shares more often stand at a discount on their nominal value.

If the company cancels paid-up capital to eliminate losses and the preference shares carry a priority right to repayment of capital in liquidation the reduction should generally fall on the ordinary shares since this is where the deficiency would fall in liquidation, ie the remaining assets would be applied first in repayment of preference capital.

If the preference shares rank equally with ordinary shares in any return of capital any repayment or cancellation of paid-up capital should apply equally to shares of both classes, even though the amount of preference dividend at a fixed rate on paid-up capital would thereby be reduced.

It has been explained that a public company may be required to cancel its shares which the company has forfeited, accepted on surrender or otherwise acquired (5.21). In any such case the reduction is an automatic consequence of the company's ownership of its shares and so the reduction may be effected by the directors under statutory powers given for that purpose: s 146. It is not a reduction of capital to which the procedure described above applies.

For some purposes a resolution signed by all the members is accepted in substitution for a resolution passed at a general meeting (Chapter 11: 11.16). The articles (Table A Art 53) may expressly recognise this practice. But the court, although it has discretion to do so in an exceptional case, will not generally permit a reduction of capital to be agreed within the company by this means without passing a special resolution, since a resolution is expressly prescribed by s 135(1).

Chapter 6

Prospectuses

A PROSPECTUS PROCEDURE

6.1 Methods of raising capital

A public company is permitted to invite the public to subscribe for shares or debentures (referred to as 'securities' in this chapter) so that the company may raise additional permanent capital. The written invitation, issued to investors and also advertised in the press, is a 'prospectus'. The main purpose of the elaborate statutory rules on prospectuses is to ensure they contain sufficient information and that the directors of the company, and others who assist in the issue of the prospectus, accept legal liability for its accuracy.

An established company usually gives its existing members a first refusal of new shares issued for cash by a rights issue (Chapter 5: 5.11). This is a prospectus but it need not contain all the information which is required of a company which is 'floated' ie issues securities to the public for the first time (see 6.4 below).

When a prospectus is issued there is a choice of three methods of raising capital from the public. First, the company may invite the public to apply to it direct for the allotment of its securities. Secondly, the company may allot securities by a single large allotment to the issuing house which then offers them to the public. This is an *offer for sale* to which additional legal rules apply which are explained below. Thirdly, the issuing house may arrange a *placing*, ie the issue of securities (usually in large holdings) to a limited number of financial institutions or clients of the issuing house. The securities may be allotted en bloc to the issuing house for resale to its 'placees' but it is also possible for the allotment to be made by the company direct to placees nominated by the issuing house. For a placing, as in the other cases, it is essential that the securities be granted a Stock Exchange listing since the placees may intend to sell all or part of their holdings through the Stock Exchange later on. Hence it is necessary to make a placing subject to prospectus rules.

Whenever a company allots, or agrees to allot, securities 'with a view' to the sale of all or any of them to the public, the subsequent offer to the public is an *offer for sale* which is deemed to be a prospectus issued by the company and is subject to the same rules: s 58. Unless the contrary is proved, an allotment, or agreement to allot, is deemed to be made with a view to sale to the public if either:

(a) the subsequent offer of the securities to the public is made within six months of the allotment or agreement to allot by the company; or

(b) at the time of the offer to the public the company has not received the full consideration for the securities allotted.

Any document which is an offer for sale must, in addition to the other prescribed contents of a prospectus, disclose:

(i) the net consideration received or to be received by the company for the securities offered; and
(ii) the place and time at which the public may inspect the contract under which the securities have been or are to be allotted: s 58(4).

The copy of the offer for sale to the public delivered to the registrar as a prospectus, must be signed by the directors of the company and also by at least two directors of the issuing house (or if the issuing house is a firm, eg of stockbrokers, by not less than half its partners).

6.2 The definition of a prospectus

A prospectus is defined as 'any prospectus, notice, circular, advertisement, or other invitation, offering to the public for subscription or purchase any shares or debentures of a company': s 744.

Although the definition uses the word 'offer' a prospectus is in reality an invitation to the public to make offers to the company by applying for securities. The company then accepts the offers by allotting securities to the applicants. A prospectus cannot be an offer in the normal sense since the company cannot undertake in advance to meet the full public demand. A successful issue is usually heavily over-subscribed and the company then allots to each subscriber fewer securities than he has applied for.

The expression 'subscription or purchase' implies that the consideration for the securities is the payment of a sum of money. Hence 'a take-over bid' by which company A offers its shares in exchange for the shares of company B is not the issuing of a prospectus. But a take-over is regulated by the Prevention of Fraud (Investments) Act 1958 and, like a prospectus, it is subject to stringent Stock Exchange disclosure requirements.

The word 'purchase' in the definition indicates that the prospectus rules apply to an offer for sale although it is strictly an offer by the allottee (the issuing house) to sell issued shares. The purchaser in such a case does not 'subscribe' in the sense of making payment direct to the company. But the word 'purchase' in this definition does not extend the prospectus rules to a normal offer by the holder of issued securities to sell them. Prospectus rules are confined to offers made by or on behalf of a company which include an offer for sale in the special sense of that phrase.

6.3 The meaning of offer to the public

A private company (limited by shares) is prohibited from offering its securities to the public and from allotting securities with a view to such an offer. If a private company infringes that rule, even unintentionally, the company, and its officers who are in default, commit a criminal offence: s 81. A public company is not so prohibited. But if it does offer securities to the public (or allot them with a view to such an offer) the offer document is a prospectus which must comply with prospectus rules (enforced by the sanction of civil and criminal liabilities against breach). If, on the other hand, the offer is not to the public, the company is not subject to the rules. Hence the meaning of 'offer to the public' in its application to borderline cases is important.

There are some statutory guidelines:

(a) an offer may be an offer to the public even if it is an offer restricted to a section of the public. Hence an offer made to effect a placing of securities among a selected group can be a prospectus, especially if it satisfies the special criteria of an offer for sale: s 59;
(b) an offer by a company to existing members or debenture holders may (subject, however, to (c) below) be an offer to the public. So is an offer to persons selected as clients of the persons making the offer;
(c) an offer is not an offer to the public if it can properly be regarded in all the circumstances as not calculated to result in the securities becoming available for subscription or purchase by persons other than the original offerees: s 60.

Company A issued a circular to the shareholders of companies X and Y offering to acquire their shares in those companies in exchange for its own shares. By its nature the offer could only be accepted by shareholders of X or Y, ie it was non-renounceable. This was not a prospectus because (1) the consideration for the shares to be allotted by company A was not cash (see comment on 'purchase' above) and (2) the offer could only be accepted by the persons to whom it was made and so it was not 'an offer to the public': *Government Stock and Other Securities Investment Co Ltd v Christopher* [1956] 1 All ER 490;

(d) it is not an offer to the public if it can properly be regarded as 'a domestic concern' of the persons making and receiving the offer.

The concept of 'domestic concern' in rule (d) above has been developed by s 60 to lay down ground rules within which a private company may safely offer or invite subscriptions for its securities without infringing the prohibition against offers to the public. These rules are based on two defined terms, ie 'members of the relevant class' and 'employees' share scheme' (explained in Chapter 5: 5.12). A person is a member of the relevant class if he is an existing member, debenture holder or employee of the company or a member of the family of an existing member or employee. Member of the family is in turn defined so as to include a spouse (including a widow or widower), a child (and remoter issue) and trustee of a settlement whose principal beneficiary is the existing member or employee or a member of the family of such a person.

An offer or invitation by a private company is then regarded, unless the contrary is proved, as the domestic concern of the persons making and receiving it if it is an offer or invitation made to members of the relevant class or relates to securities to be held under an employees' share scheme. Secondly, the offer or invitation is still treated as a matter of domestic concern even if it gives limited rights of renunciation by a member of the relevant class in favour of another member of the class or in a case where the securities are offered under an employees' share scheme, a right of renunciation in favour of a person entitled to hold securities under the scheme.

When a public company whose securities already have a Stock Exchange listing issues additional shares or debentures it must obtain listing for them also (to maintain uniformity of status for its entire issued share and loan capital of the same class). This would be the probable result even if the securities were in the first instance placed with a small number of allottees by non-renounceable letters of allotment. Hence the issue, although restricted, would be a prospectus since listed securities are inherently marketable among the public. But the burden of compliance with prospectus rules is much reduced in such cases by relieving the company of the normal requirements of prospectus content (6.4 below), ie only an abridged prospectus is required though a signed copy must be delivered to the registrar since it is a prospectus.

6.4 The contents of a prospectus
In terms of content prospectuses are of two kinds. A prospectus 'issued generally' (also called a 'full prospectus') must contain a large amount of detailed information prescribed by s 57 and Sch 3. A full prospectus is required in every case except:

(a) an offer of securities of the company to existing members or debenture holders even if the offer is renounceable to others; or
(b) an offer of securities which are in all respects uniform with securities previously issued and currently listed on a prescribed stock exchange: s 57(2).

This exemption is granted because in these cases the investing public already has available the information which a full prospectus must contain; in particular the company will have issued annual accounts (Chapter 14 outlines the very detailed information which the accounts must provide). To prevent evasion it is unlawful to issue a form of application for securities without an accompanying full prospectus in any circumstances in which full prospectus requirements would apply. But here there is an additional exemption; a form of application without a prospectus (which will not have been completed and issued at that point) may be issued to a prospective underwriter: s 56(2). But this is largely theoretical since an underwriter in practice requires to see the final draft of the prospectus before agreeing to underwrite the issue (6.8 below). As already explained an 'offer for sale' by an allottee is treated as a prospectus (6.1): s 58. This rule incidentally closes what would otherwise be a loophole.

In addition to satisfying prospectus requirements an offer of securities for which a Stock Exchange listing is to be obtained must comply with Stock Exchange requirements. The Stock Exchange (Listing) Regulations 1984, SI 1984/716 impose on the United Kingdom the requirements of an EC directive on this subject and delegates to the Stock Exchange power to supervise and enforce the directive in this country.

Every prospectus, whether it is issued generally as a full prospectus or whether it falls under the exemptions (a) or (b) above, must be dated, state that a copy has been delivered for registration (6.6 below) and specify the documents (if any) which are by law (6.6) required to be indorsed on or attached to the copy delivered for registration: s 64.

Where a full prospectus is issued Sch 3 requires it to contain information on the following main subjects:

(a) *share capital* – the rights attached to different classes of shares; any deferred or management shares and the interests of the holders of those shares in the property and profits of the company; particulars of any options relating to shares and particulars of issues within the preceding two years and consideration (in cash or otherwise) received;

(b) *property acquired* – property purchased or to be purchased out of the proceeds of the issue (unless by a contract made in the ordinary course of business or of trivial value) with particulars of the vendors, the consideration given, and any transaction completed within the preceding two years in which any vendor, promoter, director or proposed director had an interest direct or indirect;

(c) *financial position* – a report by the auditors of the company on the profits and losses of the company and its subsidiaries (and the dividends paid by the company on its various classes of shares) in respect of each of the five years preceding the issue of the prospectus and on the assets and liabilities of the company and its subsidiaries at the latest date to which accounts were made up;

(d) *new business to be acquired* – if the proceeds of the issue or any part of them are to be applied directly or indirectly in the purchase of a business or of the shares of another company an accountants' report on the profits or losses of the business in each of the previous five financial years and on its assets and liabilities at the latest date at which the accounts are made up;

(e) *the securities offered* – the time of opening of the subscription lists, the amount payable on application and allotment and in the case of an offer of shares to the public, the *minimum subscription*, ie the minimum amount which must be raised by the issue of shares:

    (i) to pay the purchase price of any property to be purchased out of the proceeds of the issue;

    (ii) to pay any preliminary expenses and any commission payable to underwriters, etc;

    (iii) to repay any sums borrowed for these purposes; and

    (iv) to provide working capital.

If any of these amounts is to be provided otherwise than out of the proceeds of the issue the amounts and their source must be given. If the company reserves the right to allot shares in spite of any failure to obtain applications for all the shares offered by the prospectus that reservation must be stated: s 84 (see 6.9 below);

(f) *material contracts* – the dates, parties and general nature of every material contract of the company made within the previous two years otherwise than in the ordinary course of business; when the prospectus is filed (6.6) copies are attached;

(g) *preliminary expenses* – the amount or estimated amount of the preliminary expenses and of the expenses of the issue and by whom these expenses have been paid or are payable;

(h) *commissions* – any commissions (other than commissions payable to sub-underwriters) for subscribing or procuring subscriptions for any securities of the company;

(i) *promoters* – the amount of benefit paid or given within the previous two years or intended to be paid or given to any promoter and the consideration for it;

(j) *directors* – personal particulars, remuneration, qualification shares, and interest in the promotion or in property which the company is to acquire;

(k) *auditors* (if any) – names and addresses.

If a prospectus is issued more than two years after the date on which the company became entitled to commence business certain requirements of Sch 3 relating to directors and preliminary expenses need not be included.

If a prospectus is issued which fails to comply with the requirement of Sch 3, where they are applicable, the subscriber cannot on that account rescind the allotment (6.14 below). It has been said that his only remedy is to claim damages from those responsible for the issue of the prospectus. A person in default may escape liability by showing that he was unaware of the matter which should have been disclosed, or that he made an honest mistake of fact, or if the matter was one which the court considers immaterial or otherwise such that he should reasonably be excused. But a condition of the offer that an applicant for securities shall waive compliance with the rules or be deemed to have notice of matters not disclosed in the offer is void: s 57(3). These provisions for relieving liability only apply to omissions. If a prospectus contains statements which are untrue or otherwise misleading other principles of liability apply (6.13). Omissions may often render what is included misleading.

6.5 Consents incidental to the issue of a prospectus
The copy of the prospectus which is delivered to the registrar before publication (6.6 below) must be signed by every person named in it as a director or proposed director of the company: s 64. In this way each director both accepts responsibility for the prospectus and gives his consent to its publication. Responsibility and consent are interrelated. If a claim is later made against a director for statutory compensation for loss due to an untrue statement in it, he may in theory raise the defence that the prospectus was issued without his consent (6.19 below). As he has signed the prospectus, however, that defence is not open to him.

If a prospectus includes a statement purporting to be made by an expert, ie an accountant, valuer, engineer or other person whose profession gives authority to a statement made by him, the prospectus may not be issued unless the expert has given and has not withdrawn, before the prospectus is delivered to the registrar for registration, his written consent to the issue of the prospectus with the statement in the form and context in which it is included: s 61.

6.6 Registration of a prospectus
No prospectus of any type may be issued by or on behalf of a company or in relation to an intended company unless on or before the date of its publication there has been delivered to the registrar for registration a copy of the prospectus and of certain supporting documents which comply with ss 64–5.

The copy delivered for registration must be signed by every person named in it as a director or proposed director of the company or by his agent authorised in writing. If the prospectus is an offer for sale it must also be signed (6.1 above) on behalf of the company or firm which offers the securities to the public. The prospectus must also be dated, state that a copy has been sent for registration and specify the documents referred to below.

There must either be endorsed on the copy delivered for registration or attached to it:

(a) the written consent (6.5 above) of any expert to whom a statement is attributed in the prospectus;

(b) if the prospectus is issued generally (6.4):
    (i) a copy of every material contract;
    (ii) a written statement by the auditors or accountants of any adjustments made in calculating the profits and losses, assets and liabilities on which they have reported for inclusion in the prospectus.

The registrar ensures that these requirements are satisfied before accepting the prospectus and attached documents for registration.

It is an offence punishable by a fine (at a daily rate over the period of default) knowingly to issue a prospectus before these registration requirements have been duly satisfied.

6.7 Action after issue of a prospectus

Any applications which the company may receive in response to its prospectus are treated as offers to subscribe for the securities. The allotment of securities to the applicants is an acceptance by the company of the offers received, so that allotment is a form of contract. But the company may only proceed to allotment if, in the case of a prospectus issued generally, two clear days have elapsed since the prospectus was issued (6.10). There are also conditions regarding the volume of applications received (6.9) and obtaining a Stock Exchange listing (6.11). These rules are usually referred to as 'restrictions on allotment'.

B RESTRICTIONS ON ALLOTMENT

6.8 Underwriting

To ensure that the offer is fully subscribed it is standard practice to arrange for it to be underwritten. The company (or in the case of an offer for sale the issuing house) arranges with financial institutions ('the underwriters') that they will apply, or find other responsible persons to apply, for all or a specified proportion or number of the securities (if any) for which applications are not received from the public. For this purpose the underwriters receive a copy of the final proof of the draft prospectus which may not thereafter be altered in any material respect without thereby releasing the underwriters from their commitment. The underwriting contract takes various forms. It may be a letter from the underwriter which the company accepts by notice in writing; alternatively the underwriter may irrevocably authorise some person connected with the company to apply for the securities which he is committed to take if the occasion arises.

The underwriters often sub-contract their obligations to a wider circle of sub-underwriters with whom they share their commission. This is a matter in which the company or its issuing house is not directly concerned and details need not be disclosed in the prospectus. The liability of an underwriter who dies continues to be binding on his estate.

The consideration payable to the underwriters for their commitment is a commission to which they are entitled in any event, ie even if they are not required to subscribe for any securities. The underwriters may wish to subscribe for securities unconditionally to hold as investments. In that case they underwrite 'firm', ie they apply for shares unconditionally but they are still entitled to their commission.

Payment of commission for underwriting an offer of shares (but not debentures) is regulated by s 97. Payment of such commission must be authorised by the articles and must not exceed ten per cent of the offer price. This limit is to prevent the issue of shares at a substantial discount; in practice the commission is very much less than ten per cent.

There are no restrictions on the payment of commission for underwriting an issue of debentures since there is no objection to the issue of debentures at a discount.

A prospectus which offers either shares or debentures to the public for subscription or purchase must disclose the amount of any commission payable (or paid within the two previous years) to underwriters: Sch 3 para 10. If an issue of shares is made without a prospectus (by a public or private company) the underwriting commission (if any) must be disclosed in any circular or notice which may be issued and a statement giving particulars of it must be delivered to the registrar. The annual return must contain particulars of any 'discount' allowed on the issue of shares (so far as not written off) or of debentures (if issued since the last return).

Brokerage is payment for services in finding subscribers for securities where the broker is an intermediary who does not himself undertake to subscribe. A bank or a firm of stockbrokers may, for example, distribute prospectuses to their clients with a view to interesting them in the offer. A company may pay brokerage for these services if the articles authorise it: (Table A Art 4): s 97.

Apart from underwriting commissions or brokerage it is not lawful for a company to make payments out of its capital to procure subscriptions for its securities. There is no objection to payments for such purposes out of profits.

6.9 Minimum subscription

Every prospectus issued generally offering *shares* to the public for subscription must give particulars of the minimum amount which the directors estimate must be raised by the issue of those shares to finance certain commitments (6.4(e) above).

If the prospectus is issued with a view to a *first* allotment of *shares* by the company, the company is prohibited from allotting any shares to applicants unless applications have been received for shares sufficient to raise the amount of capital specified as the minimum subscription: s 83. The applications must be accompanied by remittances of at least one-quarter of the nominal value of the shares plus the whole of any premium since a public company may not (whether on a prospectus issue or otherwise) allot shares unless they are paid up at least to that extent on allotment: s 101. Cheques received with applications may be treated for this purpose as payment, ie it may be assumed that they will be honoured, if the directors acting in good faith have no reason to doubt that the cheques will be paid: s 83(2).

If this condition is not satisfied within 40 days from the first issue of the prospectus the company must then repay to applicants the subscription moneys received. If the money has not been repaid by the 48th day the directors become personally liable to repay the money with interest on it at the rate of 5 per cent pa from the expiry of the 48th day until actual repayment. But a director is not liable if he proves that the default was not due to any misconduct or negligence on his part.

Any condition requiring an applicant to waive compliance with these rules is void and an allotment made in contravention of the rules is voidable within one month. A director who knowingly contravenes or permits or authorises contravention is liable to compensate both the company and the applicant for any loss which they may suffer thereby: s 85.

The above rules do not prohibit an allotment of shares if either:

(a) the company is making a second or subsequent prospectus issue; or
(b) the application for shares received in response to a first prospectus equal or exceed the minimum subscription level but are less than the full number of shares offered by the prospectus.

If in case (a) the offer is fully subscribed there are no restrictions on allotment. But if in either case the number of shares applied for is less than the number offered the company may not allot any shares unless in the prospectus it has reserved the right to do so, stating either that it will allot shares up to whatever number is applied for or, alternatively, that it will allot shares if the number applied for reaches or exceeds a specified minimum (below the full amount offered).

As a prospectus issue is invariably underwritten the underwriters take any shares which the public do not apply for. Accordingly the minimum subscription rules are entirely theoretical – though not to be ignored on that account in the study of prospectus law.

6.10 The opening of the subscription lists

When a prospectus is issued generally, i e if it offers securities for subscription direct to persons other than its existing members or debenture holders, then no allotment of securities may be made before the beginning of the third day ('the time of the opening of the subscription lists') after the day on which the prospectus is first issued generally which, in a normal case, is the day of publication in the newspapers: s 82(1). If a prospectus is issued generally on a Monday the following Thursday morning is the time of opening of the subscription lists.

If an allotment is made in breach of this rule it is valid but the company and its officers responsible for the default may be fined.

The purpose of the rule is to allow time for prospective subscribers to obtain advice or to consider comment in the financial press before sending in their applications. The applications made in these circumstances are irrevocable until after the expiry of the third day after the time of opening of the subscription lists: s 82(7). The purpose of this last rule is to enable the directors to deal with the applications before them (when the lists open) without any risk that notice of revocation could be given before the allotments are made. This procedure is necessary to restrain the practice of 'stagging' a new issue by making speculative applications for securities in the hope that their market price will immediately rise above the offer price so that the allottees can resell at a profit before their cheques are cleared through the banking system. There is a risk, however, that the market price will prove to be lower than the offer price. The 'stags' (if not prevented by this rule) would then try to revoke their applications before allotments could be made to them.

6.11 Applications for Stock Exchange listing

It is usual not obligatory, to state in a prospectus that application is to be made for a Stock Exchange permission to list the securities offered by the prospectus. Listed securities are much more easily sold than unlisted securities and this factor raises the price at which the public will subscribe for them. Without a prospect of listing it is difficult to find subscribers (or underwriters).

If the prospectus states that application for listing is to be made then any allotment is void if either:

(a) application has not been made before the third day after the issue of the prospectus; or
(b) the application has been refused within three weeks of the closing of the subscription lists or such longer period not exceeding six weeks as the Stock Exchange may (within the three weeks) notify to the applicant. An intimation that the application, although not granted will be given further consideration, is not a refusal: s 86.

If application is not made or is refused the company must forthwith repay all money received from applicants pursuant to the prospectus. If it is not repaid within eight days after the company becomes liable to repay it, the directors are liable to repay it with interest at five per cent pa from the eighth day (with exemption for any director who proves that the default was not due to misconduct or negligence on his part). All money which the company may become liable to repay must be kept in a separate bank account until permission is obtained or the money repaid.

There are suitable modifications to extend these rules to offers for sale. The rules also safeguard underwriters although they do not strictly apply under the prospectus.

In practice repayment is never necessary, as it is usual to submit the draft prospectus to the Stock Exchange long before it is published. In its published form it already satisfies Stock Exchange requirements. Unless there were some last-minute irregularity the grant of Stock Exchange permission is a final formality which is completed in the interval between publication of the prospectus and the third day when the subscription lists both open and close.

6.12 Private companies
A private company should be careful in arranging to raise share or loan capital that it does not unwittingly make 'an offer to the public'. In particular:

(a) the offer of securities to existing members or debenture holders may only be renounceable within defined limits (6.3);
(b) any approach to persons who are not members or debenture holders should be on a personal basis and not by general circulation.

One of the directors passed some typed documents to a friend who passed them on to a friend of his. The House of Lords held that 'a single private communication between friends' is not the issue of a prospectus: *Nash v Lynde* [1929] AC 158. In an earlier case (*Re South of England Natural Gas and Petroleum Co Ltd* [1911] 1 Ch 573) the issue of copies of a document headed 'For private circulation only' to a considerable number of people was a prospectus.

Within the limits set by these rules a private company may, and often does, issue forms of application for its securities without attaching a prospectus (6.4 above). So long as there is no 'offer to the public' the requirement does not apply: s 56(2).

When a private company reregisters as public (Chapter 1: 1.17) it often does so with the intention of immediately issuing a prospectus. But it need not do so and, if it does not, is no longer required to deliver to the registry a 'statement in lieu of prospectus'.

C LIABILITIES IN RESPECT OF PROSPECTUSES

6.13 Remedies available

The allotment of securities following the issue of a prospectus is a contract by which the company accepts the applicant's offer to subscribe. If he was induced to apply by an untrue or misleading prospectus he can possibly rescind the contract for misrepresentation or recover damages in tort for deceit or negligence in certain cases. Section 67 also gives him a statutory claim to compensation and he may rely on the Misrepresentation Act 1967. Apart from civil liability the persons who issue such a prospectus or accept responsiblity as experts for statements in it attributed to them may commit a criminal offence punishable under the Companies Act or other statutes if the material for which they are responsible is untrue.

This multiplicity of remedies and sanctions reflects the difficulties which company law has encountered in providing efficient safeguards to the investing public. The modern practice of basing a prospectus on thorough preliminary investigation of the company by outside experts probably affords better investor protection than any legal code. But the rules remain as sanctions of last resort.

6.14 Rescission

The right to rescind the allotment and recover the subscription money is not confined to issues of securities by public companies following the publication of a misleading prospectus. The right exists when a person has applied for securities of any company, public or private, and has been induced to do so by misrepresentation of any kind, eg a verbal statement.

Rescission is a remedy against the company. To obtain rescission the allottee must show that:

(a) an untrue statement of fact was made to him by the company or on its behalf; and
(b) the statement related to a material point; and
(c) in applying for securities he relied on the statement.

But even if he establishes his case on these points he may, for any one of various reasons, lose his right to rescind. He does not, however, have to establish that the person who made the statement was aware that it was untrue (deceit) or lacked reasonable grounds for believing it to be true (negligence).

It is doubtful whether the Misrepresentation Act 1967 has made any significant improvement in the legal position of an allottee who wishes to rescind the allotment. If he cannot or does not rescind he apparently cannot claim damages from the company instead since that would be inconsistent with the contract between members.

The plaintiff unsuccessfully claimed damages from an unlimited company (then in liquidation) on the grounds that he had been induced to take his stock by fraudulent misrepresentation. It was held that his claim must fail since as a member (he had not rescinded the allotment) he could not recover damages at the expense of other equally innocent members. This decision of the House of Lords seems inconsistent with the principle that a company is a person separate from its members. But the court appeared to be implying a contract between members on the lines of s 14 (Chapter 4: 4.4). There is no decision that this precedent must apply to statutory rights conferred by the Misrepresentation Act 1967 but it is generally considered that it would: *Houldsworth v City of Glasgow Bank and Liquidators* (1880) 5 App Cas 317.

The statement made must be one of fact. What is expressed as a statement of fact may, on examination, prove to be an opinion if it expresses something which is merely a personal judgment, eg a statement that property is worth a specified amount. On the other hand an expression of opinion by an expert may imply that there is a basis of fact for his opinion. A statement that one has a certain opinion or intention is an untrue statement of fact if the opinion or intention does not exist at all: 'the state of man's mind is as much a matter of fact as the state of his digestion'.

An advertisement offering a hotel for sale stated that it was let to 'a most desirable tenant'; in fact he was in arrears in payment of rent and otherwise most undesirable. The court said that:

'If the facts are not equally well known to both sides, then a statement of opinion by the one who knows the facts best involves very often a statement of material fact, for he impliedly states that he knows facts which justify his opinion' (per Bowen LJ).

(Although this is not a company prospectus case it illustrates the implications of expressing an opinion in a prospectus or elsewhere): *Smith v Land & House Property Corp* (1884) 28 Ch D 7.

The directors induced the plaintiff to lend money to the company by stating that they intended to use it in improving and expanding the business. They had no such intention at all but planned to use the money to pay existing debts of creditors who were pressing for payment. Held to be a misrepresentation of fact, ie that the intention existed. The much quoted comparison of states of mind and of digestion was made in this case: *Edgington v Fitzmaurice* (1885) 29 Ch D 459.

If the prospectus includes a report by an expert or other statement of a third party and it puts this forward as part of the company's exposition of its case, it will readily be concluded that the company has adopted the report so that, if it is untrue, this is a misrepresentation by the company.

The prospectus of a rubber company included an expert's report on the condition of rubber estates. This was a central element of the picture given by the prospectus. It was held that by this use of the report, which was inaccurate on important points, the company had made the accuracy of the report the basis of the contract with allottees: *Re Pacaya Rubber and Produce Co Ltd* [1914] 1 Ch 542.

On the other hand, if the prospectus refers to a report without giving the impression of relying on it (still more if responsibility for its accuracy is expressly disclaimed) the citation of the report in the prospectus is not a representation that it is an accurate statement of fact.

It is permissible to omit information unless the statutory rules require it to be included in the prospectus (6.4 above) or the omission renders what is written in the prospectus a misleading half-truth. There is no duty, however, to disclose facts (additional to what is required by the statutory rules) because a prudent investor would be influenced by the information if he had it. But omission of material information is very likely to produce a misleading picture of the situation described.

The prospectus did not disclose that the promoter had made gifts of shares to directors to induce them to accept directorships. It was held that it was not misrepresentation to withhold this information (which did not have to be disclosed under statutory rules): *Heymann v European Central Rly Co* (1868) LR 7 Eq 154.

The prospectus issued by a gold-mining company stated that the mine to be acquired had rich deposits and merely needed to have machinery installed in order to begin production. It failed to disclose:

(a) that three companies had failed to work the mine successfully;
(b) the report that the deposits were rich was three years old; and
(c) the price to be paid for the mine would use up so much of the proceeds of the share issue that there would be insufficient money left for working captial.

It was held that these omissions made what was said misleading: *Aaron's Reefs v Twiss* [1896] AC 273.

It was said in *Twiss's Case* above that:

'if by a number of statements you intentionally give a false impression and induce a person to act on it, it is not the less false although if one takes each statement by itself there may be difficulty in showing that any specific statement is untrue'.

The test for rescission is whether the statements which are made in the prospectus mislead by reason of omission or inaccuracy. Apart from that there is no right to rescind merely because material or even statutory information is omitted.

If a statement is made which can be understood in two senses, one true and the other false, and the allottee reasonably understood it in the latter sense, the company may not justify it by saying that he might have understood it in the sense in which it was true. But where it is material (6.16 below) whether the statement was made honestly (as a defence to a claim for damages for deceit) it is open to the person who made it to show how he intended it to be understood and that he himself understood it in that sense.

What is *material* is an objective test of the importance of the matter to anyone concerned with it. If the statement of fact is material it will readily be accepted that it induced the allottee to apply for the securities offered. But if it is clear that he did not in fact attach any importance to the matter but relied on other inducements then he cannot rescind.

Among other points it was argued that the prospectus was untrue in stating that a Mr X, a member of parliament, was a director. But in cross-examination the plaintiff admitted that he had never heard of Mr X and was in no way influenced by the statement that he was a director: *Smith v Chadwick* (1884) 9 App Cas 187.

The prospectus contained a very important untrue statement about the company's mine. But there was no liability for it since the plaintiff had inspected the mine and relied on his own conclusions, not the prospectus, in deciding to subscribe for shares: *Jennings v Broughton* (1853) 5 De GM & G 126.

Only a person to whom the prospectus is addressed, ie one who in reliance on it subscribes for securities issued by the company can rescind the contract with the company. A purchaser of securities in the market after issue, who has read the prospectus, cannot rely on it as it was not addressed to him.

A person who subscribes for securities in reliance on the prospectus does not lose his right to rescind because he had the opportunity to discover the untruth. He has no duty to investigate. But if he does do so he is deemed to discover whatever is reasonably ascertainable from the documents, etc, which he reads and cannot any further assert that he was induced by the prospectus to believe the contrary.

The prospectus was misleading on the financial resources and commitments of the company. It stated that reports and other information, which would have disclosed the true position, were available at the offices of the company. The plaintiff's claim for rescission could not be defeated by showing that if he had inspected the reports, etc, he could have discovered the true position: *Central Rly Co of Venezuela v Kisch* (1867) LR 2 HL 99.

6.15 Loss of the right to rescind
The right to rescind is lost in any of the following circumstances:

(a) where the allottee discovers the true facts and thereafter affirms the contract (even without any intention of doing so). This can occur if he exercises the rights of a member, eg by attending a meeting of the company or by accepting and retaining a dividend, or if he treats the securities as still his property by selling or attempting to sell them. But if he definitely elects to rescind, eg by commencing proceedings, his subsequent conduct of this kind is not implied affirmation of the contract;

(b) if he discovers the truth but fails within a reasonable time to exercise his right to rescind. It has been held that even a delay of a fortnight is too long. But if he needs time to investigate, allowance will be made for that. The principle is that he should not be permitted to 'keep the options open' while the situation develops. It would be unfair to others;

(c) if he can no longer restore the pre-contract position, ie if he has sold his shares;

(d) if the company goes into liquidation since its creditors have a first claim against the liquidator in respect of the remaining assets. The allottee can then no longer withdraw his subscription money from the pool at the expense of the creditors.

6.16 Action for damages for deceit
In contrast to rescission this is a claim primarily against the directors and any other persons responsible for the issue of the untrue prospectus. There may possibly also be a claim against the company itself for the deceit of its agents if they were acting within the scope of their authority. But if the allottee sues the company he must first rescind: *Houldsworth's Case* (6.14).

If the prospectus is an offer for sale the allottee can sue the issuing house who issued it as well as the directors of the company.

To recover damages for deceit the allottee must establish that:

(a) the defendants by the prospectus made to him an untrue statement of fact with intent that he should act on it; and

(b) it was a material inducement upon which he relied in subscribing for the securities allotted to him; and

(c) he has suffered loss thereby.

But his action will fail if the defendants show that they honestly believed the untrue statement to be true.

What is an untrue statement of fact and a material inducement upon which the allottee relied is determined in the same way as in a claim for rescission. The main difference is the allegation of fraud. But there is usually no difficulty in establishing who are responsible for the issue of a prospectus since the directors (and if it is an offer for sale the issuing house) will have signed the copy delivered for registration. A prospectus issued to the public generally or to existing members or debenture holders with a right to renounce is clearly addressed to the persons who in fact subscribe for the securities.

The main difficulty in the action for deceit is to establish fraud, ie that the untrue statement was made '(1) knowingly, or (2) without belief in its truth, or (3) recklessly, careless whether it be true or false'. It is almost impossible to show how much the directors knew at the time of issue of the prospectus.

The company was incorporated by special Act of Parliament to operate tramway services in Plymouth, using horse-drawn trams or, with the consent of the Board of Trade, steam or other mechanically propelled trams. The directors, believing that official consent was a mere formality, issued a prospectus which stated that the company had the right to use steam or mechanical power. Application for consent to this was later refused. The action against the directors failed, twice, because although they had made no enquiries, they honestly believed that consent would be given. It may have been negligence but it was not fraud: *Derry v Peek* (1889) 14 App Cas 337.

6.17 Action for negligence

At the time of the decision in *Peek's Case* it was generally believed that in the absence of a contract, and there is none between the directors and the intending subscriber, there was no liability for negligence in making a statement. It has of course been established since 1964 (*Hedley Byrne & Co Ltd v Heller & Partners Ltd* [1964] AC 465) that, in the absence of a contractual relationship, a person who makes a statement owes a duty of care to anyone whom he knows or perhaps has reasonable grounds for expecting will rely on his statement. If he fails in that duty of care, and the party misled suffers loss, there can be liability for negligence.

The Misrepresentation Act 1967 gives to a person who is induced to enter into a contract by reason of a negligent misrepresentation, a right to recover damages in addition to his right ro rescind the contract. A misrepresentation is negligent if it is made without reasonable grounds for making it.

There are a number of doubts about the efficacy of these remedies in a case of a misleading prospectus, including the difficulty raised by *Houldworth's Case* (6.14). The right to statutory compensation (6.18 below) is much easier to enforce since the plaintiff has only to show that he relied on a prospectus which contained an untrue, ie misleading, statement. He does not have to prove negligence; it is up to the defendants to show in effect that they were not negligent.

Hence actions for negligence are not important as a remedy in cases of untrue prospectus liability.

6.18 Statutory right to compensation

The original remedies of rescission and an action for deceit proved inadequate. Following the decision in *Derry v Peek* (6.16) on the nature of fraud the law was altered by statute to enact what is now s 67. The general result of this safeguard is that if the prospectus is shown to contain an untrue statement a person who subscribed for securities on the faith of the prospectus may recover compensation for loss or damage from directors (including a person named as director or prospective director with his consent), promoters and other persons who authorised the issue of the prospectus unless they can escape liability by reason of any of six statutory defences (6.19 below).

It is also expressly provided that a statement included in a prospectus shall be deemed to be untrue if it is misleading in the form and context in which it is included and that a statement is included in the prospectus if it is actually contained in it or in any report or memorandum referred to or issued with the prospectus: s 71.

6.19 The statutory defences: s 68

The six defences available to a director or other person responsible for the issue of a prospectus which contains any untrue statement are:

(a) that after he had consented to become a director he withdrew his consent before the issue of the prospectus and that is was issued without his authority or consent;

(b) that the prospectus was issued without his knowledge or consent and on becoming aware that it had been issued he gave reasonable public notice that it was issued without his knowledge or consent;

(c) that after the issue of the prospectus and before allotment thereunder he became aware that it contained an untrue statement, withdrew his consent and gave reasonable public notice of the withdrawal and of the reason for it;

(d) that in a case in which (e) and (f) do not apply he had reasonable grounds to believe and did up to the time of the allotment of the securities believe that the untrue statement was true;

(e) that in so far as the untrue statement purported to be a statement by an expert (or to be a statement contained in a report or valuation by an expert) it fairly represented the statement (or was a correct and fair copy or extract from a report or valuation by the expert) and that he had reasonable ground to believe and did up to the time of the issuing of the prospectus believe that the expert was competent to make his statement and had given and not withdrawn his consent to the issue of the prospectus before it was delivered for registration or (to the defendant's knowledge) before securities were allotted under it;

(f) that in so far as the untrue statement purported to be a statement by an official person or was contained in what purported to be a copy of or extract from a public official document, it was a correct and fair representation of the statement (or copy or extract as the case may be).

The statutory rules were a direct consequence of the decision in the *Plymouth Tramways Case*. If those rules had been in force at the time of the decision the directors, who had clearly issued a prospectus containing information which was misleading and therefore untrue, could not have relied successfully on any of these six defences. Defences (a)–(c) could not be relevant. They had not accurately reproduced the terms of an official document, they did not rely on the report of an expert and they did not have reasonable grounds for their statement however much they believed it to be true.

In relying on information obtained from others the directors must be able to show that they took some steps to verify it. The mere receipt of information from an interested party, such as a vendor of property or a promoter, without any inquiry can hardly suffice.

An expert who has given the necessary consent to the issue of the prospectus with the statement attributed to him in the form and content in which it is included has a separate range of defences if his statement proves to be untrue. To escape liability to pay compensation he may rely on the grounds:

(i) that he gave but had withdrawn his consent in writing before a copy of the prospectus was delivered for registration;

(ii) that after delivery of a copy of the prospectus for registration he became aware of the untrue statement, withdrew his consent in writing, and gave reasonable public notice of the withdrawal and of the reason for it;

(iii) that he was competent to make the statement and had reasonable ground to believe and did believe up to the time of allotment of the securities that the statement was true.

Where a director or expert has not given his consent or has withdrawn it he has a right of indemnity against those who knowingly issued the prospectus with misleading information about his position.

6.20 Criminal penalties: s 70

Any person who authorises the issue of a prospectus which includes any untrue statement is liable on conviction to be punished by imprisonment (up to two years on conviction on indictment) or by fine unless he establishes that either the statement was immaterial or that he had reasonable ground to believe and did, up to the time of the issue of the prospectus, believe that the statement was true.

Section 70 applies to directors and others who may authorise the issue of a prospectus but not to experts who merely give consent to its issue. It need not be proved that the prospectus was issued with intent to deceive, ie mere negligence (absence of reasonable grounds for a belief that it was true) would suffice in criminal proceedings.

There are also special provisions in other legislation (Theft Act 1968 s 19; Prevention of Fraud (Investments) Act 1958 s 13) under which in particular circumstances there could be criminal liability for an untrue statement made in a prospectus. Here too a prescribed degree of knowledge, intent to deceive, recklessness or other mens rea is an essential part of the offence which the prosecution must prove.

Chapter 7

Shares

A SHARES, SHARE CERTIFICATES, SHARE WARRANTS AND STOCK

7.1 The nature of a share

A share in the capital of a company has been described as

'the interest of a shareholder in the company measured by a sum of money, for the purpose of liability in the first place, and of interest in the second, but also consisting of a series of mutual covenants entered into by all the shareholders inter se in accordance with s 14': *Borland's Trustee v Steel Bros & Co Ltd* [1901] 1 Ch 279.

It is the unit by which a member's interest in and liability to the company is measured. If he is allotted a £1 share he or his successor in title to it must pay for it, sooner or later, at least £1 in money or money's worth (more than £1 if it is issued at a premium – Chapter 5: 5.10 above).

As holder of his share the member has a contractual entitlement (under the memorandum and articles) to participate (in proportion to his share(s) as a fraction of the issued shares of that class) in profits distributed as dividend, return of capital and also to vote (if his share(s) carry vote(s)). In addition by statute a member or group of members holding shares which are a certain percentage of the issued capital have statutory rights of which they cannot be deprived by the memorandum or articles. As one example among many a holder or holders of 15 per cent of the issued shares may apply to the court to cancel or modify an alteration of the objects clause (Chapter 3: 3.18). But in other cases any member, even if he holds only one share, has rights, e g to petition the court for minority protection (Chapter 15: 15.6) or for compulsory liquidation (Chapter 18: 18.5).

A share is a species of intangible property (chose in action) which is transferable by a special procedure. But it is not a proprietary interest in the assets of the company (*Macaura's Case* in Chapter 1: 1.3).

7.2 Share certificates

Within two months of allotting shares or receiving a transfer of its shares a company must have ready for delivery a certificate of the shares allotted or transferred: s 185. If it fails to do so the company and its officers are liable to be fined. But the company is not required to issue a certificate if the transfer is not properly stamped or if it refuses to register the transfer under powers given by the articles (7.16 below).

The form of a share certificate and its maximum contents may be fixed by the articles. The standard requirement is that a share certificate shall be under the common seal and shall specify the number of shares to which it relates and the amount paid up thereon: Table A Art 6. If a company has a Stock Exchange listing its share certificates must comply with Stock Exchange requirements as to size, form and content. The Stock Exchange also requires that share certificates shall be issued within two weeks, instead of the statutory two months, from the relevant event. For convenience a company may have a second (official) seal for sealing share certificates; it is a facsimile of the common seal with the addition of the word 'Securities': s 40. In normal practice the application of the company seal is witnessed by adding the signatures of a director and the secretary or of two directors, as required by the articles, eg Table A Art 101. A public company with a very large number of shareholders may, however, provide that the sealing of share certificates, of which a considerable number are issued each month, shall not require witnesses' signatures.

The standard wording of a share certificate is:

'This is to certify that [name and address] is the registered holder of [number] of ordinary shares of [nominal value] fully paid in the above-named company, subject to the memorandum and articles of association of the company.

Given under the common seal of the company on [date]

. . . . Director
. . . . Secretary

No transfer of any of the above-mentioned shares can be registered until this certificate has been deposited at the registered office of the company'.

The certificate is a formal declaration by the company of the entry in its register of the holder as the legal owner of the shares so described. If there is more than one registered holder the certificate names the joint holders who are entitled to only one certificate in respect of their joint ownership. But if the articles permit, a company may issue two or more share certificates (eg for 400 and 600 shares representing a total holding of 1,000 shares) and demand a fee.

If a share certificate is defaced, lost or destroyed the holder may, if the articles so provide (eg Table A Art 7), be able to obtain a duplicate. But the company then demands an indemnity from the holder in respect of the issue of a duplicate certificate.

A share certificate is not a document of title. It is merely evidence of ownership which the holder must deliver to the company for cancellation on transfer of his shares. A share certificate is not in itself transferable property like a negotiable instrument (in contrast to share warrants described at 7.4 below).

7.3 Estoppel by share certificate
A share certificate issued under the common seal of the company specifying any shares held by a member is prima facie evidence of his title to the shares:

s 186. But if the share certificate is incorrect the company may, unless it is estopped from so doing, deny that it is correct.

A company is estopped, ie prevented from denying that the certificate is correct, against a person who has relied on it and thereby suffered detriment. The company is not liable in damages for issuing an incorrect certificate but it must deal with the person who has it as if the certificate were correct, or pay him compensation for its inability to do so. The simplest case is where a person purchases shares and pays the price in exchange for a transfer signed by the seller and his share certificate as evidence of his title. If it later appears that the seller's share certificate was obtained by the earlier registration of a forged transfer in favour of the seller the company cannot deny against the purchaser from him that the certificate is correct.

The registered holder (X) left her share certificate in the possession of her broker who forged her signature on a transfer and delivered it with the share certificate to a purchaser (Y) who presented the transfer for registration with the old share certificate. Under the standard procedure current at the time the company sent to the holder a 'notice of transfer' to which she did not reply. The purchaser (Y) obtained a new share certificate in his name and later delivered it to another person (Z) with his transfer to Z on resale. That second purchaser (Z) was entitled to damages from the company because he had paid for the shares in reliance on the share certificate issued to Y: *Re Bahia and San Francisco Rly Co* (1868) LR 3 QB 584.

Estoppel by share certificate is less of a problem to companies than might at first appear. The following principles limit its scope:

(a) the company is only estopped against a person who obtained the certificate without fault on his part. A transferee who obtains a share certificate in his name by presenting for registration a forged transfer and a stolen share certificate is by his action, however innocent, deceiving the company and has no claim on the new certificate issued to him;

(b) the claimant must show not merely that he has a share certificate but also that he has relied on it to his detriment. Merely to receive and retain it is not enough;

By presenting a transfer of shares which the named 'transferor' did not hold the secretary of the company induced the directors to approve a transfer to the plaintiff and to issue a share certificate to him as transferee. A year later the secretary was dismissed. The plaintiff was awarded damages against the company because the share certificate had led her to believe that she had good title to the shares and so she had lost her opportunity to recover the price from the secretary who was now bankrupt: *Dixon v Kennaway & Co* [1900] 1 Ch 833.

In *Balkis Consolidated Co v Tomkinson* [1893] AC 396 the estoppel arose because the person to whom the certificate had been issued had resold his shares in reliance on it.

(c) if the share certificate itself is a forgery the holder has no rights on it even if it was issued by an apparently reliable agent of the company.

The plaintiff was issued with a certificate on which the secretary had forged the signatures of two directors (as witnesses to the sealing of the certificate). The company was held not liable either for the fraud of the secretary or for the issue of the certificate which he had forged (on the grounds that in issuing it he had acted outside his authority). The certificate was a document to which the company was not a party and for which it was not responsible: *Ruben v Great Fingall Consolidated* [1906] AC 439.

This decision has been much criticised on the ground that if the company is not estopped by the certificate it should be estopped from denying that its secretary was its authorised agent whose action in supplying an apparently valid certificate should be binding on the company. But this case has now stood for 80 years without being overruled.

Where there is an estoppel against the company it is prevented from denying the information in the certificate as much as its general validity.

The plaintiff lent money to the company on the security of fully paid shares. The company issued a share certificate to him which described the shares as fully paid. He believed that the shares had been fully paid by a previous holder. The company, by then in liquidation, was held to be estopped from denying that these were fully paid shares on which the plaintiff had no further liability although the shares were in fact nil paid: *Bloomenthal v Ford* [1897] AC 156. (But in such a case the company has a claim for lost capital against the directors who issued the certificate: *Hirsche v Sims* [1894] AC 654.)

7.4 Share warrants

A company limited by shares may, if so authorised by its articles (Table A does not provide for this), issue under its common seal a warrant stating that the bearer is entitled to the shares to which it relates: s 188.

A share warrant includes detachable numbered coupons which the holder sends in, one by one, to obtain payment of dividends due on his shares. A share warrant may only be issued in respect of fully paid shares since the company would have no practicable means of making calls on the holders of share warrants relating to partly paid shares.

It is usual for the terms of issue of share warrants to provide for the giving of notice of general meetings and payment of dividends to holders of warrants by publishing the notice in certain newspapers and for the temporary deposit of warrants with the company as evidence of the holder's right to attend and vote.

When a company issues a share warrant the company removes from its register of members the name of the former registered holder and enters in the register particulars of the shares and the fact and date of issue of the warrant: s 355. The bearer of the warrant may at any time on surrender of the warrant be restored to the register as the registered holder. The holder of a warrant is given rights as a member only to such extent as the articles may provide. To 'hold' shares is to be entered in the register of members as the holder. Possession of a share warrant does not, for example, satisfy any requirement of a director's qualification shareholding (Chapter 12: 12.4).

The annual return must state the total number of shares for which share warrants are outstanding and the shares for which warrants have been issued or surrendered since the date of the last return and the number of shares comprised in each warrant.

As a negotiable instrument a share warrant is transferable by mere delivery and the transferee may have good title even though his transferor did not. Since there is no written form of transfer the share warrant itself bears stamp duty at the specified ad valorem rate of the issue price or value at the time of issue. If the articles so provide the owner of a share warrant which is lost or destroyed may obtain a duplicate from the company. But he will be required to give an indemnity.

The use of share warrants in this country is much less common than in Europe and the USA. On the whole, companies do not encourage resort to this device though the lifting of UK exchange control has removed what used to be a strong disincentive (to owners of shares).

7.5 Serial numbering of shares

A company is required to enter in its register of members the identifying numbers of the shares held by each member 'so long as the share has a number': s 352. The corresponding numbers would also be shown on each share certificate. Where this principle applies each share issued in a series of, say, a million shares would have to bear a number in the series 1–1,000,000. With sub-division and accretion of shareholdings by transfer, members soon cease to hold shares numbered in unbroken sequence. The system is in practice almost unworkable unless the number of members is very small and transfers are made only infrequently.

To avoid these difficulties companies often converted their issued shares into stock (7.6 below). But the problem may now be obviated by more direct means under s 182(2). This section, which requires that shares shall have distinguishing numbers also provides that when all the issued shares in a company (or all the issued shares of a class) are fully paid up and rank pari passu for all purposes, ie when there is no longer any need to distinguish one share from another in terms of rights or liabilities, the shares need not (so long as these conditions obtain) have distinguishing numbers. A company which has issued numbered shares may abolish these numbers by passing a 'denumbering resolution' in general meeting.

7.6 Stock

A company, if so authorised by its articles, may by resolution passed in general meeting, convert fully paid shares into stock or reconvert stock into shares of any nominal value: s 121. If it makes this change notice must be given to the registrar within one month and also a copy of the memorandum as altered (in respect of the authorised capital) must be delivered to him within 15 days.

A company cannot issue stock. It may, however, issue shares and convert them into stock as soon as they are fully paid.

The effect of conversion is that what were, say, one million £1 shares fully paid become £1 million stock in which each member has a holding corresponding with his previous holding of shares. The articles usually provide that stock is only transferable in units of the same value as the original shares from which the stock was converted.

Some companies which converted shares to stock to avoid problems of share numbers (7.5) still retain that stock. It is not normal practice now to convert shares to stock.

References to 'shares' include stock in the Companies Act unless the distinction is expressed or implied: s 744.

B CLASS RIGHTS

7.7 Classes of shares

The rights attached to all shares of a company may be uniform. It is then unnecessary to define the shares as a class, since there is only one class, but it is quite usual to describe them in the company's memorandum as 'ordinary' shares.

It is, however, possible to issue shares to which different rights are attached. The most common example is the issue of preference and of ordinary shares (7.8 below). All shares which carry the same rights, eg preference shares (in contrast to ordinary shares) then form a 'class' of shares. To give another example, if some ordinary shares carry voting rights and others do not, there are two classes, voting and non-voting, even though they are all described as 'ordinary' shares and may in all other respects, eg dividend rights, have no difference between them.

When a company has shares of two or more classes, three main principles apply. First, the differences between the classes only exist to the extent that the differences are expressly described. The presumption is that all shares carry similar rights; that presumption may be overridden but only by express differentiation. This point is further explained below in connection with preference shares.

Secondly, the rights attached to a class of shares may be varied but the correct variation procedure must be followed (7.12 below).

Thirdly, information of the different rights of classes of shares must be available to the public from documents on file at the registry. Class rights are usually defined by the memorandum or articles or by a special resolution passed at the time when the class of shares is created. All these documents are delivered to the registrar who encloses them on the company file at the registry. But the memorandum or articles may provide that the rights of shares may be fixed or varied or shares may be reclassified by some internal procedure such as a resolution of the directors or an ordinary resolution passed in general meeting (eg Table A Art 2).

There is a procedure under which a company must give notice to the registrar within one month of allotting or creating shares with special rights in those cases where the information would not reach the registry in some other document: s 128. There is a similar procedure where a company creates or varies the rights of a class of members in a case where there are no shares. For example, a company limited by guarantee might have non-voting and voting members: s 129. Again notice must be given within one month if the information does not reach the registrar by other means.

7.8 Capital structure

A company may adopt whatever capital structure it deems convenient provided that it conforms to the rules of procedure and disclosure. In the past companies often raised part of their capital in the form of preference shares on which a fixed dividend was payable, leaving the balance of the distributable profits available for distribution to ordinary shareholders. But for tax reasons fixed interest loan capital is now a more advantageous alternative since the interest, unlike the preference dividend, is deductible as an expense from the gross profits. Many companies have reconstructed their capital so as to replace preference shares by loan stock.

In the past company promoters sometimes arranged to take payment for services or for assets transferred to the company by the allotment to them of 'deferred' or 'founders' shares, which did not participate in dividend distributions until the holders of the ordinary shares had been paid a specified rate of dividend. But this feature of public company capital structure has become obsolete and is now uncommon.

Where there are preferences or deferred shares they often carry different voting rights from ordinary shares. Preference shares may have no voting rights and deferred shares often carry enhanced voting rights. Voting rights may also be different in different circumstances (as illustrated by *Bushell v Faith* in Chapter 12: 12.7).

7.9 Preference shares

The essential characteristic of preference shares is that they carry a right to receive dividends of specified amount, eg 6 per cent of their nominal value, out of the profits of each year before any dividend may be paid to holders of ordinary shares (or other classes of shares of lower priority, eg second preference shares). In all other respects preference shares may rank pari passu with other shares but they often carry an express right to repayment of capital in priority to other shares and have no voting rights or only restricted voting rights.

A participating preference share is a hybrid type. For example such shares may have a prior entitlement to dividends up to, say, 6 per cent and then, if the dividend paid on the ordinary shares exceeds 6 per cent a right to participate equally in any distribution in excess of 6 per cent paid on the ordinary shares.

The rights of preference shares are a matter of construction of the terms of issue. There are, however, two presumptions. First, preference shares have the same rights as ordinary shares, no more and no less, unless the contrary is expressly stated. If, for example, nothing is stated concerning priority in a return of capital the preference shares have no rights to priority in repayment but they share equally (with the ordinary shares) in any surplus assets available after paid-up capital on all shares has been repaid.

Secondly, it is presumed that any express definition of class rights is 'exhaustive', ie that what is expressly given is *all* the benefit which the shares carry. As an example, if it is stated, as is common practice, that in a liquidation the capital paid up on preference shares is to be repaid in full before any repayment is made to holders of ordinary shares, then if the assets suffice to repay both classes to the full amount paid up on the shares, the ordinary shares take the whole of any surplus and the preference shares, having been repaid in full, get nothing more.

A company which had received compensation following the nationalisation of its collieries proposed to repay its preference shareholders their paid-up capital by a reduction of capital (Chapter 5: 5.28). The preference shareholders, to whom the articles gave a prior right to repayment of capital, argued that by this means they would be deprived of all participation in any surplus assets on liquidation (which was likely to follow later). Their objection failed – 'reading the relevant articles as a whole . . . articles 159 and 160 are exhaustive of the rights of the preference stockholders in a winding up' (per Lord Simonds). They also objected unsuccessfully that they would lose an income from the preference shares which was higher than they could get from reinvesting the cash to be paid to them, ie that observance of their rights would be financially detrimental to them: *Scottish Insurance Corp v Wilsons and Clyde Coal Co* [1949] 1 All ER 1068.

7.10 Preference dividends

A holder of preference shares like a debenture holder expects to receive a fixed and regular income from his investment. But he is not a creditor and his entitlement is to receive the first 'slice' of profits (if any) which the company may decide to distribute as a dividend.

The company had at the beginning of its financial year reserves of £240,000. It had suffered losses of £200,000 (in respect of assets which the court found to be 'circulating capital', ie current assets) and an unrealised loss of £50,000 on the basis of the directors' estimate of a fall in value of retained fixed assets. The court refused an application by the preference shareholders for an order for the payment of their dividend (claiming that unrealised losses at least need not be made good out of profits) and held that the directors' judgment 'that the state of the accounts did not admit any such payment' should not be overruled. It was also held that whether provision should be made for depreciation of fixed assets is a matter of commercial judgment as to whether the assets have declined in value: *Bond v Barrow Haematite Steel Co* [1902] 1 Ch 353.

NB Since 1980 both points (depreciation and unrealised losses) are regulated by statute (Chapter 5: 5.22).

If there are no profits available, either because none have been earned or because the directors decide to transfer all the profits to reserve, the preference shareholder cannot sue the company for his dividend. A dividend is not due to him unless and until it is declared. The articles may, however, provide that available profits must be applied to payment of preference dividends or give special rights to the preference shareholders if their dividends are not paid.

If the company fails to pay, ie 'passes', its preference dividend, the right to it as a priority claim is usually carried forward. If for example no dividend is paid on 6 per cent cumulative preference shares in Year 1 the holders of those shares (even if not the same persons as held them in Year 1) have a priority entitlement to 12 per cent in Year 2 – and so on. Preference shares may be expressly designated as 'cumulative' to indicate the right to carry forward entitlement to arrears. Preference shares are deemed to be cumulative unless a contrary intention, ie that they are non-cumulative, is expressed or clearly implied, as in the case below.

The preference dividend was expressed to be payable 'out of the net profits *of each year*'. This was a sufficiently clear indication that the dividends were non-cumulative and arrears could not be paid out of the profits of a later year: *Staples v Eastman Photographic Materials Co* [1896] 2 Ch 303.

This is the only case of conferring a special right on preference shares by implication from the term 'preference'.

If the company has accumulated arrears of dividends on its cumulative preference shares at the time when it goes into liquidation, the right to the arrears lapses unless there is a sufficient indication in the terms of issue of the shares that arrears are to be paid as a distribution in winding up. Where that right exists the preference shareholders may receive their arrears as a capital payment not as income. It is usual to provide expressly that arrears shall or shall not be paid at this stage since the case law on what words do create a continuing right to receive the arrears even in liquidation is rather confused and uncertain.

Preference shares carry no right to participate in profits distributed as dividend after the fixed preference dividend has been paid unless a right to participate is sufficiently clearly expressed usually by the word 'participating' and details of the level of ordinary dividend at which the preference participation in further distributions begins.

7.11 Preference shares – other points

In a reduction of capital preference shares are treated according to their rights in liquidation. If the shares have an express right to priority in repayment of capital, they cannot object to being paid off in a reduction of capital (7.9 above and the *Chatterley-Whitfield Case* in Chapter 5: 5.28). Repayment is an observance of their rights and not a variation of them. If, as is less common, the preference shares have no such priority, they should be paid off, or reduced, according to the circumstances, on the same basis as the ordinary shares.

The holders of preference shares have the same voting rights as holders of ordinary shares unless, as is usual, their rights are restricted. Voting rights may be restricted in any way, eg to voting only when preference dividends are arrears or the rights attached to the shares are to be varied, or the company proposes to go into voluntary liquidation. The restricted right to attend and vote at general meetings should be distinguished from the right to vote at a class meeting of preference shareholders on a resolution to approve a variation of class rights. Every preference shareholder may vote at a class meeting.

Preference shares may be, and sometimes are, issued as redeemable shares. But since 1981 it has also been possible to issue redeemable ordinary shares so that this is no longer, as it once was, a special feature of preference shares. (See Chapter 5: 5.16 on issue and redemption procedure.)

7.12 Variation of class rights: procedure

In connection with any proposed variation (which includes abrogation) of the rights of a class of shares three questions may have to be considered:

(a) What is the appropriate procedure for variation? Unless it is followed the variation may be invalid;
(b) What rights have a dissenting minority to appeal against a majority decision (within the class)?
(c) In what circumstances may changes be made which affect the rights attached to shares but do not amount to a variation to which alone the rules under (a) and (b) relate?

Topics (b) and (c) are discussed in the next section of this chapter.

There is a well-established procedure for variation of class rights which is applicable to most companies. It requires that the company shall obtain a consent of the class of shareholders in one or other of the following ways:

(a) the holders of at least three-quarters of the issued shares of the class give their consent in writing; or
(b) at a separate class meeting an extraordinary resolution (Chapter 11: 11.14) is passed by a three-quarters majority of votes cast giving consent

to the variation. The quorum (Chapter 11: 11.8) is the presence of holders of at least one-third of the issued shares of the class and any of them regardless of the number of his shares may demand a poll: s 374.

This formula ('consent of a three-quarters majority') is now found in s 125. As an example suppose that there are 100 issued shares of the class. To satisfy (a) the consent of holders of at least 75 shares is required. But under (b) a quorum requires only that holders of 34 shares attend and, if they all vote, that holders of 27 shares vote in favour. In either case those who do not consent are bound unless an objection under s 127 (7.13 below) prevails.

Almost all companies, if they have more than one class of shares, are subject to this procedure for variation of class rights. Either they have included it in their memorandum or articles, because it was normal to do so up to 1981 when it was given statutory recognition, or they have no variation procedure in the memorandum and articles and so s 125 makes it applicable (with one exception mentioned below).

However, there are some infrequent and therefore rather unimportant other possibilities. If the rights of the class are found in the memorandum and there is no procedure for variation set out in either the memorandum or the articles, the rights can only be varied with the agreement of all members of the company (not just of the class): s 125(5).

If the company has some non-standard variation procedure in its memorandum or articles, it follows that – and not the standard procedure above. But if the variation of rights is connected with an authority to the directors to allot shares or with a reduction of capital (Chapter 5: 5.4 and 5.28) the company must also obtain the consent of a three-quarters majority if its special procedure does not incidentally require it – as it often will: s 125(3).

An alteration of the articles to include a variation procedure for the first time or to modify an existing procedure is itself a variation of class rights for which class consent is required: s 125(7).

7.13 Minority rights of objection

Before the company in general meeting may alter its articles or other definition of class rights, it must obtain the binding consent of the holders of shares of that class. But even that procedure does not necessarily conclude the matter.

When class rights are varied under the procedure contained in the memorandum or articles, or under the statutory provision for variation with the consent of a three-quarters majority, the holders of not less than 15 per cent of the issued shares of the class, if they did not consent to or vote in favour of the variation, may within 21 days apply to the court (through one or more of their number previously appointed by them in writing) to have the variation cancelled: s 127.

The court can only approve or cancel the variation; it cannot alter it nor impose conditions for its approval. It may only cancel the variation on grounds of 'unfair prejudice'. Accordingly, orders for cancellation are only rarely made, eg if it appears that the majority who gave their consent did so not bona fide in the interests of the class but to secure themselves incidental advantages as members of another class. The *Holders Investment Trust Case* (Chapter 5: 5.28) is the leading modern case on this subject. Although the issue there was approval by the court of a reduction of capital the consent of the class was required to repayment of their capital by the issue of loan stock in place of the cash to which they were entitled.

The elaborate safeguards of variation of rights procedure and the right to appeal to the court are less effective than they may appear because of case law which has interpreted 'variation' of rights in a very restrictive way. It is possible to make changes which alter the value and effectiveness of rights attached to a class of shares without technically varying those rights. What is not a variation is not restricted by the safeguards referred to above.

A repayment of capital to preference shareholders in accordance with their priority entitlement is a recognition not a variation of their rights (see 7.11 above and the cases cited there). A sub-division of shares of *another* class which increases the number of votes attached to those shares or the issue of additional shares of the same class is not a variation of the rights of the class since it leaves the holders of the shares with the same rights, attached to their shares, as before. In either case the value of the rights is reduced by the creation of rights given to others. But that is not a 'variation' in the technical sense.

G held most of the 2s shares and in consequence had about 40 per cent of the total votes which could be cast at a general meeting. However, the other members, who held 10s shares, were able to pass an ordinary resolution by a simple majority and did so to sub-divide their 10s shares into five 2s shares. As the articles gave one vote to each share they quintupled their votes and reduced G's votes, undiminished in number, to less than 25 per cent of the increased total. They could then carry a special resolution to alter the articles – to which G was opposed. It was held that this was not a 'variation' of the rights of G's shares as 'they remain what they always were': *Greenhalgh v Arderne Cinemas Ltd* [1946] 1 All ER 512. (See Chapter 4: 4.7 for the distinct but related dispute over the alteration of the articles between the same parties in the 1951 *Greenhalgh Case*).

The articles required consent of the class of shareholders (preference) to any change which might 'affect' their rights. The company resolved to make a bonus issue of new preference shares (Chapter 5: 5.11) to the holders of the ordinary shares. As a result the original preference shareholders were no longer all, but only part, of the members of the class and the weight of their votes (unaltered in number) was diminished. The court held that the bonus issue did not 'affect' the rights of the preference shareholders since those rights did not extend 'to preserve anything in the nature of an equilibrium' with the ordinary shareholders: *White v Bristol Aeroplane Co Ltd* [1953] 1 All ER 40.

Even a change in the place of payment of dividends on preference shares is not a variation of rights attached to the shares.

The articles provided that dividends on preference shares should be paid in 'pounds' in England. The place of payment was altered to Australia so that the dividends were thereafter paid in Australian 'pounds' of lower value than English pounds sterling. It was held that as the dividends continued to be paid in 'pounds' there had been no variation of class rights: *Adelaide Electric Supply Co Ltd v Prudential Insurance Co Ltd* [1934] AC 122.

From these cases it would appear that nothing less than a direct subtraction from existing rights, as defined by the words used in the articles, will amount to a 'variation' to which variation of rights procedure and the s 127 right of objection to the court applies.

C TRANSFER OF SHARES

7.14 Restrictions on transfer

A share in the capital of a company is a form of intangible property which is by its nature transferable. There are certain requirements as to the form of transfer (7.17). Apart from those conditions the articles may impose restrictions on the transfer of shares. The shareholder is bound by those restrictions as part of the contract between the company and himself.

A private company is no longer required to include in its articles a restriction on the transfer of its shares. But it is likely to remain a common feature of such articles since the members of a private company, and the directors who represent them, generally prefer to exercise some control over the admission of new members. The restrictions imposed are of two kinds – rights of pre-emption and a power given to directors to refuse to register a transfer.

7.15 Pre-emption clauses

A pre-emption clause, when it is included in the articles, usually provides that any member who wishes to transfer his shares shall give notice to the directors of his intention; that the directors shall inform other members of it; and that the other members may purchase the shares within a specified time; if no purchaser or purchasers can be found from among existing members then the intending transferor may transfer his shares (but subject to the directors' power to veto the transfer) to an outsider.

A pre-emption clause is usually precisely expressed in terms of notices, time-limits, fixing a price for the shares, etc. It is strictly construed both against the intending transferor and the other members who may wish to acquire his shares. Unless the articles so provide the transferor cannot be compelled to sell part only of the shares to other members but he cannot refuse to sell because the total number of shares is to be divided between two or more members. He cannot evade his obligations under a pre-emption clause by contracting to sell his shares to an outsider and remaining his nominee (and voting as he may direct) until the transfer is registered.

The articles provided that any member 'desirous' of transferring his shares should give notice to the company in conformity with the pre-emption procedure. Joint holders agreed to sell their shares, received the price and gave to the purchaser a proxy in respect of the shares so that he might vote at general meetings. It was contended that as they had sold the shares and merely held them as nominees of the purchaser they were no longer 'desirous' of transferring them. It was held on the fact that they were 'desirous' of transferring the shares and must give notice so that other members might exercise their pre-emption rights: *Lyle & Scott Ltd v Scott's Trustees* [1959] 2 All ER 661. See also *Rayfield v Hands* (Chapter 4: 4.4) on the articles as a contract between members in respect of rights against each other as shareholders.

To prevent evasion and avoid dispute the pre-emption clause usually provides that the shares are to be offered at a fair price or alternatively that in case of disagreement about price they are to be sold at a fair price, to be fixed in either case by the auditors (Chapter 14: 14.18). The auditor or other valuer employed must conform to any basis of valuation prescribed by the articles. If, however, there is none he may exercise his professional judgment as to the basis adopted and his determination of the price is binding on both parties. This is so even if it is clear that the valuer has made a mistake.

The vendor was dissatisfied with the auditor's valuation of the shares. The auditor showed her his calculations. It was held that he was under no obligation to do so. His valuation was criticised on the ground that he ignored the value of control (it was a 70 per cent holding) and valued the assets (of an unprofitable business) on a break-up instead of going concern basis. The Court of Appeal held that in the absence of bad faith or manifest error (and there was neither here) the valuation should not be upset. The value of control was properly disregarded in this case because the article required a valuation of the company shares on the basis of fixing a price for any individual share in it: *Dean v Prince* [1954] Ch 409.

The valuation was criticised on various technical grounds. It was held as a matter of principle that the parties were bound by the decision of the expert, to whom they had entrusted the valuation, if he acts honestly. The remedy of a party who is dissatisfied is to sue the valuer to recover damages for loss caused by his alleged negligence (Chapter 14: 14.18): *Baber v Kenwood Manufacturing Co Ltd* [1978] 1 Lloyd's Rep 175.

7.16 Directors' power to refuse to approve a transfer

A share is by its nature transferable property (7.14). The company through its directors may have the power to refuse to register a transfer. But this is a power given by the articles and is only binding on a shareholder if the directors exercise the power in a proper manner. If they fail to do so the transferor can compel the company, by obtaining a court order for rectification of the register of members under s 359, to enter the name of the transferee as the new holder of the shares. There are three principles to which the directors should conform.

First, the directors fail to exercise their power at all unless they take a positive decision to do so. If they fail to consider the transfer or if they are equally divided and no resolution of the board is passed it is treated as accepted by default.

The three directors also held the issued shares in equal proportions. One died and his executrix sent in for registration a transfer of his shares to her. The two surviving directors held a board meeting to consider the transfer but there was deadlock between them. It was held that the power of refusal must be positively exercised. As it had not been in this case the executrix succeeded in her application to have the register rectified by entering her name as holder: *Re Hackney Pavilion Ltd* [1924] 1 Ch 276.

Secondly, in order to exercise the power effectively the directors must do so within a reasonable time. The company is required to give notice of any refusal to register a transfer within two months of the receipt of the transfer: s 183(5). Accordingly the directors must normally reach their decision within this period but meanwhile mere silence on their part is not acquiescence.

The articles provided that a quorum at board meetings should be two directors but a sole surviving director had power to co-opt a second director to make up the required number (Table A Arts 89 and 90). In August, when there was only one director in office he purported to refuse a transfer of shares. In December the transferee began proceedings for rectification of the register so that the transfer to him might be entered in the register on the grounds that the previous refusal was invalid owing to lack of a quorum at the meeting. The surviving director then co-opted a second director and they purported to refuse the transfer. It was held that it was then too late; after an interval of 4 months the directors no longer had a power to refuse the transfer which must be registered: *Re Swaledale Cleaners Ltd* [1968] 3 All ER 619.

Last – but most important of all – the directors must exercise their power to reject a transfer on the specific grounds (if any) stated in the articles and also in good faith in what they consider to be the interests of the company. The articles often give to the directors of a private company an unfettered discretion to refuse a transfer 'in their absolute discretion'. Alternatively the articles may specify grounds of refusal such as refusal when the directors' opinion is that it is not in the interests of the company to admit the transferee to membership. A refusal on any other ground is then invalid.

The articles gave to the directors power to refuse to approve a transfer if in their opinion the admission of the transferee to membership would be contrary to the interests of the company. It was held that this wording restricted the directors' power to cases where objection could be made to the transferee personally, e g because of his temperament or his connection with a rival company. The directors had therefore exceeded their power in refusing to approve transfers of single shares by a large shareholder to persons previously unconnected with the company because their objections were to the transfers and not to the transferees personally: *Re Bede Steam Shipping Co Ltd* [1917] 1 Ch 123.

Whether the directors are given absolute discretion to refuse or are limited to certain grounds of refusal they cannot (unless the articles so provide) be compelled to disclose in detail the reasons for their decision. When there is a refusal of a transfer it is usual to enter in the minutes of the board meeting a simple statement that the transfer was considered but not approved (with any relevant grounds for the decision as given in the articles) and then to give notice of the refusal in equally brief terms. Neither transferor nor transferee can require the directors to explain their decision. If, however, the directors volunteer (or are required by the articles to state) reasons for their decision these may be challenged as inadequate.

As the reasons for refusal are not usually disclosed it is very difficult for the transferor or transferee to show that the directors have failed to exercise their power of refusal in good faith. When the articles confer on the directors a wide discretion to refuse if they see fit, the court is not usually prepared to interfere or to overrule them.

The articles gave to the directors absolute discretion to refuse to register any transfer. There had been two directors who were the only shareholders and they held 4,001 shares each. One died and his executors presented a transfer of his shares to themselves. The surviving director had co-opted another and they refused to register the transfer. The original surviving director offered to register a transfer of 2,001 shares and to purchase the balance of 2,000. The court held that the article was intended to confer a complete discretion as to what the interests of the company might require and that without evidence of bad faith it must assume that the directors reached their decision in what they regarded as the interests of the company. The argument advanced to justify the directors' decision was that they considered it to be in the interests of the company to ensure continuity in its management by conferring on one of the directors control of the company as a shareholder: *Re Smith and Fawcett Ltd* [1942] 1 All ER 542.

When the directors refuse to approve a transfer on sale the transferor holds the shares as nominee of the transferee who is the beneficial owner.

7.17 Transfer procedure

A company may only register a transfer of shares (or of debentures) if a proper instrument of transfer has been delivered to it: s 183(1). The purpose of this rule is to enforce payment of stamp duty on a transfer of shares.

The articles of association may authorise the company to lay down a form of transfer but the Stock Transfer Act 1963 provides a standard form of transfer which may always be used, as an alternative to any special company form, for the transfer of fully paid shares. The Act also provides that the transferor's signature need not be witnessed (another old-fashioned requirement of some company articles) and that, except in the case of a transfer of partly paid shares, the transferee need not sign the transfer. In the normal course, therefore, a standard form of transfer is completed, and signed by the transferor.

It is necessary to require the transferee's signature on a transfer of partly paid shares since he is accepting liability to pay the amount unpaid on the shares if called upon to do so.

It is usual for a company transferor to execute a transfer (of shares of another company) as a deed by affixing its seal.

The Stock Exchange has special procedures to facilitate the transfer of listed securities. The main element of the system is a central shareholding nominee company (Stock Exchange Pool Nominees Ltd – SEPON for short) to which securities sold are temporarily transferred and from which they are later transferred to each buyer. By this means (the TALISMAN system) all sales and purchases during a Stock Exchange account period of two or three weeks can be pooled. These very special procedures are not part of general company law and practice and are not further considered here.

The simplest situation of share transfer is where by a single transfer the existing shareholder transfers his entire shareholding. He signs the standard form of transfer, on which the appropriate details have been inserted, and hands it with his share certificate, as prima facie evidence of his title (7.2 above) to the transferee. If it is a sale the transferee pays the price in exchange for the transfer and the certificate.

If, however, the transferor's share certificate includes more shares than are comprised in the transfer he delivers his share certificate to the company (or in the case of listed shares to the Stock Exchange). The certificate is retained for cancellation and the transfer is endorsed with the words 'certificate lodged' and returned to the transferor who in turn delivers it to the transferee. The legal effect of certification is explained later (7.18 below). On registration of the transfer the company issues two new certificates, ie one to the transferee and another to the transferor for the balance of his shareholding which he retains. The same certification procedure is followed if the transferor's shares comprised in the same share certificate are transferred to two or more transferees.

The transferee enters his name (or the name of his nominee) on the transfer and presents it to the Stamp Office for stamping (½ per cent ad valorem on the price or value). This should be done within 30 days to avoid penalties. The transfer (with the old share certificate in appropriate cases) is delivered to the company which should satisfy itself that the transfer is correct in its particulars, is properly executed and adequately stamped. The company may as a precaution write to the transferor to give him notice that the transfer has been lodged (in case it is a forgery) but he has no duty to reply and does not lose his rights against the company if he ignores it. (See *Bahia Rly Case* in 7.3 above).

Accordingly the issue of transfer notices of this type is no longer standard procedure and companies prefer to insure against any liability falling on them through a forged transfer.

If the transfer is found to be in order it should be submitted to the board of directors (or a committee or other person to whom authority to approve transfers has been delegated). If the directors have power to refuse to register the transfer they may do so. They are also entitled to refuse a transfer which appears to be inadequately stamped or which they know is made fraudulently or in breach of trust. If a stop notice (Chapter 8: 8.12) has been received the person who has served the notice should be informed that the transfer has been lodged.

Unless there are obstacles of these various types the transfer may be approved, the name of the transferee is entered in the register (or the shares are added to his existing holding) and a new share certificate is issued to him. At the same time the transfer of the shares out of the transferor's holding is also registered and if he then has no shares left the date of his ceasing to be a member is inserted. Either the new share certificate or notice of refusal of the transfer should be delivered to the transferee within two months of the date on which the transfer is lodged: ss 183 and 185.

7.18 Legal effect of certification

The practical purpose of certification of a share transfer has already been explained. It is a representation by the company to any person acting on the faith of the certification that documents have been produced to the company which on the face of them show a prima facie title of the transferor to the shares (or debentures) comprised in the transfer: s 184. It is not a representation that the transferor has any title.

If the certification is made by a duly authorised officer or agent of the company, the company is bound by it even if the officers or agent acted improperly: s 184. But it is not bound by a certification made by a person who had not been authorised to make it. The words 'certificate lodged' imply that the certificate will be retained pending registration of the transfer.

The representation is made only to the person who acts on the faith of the certification. A person who takes the certified transfer and gives value for it or otherwise takes action in reliance on it can hold the company liable if either:

(a) the transferor did not send in his share certificate; or
(b) the company failed to retain it.

The company would, for example, be liable if the transferor transferred his shares to a third party (with the share certificate) and the latter was registered as holder of the shares before the holder of the certified transfer applied for registration (and was refused).

There is no representation to any person who does not act on the faith of the certification nor has the company any duty to him to retain the share certificate.

A transfer of shares to B was registered and a share certificate in his name was prepared but not immediately sent to him. B delivered a transfer of his shares to H who sent it in for certification and this was done as the company held B's certificate at the time. Later the company by oversight sent to B his share certificate and B deposited it with L as security for a loan. L's claim against the company failed. The certificate was accurate at the time when it was prepared. It was superseded by the transfer to H. L had never seen the certified transfer to B and so he could not rely on it: *Longman v Bath Electric Tramways Ltd* [1905] 1 Ch 646. (If H had suffered loss he could of course have claimed on the certified transfer issued to him).

7.19 Sale of shares

A contract of sale of shares may be oral or written. Beneficial ownership passes as soon as shares are identified as the subject of the contract. The contract may be enforced by an order for specific performance.

The company continues to treat the vendor as the registered holder and legal owner of the shares until his transfer to the purchaser is registered. The vendor will receive any dividend or other payments made to members by the company and he is liable to pay any calls made in respect of partly paid shares. Unless otherwise agreed the vendor must account to the purchaser for dividends, etc, which may be both declared and paid to him after beneficial ownership has passed. But he may retain a dividend declared before beneficial ownership has passed but paid to him afterwards. He is entitled to be indemnified by the purchaser against any liability for calls made on the partly paid shares after the passing of ownership.

The vendor so long as he is the registered holder is entitled to attend and vote at meetings of the company. The purchaser has no right to instruct him how to vote unless the purchase price has been paid.

These general rules may be varied by the terms of the contract. In particular a sale of shares through the Stock Exchange is made expressly on a *cum div* or *ex div* basis which determine the parties' rights to dividends.

The duty of the vendor is to deliver a duly executed transfer with his share certificate (or a certified transfer instead) to the purchaser in exchange for the payment of the purchase price. Unless he sells with 'registration guaranteed' he has no obligation to secure that the transfer is registered and no liability if it is refused, but he then continues to hold the shares as nominee of the purchaser. But he must not take any active steps to impede registration of the transfer nor act for a principal (as in the case below) who does so. If he delivers a transfer without receiving payment of the price he has a lien, unless otherwise agreed, on the shares until the price is paid.

Solicitors instructed stockbrokers to sell securities and delivered to the brokers a share transfer in blank executed by a third party and her share certificate. After the stockbrokers had sold the stock but before the transfer had been registered the transferor instructed the company not to register the transfer. The solicitors were held liable to indemnify the stockbrokers for liability incurred as a result of these events since it was their duty to deliver a transfer by a transferor who was willing to complete the transaction: *Hichens, Harrison, Woolston & Co v Jackson & Sons* [1943] AC 266.

7.20 Mortgage of shares

Under a *legal* mortgage of shares there is a transfer of the shares into the name of the mortgagee as registered holder. The mortgagor's right to redeem and the other matters, such as who is to be beneficially entitled to the dividends, are usually expressed in an agreement with which the company is not concerned. The mortgagor may protect his position, however, by serving a stop notice on the company (Chapter 8: 8.12).

The essential feature of an *equitable* mortgage is the deposit of the mortgagor's share certificate with the mortgagee. The latter must then apply to the court for an order to enforce his security by sale unless other arrangements are made. To avoid these difficulties the mortgagee may demand from the mortgagor a power of attorney authorising him to sell the shares or alternatively a transfer in blank (see below). Again there is likely to be an agreement setting out the terms of the loan and of the mortgage. The mortgagor remains the registered holder of the shares and so the mortgagee runs the risk that even without his share certificate the mortgagor may find some means of selling or mortgaging his shares to another person unaware of the fraud.

The delivery to a mortgagee of a blank transfer, ie a transfer signed by the mortgagor but lacking the name of the transferee, is (as regards fully paid shares) implied authority to the mortgagee to complete the transfer by inserting his own name or that of a purchaser from him. The mortgagor, if he has defaulted on the mortgage, is then estopped from denying that the transfer as thus completed is valid and binding on him.

7.21 Competing claims to shares

Two persons may have competing claims to the beneficial ownership or other rights over the same shares. An illustration will suffice to show how the basic rules are applied to settle such disputes.

Suppose that T is the registered holder of shares as trustee for B. In breach of his trust T mortgages the shares to M as security for a loan by M to T. Does M have rights which prevail over B or vice versa?

If T mortgages the shares to M by a *legal* mortgage, there must – under that form of mortgage – be a transfer to M who becomes the registered shareholder. Unless he was aware of B's rights under the trust at the time when M took his legal mortgage (or if he made a purchase) giving value for the shares, M's rights prevail over B's rights since M is the legal owner and B's rights (under the trust) are equitable. There is a procedure (Chapter 8: 8.12) by which B could serve a stop notice on the company to prevent the mortgage of the shares to M, but few beneficiaries are so distrustful of their trustees as to take this precaution.

If, however, the mortgage to M is equitable, ie a mere deposit of T's share certificate with M, then B's equitable rights prevail over those of M, under the principle that priority of competing equitable interests is determined by the order in which those interests are created. In the example given the trust precedes the mortgage. B would, however, lose his priority if by his conduct he had represented that T had authority to dispose of the shares. But merely to leave a share certificate in the hands of a trustee does not have that effect.

7.22 Forged transfers

A forged transfer is a nullity and the holder of the shares whose signature is forged on the transfer can compel the company to restore him to the register as holder of the shares.

A person who presents a transfer to a company for registration warrants that it bears the genuine signature of the transferor. If in fact the signature is a forgery, then, however innocent the transferee may be, he has no rights against the company under any share certificate which may be issued to him and he must compensate the company if it suffers loss by reason of the forged transfer.

T and H were the joint owners of corporation loan stock. T forged the signature of H on a transfer and added his own. The transfer was in favour of B who obtained registration and later resold the stock to a third party. The third party accepted B's transfer with the certificate issued to B. The corporation was estopped against the third party by the certificate issued to B and could not deny to him that B was at the time the registered holder. It therefore left the stock in the name of the third party and purchased a similar amount of stock to be registered in the name of H. It was, however, entitled to be indemnified by B who had presented the forged transfer with the implied warranty that it was genuine: *Sheffield Corp v Barclay* [1905] AC 392.

7.23 Transmission
Transmission is a transfer of ownership of shares by operation of law. The most common instance is the transfer of shares on death of the holder. This subject is considered later (Chapter 8: 8.4 and 8.5).

D CALLS, FORFEITURE, SURRENDER AND LIEN

7.24 Calls on shares
In modern practice a company usually obtains the whole amount due on its shares at the time of allotment or, in allotting the shares, it lays down a timetable with precise dates on which the amount due is to be paid by successive instalments. It is however permissible to allot shares as partly paid (Chapter 5: 5.1) and then make demands ('calls') on shareholders at some later date(s) for all or part of the amount outstanding. This practice is unusual because investors do not like to hold shares carrying outstanding liabilities which may be called up at some inconvenient moment.

The articles (Table A Arts 12–22) contain a detailed procedure for making calls. It is essential that the directors, in whom the power to make calls is vested, should follow that procedure exactly. If they fail to do so the call will usually be invalid.

If a call is properly made by resolution passed at a board meeting and communicated to members (Table A Art 12 provides for a minimum of 14 days' notice to pay) each shareholder is liable to pay the amount of the call at the due date and may (Art 15) also be liable to pay interest at the prescribed rate.

The final sanction against a member in default is forfeiture of his shares by resolution of the board to that effect. The member ceases to be a member in respect of the forfeited shares but he is still liable for the amount due at the date of forfeiture. The directors may reallot forfeited shares or dispose of them in some other way, eg by sale. As already stated (Chapter 5: 5.21) a public company has a limited period only in which to cancel or otherwise dispose of forfeited shares.

A limited company may by special resolution declare that any part of its uncalled capital shall only be called up when the company is in liquidation: s 120. In effect the members' liability on their shares become a reserve (called 'reserve capital') which cannot be used while the company is a going concern but is available to meet the liabilities of the company in liquidation. The decision once taken is irrevocable.

In a case where the company has power to forfeit shares it may accept a voluntary surrender of shares by a member who is unable to pay the call made on him. But this power must be exercised in the interest of the company and not for the purpose of relieving shareholders of their liabilities if they have the means to discharge them.

The company suffered a loss of £4,000 and the directors surrendered 4,000 shares of £11 each (nominal) £10 paid to offset the loss. This was invalid since there had been no default in payment of calls nor was surrender due to inability to pay the uncalled capital: *Bellerby v Rowland & Marwood's SS Co Ltd* [1902] 2 Ch 14.

7.25 Lien

A lien is an equitable charge over the shares of a company for sums owing to the company by the shareholder. It is created by the relevant provisions of the articles which define its scope and how it may be enforced, ie there is no right of lien unless the articles confer it.

Lien is usually restricted to a charge on partly paid shares to secure the amount of capital unpaid on those shares. A *public* company (with minor exceptions) is restricted by law to liens of that type: s 150(2). Although a private company may by its articles have a lien on fully paid shares for any debt owing to the company by the holder, it is no longer common practice to do so. The 1985 Table A (Art 8) is expressly limited to lien on partly paid shares for the amount due on those shares. As most shares are, or become soon after allotment, fully paid, a lien so expressed does not apply to them.

If a company has occasion to enforce a lien on its shares they are sold and the proceeds applied in discharge of the debt to the company. The former holder of the shares is entitled to any surplus (Arts 9–11).

If a holder of shares over which a company has a right of lien mortgages the shares to a third party at a time when he has no existing debt to the company and the third party gives notice of his charge to the company he will have priority over the company's lien in respect of some subsequent debt to the company.

The articles gave the company a first and paramount lien on members' shares for all debts owing by them to the company. A shareholder deposited his share certificate with a bank as security for a loan and the bank gave notice to the company of the transaction. Later the shareholder became indebted to the company. It was held that the bank has priority in its claim to the shares since the company already had notice of the bank's charge before its own claim arose against the shareholder. The prohibition in s 360 against receipt of notice of a trust relating to the company's shares does not prevent the company from being affected in respect of its own rights as a creditor by notice of the interests of third parties: *Bradford Banking Co Ltd v Henry Briggs Son & Co Ltd* (1886) 12 App Cas 29.

On the other hand, if the member is already indebted to the company at the time when it receives notice of a third party's interest in his shares, any lien over those shares in favour of the company takes priority. The amount paid on a share does not become a debt until a call has been made (7.24).

7.26 Charging order

A person who obtains judgment for debt against a shareholder may levy execution by obtaining an order of the court charging shares of the debtor with payment of the judgment debt. This order cannot, however, give to the creditor any better rights than the shareholder has. If the shareholder has previously created an equitable mortgage the mortgagee's rights take priority over those of the judgment creditor, ie he is restricted to the mortgagor's equity of redemption. The shareholder may also resist the application for a charging order by showing that he holds the shares as trustee and has no beneficial interest.

If a charging order is made the company may not register a transfer of the shares nor pay a dividend on them except with the leave of the court. Six months after the charging order has been made absolute the creditor may, if the debt has not been paid, apply to the court for an order for sale of the shares and payment of his debt out of the proceeds.

This procedure is regulated by the Charging Orders Act 1979.

Chapter 8

Membership

8.1 Becoming a member

The first members are the subscribers to the memorandum who, by subscribing, are deemed to have agreed to become members. On its incorporation the company should enter their names in its register of members: s 22(1).

Thereafter a person is a member of a company if:

(a) he has agreed to be a member; and
(b) his name has been entered in the register of members: s 22(2).

In applying for shares to be allotted to him the applicant by implication agrees to become a member. But the issue to him of a letter of allotment does not make him a member unless he has also been entered in the register of members as the holder of the shares. If, therefore, the original allottee renounces his letter of allotment to another person before he is entered in the register, he is never a member. The renuncee agrees to become a member by presenting the letter of allotment so that the shares may be registered in his name and he becomes a member when he is entered in the register.

A person to whom shares are transferred by a transfer in the form prescribed by the Stock Transfer Act 1963 does not sign it. But the form includes a request for registration of the shares in the name of the transferee. In presenting the transfer for registration the transferee agrees to become a member. But he too, although he may already have become the beneficial owner of the shares, is not a member until his name is entered in the register. If he does not present the transfer, his agreement to becoming a member may be inferred from his conduct, eg in attending general meetings or retaining dividends paid to him.

The personal representative of a deceased member and the trustee of a bankrupt member may by the appropriate procedure (8.4 and 8.5 below) agree to become a member and he then becomes a member on entry in the register. The holder of a share warrant (Chapter 7: 7.4) is not a member, since he is not on the register, but he may by the articles be given some or all of the rights of a member.

A member of a company which has a share capital is also a 'shareholder'. the two words are used interchangeably in most contexts.

8.2 Subscribers' shares

In signing the memorandum each subscriber agrees to take the number of shares (by convention usually one) set opposite his signature. He becomes a member as soon as the company is formed and is bound to pay for the shares for which he has subscribed in the memorandum. If the company is incorporated as a public company he must pay for the shares (including any premium) in cash: s 106. The contract to take and pay for subscribers' shares cannot be rescinded for misrepresentation since the company, which did not exist when the memorandum was signed, cannot be held to have adopted a misrepresentation made by a promoter before the company existed.

The directors cannot relieve a subscriber of his obligation to take his subscriber's shares. Their duty is to enter his name in the register as the holder (allotment is not a necessary nor a correct procedure in respect of subscribers' shares). But if the directors allot all the existing shares to other persons so that there are no available shares, of which the subscribers can become the registered holders, this is a breach of contract by the company which relieves the subscribers of their obligations. The allotment to subscribers of shares, to which someone else is entitled, does not relieve them of their obligations to take and pay for their subscribers' shares.

The vendor of property to the company at a price to be satisfied by the issue of shares directed that sufficient shares should be allotted to a subscriber to discharge his obligations under the memorandum. It was held that he was still liable to pay for his subscriber's shares: *Migotti's Case* (1867) LR 4 Eq 238.

8.3 Minors as members
The ordinary rules of capacity to enter into contracts apply to minors as shareholders. During his minority and within a reasonable time thereafter the minor may avoid the contract of allotment and disclaim the shares. Unless and until he does so he has the normal rights and liabilities of a shareholder. It is not clear from the cases (some of doubtful authority since they were decided before the Infants Relief Act 1874) what is a reasonable time for avoidance of the contract. But the period can apparently extend for a year or two after attaining majority. If the minor avoids an allotment of shares made to him as first holder, the shares are treated as though they had never been issued. If he repudiates shares which have been transferred to him, the transferor becomes the holder again of those shares.

The minor is a member until he repudiates his shares and he remains liable to pay sums due on them. But if he repudiates the shares he ceases to be liable even for payments which had become due before he did so. He cannot, however, on repudiation recover sums paid to the company for his shares unless the shares have at all times been worthless so that he received no consideration for his money.

The minor applied for 500 £1 shares and paid the amount due on allotment, i e 10s per share. She received no dividend and the shares stood at a discount in the market. While still a minor she repudiated the shares and claimed repayment of the amount which she had paid. It was held that she was entitled to rescind the contract and was not liable for the amount unpaid on the shares. But as the shares had some value there had not been a total failure of consideration. She could not recover the money paid: *Steinberg v Scala (Leeds) Ltd* [1923] 2 Ch 452.

A company can refuse to register a transfer of shares to a minor. It can probably cancel a transfer of shares to him after the transfer has been registered unless the minor has meanwhile transferred the shares to someone else. But if the company, on becoming aware that he was a minor, has allowed his name to remain on the register for a long time it loses its right to cancel the entry. In a winding up the liquidator may always cancel a transfer of shares to a minor and restore to the register the name of the person who transferred his shares to him since the minor is not liable for any amount unpaid.

8.4 Personal representatives of a deceased member

On the death of a member his membership ceases, eg he can no longer be counted for purposes of the minimum membership rule, but his estate continues to be entitled to the benefits and subject to the burdens incidental to ownership of his shares until some other person is registered as the holder. This rule applies only where the deceased was the sole registered holder of the shares. If he was a joint holder the survivors are still members and the shares are held by them as legal owners by right of survivorship.

Any person to whom the deceased has given an interest in his estate, even if it be a specific legacy of the shares, only has rights against the personal representatives in whom the assets vest pending completion of administration of the estate. If the articles provide that on death of a member his shares shall pass to someone else, that provision is ineffective since it is not a proper instrument of transfer.

The deceased as subscriber to the memorandum had also signed the original articles (Chapter 2: 2.1(b)) which provided that on his death his shares were to pass to his widow. However the articles were at his death held not to be 'a proper instrument of transfer' as required by s 183. Apart from the inappropriate form the articles did not sufficiently identify the intended 'transferee'. No one could be certain that his wife (at the time of signing the articles) would be his widow at his death: *Re Greene* [1949] Ch 333.

The personal representatives cannot require the company to recognise their rights in respect of the shares unless they have produced to the company probate of the will of the deceased or, if he died intestate or without executors, letters of administration: s 187. The normal procedure is that the personal representatives send an office copy of their grant together with the share certificate of the deceased to the company. The company makes an entry in the register of members of the death of the deceased, the name and address of the personal representative(s) and the date on which the grant was produced for registration. Similar entries are indorsed on the share certificate which is returned to the personal representative together with a form of 'letter of request'. The legal position at this stage is that neither the deceased nor his personal representatives are members.

The personal representatives then have a choice of two alternative courses. They can let matters rest as they are until they are ready to transfer the shares, either to the beneficiary entitled to them or to a purchaser on sale in normal course of administration of the estate. If they opt for this course they do not become members and the rights attaching to the shares may be restricted (eg Table A Art 31 excludes the right to attend and vote at meetings). The second alternative open to the personal representatives is to apply by letter of request for registration as holders of the shares (subject to any right of the directors under the articles to refuse it – see Table A Art 30). If they are registered as shareholders they become members with the full rights and liabilities of membership. Whichever alternative the personal representatives may adopt they always have the power (subject to any restrictions imposed by the articles) to transfer the shares either as members or, if they do not become members, by statutory provision as personal representatives: s 183(3).

The personal representatives, even if they are not registered as members, may petition for the compulsory winding up of the company as contributories or for relief against conduct of the affairs of the company in a manner prejudicial to members: IA s 81 and CA s 459. The estate is still entitled to benefits arising from the shares such as participation in bonus issues, and is liable for any amounts payable on partly paid shares.

8.5 Trustees in bankruptcy
The trustee in bankruptcy of a member has a statutory title to the shares and a power to transfer them. He has the same choice as personal representatives whether to apply to be entered in the register. If he does become a member he becomes personally liable for amounts due on partly paid shares. If he leaves the shares in the name of the bankrupt the latter may vote at meetings or appoint a proxy but in doing so he must exercise these powers as the trustee directs. The trustee can disclaim partly paid shares of the bankrupt but it is not clear whether he can disclaim fully paid shares. He has the same right to present a petition as a personal representative.

8.6 Other companies
A company or other corporation may be a member of another company only if its objects clause gives it power to be so. It may be represented at general meetings of the company of which it is a member by any person authorised for this purpose by resolution of the board of directors of the shareholder company: s 375. Such a representative is not a proxy but has the same rights (for the body he represents) as an individual shareholder present in person. In all other respects a company shareholder has the same rights as an individual.

A company which is a subsidiary may not be a member of its holding company otherwise than as trustee: s 23 (Chapter 5: 5.20). It cannot be a member of itself.

8.7 Ceasing to be a member
In the ordinary course a member ceases to be a member when he transfers all his shares to another person who is entered in the register in his place. He also ceases to be a member when he dies or when his trustee in bankruptcy disclaims his shares or when as a minor he repudiates his shares. His shares may be forfeited or he may surrender them instead or the company may sell them in exercise of a lien or may redeem or purchase his shares (Chapter 5 Part B). In these cases the member ceases to be a member either because the shares are no longer registered in his name or (if he dies) because he no longer exists. He may also cease to be a member when the company is wound up and itself ceases to exist.

8.8 Register of members
Every company is required by s 352 to keep a register of members and to enter therein the following particulars:

(a) the names and addresses of the members. If the company has a share capital, it must also state the shares held by each member (with distinguishing numbers, if any) and the amount paid or agreed to be considered as paid on the shares of each member and, if there is more than one class of shares, the class. Similarly if there is no share capital but different classes of members, the class to which the member belongs must be stated;

(b) the date at which each person was entered in the register as a member;

(c) the date at which any person ceased to be a member.

If, however, shares have been converted into stock (Chapter 7: 7.6) the particulars to be stated in the register are of stock held instead of shares.

The register of members may be in the form of a bound book. It may also be kept in some other form such as looseleaf cards provided that adequate precautions are taken to prevent falsification and to facilitate its discovery: s 722(2). For this purpose a looseleaf register usually has some locking device.

Companies may also keep the register in non-legible form, ie on computer, provided that the register is capable of being reproduced in legible form: s 723. In effect, there must be a computer printout on request.

In addition to providing a record of present members the register must include entries of former members until the expiry of 20 years from the time when they ceased to be members: s 352(6).

The register must be held at the registered office or at some other place in the country of incorporation and be open to public inspection (Chapter 3: 3.10).

If the company has more than 50 members it must keep an index (to be updated within 14 days of any alteration) unless the register itself is kept in such form, eg a looseleaf card register in alphabetical order of names, that it is itself an index: s 354.

A company is not legally obliged to make more than one entry in the register for each member by splitting his shareholding. In practice banks and other institutions which hold shares as nominees or trustees for more than one customer require shareholdings in their names to be split and designated by distinguishing numbers or letters. A public company whose shares are listed on the Stock Exchange is required as a condition of its listing agreement to provide this service.

The articles usually provide that, if shares are registered in the names of two or more joint holders, notices of meetings, etc, shall suffice if sent to the first-named joint holder only (eg Table A Art 112). But an article in this form does not deprive another joint holder of his right to exercise his powers as a member. Joint holders may therefore require that their holding shall be split into parts which are each entered separately in the register so that every joint holder's name appears first in respect of some part of the holding. It is normal practice to register split holdings by making transfers out of the original combined joint holding for this purpose. But an order for rectification of the register (8.10 below) can be obtained if necessary.

Any person may inspect the register of members, unless it is temporarily closed, and may obtain a copy of the register or of any part of it: ss 356–358. The statutory rules on these matters have been explained in connection with the registered office at which the register of members is normally kept (Chapter 3: 3.10). Failure to comply with a demand to inspect or have copies of the register may lead to a fine on those at fault or a court order requiring compliance.

A company may close its register for up to 30 days in a year, on giving due notice in advance in a local newspaper: s 358. This remission is made so that companies may have a standstill on changes in the register while preparing lists of members entitled to dividends. In practice, however, companies simply work from the register as it stands at the close of business on the chosen 'record date' (for a dividend) and continue to accept and register transfers thereafter, without having a standstill, during which arrears of registration work would accumulate.

8.9 Overseas branch registers

A company which has a share capital and whose objects comprise the transaction of business in any of the countries listed in Sch 14 Pt 1 may keep in the relevant country or countries a branch register or registers of members resident therein: s 362. Similar provisions of the Companies Act 1948 referred to 'dominion registers'. The countries in question were generally formerly British dependencies.

Part II of Sch 14 contains rules for maintaining registers of this kind. When such a register is first set up notice of the address at which it is held must within 14 days be given to the registrar.

The overseas branch register is treated as part of the company's register in England ('the principal register'). A copy of every entry made in the overseas branch register must be sent as soon as possible to the registered office in this country. With its principal register the company must keep a duplicate of its overseas branch register, which is deemed to be part of the principal register, and is subject to the same statutory rules on inspection, supply of copies and rectification by court order.

There are two main advantages in having an overseas branch register in a country where the company does business – though it is entirely optional whether the company decides to do so. First, the company may obtain a quotation for its shares on a stock exchange in the country and be required, as a condition of that facility, to maintain a local register for the convenience of residents in that country who hold its shares. Secondly, a transfer of shares held on an overseas branch register is deemed to be a transfer of property outside the UK and, unless the transfer is executed in the UK, is not subject to UK stamp duty. It is also a general principle of UK capital taxes that shares on a foreign register of any kind are properly situated where the register is held. For a transferor who is not a UK resident this principle may carry exemption from UK tax.

8.10 Rectification of the register

The register of members is only prima facie evidence of matters which by law must be entered in it: s 361. The court has a statutory power in its discretion to order rectification of the register: s 359. Where however there is an undoubted error or a trivial one and there is no dispute, a company will in practice make the necessary correction without obtaining a court order.

The statutory power to order rectification may be exercised when the name of any person has been entered in or omitted from the register of members without sufficient cause or there is default or delay in entering on the register the fact that a person has ceased to be a member. Application to the court on these grounds may be made by the person aggrieved, or any member of the company, or by the company itself: s 359(1). Application is made by the summary procedure of originating summons or motion for an order for rectification. For example, application might be made to remove the name of an allottee of shares from the register on the grounds that the allotment was procured by misrepresentation and is void or voidable. An action for rectification is the standard method of challenging a refusal by the directors to enter a transfer of shares in the register (see the *Swaledale Cleaners Case* in Chapter 7: 7.16).

It is possible to bring more complicated questions before the court by this means, such as disputes over the ownership of shares or cases in which other parties are involved besides the immediate contestants. However in such instances the court is very likely to dismiss the application for rectification of the register, but leaving the parties free to resolve their dispute by other legal proceedings related to the basic issue between them and the other persons involved.

In making an order for rectification the court may award damages payable by the company or order either party to pay legal costs. But if the effect of the court order is to deny that some person, who is not involved in the action, can remain the registered holder of shares, the court would not award costs against him.

8.11 Equitable interests in shares

An entry in the register of members is evidence only of the *legal* title of the member to the shares registered in his name. But the member may hold his shares in trust for another person or have created an equitable interest in favour of another by, e g mortgaging or selling the shares to him. A company in England, but not in Scotland, is however forbidden to receive or to enter on its register any notice of a trust express or implied: s 360. The same principle is often elaborated by a more detailed prohibition in the articles (Table A Art 5).

The general effect of this rule is that the company deals only with the registered holder of the shares in connection with rights and obligations incidental to the shares. Any dividends payable on the shares should be paid to the registered holder unless, of course, he has authorised the company by mandate to make payment to someone else. Trustee shareholders may, for example, by dividend mandate authorise payment of their dividends direct to the beneficiary entitled to the trust income. In the same way the company's claim for money due as a result of making a call on partly paid shares is solely against the registered holder. Even if the company is aware that he is a mere nominee for another the company cannot recover the call from the latter.

Under the same principle if the registered holder transfers his shares the company (unless it has received a stop notice as described below) must register the transfer as a disposition by the legal owner within his powers as owner. This is so even if the company is aware that the transfer is in breach of trust.

The estate of a deceased person included shares of a banking company. A copy of the will was deposited with the bank. One of the executors, who were the registered holders, was also president of the bank. The executors presented a transfer of the shares which was in breach of the terms of the will and the bank registered the transfer. An action against the bank by a residuary legatee of the estate failed because under Canadian law similar to s 360 the company was expressly prohibited from taking notice of a trust of its shares: *Simpson v Molson's Bank* [1895] AC 270.

Because notice of an equitable interest in its shares may not be entered in the register of a company the ordinary rule of priority of equitable interests by giving notice has no application.

A registered holder had made two transfers of the same shares. The persons to whom the second transfer was made were the first to inform the company of their rights by presenting their transfer for registration. But as they could not produce the transferor's share certificate registration was refused. It was held that in giving notice to the company in this way they had not obtained priority over the holders of the first transfer (who also held the share certificate). The latter obtained registration: *Société Générale de Paris v Walker* (1885) 11 App Cas 20.

The statutory rule against entry on the register of notice of an equitable interest in shares does not give the company itself any priority in asserting its own rights against some other person of whose adverse rights it has received notice. Thus, if a company has a lien under the articles on its shares for sums owing by shareholders, the lien is postponed to rights of third parties of which the company already had notice when the debt first became due from the shareholder (Chapter 7: 7.25 – *Briggs' Case*).

Section 360, by which a company may not recognise that shares are held in trust, and is not liable for its refusal to do so, applies only to registration of transfers and other routine company administration. A company which takes an active part in transactions, knowing that they are a breach of trust, is liable as a constructive trustee under normal rules of trust law.

8.12 Stop notices

A person who has an interest in shares registered in the name of a shareholder other than himself may, however, protect himself by obtaining and serving on the company a 'stop notice' (which replaces the former 'notice in lieu of *distringas*').

The applicant files at the Central Office of the High Court an affidavit (sworn statement) which sets out the nature of his interest in the shares together with a copy of a notice to the company. The notice to the company does not include particulars of his claim to the shares but merely that he has an interest in them. The notice is issued to prevent registration of any transfer of the shares. If the applicant claims a beneficial interest in the shares the notice may also stop payment of dividends on the shares to the registered holder. The company cannot enter the notice itself on the register but it marks the relevant page in the register of members to indicate that a stop notice has been received and holds the notice on file for reference.

If a transfer is presented (or a dividend is about to be paid where there is a stop on dividends) the company sends a letter to the equitable owner named in the stop notice and must wait 14 days before registering the transfer or paying the dividend. In this period the equitable owner has time to obtain an injunction to restrain registration or payment. The company may not defer action for more than 14 days unless the court orders it to do so. If the company fails to comply with stop notice procedure the directors are deemed to have participated in any breach of trust which may result and are liable to compensate the owner of the equitable interest.

8.13 Disclosure of substantial interests in shares

It is possible for a person to conceal his beneficial ownership of shares and his control of the votes attached to them by causing his shares to be registered in the name of some other person as his nominee. The use of nominees is a common and convenient practice which is generally unobjectionable. But it can be abused when shares are acquired and held in the name of nominees in order to build up a position of influence (sometimes with a view to making a take-over bid for the rest of the share capital) without disclosing the identity and/or the number of shares owned by the person concerned. This manoeuvre is particularly objectionable in the case of a public company whose shares are listed on the Stock Exchange since one significant combined block of votes (although a minority only) can effectively outweigh the dispersed and smaller holdings of members who may find it difficult to combine effectively to mobilise their voting strength (see also Chapter 17: 17.5 on the City Code in relation to those situations).

In 1981, what are now ss 198–220, some 7,000 words of complex legal prose, were enacted to replace some earlier efforts to enforce disclosure which had proved ineffectual. This and the next following section summarise these provisions with reference to (1) the circumstances in which disclosure is required (2) what information is disclosed and how it is made available to the public and (3) the means by which a public company may seek to enforce disclosure.

The requirement of disclosure relates to interests in those shares of *public* companies which carry unrestricted voting rights at general meetings. In the remainder of this passage the word 'shares' is used in that sense; in the Act shares are defined as 'relevant share capital': s 198(2). All shares of private companies and, for example, preference shares of public companies with limited voting rights only (Chapter 7: 7.11) are outside the scope of the disclosure system.

Secondly, it is only interests of a substantial size in shares which require disclosure. The standard measure of size for disclosure is 5 per cent of the issued shares of the company or of a class of its shares. But the level may be fixed by regulation, for companies of particular types, at some other percentage. It is of course the size of the interest which is material. If, for example, X has an interest in shares held in the names of two nominees, P and Q, those holdings are aggregated for the purpose of these rules.

The current rules seek to counter an avoidance device by which two or more persons, who are independent of each other, enter into an agreement or understanding to act in concert (colloquially they become 'a concert party') with a view to common action. In such cases the members of the group are treated as if they were a single person. If, for example, A and B, acting in concert, each have 4.99 per cent of the shares, each of them is subject to the rules of disclosure of his own *and* the other person's interest as if he had 9.8 per cent: s 205.

The obligation to disclose begins as soon as a person acquires an interest at or in excess of the notifiable percentage. Thereafter he must give notice each time there is a change in the size of his interest of one percentage point: s 200. If his interest decreases to less than 5 per cent he gives final notice of that fact. In giving notice on each occasion he must supply prescribed particulars which include the number of shares and the name of the person who is the registered holder of those shares.

There are subsidiary rules which define elaborately what is a notifiable interest and what interests may be disregarded: ss 208–9. For example, there is a notifiable interest when a person contracts to purchase shares, or has obtained control of votes attached to shares, or is a beneficiary of certain kinds of trust which have an interest in shares. On the other hand the appointment of a person to be a proxy, to vote for a shareholder at a general meeting, does not constitute the proxy a person with a notifiable interest.

The notices are given to the company, which is required to enter them in a register. The register is held at the same place as the company's register of directors' interests (Chapter 12: 12.10). Anyone may inspect it without charge and on payment of a fee obtain a copy: s 219. The listing agreement with the Stock Exchange, in the case of a public company whose shares are listed, also requires that the information obtained from the notices shall be passed on to the Stock Exchange.

8.14 Disclosure by nominees and others

Within the limits of the rules described in the previous section a public company may require any person, who need not be a member of the company, to provide information, if the company has reasonable cause to believe that this person has, or within the previous three years has had, an interest in the company's shares: s 212. The company may by this means both require the person to confirm his interest and, where appropriate, to give particulars of his own or other interests in the shares known to him. If he had an interest which has now ceased he may be asked to give the identity of the person who took it over from him.

The information so obtained must be entered in the company's register of interests already described.

If the information demanded is not given, the company may apply to the court for an order, imposing on the relevant shares the same restrictions as are available in an investigation of the ownership of shares by inspectors appointed by the DTI (Chapter 15: 15.10). This sanction is particularly useful if the nominee shareholder resides in a foreign country or does not himself know who is the ultimate and real owner of the shares.

A minority of members, if they hold at least one-tenth of the shares of the company carrying unrestricted voting rights, may serve a requisition on the company, requiring it to investigate interests in its shares. The company must report at three-monthly intervals until the investigation is completed. This provision is to prevent obstruction in cases where the persons whose interests are to be investigated, already control the company through their nominees.

8.15 Annual return

Every company is required once in every calendar year to make an annual return to the registrar. There are different rules on the prescribed contents of annual returns made by companies which have and companies which do not have a share capital: ss 363–4.

Both the form and content of an annual return are prescribed. The company must in practice insert on a standard printed form (or attach sheets to it) the information required by law.

The annual return must be made up to contain particulars of the company as at the fourteenth day after the annual general meeting of the year and be signed by a director and by the secretary of the company. It should be delivered to the registrar within six weeks after the meeting. But no return need be made in the year of incorporation or the next year, if the company holds its first annual general meeting within 18 months of incorporation. If there is default in delivering the annual return when due the company and its officers in default are liable to a fine: s 365. It is no longer necessary to attach a copy of the accounts to the annual return since there are other rules which require the accounts to be delivered to the registrar separately (Chapter 14: 14.4).

The particulars which must be given in the annual return of a company which has a share capital are specified in Sch 15 as follows:

(a) the address of the registered office;
(b) the address at which the register of members and any register of debenture holders is kept if they are not kept at the registered office;
(c) a summary of nominal, issued, called-up and paid-up capital with particulars of consideration received, commissions paid, discounts allowed on the issue of shares and debentures, shares forfeited and shares in respect of which share warrants have been issued;
(d) a statement of the total indebtedness of the company secured by mortgages or charges requiring to be registered at the registry;
(e) a list of members with their addresses and the number of shares which each member holds together with a list of persons who have ceased to be members and of shares transferred since the date of the last return (or since the incorporation of the company if it is the first return made);
(f) the same particulars of the directors and of the secretary as are required to be entered in the register of directors and secretary.

As an alternative to the full list of members required in (e) above a company may provide a list once in three years with only particulars of changes for the intervening years: s 363(5). But this remission is little used since most companies find it more convenient to reproduce the full list by mechanical means each year.

The annual return is a useful summary of basic information about the company. A study of the sequence of annual returns on file at the registry can provide a clear account of the main events over the period of a company's existence. But an annual return is already beginning to be out of date at the time of delivery to the registry. In the interval of about a year before the next return is received it becomes less and less useful as a source of current information.

In recent years the registrar has become increasingly strict in enforcing the prompt delivery of the annual return (and also the annual accounts). Those at fault persistently may be fined or disqualified by court order from being directors of any company for up to five years: CDDA s 3 (Chapter 12: 12.3). A member or creditor (and also the registrar) may apply to the court for an order requiring the company to deliver an overdue annual return within 14 days: s 713. In practice creditors who find that the latest annual return is overdue and not on file complain to the registrar, who brings pressure to bear by threatening to impose a fine or in a bad case to strike the company off the register if default continues. But a private citizen cannot compel the registrar to take action.

Chapter 9

Loan capital and charges

A BORROWING AND DEBENTURES

9.1 Loan capital

A company may finance its business in a variety of ways and it is usual to make use of a combination of methods. The money subscribed by members for their shares is permanent capital for the use of which the company makes no payment except by distribution of dividends out of its profits. The company may also be able to obtain goods and services on short-term credit or install plant and equipment procured on hire or hire-purchase terms. The liabilities which arise from these transactions are not, however, usually regarded as borrowing since no money is paid to the company. The third main source of company finance is borrowing money.

The terms of such loans vary widely according to the form of contract. A bank overdraft, for example, is repayable on demand though the bank will usually undertake not to exercise its rights on this basis but agrees to provide these facilities subject to renegotiation, say, at annual intervals. Banks and other lending institutions will provide short- or medium-term loans for fixed periods, if satisfied that the company is likely to be able to fulfil its contractual repayment obligations. In other cases the members of the company agree to provide a proportion of the required capital as lenders, and not as shareholders, since they then rank as creditors if the company becomes insolvent, can receive income as interest if there are no profits, and can withdraw capital surplus to requirements without formality. Finally a large public company may raise loan capital repayable after a period of years by the offer of debentures, or more usually debenture stock, to the public as investors.

From whatever source loan capital is procured, it tends to be part of the permanent or semi-permanent capital of the company. There is a continuing relationship between the company and its loan creditors which has something in common with the relationship between a company and its shareholders. The loan creditors are risking their money on the solvency and financial success of the company. Their concern is reflected in the terms of the loan which often give them security, i e a priority claim on the company's assets in case of default. The issue of loan capital by the offer of debentures to the public is regulated by the same general rules of prospectus law as apply to similar offers of share capital. The lender's rights to repayment and to receive interest meanwhile are a form of property which is transferable. The transfer procedure for registered debentures or debenture stock is similar to that for the transfer of shares.

Despite the similarities between share and loan capital there are more fundamental differences. A lender is a creditor whereas a member is a proprietor. In a reduction of share capital or a liquidation loan capital must be repaid (or in a reduction of capital safeguarded) out of available assets before capital subscribed by members can be repaid. Interest on loan capital is a debt which must be paid whether or not the company is making profits. The profits available for dividend are calculated after charging loan interest as an expense. Because the loan creditor is not a member he usually has no right to attend and vote at general meetings and no right to participate in any surplus assets available for distribution in a liquidation. A company may issue debentures at a discount and may purchase its own debentures without in either case being subject to statutory rules such as apply to shares (Chapter 5: 5.7 and 15).

9.2 Borrowing powers

In modern practice the objects clause of a company's memorandum includes, among other express powers, a power to borrow. But the power to borrow is implied in the case of a company whose objects are to carry on a trade or business since borrowing is incidental to those activities. A company with non-commercial objects does not, however, have the power to borrow unless it has been expressly conferred by the objects clause. Any power to borrow, express or implied, is a power limited to borrowing for the purposes defined as the objects of the company (Chapter 3: 3.13 – the *Introductions Case*). Much of the case law on the ultra vires doctrine turns on this point.

If a company has power to borrow it also has implied power to give security by creating charges over its assets. But a power to give security in this way is, like the power to borrow, usually expressed in the objects clause. There is, however, no implied power, though it can be given expressly, to mortgage the uncalled capital. If, for example, a company has issued 100,000 £1 shares 75p paid up it can at liquidation or some earlier stage call up the outstanding £25,000 on its issued shares. But it cannot charge that potential resource to a lender as security for his loan unless there is an appropriately worded power to do this in the objects clause. Uncalled capital is not 'property'; it is merely a right to call on members to contribute more capital. If, however, the objects clause provides a power to borrow on the security of a charge on any property or *any other security* then the power does extend to charging uncalled capital.

If there is a power to borrow, express or implied, it is a power to borrow without limit as to the amount unless the objects clause expressly restricts it – which is not usual. The directors under the general powers of management delegated to them by the articles (eg Table A Art 70) may exercise the company's powers to borrow. It is usual, however, to impose a limit on the amount which the directors are authorised to borrow under their delegated authority. The limit may be a specified amount, eg £1 m, but is more usually related to the amount of the issued share capital and reserves. The 1985 Table A articles include no limit on the directors' borrowing powers but many companies, public and private, continue to have in their articles a limit modelled on the 1948 Table A Art 79 (the issued share capital).

If the directors wish to raise loans in excess of the limit of their delegated authority they may obtain approval from the company in general meeting since the company itself has unlimited powers (unless the objects clause otherwise provides). If the directors have borrowed in excess of their limit without prior authority the company in general meeting may ratify the loan agreement, always provided that the purpose of the loan does not make it ultra vires. The company may, however, as a condition of a loan, agree to restrict its total borrowings to a specified limit (this is a normal condition of a debenture trust deed). The company is then still able to borrow in excess of the agreed limit but is in breach of contract if it does so.

A public company, incorporated as such, may not exercise its borrowing powers until it has obtained an appropriate certificate (Chapter 2: 2.4) pursuant to s 117. But the loan agreement is valid even if made in breach of this rule.

9.3 Debentures

The statutory definition provides that the term debenture 'includes debenture stock, bonds and any other securities of a company whether constituting a charge on the assets of the company or not: s 744. A court has said 'a debenture means a document which either creates a debt or acknowledges it . . . it is not either in law or commerce a strictly technical term': *Levy v Abercorris Slate and Slab Co* (1887) 27 Ch D 260.

Broadly a debenture is any document which sets out the terms of a company borrowing, i e the conditions of a loan contract. It includes, for example, a legal mortgage of land.

The company had mortgaged freehold properties to secure a loan repayable, with interest, by half-yearly instalments over a period of 40 years. General mortgage law may invalidate a condition which requires repayment of the loan over a very long period (as being a 'clog on the equity of redemption' i e a restriction on the mortgagor's right to pay off the loan and discharge the mortgage). However s 193 expressly provides that a debenture shall not be invalid on that account. The issue was whether the company's mortgage was also a 'debenture' to which this saving provision applied. The House of Lords held that it was a debenture: *Knightsbridge Estates Trust Ltd v Byrne* [1940] 2 All ER 401.

As stated above the statutory definition of 'debenture' expressly includes an *unsecured* borrowing. Commercial practice is to apply 'debenture' only to secured company loans and distinguish others as 'unsecured loans'; in company law both are debentures.

In general an obligation requiring a repayment of money by a company will be treated as a debenture even though it is not strictly a loan.

Money was deposited with a company on terms that it should be repaid at a fixed future date. Although it was not strictly a case of borrowing it was closely akin to it. The deposit receipt was a debenture: per Diplock LJ at p 988. (If a debenture or debenture trust deed imposes a limit on total borrowings it usually states what liabilities are to be reckoned as borrowings for this purpose); *United Dominions Trust Ltd v Kirkwood* [1966] 1 All ER 968.

The type and form of a debenture varies with the context in which it is issued. It is usual but not legally necessary to issue a debenture as a deed under the seal of the company. Since the use of the seal is controlled by the directors (Table A Art 101) a document under seal clearly relates to a transaction decided on by the directors and so s 35 may afford protection to the lender. Another advantage to the lender is that a secured debenture issued under seal is a mortgage created *by deed* and this gives to the mortgagee some legal powers under the Law of Property Act 1925 if he has to enforce his security.

If money is borrowed from a bank or other financial institution whose business is lending money the lender is likely to insist on the use of its standard form of loan agreement (including security by way of floating charge).

9.4 Registered debentures

The company may borrow money from a small number of lenders who may be, but need not be, otherwise connected with the company as directors or as members. In such cases it is usually agreed that the lenders, even if they provide different amounts or on different dates, shall be treated as participants in a common arrangement and with similar rights to repayment or to remedies in case of default. In such a case the debentures issued are expressed to form part of a series ranking pari passu and relating to the borrowing of an aggregate amount (of all the debentures).

As there are several debenture holders who may have occasion to transfer their debentures it is convenient, though it is not legally necessary, to provide for a register of debenture holders in which the original issue and any subsequent transfer of the debentures can be entered. Each debenture holder is a separate lender to the company but his contractual rights are regulated by a document which is in standard form and which is expressed to be one of a series ranking equally, regardless of the date of issue, with others of the same series. The individual debenture, issued under the company seal, provides for the repayment of the principal sum at a specified or determinable date, and for the payment of interest half-yearly on specified dates at a specified rate. Then follow the conditions on which the loan is made.

The conditions cover such matters as the series of which this debenture is one; the principle that all holders of debentures of the series rank pari passu; a register of debenture holders is to be maintained; the company is not bound to recognise any one except a registered holder as having title to the debenture nor to receive any notice of a trust for entry on the register; provisions for transfer of the debenture; the holder for the time being is not to be affected in his dealings with the company by any 'equities', ie adverse rights of the company against a previous holder; the principal and interest are to be repayable at the registered office or some other specified place; the company is to have the right to purchase any debenture; the circumstances of default on the happening of which the principal sum is immediately to be repayable.

The specified circumstances of default usually include default in payment of interest for a specified period after it falls due, commencement of winding up the company and action taken to enforce any security created by the debenture.

Since the individual debenture holders have equal rights it is reasonable that they should be subject to co-ordination in the exercise of their rights. An individual debenture holder's action against the company is usually treated as a representative action on behalf of all and for the benefit of all. This problem may be anticipated and resolved by including a standard condition in every debenture of the series whereby only the holders of a majority in value can enforce any security obtained, by appointing a receiver and a similar majority is empowered to approve modifications of the terms of the debenture which are then binding on all debenture holders.

The need for co-ordination may alternatively be met by appointing a trustee for the debenture holders who is required and authorised by the trust deed to represent the interests of them all (see 9.5 below). But the debenture holders are still treated as individual lenders to the company in their own right. In all other respects, however, the effect of a trust deed is similar to that described below in connection with debenture stock.

9.5 Debenture stock

When loan capital is raised from a considerable number of individual subscribers it is the convenient and standard modern practice to treat it as a single loan to which subscribers contribute and in which they have an interest corresponding to their contributions. This secured debenture or unsecured loan stock, as the case may be, is transferable (and therefore divisible in terms of ownership) in units of, for example, £10 or £100. The registered holders of the stock receive their half-yearly interest payments and eventually the repayment of their capital direct from the company. But they are not the creditors of the company and cannot bring legal proceedings (as holders of separate debentures may) in their own name.

Throughout this book references to 'debentures' and 'debenture holders' include debenture stock and debenture stockholders unless the context distinguishes between them. Similarly references to conditions on which debentures are issued include the conditions contained in a debenture trust deed, if any.

In the case of a substantial issue of debenture stock it is usual for the company first to arrange with a financial institution, eg a bank, an insurance company or one of the companies which specialise in this work, to agree to accept appointment as trustee. The standing of the trustee is the essential guarantee that proper safeguards for the future debenture stockholders will be secured. The trustee designate instructs its legal advisers in consultation with the company's advisers to settle the terms of the trust deed. An elaborate standard draft deed, which embodies the hard-learnt experience of the past, is adapted to the particular circumstances of the case. The object of the trustee designate is to impose the strictest safeguards. The company on its side aims to retain reasonable flexibility in the conduct and organisation of its business.

The essential elements of a debenture trust deed are:

(a) the appointment of the first trustee by the company. Power is reserved to the debenture stockholders to appoint a different trustee if ever they wish to do so;

(b) a covenant by the company to repay the amount of the debenture stock and to pay interest usually at fixed half-yearly intervals meanwhile. The deed may provide for further borrowings but imposes an overall limit on the total amount of the stock;

(c) if the stock is secured the company (and usually its principal subsidiaries as guarantors) grants to the trustee a fixed charge on assets such as land and buildings and creates a floating charge over the general undertaking and assets of each company. If the stock is unsecured the trust deed imposes a prohibition against the creation of charges in favour of other creditors;

(d) a clause which specifies the events in which the security becomes enforceable, such as default in payment of interest or repayment of the principal of the debenture stock, commencement of winding up, appointment of a receiver, cessation of business, breach of the conditions of the trust deed by the company. If it is an unsecured loan stock the clause may provide that the principal money is to become immediately repayable on the happening of any of these events. There may also be commercial covenants by which the company undertakes to maintain its profits at a specified level above the annual interest payable on the stock and its net assets at some multiple of the loan stock or to keep its overall borrowings within some specified limit. If these conditions are not satisfied the capital becomes immediately repayable;

(e) the trustee is given express powers to enforce any security given, when it becomes enforceable, eg by taking possession of assets charged or appointing a receiver. In any such case assets may be realised and the proceeds applied in repayment of the principal sum with interest; any surplus is to be paid to the company;

(f) additional clauses and schedules provide for such matters as the trustee's remuneration, the power to the trustee to consent to minor modification of the terms of the trust deed, holding meetings of debenture stockholders which are empowered (usually by passing an extraordinary resolution) to take decisions binding on all debenture stockholders, covenants by the company to insure its property and not to make substantial disposals of assets without the consent of the trustee, the keeping of a register of debenture stockholders, procedure for transfer of holdings of debenture stock and the issue of certificates to debenture stockholders;

(g) as with registered debentures it is expressly provided that the company deals with the registered debenture stockholder as the owner of the stock registered in his name, ie 'equities' between the company and any other previous holder and any rights of third parties are excluded (but see 9.9 and 9.10 below).

The principal advantage of a debenture trust deed is that any security by way of charge over the company's assets is vested in the trustee. It would not be practicable to grant such security to a large and constantly changing body of debenture stockholders. Secondly, the trustee is given precise powers and duties to protect the interests of the debenture stockholders and the events are specified in which their rights may be enforced against the company. A considerable number of restrictions and obligations are imposed on the company to safeguard the lenders even in the case of an unsecured loan stock.

The company on its side finds it convenient to deal with a single representative of the debenture stockholders. The trustee is not usually authorised to consent on their behalf to any but technical or minor changes. But there is provision for calling meetings of debenture stockholders at which their approval can be sought for more significant changes.

The system expressed in the trust deed recognises that there is a continuing relationship between the company and its debenture holders. The latter need flexible and effective safeguards which can be operated in the changing circumstances of the company over the period of years before the capital money is repaid. The company can through the trustee obtain sensible remissions, eg the substitution of new assets as security in place of obsolete equipment or buildings which are sold, in order to carry on the business profitably to the common advantage of shareholders as proprietors and debenture holders as creditors.

9.6 Convertible debentures
A debenture may be issued with the right at the debenture holder's option to convert it into ordinary shares at a prescribed issue price and usually at

specified conversion dates. The investor who wishes to have the status of a creditor at the outset may then later become a shareholder on advantageous terms if he deems it worthwhile.

The exercise of the option to convert a convertible debenture is in legal terms two transactions, ie a repayment of a loan and the immediate application of the money then due to debenture holders in paying up shares to be allotted to them instead. A return of allotment of shares for cash must be delivered to the registrar.

Since a convertible debenture offers an indirect opportunity of obtaining shares certain rules which apply to the issue of shares extend to convertible debentures also. The directors need the same authority to issue convertible debentures and the same rules of pre-emption apply: ss 80 and 89. Secondly, a convertible debenture issued at a discount, say £80 cash for £100 nominal, with an immediate right of conversion into shares at par, would enable the allottee to obtain £100 (nominal) in shares for £80 cash. It has been held that such a device is illegal as a means of issuing shares at a discount.

The facts of the case are as given above. In deciding that an issue on those terms was illegal the court placed much emphasis on the fact that the debentures carried an *immediate* right of conversion into shares (on the 80/100 basis): *Mosely v Koffyfontein Mines Ltd* [1911] 1 Ch 73.

The essence of the *Mosely* decision was that convertible debentures are not to be used as a device for achieving the issue of shares at a discount. In normal circumstances, however, the option to convert is not exercisable until some years after the issue of the debentures; the court expressly reserved the question whether a *deferred* right to convert at a discount (on the nominal value of the shares) would be found illegal. In modern practice the terms of conversion are usually so devised that there is no possibility of obtaining less for the shares than their nominal value. The £1 debenture, if issued at a price of say 75p, carries a right to convert into shares at a premium, e g £1.50 per £1 share; hence it takes 3 debentures, costing £2.25 in cash, to obtain two £1 shares (valued at £3). The effect of the conversion (in this example) is that the company redeems £3 of debt and issues £2 in share capital, for which in cash it has received 25p more than their nominal value; there is no issue of shares at a discount.

9.7 Bearer debentures
There are statutory rules for the register of debenture holders when it exists (9.9 below) but no legal requirement that there shall be a register: s 190. It is possible to issue debentures expressed to be transferable merely by delivery. In this case, as with share warrants, there are coupons attached to the debenture which are cut off and presented to the company on successive interest payment dates to claim payment of interest when due. Bearer debentures are negotiable instruments which the company undertakes to redeem at the due date from the holders when they present them.

B TRANSACTIONS AND DEALINGS IN DEBENTURES

9.8 Issue of debentures
Debentures or debenture stock are issued to borrow loan capital (or to secure an existing debt). As the exercise of the company's borrowing powers is

usually delegated to the directors they must approve the issue of debentures
and usually authorise them to be issued under the common seal. If it is an issue
to the public, the prospectus rules apply (Chapter 6) and so do the rules
(6.10–6.11) on opening of the subscription lists and obtaining a Stock
Exchange listing. But the minimum subscription rule (6.9) does not apply to
an issue of debentures. In making an issue of debenture stock to the public a
company usually follows the same procedure, eg the use of renounceable
letters of allotment, as in an issue of shares.

Whether it is a large issue of debenture stock to numerous subscribers or a
single debenture issued to one lender such as a bank, or some intermediate
type, the debentures create and provide evidence of contract by which the
company borrows money. The contract is subject to the same general
principles as apply to determine the validity of any contract made by the
company. These are explained elsewhere (Chapter 13: 13.5). By special
statutory provision a preliminary contract with a company to take up and pay
for debentures may be enforced by an order for specific performance: s 195. If
the debenture is secured by a charge on land the contract relates to an interest
in land and is unenforceable unless there is the written evidence required in
such a case. The prospective subscribers' written applications usually provide
that evidence.

A debenture holder is entitled to receive his debenture (or debenture stock
certificate) within two months of the date of allotment unless the issue
otherwise provides: s 185. He also has a statutory right on payment of a fee to
obtain a copy of any debenture trust deed: s 191. His right to inspect the
register (if any) of debenture holders and to obtain a copy has been explained
(Chapter 3: 3.10).

There is no objection to the issue of debentures at a discount unless this is
used to circumvent the rules against issue of shares at a discount (9.6 above). If
any commission is paid or allowance or discount is given to any person in
consideration of his subscribing or procuring subscriptions for debentures,
particulars of the amount or rate must be sent to the registrar within 21 days:
s 397(2). Similar information must also be given in the next annual return:
Sch 15 para 3(h).

A company may issue debentures on condition that they shall be repaid at a
premium, eg £100 (nominal) issued in exchange for £100 cash but with an
obligation to pay £105 to the holder on redemption. The premium must
usually be included in any calculation of actual borrowings compared with the
amount which the directors are authorised to borrow. On redemption at a
premium the premium may be provided out of share premium account or out
of profit: s 130(2).

9.9 Transfer of debentures

Except where a single debenture is issued (or debentures in bearer form) the
conditions of the debenture or debenture stock usually impose on the company
a contractual obligation to maintain a register of debenture holders to
facilitate proof of ownership and also transfer of debentures. Although the
Companies Act does not impose on a company an obligation to maintain a
register of debenture holders it does contain rules for such a register if it exists.

Where there is a register it must be held at the registered office or other place
in England (for an English company) of which notice has been given to the

registrar: s 190. There is a public right to inspect the register and to have a copy: s 191.

Whether or not the company maintains a formal register of debenture holders it may not register, ie record in its books, a transfer of debentures, unless a written instrument of transfer has been presented: s 183. In most cases the same procedure is followed as for a transfer of shares (Chapter 7: 7.17). The transferor executes a transfer in the standard form introduced by the Stock Transfer Act 1963 and delivers it to the transferee together with the debenture or, as the case may be, debenture stock certificate. The transferee has the transfer stamped and delivers it for registration with the debenture or debenture stock certificate. The company registers the transfer and issues a new certificate or returns the debenture with an indorsement recording the change of registered holder. On the death of a holder his personal representatives must establish their title to the debenture as with any other asset of the deceased. A bearer debenture is transferred by delivery.

The transfer of a debenture is an assignment of a chose in action which, under normal principles of law, gives to the new holder no better rights than his transferor had. To safeguard the transferee it is usual to include in the conditions applicable to the debenture a stipulation that:

(a) the registered holder will be regarded as exclusively entitled to the benefit of the debenture and all persons may act accordingly:
(b) principal moneys and interest will be paid without regard to any equities between the company and the original or any intermediate holder or to any right of set-off or counterclaim.

The practical effect of these rather complicated clauses is fairly straightforward. Under (a) the holder of a registered debenture is assured that, once he is on the register, the company cannot challenge his title. A third party who makes a claim to his registered debenture cannot be disqualified by the terms of a contract between the holder and the company. But the third party will have to establish his claim in proceedings against the holder in which the company is not concerned.

The effect of (b) is that if the company was a creditor of a previous registered holder, it may not set off that debt against the present holder: *Re Rhodesia Goldfields Ltd* [1910] 1 Ch 239, where the company's claim on this basis failed.

9.10 Third party claims
The prohibition against entering in the register of members notice of a trust (Chapter 8: 8.11) is limited to shares and does not extend, as a statutory rule, to debentures. However the conditions of a debenture usually include that prohibition as a contractual term.

The conditions also provide that the receipt of the registered holder of a debenture, for interest or capital paid to him, shall be a good discharge to the company of its liability to make that payment.

It is possible to obtain a stop notice in respect of a debenture with the same effect as when a stop notice is issued in respect of shares (Chapter 8: 8.12).

9.11 Redemption of debentures
The date (if any) on which the company may redeem its debentures or the holder of a debenture is entitled on his side to repayment of the principal of the debt is specified in the debenture as a term of the loan contract.

The company may, however, borrow for a long period of years without the right to repay the loan during that period or may issue irredeemable debentures with no specified date for repayment. (See *Knightsbridge Case* in 9.3 above on long-term debentures secured by a mortgage).

Debentures which have no date for repayment or a repayment date which has not yet arrived nonetheless become immediately due for repayment if the company makes default, eg in payment of interest, since it is then in breach of the loan contract, or if the company goes into liquidation since in that event it is the duty of the liquidator to discharge all debts out of available assets before making a return of capital to shareholders.

Irredeemable or perpetual debentures are much less common than debentures due for repayment at a specified date or at a date to be selected by the company within a specified period.

The company may intend to raise a new loan to finance the repayment of the debentures. But to provide a safeguard against default the debentures may require the company to establish a sinking fund and to appropriate a fixed amount each year for transfer into the sinking fund for the eventual redemption of the debentures. In that case debenture holders have no right (unless it is expressly so agreed) to have their debentures redeemed out of moneys available in the sinking fund before the due date for redemption arrives. It is also common to provide that the company may discharge its sinking fund obligation in any year by purchasing its debentures (or equivalent amount) in the market for cancellation. In a period of high interest rates the debentures may be obtained by purchase in the market at a price well below their nominal amount.

Another possible method of progressive redemption, for which the conditions of the debentures may provide, is selective redemption by drawing lots or by inviting debenture holders to tender (with acceptance by the company of those debentures tendered for repayment at the lowest price).

Although the right to redeem may be postponed indefinitely or for a long period of years general mortgage law requires that the right of redemption of a secured debenture shall not be 'clogged' by the imposition of some advantage to the debenture holder which is considered harsh or unconscionable. But this principle does not prohibit the grant by the company to the debenture holder of an advantage distinct from his right to repayment even if that advantage is to continue after repayment. The test is whether it is a fair commercial bargain.

The debenture was for a period of five years but with the option to the company to repay before the expiry of the period. It was secured by a floating charge. In addition the debenture holder was given the right for five years, whether or not the debenture was outstanding, to purchase at an agreed price the by-product (sheepskins) of the company's meat canning business. It was held that there was no rule which precluded the grant to a mortgagee of a collateral advantage of this kind continuing after repayment. It was simply a question whether the condition was unfair or designed to fetter the company's freedom to redeem: *Kreglinger v New Patagonia Meat and Cold Storage Co Ltd* [1914] AC 25.

On the other hand, in a case where the commercial advantage to the mortgagee was to continue 'always hereafter', the term was void as repugnant to the mortgagor's equity of redemption: *Bradley v Carritt* [1903] AC 253 (not a company law case but it serves to illustrate mortgage law applicable to companies).

Debentures which have been redeemed may be reissued (on the same terms as applied on the original issue) unless either the articles or any contract, i e the conditions of the debenture, forbid it or the company by resolution of its directors or otherwise has cancelled the redeemed debentures: s 194.

A company may deposit its debentures with a lender such as a bank as security for amounts owing from time to time on current account. The deposit is an issue of the debentures. But they are not redeemed and then reissued if the company's account moves temporarily into credit and then back into debit in the lender's books: s 194(3).

Particulars of any redeemed debentures which the company has power to reissue must be included in the annual balance sheet: Sch 4 para 41(2).

C CHARGES

9.12 Fixed and floating charges

A fixed charge attaches to identified property at the time of the creation of the charge (or in the case of property not yet created or acquired when it becomes the company's property). Thereafter the company cannot deal with the property except subject to the charge. If the charge is properly registered (when registration is necessary) it takes priority over the claims of any other person to the same property.

A fixed charge is in the nature of a mortgage. It is a suitable and convenient method of giving security over fixed assets such as land, buildings or plant which the company is likely to retain for a considerable period.

A floating charge is an immediate security (and must therefore be registered within 21 days of creation: s 395). But it does not immediately attach to specific property but only later when the charge 'crystallizes'. A floating charge is appropriate where the property subject to it is current assets such as materials and stock in trade or trade debts which are disposed of and replaced by the company in the course of carrying on its business. Indeed a company could not trade without this power to dispose of current assets free of the incumbrance of a floating charge.

The floating charge may be described either as an immediate charge with a licence to the company to deal freely with the assets subject to the floating charge or as an immediate charge on future assets existing at the moment of crystallization. In many respects it does not matter which of the two alternative bases (the licence theory and the mortgage of future assets theory) is preferred. But it is material to the 'automatic crystallization' issue which is explained below.

Although a floating charge is by its nature appropriate to forming a general security over the current assets of a company, it is not restricted to assets of that category. A floating charge over 'all the property' of the company covers its fixed as well as its current assets.

Charges may be – and usually are – created by express words such as 'the company hereby charges by way of legal mortgage [specified] property and by way of floating charge its undertaking and all its other assets'. A formula of this type extends the floating charge to all assets including fixed assets. But any form of words which creates a charge 'ambulatory and shifting in its nature', i e which leaves the company free to deal with assets free of any immediate incumbrance is a floating charge. It has been said that the characteristics of a floating charge are that:

(a) it is a charge on a class of assets of the company present and future; and
(b) the class is one which in the ordinary course of business of the company would be changing from time to time; and
(c) the company is free to dispose of its assets of that class in the course of carrying on its business in the usual way.

This celebrated formulation was laid down in *Re Yorkshire Woolcombers Association Ltd* (confirmed in the House of Lords as *Illingworth v Houldsworth* [1904] AC 355 – the facts are not material). Recent decisions (9.14 below) on retention of title to goods until the price is paid ('Romalpa clauses') have incidentally illustrated the point that a floating charge can exist if the above conditions are met, even though no words are used to indicate an intention to create such a charge. A retention of title clause which is invalid as such, is often deemed, by its wording, to be a floating charge.

Goods were supplied under a contract which provided that the purchaser company might resell them or use them in manufacture. But until the full price had been paid the supplier was to retain *beneficial* ownership of the goods or the proceeds of sale. It was held that by implication *legal* ownership passed to the company at once and the supplier's rights amounted to a floating charge on the goods or sale proceeds; the charge was void as it had not been registered (9.19): *Re Bond Worth Ltd* [1980] Ch 228.

It is still a floating charge even if it is confined to assets of a particular class such as trade debts. The expression 'undertaking' (or 'property' or 'estate') brings within the charge all assets, fixed or current, of the company, but subject to any fixed charges existing or created thereafter with priority over the floating charge. If it is intended to charge the uncalled capital on partly paid shares this must be expressly stated since uncalled capital is not property (see 9.2 above).

9.13 Crystallization of a floating charge
The intention of a floating charge is that the company should be left free to deal with its property, unencumbered by the charge, for the purpose of carrying on its business in the ordinary course. Yet, at the appropriate time, the charge crystallizes, ie it becomes a fixed charge attaching to all the assets of the company, of the categories subject to the floating charge, which the company owns at the moment of crystallization.

It is generally accepted that crystallization occurs in any of the following circumstances:

(a) if the company goes into liquidation; or
(b) if a receiver is appointed (or presumably an administrator – see Chapter 10: 10.11); or
(c) if the company ceases to carry on business.

The common characteristics of these three events is that the company thereby ceases to carry on its business under its normal arrangements and each event is an ascertainable change in the company's situation, which creditors can discover. Ceasing to carry on business however may result informally rather than by a public declaration.

From a standpoint of a bank or other lender, to which a floating charge is most often given, the drawback of a floating charge (apart from some other features mentioned in 9.14 below) is that until crystallization the company is free to create fixed charges over valuable property, which if certain conditions are satisfied (9.14) take priority over the floating charge at the time when that charge crystallizes.

In an attempt to prevent the loss of priority in this way, lenders may include in the terms of the floating charge a condition whereby crystallization is to occur *automatically* at the moment before the company creates any other charge which would otherwise take priority over the floating charge. The validity of 'automatic crystallization' is well recognised in the legal systems of Australia and New Zealand. There are judicial dicta in its favour but no clear-cut recognition of its validity in English law. The Cork Report recommended that legislation should make it clear that only liquidation or receivership could cause a floating charge to crystallize. But any action of this point awaits the outcome of a current review of company charges generally.

There are practical arguments against automatic crystallization. For example, the holder of the floating charge will be unaware of the change in the nature of his security. In view of its potentially damaging effect on the debtor company's commercial activities, he might prefer to waive his right to a fixed charge on all its assets. But, as it is automatic, he cannot do so. There are also objections of principle.

One of those objections is that it should not be left open to the company and a secured creditor to settle by private agreement how the charge is to crystallize. Yet it now appears (*Re Brightlife Ltd* [1986] 3 All ER 673) that they are entitled to do so. In the *Brightlife Case* the floating charge contained a clause by which the creditor might serve notice on the company requiring that the floating charge should become a fixed charge. The purpose of this clause was to enable the creditor to obtain a fixed charge which would take priority (as regards the company's book debts) over the claims of preferential unsecured creditors. Preferential debts rank before a floating charge (Chapter 20: 20.9).

It has been suggested that the holder of a floating charge who claims that his charge has crystallized, whether by his action or some other event, should be required to give notice to the registrar, under penalty of losing his claim to the priority given by a fixed charge (crystallized floating charge) if he failed to do so. That would relieve the problems raised by the *Brightlife* decision. But the Cork Committee felt that it was insufficiently radical in its approach to crystallization in general.

Yet another device to circumvent the inherent weaknesses of the floating charge is the recent development of the practice of creating fixed charges over book debts, although these are current not fixed assets. The sums owing to an insolvent company by its debtors are often the most valuable and easily realisable part of its remaining assets. This practice too is debatable (see 9.17 below).

The whole situation as regards charges on company property is in a state of flux, and indeed of confusion. The creditor who takes a floating charge under the present rules will often achieve the desired priority over other creditors. But he needs to be alert and to take every precaution. These are topics considered further in the sections which follow.

9.14 Priority obtained by a floating charge

The holder of a floating charge is subject to major uncertainties. First, there is the commercial risk that when his charge crystallizes the remaining assets, to which the charge then attaches, will be much less in value than when the charge was created.

His other main problem is that he may not obtain the priority over other debtors which he relies on, in taking a floating charge. The device of 'automatic crystallization' is uncertain in its effect. The more conventional alternative is to include in the floating charge a prohibition against the creation by the company of subsequent charges with priority over his own. If the company nonetheless does so, it is a breach of contract by the company but it does not prevent the holder of a subsequent *legal* charge (equitable charges are discussed later) from obtaining priority if he has no notice of the prohibition. Under general principles of property law a purchaser for value (including a mortgagee) of a legal estate or interest is not affected by prior equities of which he has no notice, actual or constructive, when his charge is created.

If a floating charge includes a prohibition on the company against creating charges with priority over the floating charges (sometimes called 'a negative pledge clause') it is standard practice, though not legally necessary, to include particulars of the prohibition in the summary of the floating charge which is delivered to the registry, when the charge is registered under s 395 (9.17 below).

Information of the prohibition is then on the file at the registry open to public inspection. It is generally considered that, as this information is not one of the prescribed points for inclusion in the summary (Form 395), its actual presence does not constitute *constructive* notice to anyone who takes a subsequent legal charge on the same assets in ignorance of the prohibition. However, in practice a creditor, before taking any charge on a company's assets, would make a search at the registry as a routine precaution. If he does so he has actual notice of the prohibition since he finds it on the file.

In 1901 the company issued debentures secured by a floating charge and containing a prohibition on creation of charges ranking in priority to it. The charge was duly registered as required by what is now s 395. In 1905 the company purchased property and gave a charge over it to the vendors to secure the unpaid balance of the purchase price. The vendors were unaware of the floating charge (and of the prohibition which it imposed) and did not make a search at the registry. In 1906 the company granted a second mortgage over the same property to the plaintiff who had also acquired the first mortgage. The plaintiff who was chairman of the company was aware of the floating charge and of the prohibition in it. It was held that the 1905 charge, accepted in ignorance of the prohibition in the floating charge, took priority over it. But the 1906 charge given to a person who then had actual notice of the prohibition in the floating charge ranked after it: *Wilson v Kelland* [1910] 2 Ch 306. (To avoid misunderstanding registration always gives constructive notice of the existence of the charge and of those of its terms, such as the property charged, which it is legally obligatory to register under s 395).

The solicitor acting for the lenders to whom the fixed charge was granted knew of the floating charge but in making enquiries did not ask about the possibility of a prohibition affecting his clients' charge. He had acted honestly. It was held that his clients were not affected by the prohibition: *English and Scottish Mercantile Investment Co Ltd v Brunton* [1892] 2 QB 700.

If the subsequent charge is another floating charge or if it is an equitable not a legal fixed charge, then under general equitable principles the existing floating charge retains its priority since it was created first. There are however exceptions.

The company had created a floating charge (at a time when registration of company charges was not yet compulsory). Later it gave an equitable mortgage by deposit of title deeds to another person. The latter charge took priority over the floating charge, of which he was unaware, because the holder of the floating charge had left the title deeds in the hands of the company, contrary to normal practice, and had thereby led him to assume that there was no prior charge on the property comprised in the deeds: *Re Castell and Brown Ltd* [1898] 1 Ch 315.

A first floating charge on all assets of the company expressly permitted the company to create subsequent charges on assets with priority over the floating charge. A second floating charge on one class of assets only then took priority: *Re Automatic Bottle Makers* [1926] Ch 412.

Apart from the possibility of being postponed to a subsequent fixed charge over the same property the holder of a floating charge may lose his security before crystallization in any of the following circumstances:

(a) the company is free to sell the property since the floating charge does not yet attach to it;
(b) a judgment creditor may obtain execution of his judgment by seizure of the company's property by the sheriff followed by sale or receive payment of the debt by the company to avoid sale or the making of a garnishee order absolute. It is essential in any such case that the action shall have been completed before the floating charge crystallizes (automatically or otherwise);
(c) a landlord may levy distress for rent;
(d) a debtor of the company may set off a sum owed by the company to him against his debt to the company;
(e) a creditor of the company may obtain a lien on its property in his possession;
(f) if the company is in receivership or liquidation its preferential unsecured debts, mainly arrears of wages, take priority over a floating charge (Chapter 20: 20.9).

The holder of a floating charge which has crystallized can only enforce his charge against property of the company. He may find that fixed assets in use in the company's business are held under hire-purchase or hire agreements and belong to third parties. He may also find that goods have been supplied to the company under contracts by which the ownership of the goods remains with the supplier until his entire debt is paid. Moreover the contract may also provide that if the company resells the goods it is to hold the proceeds of sale in trust for the unpaid supplier and that if it consumes the goods in the course of manufacture the unpaid supplier is to have some claim to the resultant product. The general effectiveness of clauses of this kind was upheld in *Aluminium Industrie Vaassen BV v Romalpa Aluminium Ltd* [1976] 2 All ER 552. The same conclusion was reached when the Court of Appeal reviewed the law in *Clough Mill Ltd v Martin* [1984] 3 All ER 982. There are pitfalls to avoid (see *Bond Worth Case* in 9.12 above) and claims to goods which have been converted in the course of manufacture are difficult to enforce. But these are not problems of company law.

9.15 Validity of charges
A charge becomes invalid (though the debt which it secures is still owing by the company) in any of the following circumstances:

(a) charges of nine classes created by a company become void for certain purposes unless registered within 21 days of creation: s 396 (9.16 below);
(b) a floating charge over the undertaking or property of the company created within 12 months of the commencement of winding up becomes invalid subject to certain exceptions: IA s 245;
(c) a fixed or floating charge, like some other transactions of a company effected within six months before the commencement of winding up, may become invalid as a preference or a transaction at an undervalue (Chapter 20: 20.14–16): IA ss 238–241.

These provisions also apply if the company becomes subject to an administration order (Chapter 10: 10.11) and the periods mentioned in (b) and (c) may be extended in certain cases.

9.16 Registration of charges

To safeguard existing or prospective creditors a company is required to register charges over its property as follows:

(a) when any charges of specified types are created by a company or it acquires property already subject to any such charge, the company is required to register the charge at the registry. Failure to register such a charge if *created* by the company renders the charge void against the liquidator or administrator and any creditor: s 395;
(b) a limited company is required to enter in a register of charges kept at its registered office particulars of all charges, fixed or floating, over its undertaking or property and also to keep there a copy of every instrument (or a specimen copy in the case of a series of uniform debentures). Any person may inspect the register and a member or creditor may inspect the copy charges: ss 406–7.

There are penalties for failure to conform to these requirements. Registration of charges created by the company is perhaps more important since failure to register may prejudice the interests of the creditors who wished to be secured by the charges.

9.17 Charges created by a company which must be registered

A company is required to register any charge which it may create over its property in the following classes:

(a) a charge to secure an issue of debentures;
(b) a charge on the uncalled capital;
(c) a charge which if created by an individual would require registration as a bill of sale;
(d) a charge on land (other than a rentcharge);
(e) a charge on the book debts of the company;
(f) a floating charge on the company's undertaking or property;
(g) a charge on calls made but not paid;
(h) a charge on a ship or aircraft, or a share therein;
(i) a charge on goodwill, a patent or licence under a patent, on a trademark, a copyright or a licence thereunder: s 396.

Although not expressly excluded a charge on the share capital of the company's subsidiaries and on some commercial documents, such as bills of lading, deposited as security for short-term loans in the course of business apparently do not fall in any of these categories. Classes (a) and (f) have a very wide effect.

A company is not required to register a charge arising by operation of law, eg if it buys land and the vendor retains the title deeds (vendor's lien) as security for payment of the price. If the company acquires property already subject to a charge created by a previous owner it is required to register it, but the consequences of any failure to do so are different: s 400. In that case, unlike an unregistered charge created by the company, the charge remains valid (see 9.18 below). A charge on company land may also have to be registered as a land charge at the appropriate land registry.

A charge requires registration even though it is an equitable charge created informally by deposit of title documents.

A company paid one-quarter of the purchase price of land and granted to the vendor a mortgage to secure the payment of the balance. The vendor retained possession of the title deeds. The mortgage was not registered. It was held that the vendor's common law lien was terminated on the part payment of the purchase price and grant of the mortgage since this security was what the vendor under the contract agreed to accept. The vendor's contention that the charge (by retention of title deeds) was created before the company acquired the property and so was registrable under s 400 (and therefore not void for lack of registration) was rejected: *Capital Finance Co Ltd v Stokes* [1968] 3 All ER 625.

In such circumstances the vendor loses his common law lien and must surrender the title deeds: *Re Wallis & Simmonds (Builders) Ltd* [1974] 1 All ER 561.

An outright assignment, ie transfer of ownership, of book debts is a sale not a charge. But an arrangement by which a creditor may collect book debts of the company and recover his debt from the proceeds is a registrable charge.

The company obtained a bank loan to be repaid out of payments to be made by trade debtors. As part of the arrangement the company wrote to its customers requesting them to pay the company's bills direct to the bank. This instruction was not to be revoked without the bank's consent. This was held to be a registrable charge over future book debts since the purpose and effect was to give to the bank the right to recover its loan from these payments: *Re Kent and Sussex Sawmills Ltd* [1947] Ch 177.

It is possible to create a fixed charge, which requires registration, on a future book debt by providing that it shall be paid to the company's creditor, such as a bank, giving to the creditor complete control of it: *Siebe Gorman & Co Ltd v Barclays Bank Ltd* [1979] 2 Lloyd's Rep 142.

A security by way of third party guarantee, as when directors guarantee the company's bank overdraft, is not registrable since it is not a charge on company property nor is it created by the company.

9.18 Registration rules and procedure

To register a charge, the company should present the *original* charge (not a copy) to the registrar with prescribed particulars (Form 395) of the property charged, the amount secured, and the name of the person entitled to the charge, plus the date of its creation. This must be done within 21 days of creation of the charge.

The registrar inspects the charge – but not in detail – and returns it with his certificate of registration (see 9.21 below as to its effect). He places the particulars (Form 395) on the company's file and notes in an index at the back of the file that the charge is registered therein.

Anyone may inspect the file and will thereby discover that the charge exists and has been registered, together with brief particulars of its scope. If a creditor or member wishes to see the charge itself he may inspect it at the registered office: s 408 (Chapter 3: 3.10). Any person dealing with the company has constructive notice of the existence of the charge, if duly registered, and of the required particulars. It is doubtful however whether he has constructive notice of any additional information which the particulars may contain (see 9.14 above on 'negative pledge clauses').

The legal duty to register a charge is placed on the company; the company and its officers are liable to a fine if they default in this duty. However in practice the creditor, to whom the charge is given, usually attends to the registration, to ensure that it is done within the 21 days. This discharges the company's legal obligation of registration: s 399.

9.19 The time allowed for registration of charges

The period of 21 days for registration runs from the time when the charge is created and not, if it is different, from the time when the loan is made which the charge secures.

If therefore the charge is given to secure an existing loan, the 21 days runs from the date of the charge. If on the other hand the charge is given to secure future loans, which are not made until some interval has elapsed, the charge must still be registered within 21 days of its creation.

If a charge is given to secure debentures issued as a series, it is a single security. The issue of further debentures in the same series does not require a second registration.

The property charged is an essential part of the charge. If new property is added to the charge, either by way of addition or substitution for property released, the change does require registration of the new security, unless the original charge is expressed, as is often the case, to be a charge on the original property and all subsequent property charged under it.

By a debenture trust deed executed in 1903 and duly registered, the company created a charge on its fleet of ships. In 1904, 1905 and 1907 the company gave specific charges on new vessels, as required by the trust deed. It was held that these did not require registration: *Cunard SS Co Ltd v Hopwood* [1908] 2 Ch 564.

The charge, which requires registration, may be created informally, as when title deeds or share certificates are deposited to create an equitable charge over them. The 21 days runs from the date of deposit when the charge is effectually created (see the *Wallis and Simmonds Case* in 9.17 above).

The process of registration must be completed within the 21 days allowed.

The particulars (now Form 395) lodged with the charge for registration were defective and the registrar returned them for correction. The corrected form was redelivered to the registrar after the 21 days from the creation of the charge had expired. Under his practice at that time the registrar registered the charge. His decision to do so could not be overruled (see 9.21 below) but the Court of Appeal considered that the registrar's practice in such cases was incorrect. The registrar has now altered his practice and will no longer accept for registration corrected documents, redelivered after the 21-day period has expired: *R v Registrar of Companies, ex p Central Bank of India* [1986] 1 All ER 105.

If a charge, requiring registration under s 395, is not registered within 21 days of its creation (or such longer period as the court may allow – see below):

(a) it becomes void against the liquidator, administrator or a creditor of the company; and

(b) the loan secured by the charge becomes immediately repayable by the company. For example, a secured loan given for a period of five years may be called in by the lender at once, if the charge has not been registered within the 21 days.

The effect is that the charge may still be enforced by the holder against the company, eg by appointing a receiver. But if another creditor obtains judgment against the company for debt and seizes the property subject to the charge in execution of his judgment, or if a liquidator or administrator is appointed, the holder of the charge has no priority against them. He is still a creditor and may take normal steps to claim his debt as if he were an unsecured creditor.

The holder of an unregistered charge may apply to the court for an order permitting the registration of the charge out of time: s 404. The reasons, accident or inadvertence etc, must be given. If the court is satisfied that it was an honest mistake or oversight and not deliberate concealment of the charge, it will make an order, unless of course the company has meanwhile gone into liquidation or become subject to an administration order, or either event is impending.

In sanctioning late registration the court may impose such conditions as it deems 'just and expedient'. Normally it will not deprive another person, such as the holder of a subsequent charge which has been duly registered meanwhile, of his priority over the unregistered charge.

However the holder of a charge which is registered out of time under s 404 will be permitted to regain his priority over a subsequent charge, if the later charge was created within 21 days of his unregistered charge and was expressed to rank after it.

At the time when the two charges were created the second charge by its express terms ranked after the first. This situation continued during the 21-day period allowed for registration. During that period the holder of the second charge registered it but this did not alter his position vis-à-vis the first charge since the latter, if registered later but within the 21-day period, would have retained its priority. When the 21-day period for registration of both charges expired the rights attached to the second charge continued but no new rights were created for it after the 21-day period. It is only rights obtained *after* the un-registered charge had become void which are preserved on late registration: *Watson v Duff Morgan and Vermont (Holdings) Ltd* [1974] 1 All ER 794 following *Ram Narain v Radha Kishen Moti Lal Chamaria Firm* (1929) LR Ind App 76 (a Privy Council decision).

This decision produces a fair result, since the holder of the second charge well knew that his rights, when created, were intended to rank after those of the first charge (but see the *Monolithic Case* below on this aspect). The objection to the decision is that it adds to the wording of s 395 limitations which Parliament did not impose. In the *Duff Morgan Case* the holder of the second charge also argued that he did in fact acquire rights after the expiry of the 21-day registration period: he had appointed a receiver. But this point was dismissed; the receivership was simply an exercise of powers created under the charge and not an independent right.

Application may also be made for late registration if the company has acquired property subject to an existing charge and failed to register the charge within 21 days of acquiring the property as required by s 400. But this is a less serious situation since the charge remains valid and no question of competing rights of subsequent charges can arise.

As s 395 states explicitly that a charge not registered within 21 days 'is void' it is immaterial that the holder of a subsequent charge knew of the prior unregistered charge by some other means.

The first and second charges over freehold land were unregistered. A third charge was granted to the managing director who well knew of the existing charges. His charge was duly registered. In approving late registration of the first and second charges the court ordered that the third charge must preserve its priority over them. The words of s 395 were categorical: *Re Monolithic Building Co* [1915] 1 Ch 643.

9.20 Clearance of registered charges

When a debt secured by a charge registered at the companies registry is paid off or the property (or some of it) subject to the charge is released from it or is sold by the company, the company may deliver to the registrar a memorandum of satisfaction or part satisfaction of the charge. The memorandum under the common seal of the company must be verified by statutory declaration made by a director and the secretary. In enclosing the memorandum on the file the registrar also notes its effect in the index of charges at the back of the file so that it can readily be seen which charges are outstanding: s 403.

The company has no obligation to clear the registry file of obsolete charges in this way. If a memorandum is delivered which is incorrect the registrar has no practicable means of discovering this error unless the owner of the charge, who has no part in the preparation of the memorandum of satisfaction, objects. The latter is not, however, prejudiced in his rights by the filing of an incorrect memorandum. But the court has power to order that an omission or error be corrected: s 404.

9.21 The effect of a certificate of registration of a charge

The registrar's certificate that a charge has been registered, including the amount of the debt thereby secured, is conclusive evidence that the statutory requirements as to registration have been duly complied with: s 401(2). A copy of the certificate must be endorsed on every relevant debenture or certificate of debenture stock issued by the company. A copy is also enclosed on the registry file.

The system is intended to safeguard the persons, who may be numerous, who subscribe for debentures. The company issues debentures or debenture stock certificates on which the registrar's certificate is endorsed. This is an assurance that the proper registration of the charge cannot thereafter be challenged. Other creditors of the company have the assurance that a search at the registry will disclose secured debts created up to 21 days before the search is made. But from their point of view the system has defects and loopholes.

The certificate is merely conclusive that particulars have been delivered for registration. It does not establish that those particulars are correct (nor is the registrar responsible for verifying them by close examination of the charge – even if he did so there might be additional terms agreed orally and not included in the written instrument of charge). If the particulars delivered are incomplete or misleading as to the property charged or the amount secured by the charge the owner of the charge may nonetheless enforce the charge in accordance with its correct terms.

The 'amount secured' was limited to £18,000 plus sums owing for goods supplied. This additional item (i e cost of goods supplied) was omitted from the registered particulars. The charge was valid, i e treated as duly registered but enforceable to the full extent of the charge. *Re Mechanisations (Eaglescliffe) Ltd* [1966] Ch 20, following *National Provincial and Union Bank of England v Charnley* [1924] 1 KB 431, where the property charged was land and chattels but the filed particulars related only to the land.

The certificate is even conclusive as to the registration of the charge within 21 days of creation when on the true facts it was not registered within that period and should have been void.

An undated charge in favour of a bank was handed to its solicitor so that he might have it registered. But by oversight he failed to attend to this within the 21 days. He then inserted a current date, apparently in the erroneous belief that the charge had in the meanwhile been held in escrow (and so the 21 days had not in his view begun to run). The registrar's certificate of due registration within 21 days was held to be conclusive: *Re C L Nye Ltd* [1970] 3 All ER 1061. This followed an earlier decision on rather similar facts, where it was held that the registrar's certificate was conclusive but the issue of the charge was set aside on other grounds: *Re Eric Holmes (Property) Ltd* [1965] Ch 1052.

In the *Nye Case* (and also in the *Central Bank of India Case* in 9.19 above) the court noted that there was no suggestion of fraud. In the *Holmes Case* there was fraud but it related to the whole transaction and not just to the registration of the charge. In the *Charnley Case* above the court left open the question whether it would treat the registrar's certificate as conclusive if it had been obtained by fraud. In any such case much would depend on the particular facts.

The registrar has no duty to check the accuracy of the information given to him. He could not possibly scrutinise the whole original charge, usually a long and complicated document, to reach his own view of the accuracy and completeness of the accompanying particulars (Form 395) which is all which he retains for enclosure on the company file at the registry.

He does of course consider whether the documents are complete and whether there is an obvious error. If it is a very minor mistake, eg the wrong company number on the Form 395, he might contact the presenter and obtain his consent to making a correction of the document in his possession. In any other case, the registrar returns the documents to the presenter for correction and re-presentation. If they are not returned within 21 days of the creation of the charge, the registrar will refuse to register it. The presenter must then go to the court for an order for late registration under s 404 (9.19).

9.22 The company's register of charges

Every limited company is required to keep at its registered office a register of charges and to enter in it all charges affecting its property: s 407. The particulars to be registered are a description of the property charged, the amount secured by the charge and the names of the persons entitled to it (unless it relates to a bearer debenture). All companies must keep a copy of the instruments (or a specimen copy of debentures issued as a series) by which such charges are created. There is a public right of inspection of the register but only a creditor or member may inspect the copy documents. The company cannot object to the making of his own copy or extracts by the person who inspects the register and related documents but has no obligation to supply a copy: s 408.

If there is default in compliance with these rules the company's officers are liable to a fine and the court may order the company to open its register to inspection. But the charge remains valid in all such cases.

Chapter 10

Company insolvency

10.1 Introduction

In the last edition of this book this chapter was entitled 'Debenture Holders' Remedies'. That is also the main subject considered in this chapter. But recent changes in statute law have served to emphasise that debenture holders as secured creditors operate within the context of wider problems than merely enforcing the security for what is owing to them by the company. Debenture holders are very properly concerned with promoting their own interests but these may best be served by co-operating in measures which preserve the company's undertaking, perhaps reduced in size. They may also seek to assert claims against the directors of an insolvent company if there is evidence that the insolvency is attributable to the incompetence (or worse) of the directors. Hence it is useful to study debenture holders' remedies, which generally come down to putting in a receiver, in a wider context including 'rescue' operations and review of past management performance.

The commonest form of security for a debenture is a floating charge, either created independently or in support of specific charges on fixed assets, on the company's undertaking as a whole. In this situation when the floating charge is enforced by putting in a receiver, he takes charge of the company's business and manages it – unless of course the company ceases to trade before the receivership or in the course of it. The receiver's task is to obtain payment for the secured creditor(s) (whom he represents) of the money owing to him (them). For this purpose he may close down the business and sell off the assets piecemeal, or sell the business and the assets used in it as a going concern, or reorganise the business and improve the standards of management in the hope of restoring it to profitability and thereby to solvency. If the receiver is unable to obtain payment in full of the amount owing to the debenture holders whom he represents (plus the costs and expenses incidental to the receivership), receivership may be followed by liquidation. The temporary administration of an insolvent company by a receiver is then followed by the winding up of the company's affairs and its eventual dissolution. Liquidation is, however, a large subject to which several later chapters are devoted.

The work of a receiver requires personal skill, judgment and integrity of a high order. For that reason it is the well-established practice to appoint as receiver only a member of a profession specialising in insolvency work, typically a professional accountant. In the exceptional cases where it is necessary to invite the court to appoint a receiver, the court would not appoint anyone but a suitably experienced professional. However until 1986 there was no general legal rule which required a debenture holder to appoint such a person. This loophole led to abuse, especially if an unqualified receiver was acting in collusion with some interested party. As will be explained later that loophole has been closed and some additional duties of reporting on the conduct of company directors have been added to the normal duties of an 'insolvency practitioner'.

The wider issues briefly indicated above will return in greater detail in their proper context later in this chapter. First, however, it is necessary to consider the legal rights – the 'debenture holders' remedies' – of a secured creditor of an insolvent company.

10.2 The action which a debenture holder may take

A debenture holder, such as the company's bank, may be the only creditor of his class. He may enforce his rights, whether he is a secured or an unsecured creditor, without regard to other creditors. That is also the position of a trade creditor who has not received payment for goods or services supplied.

The position is different however if there is a series of debentures (Chapter 9: 9.4) or a debenture stock (Chapter 9: 9.5). In these cases the debenture holder is one of a group and – avoiding the technicalities of some conflicting case law – the claims of the group against the company must be enforced on a collective basis so that all benefit from the action which may be taken. When a debenture stock is issued, and sometimes when a series of debentures ranking pari passu is issued, a trustee, usually a corporate body, is appointed to act as representative of the debenture holders; the trustee takes legal action against the company when it is necessary. If however there is no trustee an individual debenture holder who sues the company does so in the form of a representative action on behalf of all debenture holders. Where there is a trust deed it often provides that the trustee may or must take action if so authorised or instructed by a specified fraction (in value) of the debenture holders.

A debenture is simply a document relating to a company liability; it may be secured or unsecured (Chapter 9: 9.3). If it is unsecured the debenture holder has the same rights as any other unsecured creditor, such as a trade creditor whose account has not been paid. Effectively an unsecured debenture holder has three available remedies:

(a) he may sue the company for debt and then 'execute' his judgment by court process which usually entails the seizure and sale of company property or the impounding of a bank credit balance or trade debts due to the company by a 'garnishee order';
(b) he may petition for the compulsory liquidation of the company so that its assets may be applied in payment of its debts generally (Chapter 18);
(c) under a procedure introduced in 1986 (see 10.11 below) he may petition the court for an administration order, which has much the same effect as the appointment of a receiver.

The position of an unsecured debenture holder may differ from that of a trade creditor or an employee whose wages are in arrears in that the latter have a claim for a debt which is already overdue. It is normal, but not inevitable, that a debenture provides for the repayment of money lent, with interest meanwhile, at some future date. A debenture holder cannot sue until money is due to him. But the debenture often stipulates that in various situations of insolvency of the company, such as failure to pay interest on the debenture or seizure of assets by a judgment creditor, the capital amount due under the debenture becomes immediately repayable.

A secured debenture holder, i e one whose claim is supported by a charge on the company's property, may – in addition to the remedies of an unsecured creditor described above – enforce his security. The basic idea of enforcement of a security is that the creditor takes control of the company asset which is his security with the right to obtain repayment from it of the amount owing to him. If it is a revenue-producing asset the income may suffice; if it is saleable it may be necessary to sell it.

Much of the law on enforcement of security is derived from the law of mortgages. When a debenture holder's security is a specific charge on a fixed asset, such as land or buildings, he is simply treated as a mortgagee (see *Knightsbridge Estates Case* in Chapter 9: 9.3). If, however, the security is or includes a floating charge, as is usually the case, the debenture holder must in the first instance assume control of the company's business before he can extract money from it as profits or the proceeds of selling off assets. He has the four recognised remedies of a mortgagee (though he may have to go to the court for its aid in obtaining some of them) – these are sale, taking possession, foreclosure by court order and appointing a receiver. Foreclosure is the transfer by court order of the ownership of the mortgaged property to the mortgagee; the others explain themselves. Immediate sale, foreclosure and taking possession are all, for technical reasons of mortgage law, not satisfactory remedies in the context of insolvency of a trading company.

Hence the standard remedy of the secured debenture holder is to appoint a receiver, i e a financial agent who on his behalf takes control of the company's business and property, or so much of it as is subject to the charge.

10.3 The purpose of receivership

As explained above a receiver's task is to take control and to exercise various powers over the company's property, usually the whole of it, as this is the security created by a charge over the property. The purpose of receivership is to extract from the security money with which to pay off the debenture holder's debt and the incidental expenses.

There is a set order of payment, i e the receiver is required to apply the funds which come into his hands in accordance with a sequence (in descending order of priority) of claims on it. He must pay the expenses of selling company property, then the fees due to the receiver himself and to the trustee (if any) for the debenture holders and the costs (if any) of a debenture holder's action leading to the receivership. After clearing the prior claims in this fashion the receiver then pays the company's debts. If he is appointed under a floating charge he must pay unsecured preferential debts (Chapter 20: 20.9), unless there are other uncharged assets available for this purpose, before he may pay the principal and interest due to the secured debenture holder(s) whom he represents. If there are other secured debts ranking after the charge under which the receiver is appointed, they are paid next and finally the non-preferential unsecured debts.

The term 'administrative receiver' has been introduced to distinguish a receiver appointed under a floating charge of the whole or substantially the whole of the company's property: IA s 29. References in the remainder of this chapter to a 'receiver' denote an administrative receiver, unless otherwise stated, since administrative receivership is the situation which is characteristic and important in the context of company law relating to companies under the temporary control of secured creditors. An administrative receiver is to be distinguished from a receiver appointed under a specific charge solely to take control of a particular asset; as already explained the law on this latter type of receiver is derived from mortgage law. Because an administrative receiver has general charge of the company's business he has in the past been referred to as a 'receiver and manager'.

To simplify and standardise the law of receivership it is now provided that an administrative receiver is by virtue of his office vested with a long list of statutory powers, unless the debenture under which he is appointed varies or excludes any of those statutory powers: IA Sch 1. These powers necessarily include a number of specific and technical powers which experience suggests may be required. The statutory powers also include the basic and general powers of a receiver (1) to sell the company's property (2) to borrow money and to give security over the company's assets for such borrowing and (3) to carry on the business of the company and to transfer it to a subsidiary ('hiving down' as explained below in 10.9).

With these standard statutory powers provided it should no longer be necessary, as it often was in the past, to apply to the court to appoint a receiver on behalf of the debenture holder(s). Such applications were usually made because the debenture, perhaps drafted many years before, did not confer the wide powers required in a modern receivership.

The purpose of appointing a receiver is limited in scope and duration. If he is able to obtain payment in full of the sums owing to the secured debenture holder(s) whom he represents he vacates his position since his task is accomplished and control of the company reverts to its directors and shareholders. This idea is sometimes expressed by saying that the function of a receiver is 'to get in and get out'. It may of course take him months or even years to accomplish this task, by improved management, reorganisation, sale of assets etc. If, however, he is unable to promote the complete discharge of the company's liabilities to those creditors whom he represents, its incurable insolvency will generally lead on to liquidation.

The differences between the functions of a receiver and a liquidator must be understood. In contrast to the receiver's task, as described above, the liquidator is concerned with the realisation of all the company's assets, not merely those which are charged to a debenture-holder, and he must pay regard to the interests of all creditors, secured or unsecured, and also to the interests of members. He does not represent one group against the others. When the liquidator's task is accomplished the company is dissolved, ie it ceases to exist.

The confusion, which sometimes exists, over receivers and liquidators arises from the fact that both are specialists in financial administration of insolvent companies. Both are imposed on a company and replace, temporarily or permanently, its board of directors. The legal procedure of receivership and liquidation has some elements in common, such as the preparation of a statement of affairs. Both often sell off or close down the business of a company. The Official Receiver, an official of the DTI, has an essential role to play in the early stages of compulsory liquidation.

Both a receiver and a liquidator now have statutory duties to discharge in the way of reporting on the management of the company by its directors and the personal performance of the directors. This topic is considered in a later chapter (Chapter 12) since it is really more an aspect of company law in relation to directors than an insolvency procedure.

10.4 Who may be a receiver?
Apart from requirements of individual qualification described below there are two basic exclusions. A receiver may not be:

(a) a corporate body or an undischarged bankrupt: IA ss 30 and 31;
(b) an individual against whom a court has made a disqualification order which may be for a specified period not exceeding 15 years: CDDA s 1.

Disqualification by court order is a sanction aimed mainly against unsatisfactory directors (Chapter 12: 12.3). But it has the effect of disqualifying an individual from being a receiver, among other company offices, and one of the grounds for such an order is conviction on an indictable offence in connection with receivership of a company or fraud while acting as manager of the property of a company: CDDA ss 2 and 4.

A receiver (and also a liquidator or an administrator) must now be an 'authorised insolvency practitioner' ie he must hold a written authority to act in that capacity issued by or under powers delegated by the DTI. The leading accountancy bodies and some other professional bodies such as the Law Society are permitted to issue authorisations to their members, not automatically by virtue of membership but by reference to individual criteria. The other method of obtaining an authorisation is by application to a 'relevant authority' established by the DTI for that purpose. Whichever method is used the authorisation will only be issued to an applicant who is:

(1) 'a fit and proper person' – anyone with an unsatisfactory record may be turned down on this ground; and
(2) up to 'prescribed requirements with respect to education and practical training and experience' – so that expertise is now required as well as good character.

An authorisation may be withdrawn before its expiry if there are sufficient grounds. But in every case it will require periodic renewal, which will entail a review of the 'fit and proper person' criterion.

This system introduced by the Insolvency Act 1985 Pt 1 and the relevant statutory provisions are consolidated in the 1986 Act.

10.5 The appointment of a receiver
In normal practice a receiver is appointed under express powers to do so contained in the debenture. This power, when it exists, must be exercised strictly in accordance with the contractual terms of the document. It must be clear that one of the events has occurred by which the power to appoint a receiver becomes exercisable. In making the appointment the debenture holder(s) or their trustee will also consider whether the powers of the receiver will suffice for the action which they intend him to take. However a receiver is now vested automatically with wide statutory powers, as explained in 10.3 above, and this is no longer likely to be an impediment to appointing a receiver under powers given in the debenture.

Apart from any express powers if the debenture has been issued under the common seal of the company and contains a charge on its property, the debenture holder, as a mortgagee, has a statutory power of appointing a receiver. There is some doubt however whether the statutory power, given by the Law of Property Act 1925 s 101, extends to a floating charge (*Blaker v Herts and Essex Waterworks Co* (1889) 41 Ch D 399). But modern commentators consider that this decision is unsound and would not now be followed. The point is not of much practical importance since appointments under s 101 in connection with company charges are rare.

A third method of appointment of a receiver is by the court on application by the debenture holder. This is a procedure of last resort since it entails delay and expense. The applicant must satisfy the court that one of the following situations exists:

(a) payment of interest or payment of the principal of the loan is overdue;
(b) the company has gone into liquidation either voluntarily or by order of the court;
(c) the security is in jeopardy.

If the debenture holders have a floating charge on the undertaking of the company the court may appoint the receiver or some other person to be manager. But a manager is appointed only with a view to selling the business as a going concern; his appointment is usually limited to a period of three months or such longer period as the court may allow.

The security may be in jeopardy even before there has been default or commencement of liquidation. The most likely occasion is that one or more creditors has obtained judgment for debt against the company (with or without taking steps to execute the judgment by seizure of assets) or has presented a petition for an order for compulsory winding up. The security has also been held to be in jeopardy if the company has or is about to close down its business or transfer its assets to its members or to some other person. But the security is not in jeopardy merely because the company's remaining assets appear to be less than its liabilities if it intends to carry on its business.

The company was about to close down its business and let off its premises. The security was held to be in jeopardy: *Re Braunstein and Marjolaine Ltd* (1914) 112 LT 25.

A receiver appointed by the court must be an authorised insolvency practitioner, unless the court decides that it is appropriate to appoint the Official Receiver. The receiver is required to give security for the proper performance of his duties. Both the receiver and any manager of the business who may be appointed to act with him are officers of the court, and are not agents of the debenture holders or of the company.

A receiver appointed under a power given in the debenture is required, not later than the following day after the written appointment is delivered to him, to signify his acceptance of the appointment which then takes effect from time of delivery. He is an agent of the company as explained below.

A receiver is dealing with the property of another person and, except where he is appointed by the court, his power to do so is derived from the debenture under which he is appointed (supplemented by the statutory powers of a receiver as explained above). If his appointment is defective, or if he takes control of property not subject to the charge, eg the property of a third party in the possession of the company, or if the charge under which he is appointed is or becomes void, he is acting without authority and may be personally liable. An experienced receiver is alert to consider all the technical aspects of these matters at the time of his appointment. He will also bear in mind that a subsequent liquidation of the company may make void the charge under which he was appointed, even though it was originally valid. It is common practice for receivers to obtain from those by whom they are appointed an indemnity against personal liability, especially if the charge was created only a short time before his appointment. The court now has power to order that a receiver shall be so indemnified against any invalidity of his appointment: IA s 34.

As at other stages of enforcing the rights given by debentures it is often the trustee for the debenture holders who takes action; references above to action by debenture holders include action by their trustee (if any).

When a receiver is appointed by the court the amount of his remuneration is fixed by the court. If he is appointed under a power contained in the debentures his remuneration is fixed by agreement. But if in this case the company is or goes into liquidation the liquidator may apply to the court to fix the amount of the receiver's remuneration with effect from his first appointment: IA s 36. A receiver appointed by the court is required to give security for the amounts which he may receive.

10.6 Action following the appointment of a receiver

Within seven days of the appointment of a receiver or manager either by order of the court or by exercise of powers given by the debentures (or trust deed) the person who obtained the order or who made the appointment must give notice of the appointment to the registrar: s 405. When a receiver or manager ceases to act he must give notice of it to the registrar. These notices are, of course, available on the company's file at the registry.

So long as there is a receivership, all business communications of the company must disclose that fact; the usual formula is the words 'in receivership' after the name of the company on letterheads etc: IA s 39.

There is a set procedure by which information of the company's affairs is provided:

(a) forthwith on his appointment the receiver gives notice to the company and publishes notice of his appointment; within 28 days he gives notice to all creditors of the company known to him;

(b) forthwith on his appointment the receiver gives notice to selected officers and/or persons connected with the company that he requires from them a statement of affairs. They have 21 days in which to comply with this request;

(c) within three months of his appointment the receiver makes a report on such matters as the events leading up to his appointment, the actual or planned disposal of company property and the carrying on of its business, the amounts owing to the debenture holders whom he represents and to preferential creditors, and any amount likely to be available for payment to other creditors.

The statement of affairs and the receiver's report are explained in more detail below.

The persons who may be required to submit a statement of affairs are past and present officers of the company (or of another company which has been an officer, eg director or secretary, of the company now in receivership), employees or other persons likely in the receiver's opinion to be able to give information, and any persons who have taken part in the formation of the company. But for those with a past connection with the company there is a time limit (in retrospect) of one year in some cases. The statement of affairs gives particulars of the company's assets, debts and liabilities, of its creditors and their respective security (if any) and any other information which the receiver may prescribe. The general effect is that the receiver may identify those who should be able to provide pertinent information and he can then, partly on a standard and partly on a selective basis, call for the information which he requires.

The receiver sends copies of his report to the registrar, to secured creditors and the debenture holders' trustee (if any). Unsecured creditors either receive a copy or are notified by advertisement that they may apply for a copy. Unless the court otherwise directs, the receiver lays his report before a meeting of unsecured creditors who may appoint a committee.

These rules establish a legal framework and timetable for the formal procedure of receivership. In practice a receiver would take control and call to account the company's management as soon as he is appointed. In this way he minimises the risks of evasion and is able to decide what emergency measures the company's precarious financial position may require.

10.7 The legal effect of the receiver's appointment

The appointment of a receiver causes a floating charge to crystallize. The company is no longer able to dispose of its assets without the consent of the receiver. The receiver appointed out of court has a right to apply to the court for directions on any matter relating to his functions: IA s 35.

The directors continue in office but they lose control of the assets comprised in the charge. If it is a charge over the whole undertaking the directors no longer have power to manage the business; that power is vested in the receiver (if also manager). But they can still convene an extraordinary general meeting, eg for the purpose of putting the company into voluntary liquidation. They also retain power to enforce claims by the company to protect its interests if the receiver fails to do so.

A bank had appointed a receiver under a debenture which provided that the receiver should have power to bring proceedings in the company's name. But the receiver failed to institute proceedings on behalf of the company against the bank itself over a breach of contract by the bank (the contract was between the bank and the company). The directors therefore began proceedings against the bank (and gave indemnity to the company in respect of liability for costs). It was held that the directors had power to protect an asset of the company, ie its claim against the bank, if the receiver neglected to do so. But any damages recovered for the company would, when received, come under the control of the receiver: *Newhart Developments Ltd v Co-op Commercial Bank Ltd* [1978] 2 WLR 636.

In respect of the company's assets under his control the receiver has the same rights as the company. In particular if a debtor of the company has a right of set-off or counterclaim he can maintain it against the receiver. If the security includes a charge on the uncalled capital of the company the receiver cannot make calls on shareholders but must apply to the directors (or the liquidator) to do so.

A receiver is by statute declared to be the agent of the company unless and until it goes into liquidation: IA s 44. This gives him power to act on behalf of the company and to manage its affairs. However, he is not in the normal position of an agent. The company, which is his nominal principal, cannot instruct him what he should do. Unlike other agents he is personally liable on the contracts which he makes for the company (10.9 below).

In the performance of his task of raising money with which to pay the debts owing to the secured creditor(s) whom he represents the receiver may have to take action which a normal company management would regard as unwise or short-sighted. His power to disclaim contracts of the company made before his appointment presents special problems which are considered later (10.9). The more general question is how far he is accountable to the company or any other person who may suffer loss if he fails to perform his duties in a proper manner.

A recent case has established that the receiver owes a duty to the company to exercise his powers honestly and also with reasonable skill and care. If he fails in that duty he is liable to the company and others to whom his default may cause loss.

A bank obtained a floating charge on the company's assets as security for its overdraft and also the personal guarantees of two directors limited to a maximum of £75,000. At the time when the bank appointed a receiver the overdraft stood at £88,432. Under pressure from the bank to expedite the recovery of its debt the receiver arranged a sale of the company's property by auction at an unsuitable time of the year. The sale was also badly advertised. There was a poor attendance at the sale and the proceeds amounted to some £42,800 which was far below the normal market value of the property sold. This sum did little more than cover the costs of realisation. The bank therefore called on the guarantors to pay the balance of the debt.

It was held that in arranging the sale the receiver owed a duty to the company and to the guarantors to use reasonable skill and care; he had failed in that duty. Although the receiver was formally the agent of the company and not of the bank, the bank by interfering in the receiver's arrangements had assumed a duty of care to the guarantors and was liable to them jointly with the receiver: *Standard Chartered Bank Ltd v Walker* [1982] 3 All ER 938. However a receiver is not an 'officer' of the company who can be held liable in misfeasance proceedings: *Re B Johnson & Co (Builders) Ltd* [1955] Ch 634. (See Chapter 20: 20.20).

10.8 The company's employees

Until 1986 the appointment of a receiver by the court or by the debenture holders as their agent, both of which were infrequent contingencies, effected a change of employer and automatically terminated the contracts of employment of employees with the company: *Reid v Explosives Co Ltd* (1887) 19 QBD 264. But, in the more usual case, the appointment of a receiver by the debenture holders, on terms (expressed in the debenture) that the receiver should be the agent of the company, did not automatically terminate contracts of employment; the company was still the employer although under different management.

However, it is now provided by statute (IA s 44) that unless and until the company goes into liquidation (see 10.10 below) every administrative receiver shall be deemed to be the agent of the company. Accordingly automatic termination of employment no longer follows.

There are nonetheless circumstances in which contracts of employment of company staff and workers may be terminated. Under the new statutory system the receiver is given a period of 14 days from his appointment in which to make up his mind whether he wishes to retain employees. At the end of that period he will be deemed to have 'adopted' existing contracts of employment, and assumed personal liability on them, unless he has meanwhile given notice of dismissal: IA s 44(2).

In due course the receiver may decide to dispose of the business and the assets used in it. If he sells the business, or part of it, in the United Kingdom as a going concern the employees are automatically transferred to the service of the purchaser under the same terms of employment as before: Transfer of Undertakings (Protection of Employment) Regulations 1981, SI 1981/1794. To prevent this result the purchaser may of course stipulate that the receiver shall terminate the employees' contracts by notice before the sale or the purchaser may terminate the contracts in the course of acquiring the business. The effect of such action on the rights of the employees is a matter of employment law not company law.

If the receiver sells the assets used in the business but does not sell the business as a going concern the 1981 regulations do not apply and the sale, since it ends the company's business activities, effects a termination of the contracts of employment of those who have worked in the business.

The receiver had been appointed by the debenture holders and under the terms of the debenture he was declared to be the agent of the company. He sold the business. This happened long before the 1981 regulations effected a transfer of the employees on sale of the business. It was held that the appointment of the receiver has not terminated the contracts of employment of employees but the sale of the business did have that effect: *Re Foster Clark Ltd's Indenture Trusts, Loveland v Horscroft* [1966] 1 All ER 43. Note that under the 1981 regulations the result of the sale would have been different.

The appointment of an administrative receiver does of course displace the senior management of the company since he assumes the duties which they have hitherto performed. For the senior management the result of the receiver's arrival is much the same as if he had sold the business or closed it down, either of which would (subject to the effect of the 1981 regulations on a sale) terminate their employment. This was recognised in the case below.

The appellant was employed as managing director to perform such duties as the board of directors might delegate to him. After a receiver had been appointed, the managing director continued to work for a period of four weeks and then resigned. The issue was whether the appointment of the receiver, who had assumed most of the duties previously performed by the managing director, terminated the employment of the latter so that he had the rights of an employee who had been dismissed rather than those of one who had resigned. It was held that this was a possible result of the receivership. But on the particular facts of the case the managing director had not been dismissed in this way. It was open to the company, now represented by the receiver, at any time to redefine the managing director's duties. In effect the receiver had done so and there was no dismissal by 'incompatibility of function'; the managing director had been given new duties under the terms of his contract: *Griffiths v Secretary of State for Social Services* [1974] QB 468.

The effect of 'hiving down', ie transfer of the company's business to its wholly-owned subsidiary, is considered below (10.9).

If a receiver is appointed under a floating charge unpaid wages of employees within certain limits (Chapter 20: 20.9) are preferential debts, as in liquidation, and take priority over the floating charge: s 196.

10.9 The receiver and the contracts of the company

Apart from contracts of employment (see 10.8 above) a receiver is not personally liable on contracts of the company existing at the time of his appointment. The company however continues to be bound by and liable on these contracts unless they contain terms providing for their termination, usually at the option of the other party, if the company goes into receivership.

Where there are outstanding contractual obligations the receiver can either let the company discharge them by performance of the contract or, in exercise of his control over the company, he can induce a repudiation of these contracts with consequent liability for damages for breach of contract. If he decides to close down or sell the business or to sell off assets in the course of recovering the amounts due to the secured creditor(s) whom he represents, he may incidentally put it beyond the company's power to perform its contracts.

He is however subject to restrictions if he proposes to repudiate contracts in such a way as will destroy the goodwill of the continuing business of the company. Before taking such action he must obtain the leave of the court. However the court will not refuse its leave if performance of the outstanding contracts will increase the losses which the company has incurred or will require borrowing by the receiver to finance them.

The receiver found that the entire output of the colliery company had been sold forward at contract prices which were now below the market price. He proposed to repudiate these contracts in order to resell the coal at higher prices and so increase the money available to pay the debenture holders. This course would have damaged the goodwill of the business and also have produced claims for damages by the buyers under the existing contracts. The court refused to sanction this scheme, saying of a receiver that 'it is his duty to do . . . everything reasonable and right for the protection of the property as an undertaking for the benefit of all the persons interested in it': *Re Newdigate Colliery Ltd* [1912] 1 Ch 468.

The company had half-built ships which it would not be profitable to complete and the receiver would have had to borrow to finance their completion. He was allowed to repudiate the contracts: *Re Thames Ironworks, Shipbuilding of Engineering Co Ltd* [1912] WN 66.

Any contracts which the receiver himself makes in the course of carrying out his functions are contracts on which he is personally liable unless the contracts otherwise provide: IA s 44. But when he is liable he has a right of indemnity out of the assets of the company. This is also the position if he 'adopts' contracts of employment of employees by retaining them beyond the first 14 days (10.8 above).

As a minimum precaution a receiver usually limits the contracts which he makes to those which are essential and for which the company has in hand the required funds to meet the incidental payments. He buys 'for cash' and so on. This precaution is not of course adequate in all circumstances. If the company continues to make and sell its products there could be liability to purchasers if the products are defective. To avoid personal liability altogether, a receiver may transfer the company's undertaking to a wholly-owned subsidiary company of which he is managing director but not receiver. Among the statutory powers of an administrative receiver there is power to transfer its undertaking to a subsidiary. It is also provided in the 1981 Transfer of Undertakings (Protection of Employment) Regulations (10.8 above) that if a transfer to a subsidiary (known colloquially as 'hiving down') is followed by a sale of the share capital of the subsidiary to a third party, the consequent

171

transfer of the employees in the business takes effect only when the subsidiary is sold and not when the initial hiving down is effected. Using a subsidiary as a means of selling the business as a going concern is common practice. A sale of shares is more straightforward than a sale of assets.

Although the receiver is the agent of the company the other party to any contract which the receiver makes has no direct claim against the company. If however the receiver defaults on the contract and incurs liability which he cannot meet the other party may claim against the company by subrogation to the receiver's right of indemnity. Hence it is not advantageous for the other party to enter into a contract by which the receiver disclaims personal liability to him on the contract. This is because in that case the receiver has no right of indemnity from the company's assets, since there is no liability to which the indemnity applies. If the receiver has no right of indemnity the other party has no claim against the company – since the receiver has none to which he can be subrogated.

10.10 The effect of liquidation

A secured creditor is not prevented from appointing a receiver even though the company has already gone into liquidation, provided always that his charge is still valid. The receiver then claims from the liquidator the assets subject to the charge which are the security (Chapter 20: 20.5).

It more often happens that the financial position of the company in receivership is found to be irretrievable and so it is put into liquidation.

In this situation the receiver must first consider whether the charge under which he has been appointed is still valid. The grounds on which subsequent liquidation may render a charge void against the liquidator are considered in a later chapter in the context of liquidation (Chapter 20 Part C). If the charge is void the receiver accounts to the liquidator for the assets in his charge and for his past transactions. He is no longer a duly appointed receiver since the basis of his appointment has gone.

If the charge is still valid the receiver is no longer the agent of the company: IA s 44. But he retains his essential powers as receiver and may act in that capacity in dealing with the assets under his control. If he is able to obtain full payment of the amount owing to the creditor(s) whom he represents, plus costs and expenses, he accounts to the liquidator for any surplus and vacates his appointment as receiver. Although there is a liquidator in office the receiver, while his tenure continues, may act without obtaining the consent of the liquidator.

There are obvious drawbacks to a situation in which two insolvency practitioners, with different responsibilities, are concerned with the same property. There is no legal objection to the same individual holding both positions at the same time. However the professional accountancy bodies have advised their members that, owing to the possible conflict of interests, it is undesirable to accept such a dual appointment.

10.11 Administration orders

There are several limitations and drawbacks to receivership. The right to appoint, or apply to the court to appoint, a receiver is restricted to secured creditors (10.2 above). The receiver once appointed has the interests of the creditors whom he represents as his sole concern. Yet his actions may affect and perhaps prejudice the interests of unsecured creditors and of members of the company. The unsecured creditors now have a right to obtain a copy of the receiver's initial report (10.6 above) and they may appoint a creditors' committee to work with him: IA s 49.

If the receiver decides to carry on the business of the company he may encounter difficulties arising from the action of other creditors (10.13 below). It is not generally worthwhile for an unsecured creditor to petition for the compulsory liquidation of the company but the receiver cannot prevent him from doing so, or from threatening to do so as a means of exerting pressure.

The purpose of the administration order procedure, introduced by the Insolvency Act 1985 (now IA Pt II), is to give to the unsecured creditor the opportunity of securing the appointment of an administrator, with similar powers to those of a receiver but with wider responsibilities to all creditors and to the company, as explained below. Even a secured creditor may benefit by the controlled and regulated management of the company under the protection of the court. This procedure is derived from practice in other countries, notably the USA, where it has been found useful.

A petition for an administration order may be presented to the court by the company itself or by its directors, or by any creditor, including a creditor for a contingent or prospective debt. But the petitioner must satisfy the court that (1) the company is already or is likely to become unable to pay its debts (by the same criteria as apply to a petition for compulsory liquidation – see Chapter 18: 18.3) and (2) that by an administration order it is likely that one or more of the following specified purposes will be achieved:

(a) the survival of the company and its business, wholly or in part, as a going concern; or
(b) a settlement of the company's debts by a composition etc with its creditors, ie on the basis of less than payment in full; or
(c) a more advantageous realisation of the company's assets than would be effected in a liquidation.

If the court is satisfied on these points it makes an administration order by which an administrator, who must be an authorised insolvency practitioner (see 10.4 above), is put in charge of the company with the same general powers as are given to an administrative receiver (10.3 above). In addition he has power to remove directors from office, to appoint directors and to convene meetings of members and of creditors: IA.

The effect of an administration order is also to stay all interference by creditors individually. No petition for compulsory liquidation may be presented; no administrative receiver may be appointed and any such receiver already appointed must vacate office (but there is an important reservation here as explained below). No creditor may take legal action to seize the company's assets and the owner of property in the possession of the company, under a hire-purchase agreement or a contract of sale with reservation of title until payment is made (a Romalpa clause – Chapter 9: 9.14), may not recover it, unless the court gives leave for such action to be taken. There is also a standstill on such action in the interval between the petition and the making of the order to prevent a creditor from moving swiftly to forestall its effect on him.

The initial procedure following the making of an administration order is in substance similar to that following the appointment of an administrative receiver, though there are differences of detail. In particular notice is given of the administrator's appointment and he is entitled to receive a statement of affairs from the company's officers etc. Similarly the administrator is given a period of three months in which to set out what he intends to do. In this case it is a statement of his proposals, which is distributed to the registrar and to creditors insofar as their addresses are known. The administrator may either send copies to members or advertise so that they may apply for copies.

The administrator must next obtain approval of his proposals for achieving the purposes specified in the administration order. He convenes a creditors' meeting by a 14-day notice. If the creditors approve the proposals they may establish a committee to work with the administrator. In any event the administrator reports the outcome of the meeting to the court; if the proposals have not been approved by creditors the court makes whatever order it sees fit but the administration order is unlikely to continue in its original shape. Any creditor or member may object to the court against the order, while it is in force, alleging unfair prejudice to himself, and the court may, if it sees fit, grant relief.

A secured creditor who has appointed, or who has power to appoint, an administrative receiver has what amounts to a veto on the making of an administration order in the first place. He must be given notice of the petition to the court for the order. He thus has time to appoint a receiver, if he has not already done so, before the court hearing of the petition. If at the time of the hearing there is an administrative receiver in office the court cannot make an administration order, since there would be a conflict of authority in the company between the administrator and the receiver, unless (1) the person by whom the receiver was appointed gives his consent or (2) the charge under which the receiver has been appointed would become void in a liquidation of the company at this point. This second proviso is aimed to counter charges obtained within the recent past (see Chapter 20 Part C).

If the secured creditor by whom an administrative receiver has been appointed gives his consent to the administration order the administrator, appointed by the court, will replace the receiver in control of the company. As already indicated there can be situations in which a secured creditor will find that the balance of advantage to himself lies in consenting to an administration in place of a receivership (see also 10.13 below). In many instances the only secured creditor of an insolvent trading company is its bank; it will have to weigh up the pros and cons of each alternative.

If of course there is no secured creditor the way is open to the unsecured creditors to petition for an administration order without the problem of competing priorities.

10.12 Voluntary arrangements
The purpose of a voluntary arrangement, another innovation introduced by the Insolvency Act 1985 (now IA Pt I) is to provide a simple and flexible method of establishing a compromise between a company and its creditors which is binding on *all* creditors. It can happen that one or more creditors, although a minority, will wreck a compromise which the majority would accept as in their best interests, but which they cannot impose on the minority against their will, unless there is a statutory power as described below or a contractual acceptance of binding majority decisions such as is often included in a debenture trust deed (Chapter 9: 9.5(f)). The minority exploit their 'nuisance value' by holding out for special treatment of their claims which the majority will not concede.

This is not a recent problem but previous attempts to provide a solution have not been satisfactory. A scheme of arrangement (Chapter 16: 16.3) entails the heavy expense of two applications to the court. Another procedure (s 601 now repealed) was almost workable.

The new 'voluntary arrangement' is more flexible and is available to a company which is in liquidation or subject to an administration order or which has not yet reached that stage. In this last case there is no insolvency practitioner in charge already and so the directors, in initiating a 'voluntary arrangement', must first find an insolvency practitioner to act for the company and he makes a preliminary submission to the court of his proposals for convening meetings of the company and of its creditors. Whoever the insolvency practitioner may be he is described as 'the nominee' at this stage.

The nominee puts the proposal for a composition, ie part payment of debts, or other schemes of arrangement, such as rescheduling, before separate meetings of members and creditors. If the proposal will affect the rights of any secured creditor or preferential creditor his individual consent is required. Apart from that the proposal must be approved by a majority at each meeting.

If approved the proposal is then implemented under the supervision of either the nominee or of some other insolvency practitioner appointed to replace him at this stage. Any member or creditor who objects may apply to the court for relief on grounds of unfair prejudice. But this will entail expense and if his objection lacks merit it may be dismissed, leaving him to bear his legal costs. A creditor who does not object is bound by the proposal once it has been approved.

10.13 Other problems of insolvency administration
In connection with administration orders it has been explained that an administrative receiver, who does not have the protection of a standstill on actions against the company and assets which it owns or merely has in its possession, may encounter difficulties created by third parties who thereby seek to promote their own interests or to obtain concessions. A secured creditor who has appointed an administrative receiver may always apply for or give his consent to the making of an administration order.

A different type of problem may confront an administrative receiver if he proposes to sell property of the company which is subject to a charge, eg premises subject to a mortgage with priority over the floating charge under which the receiver is appointed. In such cases the receiver may now apply to the court for leave to sell the property unencumbered by the charge on the basis that the charge will be transferred to the proceeds of the sale: IA s 43.

In attempting to carry on the business of the company the receiver may need to obtain essential goods or services from suppliers to whom the company is indebted for past supplies. In addition to demanding guaranteed payment for future supplies – for which the receiver is personally liable (10.9 above) – the suppliers could in the past make it a condition of continuing supplies that all unpaid bills should also be paid. This was common practice on the part of public utilities such as gas, electricity, water and telephone undertakings. However public utilities are now prohibited from making the continuation of supplies conditional on payment for past supplies: IA s 233.

If a company goes into liquidation charges created within specified periods before the commencement of liquidation may become void (Chapter 20 Part C). The same provisions apply to charges created in similar circumstances in the interval between presenting a petition for an administration order and the making of the order. This is a safeguard against attempts to frustrate an administration order by creation of charges in that interval: IA s 240.

Chapter 11

General meetings

11.1 Kinds of meetings

A company is required to hold an annual general meeting ('AGM') within 18 months of incorporation and thereafter once in each calendar year. The other kind of general meeting, ie an extraordinary general meeting ('EGM'), may be held as often as required. Meetings of members who hold a class of shares, for the purpose of considering a proposed variation of class rights, are subject to the same general principles of procedure.

The general meeting is the means by which members, with whom rests the ultimate control of the company, may extract information from and express their views to the directors, whose task is to manage the company's affairs.

An AGM need not be held on the same date in each year but the maximum interval between one AGM and the next is 15 months: s 366.

There is no obligatory business to be transacted at an AGM. But it is well understood that the main purpose of an AGM is to transact the recurrent, routine business (still called 'ordinary business' in pre 1985 articles – see 11.6 below) which the company will have to deal with in the course of the year. This business is the consideration of the annual accounts (Chapter 14: 14.4), possibly the declaration of a dividend, the re-election of directors and the reappointment of auditors. If there is also 'special business', which was not so urgent as to require that an EGM be convened to deal with it, the AGM can go on to deal with that business also, eg a technical alteration of the articles. But there is no legal requirement that routine 'ordinary business' shall be done at the AGM.

If, for example, the annual accounts are not ready at the time when the AGM is convened in compliance with the timetable set by s 366, it is permissible to consider the accounts at an EGM convened later on (though there are also time limits for laying accounts before a general meeting to keep in mind – Chapter 14: 14.4).

If the directors fail to convene an AGM within the prescribed period the DTI may on the application of a member call or direct the calling of an AGM and among other matters fix the quorum for the meeting at one member present in person or by proxy: s 367(2). This provision is to deal with the difficulty which can arise if the number of members is reduced to one or only one member is willing to attend.

The articles (Table A Art 37) always confer on the directors power to convene an EGM whenever they think fit. The directors of a public company are also required to convene an EGM if the net assets become half or less the amount of the called-up share capital: s 142 (Chapter 5: 5.26). In addition there are statutory provisions for calling an EGM of any company by or on the requisition of members or retiring auditors or by order of the court.

11.2 EGM called by or at request of members or auditors

Since normal procedure requires that the directors should resolve at a board meeting to convene a general meeting, the articles (Table A Art 37) usually provide that if there are not sufficient directors within the UK to hold a board meeting, any director or any member may convene a general meeting. In case the articles make no such provision, s 370(3) confers the right, unless the articles otherwise provide, on two or more members provided that they hold at least ten per cent of the issued share capital or form 5 per cent of the membership if there is no share capital. However the articles usually cover the point and so s 370 is a procedure of rare application. It would also be possible for a member to apply to the court (11.3 below).

If there are directors to convene a meeting but they are reluctant to do so, members may serve on the company a requisition which they deposit at the registered office. The requisition must be in writing and signed by a sufficient number of members, ie either members holding not less than one-tenth of the issued share capital carrying voting rights or, if the company has no share capital, members who represent at least one-tenth of the total voting rights of members entitled to vote at a general meeting: s 368(2). It may consist of several documents in similar form; this is to facilitate collection of signatures without having to circulate the same copy to different signatories.

The requisition must state 'the objects of the meeting'. Although very general words would suffice it is usual to set out in the requisition the text of the resolution(s) which the requisitionists intend to propose. They cannot compel the directors to include in the notice issued to convene the meeting any matter not included in their stated 'objects'. But the directors are free to add items of their own choice.

If the directors fail to call the EGM within 21 days of the deposit of the requisition any of the requisitionists representing more than one-half of their total voting rights may call it, but the meeting must then be held within three months from the deposit of the requisition. In that case the requisitionists may recover from the company their expenses in convening the meeting and the company may retain the same amount out of remuneration, etc, due to the directors. A meeting convened by the requisitionists may only transact business described as an object in the requisition.

If the directors comply with the requisition they may convene the EGM for any date however far ahead. But if they fix a remote future date application could be made to the court to order a meeting to be held at an earlier date. The directors must of course comply with anything in the articles on this subject. Table A Art 37 now provides that the meeting shall be convened for a date not later than eight weeks from the receipt of the requisition.

An auditor who resigns may state his reasons in his written notice of resignation (Chapter 14: 14.10). If he does so he may at the same time deposit a written requisition requiring the directors to convene an EGM to receive and consider his resignation. The EGM must be convened by notice issued within

21 days of the requisition to be held within 28 days of the notice convening it. If the directors do not comply they are liable to be fined: s 391.

11.3 EGM convened by order of the court

The court has an inherent power to direct that meetings shall be held of the members or of a class of members. It also has a general statutory power, on the application of a director or of any member entitled to attend and vote or of its own initiative, to order that a meeting shall be called and among other incidental matters to fix a quorum for the meeting which may be one member only present in person or by proxy: s 371.

The court will not intervene merely to overrule the directors but uses its power to resolve a deadlock.

A member who held 90 per cent of the shares requisitioned an EGM but the other two members, who were also the directors, refused to attend. The directors also had failed to convene an AGM because the controlling shareholder intended to remove them from office. The court directed that a meeting should be held: *Re El Sombrero Ltd* [1958] Ch 900.

There are a number of specific situations in which it is necessary to ascertain whether a majority of members approves some proposal, such as a voluntary arrangement with creditors (Chapter 10: 10.12) or a scheme of arrangement (Chapter 16: 16.3), or to consult them in the course of compulsory liquidations (Chapter 20 and IA s 160). In all these situations the court has power to order that meetings be held for the relevant purpose.

11.4 Issue of notice of meeting

The directors may select the date, time and place of the meeting. In doing so they must act in good faith and not make arrangements designed to frustrate the purpose of the meeting. A meeting once convened cannot be cancelled or postponed; the proper procedure is to resolve at the meeting to transact no business or to adjourn it to a later date.

A meeting can only reach valid and binding decisions if it is properly convened by notice of the required duration given to the persons entitled to receive it; if the notice also adequately describes the business to be transacted at the meeting; and if the meeting itself is properly conducted. Some of the rules on these matters which are explained below are common law rules applicable to meetings of any kind but there are also specific statutory rules imposed by the Companies Act.

Unless the articles otherwise provide, notice of each general meeting must be served on every member of the company in accordance with Table A: s 370(2). The auditor is also entitled to a copy of the notice: s 387(1).

Most articles do in fact follow the model of Table A in providing that:

(a) notice is to be sent to every member who has a registered address in the UK; to the personal representatives of a deceased member; to the trustee of a bankrupt member: Arts 112 and 116;
(b) notices shall be given personally or by post sent to the registered address. In case of joint holdings notice need only be given to the first-named joint holder: Art 112;
(c) a notice properly addressed and stamped is deemed to reach the addressee 48 hours after posting: Art 115;

(d)   accidental omission to give notice of a meeting to a person entitled to it is not to invalidate the proceedings: Art 39. But deliberate omission due to misunderstanding of the articles is not 'accidental'.

A member whose address in the register of members is outside the UK may, if he wishes, supply the company with a UK address to which notices are to be sent. He is nonetheless deemed to receive notices within 48 hours of posting.

Some public companies do in practice send notices by airmail to members who reside outside the UK.

A statutory period of 14 or 21 days' notice is prescribed for general meetings of different types by s 369:

(i)   21 days for an AGM or for an EGM at which a special resolution is to be proposed; and

(ii)   14 days' notice in any other case, i e for an EGM at which only ordinary or extraordinary resolutions are to be proposed.

The same rules apply to class meetings which are generally called on 14 days' notice to consider extraordinary resolutions for variation of class rights under s 125(2).

These are minimum periods of notice. A meeting may be called on longer notice and the articles may provide for a longer period, but this is unusual.

The statutory period of 21 days' notice of an AGM may be waived by the consent of all members entitled to attend and vote. For any other meeting it suffices to obtain a waiver from a majority of the members holding not less than 95 per cent in nominal value of the shares carrying the right to attend and vote: s 369(3) and (4).

In the case of private companies it is common practice, when all the members are present, to hand them their copy of the notice and to invite them to sign a waiver of statutory notice so that the meeting may be held forthwith. Alternatively, signed waivers are obtained in advance from members who do not attend. The waiver must, however, be in express terms and will not be implied from mere agreement to hold the meeting without interposing the statutory period of notice.

The waiver may be by word of mouth but for record purposes it is usual to invite members to sign a written waiver. If the meeting is held without notice of prescribed length or an adequate waiver, its proceedings are invalid – but may be transacted afresh or perhaps confirmed at a subsequent meeting properly convened or treated as an informal agreement of members (11.16).

The waiver procedure is limited to notice of a particular meeting. Any attempts at a general waiver, e g by the terms of the articles, is overridden by the statutory rules and would be void.

The articles always follow the model of Table A Art 38 in requiring that the 14 or 21 days shall be 'clear days notice', i e the day when the notice is received and the day of the meeting must be excluded from the reckoning. With a 48-hour interval (Art 115) allowed for transit in the post a notice posted on say Monday is deemed to arrive on the following Wednesday; the period of notice begins on the next day (Thursday) and expires on Wednesday either two weeks (14 days) or three weeks (21 days) later; the meeting can be held on the next day (Thursday) of that week or later. If the articles provide for deemed delivery within 24 hours this timetable is shortened by one day, so that notice posted on Monday will suffice for a meeting held on the appropriate Wednesday.

11.5 Special notice to the company

For three kinds of resolution *special* notice is required. These are resolutions:

(1) for the removal of a director under s 303;
(2) for the election or re-election of a director who is over the age of 70 where s 293 applies; and
(3) to appoint an auditor in certain cases or to remove an auditor; s 388 (Chapter 12: 12.5 and 12.7 and Chapter 14: 14.9).

The rules on special notice are prescribed by s 379, ie:

(a) notice of intention to move the resolution must be given to the company at least 28 days before the meeting at which it is to be moved. But if after this notice of intention has been given the meeting is called for a date which is 28 days or less after the notice has been given, it is deemed to have been properly given;
(b) the company may then give notice of the resolution at the same time and in the same manner as it gives notice of the meeting or if that is not practicable give notice to members by advertisement in a newspaper having an appropriate circulation or in any other mode allowed by the articles not less than 21 days before the meeting.

The procedural rules set out in (b) above do not, however, compel the company on receipt of a member's notice of intention to include his resolution in the notice convening the meeting. Unless s 376 (see 11.7 below) determines the matter, the directors are free to decide whether to include the member's resolution in the business of the meeting or not to do so. In the latter case the resolution cannot be moved since if it is to come before the meeting s 379 requires that members shall have notice of it as described in sub-para (b) above.

On 29 October 1975 the plaintiff, a member of the company, gave special notice of his intention to move a resolution at the AGM on 29 November 1975 for the removal of all the directors from office under s 303. He did not, however, hold 5 per cent of the voting shares so as to have rights under s 376. It was held that a member had no right to compel the company to include a resolution in the notice of a meeting (it must be an AGM) unless he was so entitled by s 376. Section 379 on special notice, was purely procedural, ie it gave members the right to have 21 days' notice of any resolution for which this procedure is prescribed. It does not give to a member the right, unless he qualifies under s 376, to insist that his resolution shall be included in the notice of the business of the meeting: *Pedley v Inland Waterways Association Ltd* [1977] 1 All ER 209.

Taken in isolation the decision in this case may be logical but its effect is to add to s 303 (removal of directors by ordinary resolution) a condition not found in s 303. It means that a member must either obtain the consent of the directors to moving a resolution for the removal of one of their number, which may well be refused, or he must as an initial condition hold or be supported by members, including himself, who have at least 5 per cent of the share capital. It is true that without that modest support he is unlikely to carry his resolution. But s 303 requires only that he shall get a majority of votes cast at the meeting – which is quite a different proposition.

11.6 Contents of the notice

Every notice of a general meeting must give information as follows:

(a) the date, time and place of the meeting must be specified;
(b) if the meeting is an AGM the notice must describe it as such: s 366(1);
(c) if it is intended to propose a resolution as a special or extraordinary resolution the notice must describe it as such: s 378(1);
(d) the text of a special or extraordinary resolution must be set out verbatim and the text of certain ordinary resolutions may be, but resolutions which by the articles are ordinary business need not be, dealt with in this way (see below);
(e) every member who has the right to attend and vote has a statutory right to appoint a proxy (or in the case of a public company more than one proxy) to attend and vote instead of him. A proxy need not also be a member. This right must be stated with reasonable prominence in the notice of every meeting: s 372(3).

It is conventional for the notice to show the date and place of issue and to bear the printed signature of the secretary with a statement that the notice is issued 'by order of the board'.

An ordinary resolution may deal with a matter of routine, such as the consideration of the accounts at an AGM. On the other hand it may be important and/or contentious, eg a resolution for the removal of a director (Chapter 12: 12.7) or a decision of a public company to expend millions of pounds in the purchase of its own shares (Chapter 5: 5.17(c)). Although the Companies Act does not draw any distinction – it would be difficult to know where to draw the line – established practice, based on case law, requires that the full text of an ordinary resolution should be included in the notice convening the meeting if the resolution deals with anything but routine matters.

The 1985 version of Table A states that the notice must 'specify . . . the general nature of the business to be transacted' (Art 38). Unlike the 1948 Table A (Art 52) it does not describe the routine business of an AGM as 'ordinary business' and all other business, including everything done at an EGM, as 'special business'. But it is well understood that the items of business which come up at the AGM each year, ie accounts, dividends (if any), election of directors and appointment of auditors, are sufficiently identified by a short description, such as 'to consider the accounts', 'to re-elect directors' etc. It is not usual or necessary to include in the notice the full text of the resolutions to be moved to transact this business. Hence it follows that a member present at the meeting may propose an unexpected resolution *if* it falls within the scope of the routine item.

The notice of an AGM specified the election of directors. The chairman refused to accept a resolution for the election of three new directors to replace a director retiring (but seeking re-election) and to fill two vacancies. It was held that his decision was wrong since the resolution was within the scope of the notice. In this case the articles did not apparently reproduce Table A Art 76, as most modern articles do, and require that advance notice shall be given to the company (but not to members) of intention to propose the election of any but a retiring director. This requirement prevents a sudden 'ambush' and allows a short time in which the board can seek support from members by the issue of a circular or otherwise: *Choppington Collieries Ltd v Johnson* [1944] 1 All ER 762.

Many companies of course still have articles based on the 1948 Table A, which distinguished between 'ordinary business' (AGM routine) and 'special business' (everything else including non-routine business done at an AGM). The change in the wording of the Table A articles does not entail any alteration in the practice of itemising ordinary business briefly so as to 'specify the general nature' of that business.

11.7 Circulars and additional information

The general requirement of proper disclosure may call for more information to be given than setting out the text of the resolution in the notice. If, for example, a special resolution is proposed to alter the articles or to adopt entirely new ones the members must be informed of the material changes which will thereby be effected. If the directors have an interest in the passing of a resolution set out in the notice, their interest must be disclosed and in sufficient detail. It is not enough to state that members may inspect documents from which the information could be obtained at the company's or other offices.

The notice convening the meeting stated that a resolution was to be proposed to approve an agreement for the sale of the company's undertaking. It did not disclose that under the agreement substantial compensation was to be paid to the directors. It was held that in the notice the purpose of the meeting 'must be stated fairly: it must not be stated so as to mislead'. The notice was 'tricky' and so the resolution was invalid: *Kaye v Croydon Tramways Co* [1898] 1 Ch 358.

A special resolution to approve remuneration paid to directors by a subsidiary was held to be invalid since the notice and accompanying circular merely disclosed the percentage of profits paid to the directors and not the exceptionally large profits to which that percentage related. This last was also treated as one of 'fraud on a minority': *Baillie v Oriental Telephone and Electric Co Ltd* [1915] 1 Ch 503.

Although the Companies Act does not refer to the issue of circulars (except in restricted circumstances such as the explanatory memorandum which accompanies a scheme of arrangement – Chapter 16: 16.3) they are commonly issued as the main means of explaining to members the significance of a notice of a general meeting which is therefore a brief and formal document. In the *Moorgate Mercantile Holdings Case* (11.9 below) it was held that a formal notice issued to convene a meeting and the explanatory circular issued with it should be treated as one document.

Members who have a sufficient stake in the company (but not any member regardless of his shareholding – see *Pedley's Case* in 11.5 above) may require the company (i) to include a resolution in the notice convening an AGM and (ii) to issue to members, entitled to notice of any general meeting, a statement not exceeding 1,000 words in length relating to a resolution or to business to be dealt with at that meeting: s 376.

In either case the requisition must be made by members representing not less than one-twentieth of the total voting rights of members (entitled to vote at the meeting) or by not less than 100 members holding shares on which there has been paid up an average sum per member of not less than £100. A requisition for the inclusion of a resolution in a notice of AGM must be deposited at the registered office at least six weeks before the date of the meeting but if after the deposit of the requisition the AGM is called for a date which is six weeks or less after the deposit it is deemed to have been properly deposited. A requisition for the circulation of a members' statement must be similarly deposited not less than one week before the meeting. The requisition, which may be in the form of several copies of the same document, must be signed by the required number of requisitionists. The requisitionists must, in delivering their requisition, deposit or tender a sum reasonably sufficient to meet the company's expenses in giving effect to it. The company is not bound to circulate a members' statement if the company (or any other person aggrieved) can satisfy the court that these statutory rights are being abused to secure needless publicity for defamatory manner. Apart from that ground of objection, default by the company in compliance renders the officers liable to be fined: s 377.

These statutory rights are little used. As *Pedley's Case* illustrates a small shareholder in a large company is not qualified to exercise the right and often finds that the expense of mobilising support from other members would be prohibitive. In a 'battle of circulars', in which competing groups contend for the support of uncommitted shareholders, each group obtains a copy of the full list of members and their addresses (Chapter 8: 8.8) in order to be able to issue the circular direct to members without disclosing its contents to the directors by submitting it to the company for issue.

11.8 Quorum, chairman and adjournment

The decisions of a meeting which has been properly convened are only valid if the meeting is also properly constituted by the presence of a chairman and the required number of members ('the quorum') and if it is properly conducted in accordance with the rules of debate, amendment of motions and voting.

Company law has adopted from the common law of meetings of all kinds the principle that there is no meeting at all unless at least two persons are present who are entitled to take part in its proceedings.

At a meeting convened to approve calls on members (Chapter 7: 7.24) for unpaid capital only one member attended, plus the secretary who was not a member. The resolution to make calls was duly passed and at the conclusion of the meeting the one member present, who had taken the chair, proposed a vote of thanks to himself. Later the company, through the secretary (Sharp), sued a shareholder (Dawes) for the money which had been called up on his shares. In holding that there had been no meeting (and so the call was invalid) the court said that 'the word meeting prima facie means a coming together of more than one person': *Sharp v Dawes* (1876) 2 QBD 26.

On the same principle one member present in person and also as proxy for another member (11.12 below) cannot by his sole presence constitute a meeting, though he may be counted as two members present in person or by proxy for purposes of a quorum: *Re Sanitary Carbon Co* [1877] WN 223. It also follows that if only two members are present at the start of the meeting and one later withdraws, the meeting is at an end and no further business can be done: *Re London Flats Ltd* [1969] 2 All ER 744.

The articles cannot override this basic common law principle but they may fix a quorum at a higher or more demanding level. The usual formula is a quorum of two members present in person or by proxy (Table A Art 40). If the articles do not fix a quorum, it is two members present in person: s 370(4). Proxies may only be counted in the quorum total if the articles so provide. A member who is a corporation may be represented by an authorised person (s 375) and is then deemed to be present in person.

If the articles fix the quorum at more than two, they may provide that the quorum is required only when the meeting 'proceeds to business' i e begins its course. If the subsequent withdrawal of member(s) reduces the attendance below the quorum level, then on this formula the meeting may continue, provided always that there are still at least two persons present: *Re Hartley Baird Ltd* [1955] Ch 143. The 1948 Table A contained this formula. But the 1985 Table A Art 40 is differently worded – 'no business shall be transacted . . . unless a quorum is present'. Table A goes on to provide for automatic adjournment (Art 41) if the meeting becomes inquorate.

There are two important statutory exceptions to the principle that there cannot be a meeting unless at least two members are present. As stated above the DTI in ordering that an AGM shall be held may fix the quorum at one (11.1 above). Similarly, if the court orders that a meeting shall be held it may fix the quorum at one (11.3 above). These powers are given as a means of getting round the difficulty which arises if there is only one surviving member of a company, or if only one member is willing to attend.

These rules apply to *general* meetings. It has been held at common law that if all the shares of a class are held by one person, he alone may constitute a meeting of the class: *East v Bennett Bros Ltd* [1911] 1 Ch 163. However, if a class meeting is called to give consent to a variation of class rights, as is usually the case, s 374(2) requires a quorum of two but permits a single member to constitute a quorum if the meeting is adjourned on the first occasion for lack of a quorum: s 374(3). The one member might of course give his consent in writing to obviate the need to convene a class meeting at all: s 125(2).

To allow a reasonable time for late arrivals the articles usually allow a short period (half an hour from the appointed time in Table A Art 41) before it is necessary to adjourn a meeting for lack of an initial quorum.

The articles usually provide that at a general meeting the chairman of the board of directors or in his absence (or if he is unwilling) another director selected by the directors present shall be chairman of the meeting: Table A Art 42. If there is no director available to take the chair the members present may choose one of themselves as chairman under the articles (Table A Art 43) or if the articles do not provide for it under s 370(5).

The general function of a chairman is to conduct the meeting in a proper fashion. He derives his authority from the members' agreement (usually expressed by the articles), that he shall be chairman. His principal duties are to preserve order, to call on members to speak, if they wish, in turn so that they have the opportunity to express their opinions, and to bring forward each item of business (within the scope of the notice convening the meeting) so that each resolution is discussed if necessary and then put to the vote. He may insist that a member who is becoming disorderly, abusive or irrelevant, shall be silent or in the last resort shall leave the meeting if the member will not submit to the chairman's ruling. He may in his discretion determine that a particular point of view has been sufficiently expressed and refuse to allow members to waste time by unnecessary repetition of their own or other speakers' remarks. Strictly he should not permit a person, such as a proxy at a meeting of a public company, to speak if he has no right to do so. But in this as in all other contentious issues the skill of a good chairman lies in knowing when to insist on and when to relax the rules of procedure so that fairness as well as good order prevail and are apparent to all.

The chairman has no general power to dissolve or adjourn the meeting unless a majority of members present so resolve. But in view of his duty to maintain order he has an overriding power to adjourn the meeting for a short time if it becomes disorderly so that order may be restored. The articles (eg Table A Art 45) may provide that the chairman must adjourn the meeting if the meeting so directs and may do so if it consents. If the chairman adjourns the meeting when he has no power to do so, the members may elect a new chairman in his place to continue the proceedings from the point reached at the time of irregular adjournment.

The notice convening the meeting specified its business as passing the accounts, considering reports and electing auditors. After a resolution to receive the report and accounts had been lost the chairman closed the meeting. The members present chose another chairman and continued the business. It was held that these later proceedings were valid. The former chairman could not halt the meeting because he disliked the course it was taking: *National Dwellings Society v Sykes* [1894] 3 Ch 159.

The articles (Table A Art 41) may provide for an automatic adjournment if there is no quorum at the start of the meeting or if it later becomes inquorate. The chairman usually has power to decide on a new date and time for resumption of the meeting. Table A (Art 45) limits the adjourned meeting to completion of the unfinished business of the original meeting but requires that seven days' notice shall be given if the meeting is adjourned for 14 days or more.

11.9 Debate and amendment of resolutions

Two main principles apply to regulate the course of discussion at a general meeting. First, the meeting may only discuss matters which are within the scope of the notice convening the meeting. If the notice merely describes the business in general terms such as the election of directors, a member may propose his own resolutions on that item as in the *Choppington Collieries Case* in 11.6 above. But if the text of a resolution is set out in the notice a member who wishes to vary it must do so by way of amendment (see below). The second principle is that only one item of business should be under discussion at one time and members should confine their remarks to that business. This principle is observed by a formal proposal of a resolution, followed by debate on it, and finally voting on it; the meeting then moves on to the next item of business.

A member may propose an amendment to a resolution under discussion. Unless the articles so require he need not give advance notice nor put forward his amendment in writing nor find a seconder among those present. In deciding whether to allow discussion of the amendment the chairman should consider whether the resolution if so amended, would still be within the scope of the notice of business to be transacted at the meeting. If the resolution is business which is described in the notice in brief general terms there may be no difficulty. If, however, the resolution is special business, its complete text is likely to have been set out verbatim in the notice (but perhaps introduced by the words 'to consider and if thought fit pass with or without modification the following resolution'). In such a case the amendment may be accepted if the resolution, as so amended, would still be within the general intention disclosed in the notice or would set a lower financial limit on the proposal. But an amendment, even if effected by deletion only, is inadmissible if it completely alters the nature of the proposal.

186

The notice stated that resolutions would be proposed to wind up voluntarily and to appoint a named person as liquidator. At the meeting it was resolved to wind up but to appoint a different liquidator. This amendment was within the scope of the notice since a company which commences voluntary winding up may appoint a liquidator without notice: *Re Trench Tubeless Tyre Co* [1900] 1 Ch 408.

The notice set out a resolution authorising the payment to the directors of a percentage of the company's profits. An amendment was proposed by which the percentage would be less than in the original resolution. This was a permissible amendment since the resolution as amended would be within the scope indicated by the notice: *Torbock v Lord Westbury* [1902] 2 Ch 871.

The original resolution provided for sale of the business and winding up: an amendment to delete reference to sale of the business so that it became a resolution for winding up was inadmissible since it altered the nature of the proposal: *Re Teede and Bishop Ltd* (1901) 70 LJ Ch 409.

A special or an extraordinary resolution cannot, however, be amended in substance at all since the statutory definition of such resolutions (11.14 below) means that the text of the resolution to be passed must be set out in the notice convening the meeting.

A special resolution as set out in the notice provided for cancellation of the entire balance on share premium account of £1,356,900.48 and the accompanying circular explained that the assets represented by this balance had been lost. After the notice had been issued it was realised that a small amount of £321.17, included in the above total, had only recently been received and had not been 'lost'. At the meeting the chairman proposed that the resolution should be amended so that it provided for a reduction of share premium account from £1,336,900.48 to £321.17. The resolution was carried on a show of hands and no poll was demanded: the chairman's declaration that it had been carried was apparently conclusive: s 378(4). But the court held that the resolution had not been properly carried since what had been passed was not the resolution of which notice had been given. It was held that the notice to be given must either be notice of the resolution as actually passed or at least notice of its entire substance. Grammatical or clerical errors could be corrected or mere drafting improved by amendment. But any alteration of substance, however minor, would not produce a resolution of which notice had been given as s 378 requires. Earlier decisions such as *Henderson v Bank of Australasia* (1890) 45 Ch D 330 were distinguished on the grounds that statute law at the time did not correspond with s 378. It was also held that a notice and its accompanying explanatory circular should be treated as one document and that any introductory formula in the notice referring to possible 'modifications' in no way alters the effect of s 378: *Re Moorgate Mercantile Holdings Ltd* [1980] 1 All ER 40.

The limits placed on the amendment of resolutions protect those members who do not vote in favour of the amendment. If of course there is complete unanimity of members different principles may apply (11.16 below).

There are more general restrictions on what is permissible as an amendment. The chairman should only accept a proposed amendment for discussion if it is relevant to the resolution then under discussion and does not amount in substance to a rejection of it, e g a proposal to reduce £100,000 to £1. The proper course in the latter case is for the member to vote against the resolution, not to seek to have it passed in a meaningless form.

If the amendment is accepted for discussion it should be debated and put to the vote before a vote is taken on the main resolution. If the amendment is carried, the resolution as amended should then be put to the vote. If several amendments are proposed the chairman should select them for discussion in the most convenient order. If he wrongly refuses to permit debate and a vote on an amendment, his error invalidates the original resolution if it is then passed without the amendment. This was the decision in *Henderson's Case* above.

11.10 Voting at general meetings

The votes attached to shares are defined by the articles. If however the articles do not determine voting rights, then every member is entitled to one vote for every share or £10 of stock held by him: s 370(6). There is no legal objection to providing that shares shall carry no voting rights (as is often the case with preference shares – Chapter 7: 7.9) or shall have enhanced votes on certain issues (see *Bushell v Faith* in Chapter 12: 12.7).

At a general meeting the normal method of voting is by show of hands, in which each member present in person has one vote, regardless of the size of his shareholding, and proxies do not vote. The chairman counts the votes, for and against the resolution, by looking round the room, and then declares the result. By this means non-contentious decisions can be taken rapidly.

If there is an equality of votes, the chairman has a casting vote only if the articles so provide, as they usually do (Table A Art 50). A resolution which is not carried by a majority is lost.

If more than one joint holder of the same shares is present, the first-named in the register is entitled (against the other) to vote if he wishes to do so. A member who is mentally incapable may vote by his receiver. A member who is in arrears in payment of calls on his shares may be debarred by the articles from voting. The decision of the chairman, given at the meeting, on a member's right to vote, cannot be challenged afterwards: Table A Arts 55–58. There is no objection to a member contracting with a third party to vote as the latter directs. But on some matters, such as protection of minorities (Chapter 15: 15.3), variation of class rights (Chapter 7: 7.13) and alteration of the articles (Chapter 4: 4.7), a member's vote may be challenged or disregarded.

The chairman's declaration of the result of a vote on a show of hands, supported by an entry in the minute book, is usually made conclusive unless a poll has been demanded: Table A Art 47 and s 378(4) (on voting on a special or an extraordinary resolution). It is not practicable to debate the number of votes cast on a show of hands after the meeting. But the chairman's declaration may be challenged if by its own terms it is manifestly wrong.

In a vote on a show of hands on a special resolution the chairman declared that 6 votes had been cast in favour and 23 against, but he added that 'there are 200 voting by proxy and I declare the resolution carried'. As proxies could not vote on a show of hands, the declaration was held to be wrong and invalid: *Re Caratal (New) Mines Ltd* [1902] 2 Ch 498.

11.11 Voting on a poll

If a poll is validly demanded, the result of a vote on a show of hands lapses and has no effect. The articles usually give to the chairman the power to call for a poll and he should use it if there is any real disagreement.

A poll should also be held if demanded by at least five members, or their proxies, or by members (or proxies) holding at least one-tenth of the shares with voting rights (or shares with such rights on which at least one-tenth of the paid-up capital has been paid): s 373(1)(b). The articles may set the minimum at a lower level (Table A Art 46 gives the right to demand a poll to two members present in person or by proxy). But any 'threshold' set by the articles above the statutory level is void. The articles are also void insofar as they seek to deny altogether the right to have a poll on any question other than the election of a chairman or the adjournment of the meeting: s 373(1)(a).

In some special situations, such as approval of a contract for purchase of the company's own shares (Chapter 5: 5.17) or variation of class rights (Chapter 7: 7.12), even a single member has a statutory right to have a poll: s 164(5)(b) and s 374(4).

Whatever the requirement a proxy has the same right to demand a poll as the member whom he represents: s 373(2). A proxy is not required to cast all his votes, nor is he prohibited from casting some votes for and others against the same resolution. He may need to do this if he represents more than one absent member.

The articles usually follow Table A Art 49 in leaving it to the chairman to decide how a poll shall be conducted. He may decide to have it on some later day so that suitable arrangements can be made.

The normal procedure on a poll is that the chairman appoints scrutineers to examine and count the votes. He usually appoints either the auditors or one representative of each opposed faction nominated by them. At a large meeting the most convenient method of voting on a poll is to distribute voting cards, which members and proxies complete and hand in. The scrutineers check the cards against the register of members, and hand to the chairman their written report of the votes cast for and against the resolution. He then declares the result.

An alternative procedure is to prepare a single voting list 'For the resolution' and another 'Against the resolution'. The voters then come up to sign the list and enter the number of votes cast. But this entails a lot of movement which can cause difficulty in a crowded room.

The result of a poll takes effect from the date of its declaration.

The articles provided that a director should cease to hold office unless he became the holder of qualification shares within two months of appointment. A poll was taken at a general meeting held on 23 December 1957 and the result declared on 24 December 1957. Two directors elected by this poll were entered on the register as holders of their qualification shares on 24 February 1958, ie 2 months and 1 day after the meeting but just within the permitted two months from the declaration of the result. It was held that they had been appointed on 24 December 1957 and so had not vacated office on 24 February 1958: *Holmes v Keyes* [1958] 2 All ER 129.

11.12 Proxies: s 372

Instead of attending a meeting in person a member has a statutory right to appoint a representative to attend and vote instead of him: s 372(1). (The right is restricted to members of companies which have a share capital and to those members who have the right (under the articles) to attend and vote in person.) The representative so appointed is called a proxy and the written form of appointment is a proxy card (also colloquially referred to as a 'proxy'). The articles may give additional rights in respect of proxies but they cannot deprive a member of his minimum statutory rights.

As stated above (11.6) every notice convening a meeting must state the member's right to be represented by proxy and that he may appoint as proxy a person who is not also a member.

In the case of a private company a member is entitled to appoint only one proxy but his proxy may speak at the meeting. In the case of a public company a member may appoint more than one proxy but his proxy has no right to speak. The purpose of the public company rules is to permit a member who is a nominee of two or more beneficial owners to appoint more than one representative to attend the meeting on their behalf but to discourage the practice of appointing professional advocates as proxies who might argue technical points at length at meetings of public companies if permitted to speak.

A proxy can vote on a poll but not on a show of hands. He can demand or join in demanding a poll just as the member could. A proxy is only counted in reckoning the quorum (11.8 above) if the quorum is prescribed in terms of members present (in person or) *by proxy*. In that case one member who is the proxy of another is reckoned as two for quorum purposes but not so as to satisfy the basic requirement that a meeting requires the presence of more than one person (11.8 above).

It is usual to provide in the articles that an appointment of a proxy shall only be valid if received by the company in advance of the meeting. This rule facilitates the checking of proxy cards in advance (in case there is a poll) and incidentally enables the directors to know – in many cases – how much support for themselves or opposition there will be at the meeting. But the articles are void in so far as they require that a proxy card, to be valid, shall be received by the company more than 48 hours before the meeting. If the meeting is adjourned or a later date is fixed for conducting a poll the articles may provide for delivery of proxy cards in the interval between the original meeting and the subsequent event: Table A Art 62. But without such provision in the articles there is no right to deliver a proxy card except in time for the original meeting. The articles usually provide for the due execution of a proxy card: Table A Art 62.

The normal practice of public companies is to issue with the notice convening the meeting a printed proxy card (in the form of a postcard) by which a member may appoint the chairman of the meeting or other directors to be his proxy. A company whose shares are listed on the Stock Exchange is required as a Stock Exchange condition to issue a 'two-way' proxy card such as appears in Table A Art 61. With this form of card it is easier for the member to instruct his proxy to vote against resolutions instead of for them.

It is permissible for the directors to solicit support for their proposals in this way at the company's expense. But if they adopt this practice they are required to issue proxy cards to all members instead of selectively to those members whom they regard as potential supporters: s 372(6).

A member who has completed and sent in a proxy card is free to revoke it and appoint a different proxy or to attend the meeting and vote in person, which is an automatic revocation of the proxy appointment. Other events such as the death or insanity of the member would, under normal principles of agency law, terminate the proxy's authority. But to avoid practical difficulties the articles (Table A Art 63) usually provide that a proxy, once duly given, remains valid unless the company receives written notice, at the place fixed for the deposit of proxy cards, not later than the start of the meeting or of the poll.

A company or other corporate body which is a member of another company is entitled to appoint a proxy just as an individual member may. But it can as an alternative by resolution of its directors authorise any person to act as its representative at a general meeting or class meeting: s 375. A representative so appointed has the same rights and power as an individual member present in person, eg he may, unlike a proxy, speak at a general meeting of a public company. A company which is a creditor or debenture holder of another company may in like manner appoint a representative to attend a meeting of creditors or debenture holders.

11.13 Minutes: ss 382–3

Every company must keep minutes of the proceedings of general meetings. The minutes may be in the form of a bound book or a looseleaf record or on computer subject to the same safeguards as apply to keeping a register of members (Chapter 8: 8.8). The minutes must be kept at the registered office and be open to inspection by any member without charge for at least two hours a day and he may have a copy on payment of a fee.

The minutes when signed by the chairman of the meeting or of the next succeeding meeting are evidence of the proceedings: s 382(2). But they are not conclusive evidence unless the articles so provide (eg Table A Art 47 on the declaration of a vote by a show of hands: 11.10). When minutes are not conclusive other evidence of the proceedings may be produced.

11.14 Resolutions: s 378

There are three kinds of resolution which are distinguished by the size of majority required to carry them and the notice to be given, ie:

(a) an ordinary resolution is one of which due notice has been given and which is passed by a simple majority of votes;
(b) a special resolution is one passed by a three-quarters majority at a general meeting of which at least 21 days' notice has been given specifying the intention to propose the resolution as a special resolution: s 378(2);
(c) an extraordinary resolution must be described as such in the notice of the meeting and must also be passed by a three-quarters majority. But 14 days' notice usually suffices: s 378(1).

The ordinary resolution is the residual category, ie references to 'resolution' mean ordinary resolution unless the word 'special' or 'extraordinary' precedes 'resolution'. There are, however, some references in the Companies Act to an 'ordinary resolution' as such in connection eg with the removal from office of a director or an auditor by simple majority vote: ss 303 and 386(1).

Where a matter is submitted to a general meeting for decision an ordinary resolution suffices unless the Companies Act or the memorandum or articles prescribe a different kind of resolution.

A special resolution is one which satisfies three conditions, ie:

(i) that it is so described in the notice, eg 'to consider and if thought fit pass the following resolutions as special resolutions';
(ii) at least 21 days' notice is required for the meeting at which it is passed; and
(iii) it must be carried by a three-quarters majority of votes cast (see below).

An extraordinary resolution must also be so described in the notice and must be carried by a three-quarters majority, ie conditions (i) and (iii) apply. But, like an ordinary resolution, it may be passed at a general meeting of which only 14 days' notice is given (unless the meeting is an AGM for which 21 days' notice is required or a special resolution is moved at the same meeting).

The requirement of 21 days' notice for a special resolution may be waived with the consent of members holding at least 95 per cent of the shares carrying the right to attend and vote at the meeting. Since the 21 days' notice is prescribed by statute it must be reckoned in 'clear days' in accordance with the statutory model articles, ie Table A Art 38.

The effect of point (i) on amending the resolution when it is before the meeting have already been considered (the *Moorgate Mercantile Holdings Case* in 11.9 above).

A special or an extraordinary resolution is also one defined as having been 'passed at a general meeting': s 378(1). However the statutory model articles (Table A Art 53) provide that a resolution signed by every member entitled to vote at a general meeting 'shall be as effectual as if it had been passed at a general meeting' (see 11.16 below on the 'assent principle'). The cases below suggest that the courts will recognise the effectiveness, as a special or extraordinary resolution, of such a signed resolution. If, however, the court is asked to give its sanction to a transaction, for which a special or extraordinary resolution is expressly required by statute, it will only exercise its power in exceptional circumstances.

The articles gave to the chairman a casting vote at general meetings. All three members of the company agreed that he should no longer have this casting vote but no meeting was held to pass a special resolution to alter the articles accordingly. Later the validity of this change was challenged. The court held that the alteration was valid. The statutory procedure (s 9) for altering the articles is merely a safeguard for individual members who may disagree. If all have consented there is no reason why their agreement should not be a valid substitute: *Cane v Jones* [1981] 1 All ER 533.

All four members of the company signed a resolution for the reduction of the company's capital, for which a special resolution followed by court approval is required (s 135 and Chapter 5: 5.28). When the resolution came before the court for approval the court expressed a 'strong inclination' to postpone the hearing so that a special resolution might be passed at an EGM convened for the purpose. In the end the court approved the signed resolution after it had been represented that delay would cause much difficulty to the company. But the court indicated that, although it had discretion, it would not be prepared to waive the statutory requirement of a special resolution in any future case: *Re Barry Artist Ltd* [1985] 1 WLR 1305.

Normal rules of voting at company meetings are applied to determine whether there is a three-quarters majority. If, on a show of hands, the chairman declares that a special or an extraordinary resolution has been carried, without giving the number of votes for and against, his declaration is conclusive unless a poll is then demanded: s 378(4).

A special resolution is required in many situations which affect the constitution or future of the company, such as an alteration of the objects or of the articles (Chapter 3: 3.18 and Chapter 4: 4.6), or a resolution to wind up the company (Chapter 19: 19.1). An extraordinary resolution is prescribed for voluntary liquidation on grounds of insolvency, where the decision may have to be taken urgently, and for a variation of class rights (Chapter 7: 7.12).

11.15 Registration of resolutions: s 380

One of the most important differences between special and extraordinary resolutions on one hand and ordinary resolutions on the other is that copies of the former must always be delivered to the registrar within 15 days after the resolution has been passed but only certain specific categories of ordinary resolution require registration. If the law requires that a copy of a resolution shall be registered in this way and placed on the company's file at the registry, everyone dealing with the company is deemed by 'constructive notice' to know whether such a resolution has been passed and registered and, if it has, the nature of its contents. But there is no constructive notice of the existence or content of an ordinary resolution, unless it has to be registered. This distinction is the basis of the rule in *Turquand's Case* (Chapter 13: 13.8).

Section 380 requires that a printed copy of every resolution passed in general or class meeting of members of the following types shall be delivered to the registrar within 15 days:

(a) a special resolution;
(b) an extraordinary resolution;
(c) a resolution or agreement agreed to by all the members of the company in substitution for a special or an extraordinary resolution;
(d) a resolution or agreement agreed to by all the members of a class in substitution for a resolution passed at a class meeting which would be binding on all members of the class;
(e) ordinary resolutions of the following types:
    (i) to authorise the directors to allot shares or to vary or revoke that authority (Chapter 5: 5.4);
    (ii) to approve a market purchase of the company's own shares (Chapter 5: 5.17(c));
    (iii) to wind up voluntarily in accordance with the provisions of the articles under s 572(1)(a) (Chapter 19: 19.1).

In addition s 123 requires that within 15 days a company shall register:

(f) a copy of the resolution passed to increase its share capital together with a notice of the increase (Chapter 5: 5.27).

In the ordinary way resolutions passed at a meeting of the board of directors are merely management decisions which are kept in confidence. However, there are special circumstances when directors are given statutory powers to perform a formal act on behalf of the company; in these cases a copy of the board resolution must be registered: s 380. These cases are:

(1) a resolution to alter the memorandum when the company ceases to be a public company following acquisition of its own shares (Chapter 1: 1.18);
(2) a resolution to change the name of the company on directions from the registrar (Chapter 3: 3.4);
(3) a resolution under the Companies Consolidation (Consequential Provisions) Act 1985 s 2 – no longer of any practical importance.

11.16 Informal but binding agreements of members

The normal effect of a resolution of the appropriate type passed in general meeting is to impose on the company and on all its members a binding decision. As explained above the meeting must for this purpose be properly convened and conducted; the proceedings must be recorded in written minutes.

It is, however, necessary to give legal recognition to decisions reached by unanimous agreement of the members but without the formality of passing resolutions in general meeting. The statutory period of notice may be waived (11.4) and the articles of a company may provide expressly that a resolution signed by all the members entitled to attend and vote at a meeting shall be as valid and effective as a resolution passed at a general meeting duly convened and held: Table A Art 53 (11.14 above).

In addition the mere agreement of members, formal, or even implied by conduct, may be treated as binding decisions although the appropriate procedure has not been observed. In such cases it is essential that all the members should agree since a majority cannot bind a minority in this way.

Five persons who were the only directors and shareholders of the company held a meeting of directors and took a decision to purchase property from a syndicate in which they were interested. Debentures were issued in payment of the price. But under the articles the directors were not entitled to vote on a contract in which they were interested. The issue of the debentures was void if it was treated as a board decision. It would, however, be valid if ratified by the members in general meeting (Chapter 13). It was held that all the members had in effect sanctioned the transaction and it was binding on the company although the decision had not been taken at a general meeting: *Re Express Engineering Works Ltd* [1920] 1 Ch 466.

Directors' remuneration had been paid without obtaining formal approval in general meeting as the articles required. But the payments had been made with the agreement of the holders of the ordinary shares carrying the right to attend and vote at general meetings who were also the directors. The liquidator's claim to recover these payments failed as they had been sufficiently approved under 'assent principle' established in *Parker and Cooper Ltd v Reading* (Chapter 1: 1.11), ie the assent of all members entitled to vote at a meeting is equivalent to a resolution passed at a meeting. In the present case there was no express assent but it was sufficient that the annual accounts, which disclosed the payments, were distributed to the members and approved by them: *Re Duomatic Ltd* [1969] 1 All ER 161.

The assent principle also applies to attempts to hold a general meeting, which is invalid because of procedural irregularities.

The chairman had 45,000 shares, his wife 150,000 and a third member 5,000, making a total of 200,000. The third member agreed with the proposal to pass an extraordinary resolution to wind up; the chairman's wife gave him her proxy. But the chairman was the only member present at the EGM at which the resolution was passed. It was held that there had been no 'meeting' since only one member was present (and the proxy given by a second member did not suffice). But as all three members were agreed that the resolution should be passed, the 'assent principle' of *Re Duomatic Ltd* could apply to an extraordinary resolution just as much as to an ordinary resolution since the articles included what is now Art 53: *Re MJ Shanley Contracting Ltd* LS Gaz 26 March 1980.

The *Shanley Case* goes rather further than the cases cited in 11.14 above since there was no signed resolution (in substitution for an extraordinary resolution) but merely an informal agreement.

The case below shows that if all the members are present at an invalid meeting, have the opportunity of dissenting from the proposal put to it but do not dissent, that is sufficient as evidence of their unanimity.

All five members attended a general meeting which had been called without giving the required notice, ie the meeting had not been properly convened and the extraordinary resolution to wind up passed at the meeting was as a formal resolution invalid. At the meeting the resolution was carried by the votes cast by two members; the other three members abstained. It was held that the three members had by their presence and abstention from voting created a situation of unanimous agreement with the result that the resolution was a valid decision to wind up: *Re Bailey, Hay & Co Ltd* [1971] 3 All ER 693.

Chapter 12

Directors

12.1 The office of director

A company, as an abstract person, cannot manage itself and it is not
practicable for the members in general meeting to do so. Accordingly every
company must have at least one director and a public company must have a
minimum of two: s 282. The articles usually follow Table A (Art 70) in giving
to the directors, as a body called 'the board', wide powers of management.

The test of who is a director of the company is one of function. It is provided
that 'director' includes any person occupying the position of director, by
whatever name called: s 741(1). If the members of the managing body are
called 'trustees' or 'governors', they are nonetheless company directors by
virtue of their powers.

Some companies give to senior members of their staff the title of 'director' to
confer status, eg 'sales director' or 'director of research'. But such a person is
not a director, to whom the rules of company law apply, unless he is also a
member of the board, appointed under the articles and with the right to attend
board meetings. An 'alternate director' (12.2) is a company director.

To prevent avoidance of the rules and responsibilities of directors any
person 'in accordance with those directions or instructions the directors of the
company are accustomed to act' is a 'shadow director' to whom many of the
rules relating to directors apply. But a professional adviser is not a shadow
director merely because the directors often follow his advice. The directors of a
subsidiary normally conform to the policy of the holding company, but that
company is declared not to be a shadow director for the purposes of various
rules applicable to shadow directors generally.

12.2 The appointment of directors

When a company is formed, the documents name the first directors and
secretary, and they sign to indicate their willingness to accept appointment.
They are automatically appointed by the issue of the certificate of
incorporation: s 13 (Chapter 2: 2.1). There is no objection to naming the first
directors in the articles, but if there are differences the formation documents
prevail.

The appointment of subsequent directors is regulated by the articles which
usually follow the model of Table A Arts 73–80 by which the ultimate control
of the membership of the board of directors rests with the company in general
meeting: Art 78. It is then the general meeting which elects, re-elects or
removes directors from office. But there is no legal objection to articles which

confer on some person, whether or not a member of the company, the right under the articles to nominate one or more directors. A group holding company, for example, may be authorised under the articles of each subsidiary to appoint and remove its directors from office. The articles usually (eg Table A Art 79) authorise the existing directors to co-opt a new director either to replace a director who has resigned or died, etc, or as an addition to the board. By this means the initiative in selecting new recruits to the board is usually taken by the board itself and the shareholders in general meeting merely confirm the existing directors in office under the standard (but not obligatory) rules explained below.

The duration of a director's appointment can be unlimited (subject to the rules on disqualification and removal from office under s 303). But the articles usually follow the model of Table A in requiring directors to vacate their office and (if they wish) offer themselves for re-election as follows:

(a) a director who has been co-opted by the board since the last annual general meeting under Art 79 retires at the first AGM after his appointment and may then offer himself for re-election;

(b) at the first AGM all the directors retire and at each ensuing AGM one-third of the directors (or if their number is not a multiple of three the nearest one-third) may offer themselves for re-election. Those directors retire who have been longest in office since their last election, i e a director may expect to be due for retirement and re-election at intervals of approximately three years.

When a choice has to be made between directors who were last elected on the same day this is done by agreement or by drawing lots.

A managing director or other director appointed by the board to executive office (12.8 below) does not retire by rotation (Art 84). In reckoning how many directors are to retire under the 'one-third rule' these directors are excluded from the reckoning, and so is any director retiring under rule (a) above. The chairman, however, is treated as an ordinary director for purposes of retirement by rotation. These Table A rules may of course be displaced or varied by special articles. The articles may, for example, omit altogether retirement by rotation so that each director holds office for an indefinite period. This is not uncommon in wholly-owned subsidiaries and in private companies in which the members have agreed upon a permanent composition of the board.

In a small private company, where all the shareholders are also directors, it makes no significant difference that the existing directors can co-opt a new member to the board to fill a vacancy. However in larger companies the bias of the system is towards giving the existing directors control of the future composition of the board ('a self-perpetuating oligarchy'). The members usually take little interest in the qualifications of the new director and duly re-elect him when he comes up for re-election at the first AGM after his original co-option to the board.

The justification sometimes offered for this system is that the directors must act collectively as a board in the management of the company's business. The board usually functions better if it is a group of like-minded and compatible individuals than if it is divided into warring factions.

In the same spirit the articles (Table A Art 75) usually provide that a retiring director is to be deemed to be re-elected if no other candidate is elected in his place (unless either a positive resolution for his re-election is put to the vote and is lost, or a resolution is passed that his place shall not be filled).

The 1985 Table A did however introduce a requirement that in recommending a director for re-election, other than a director retiring by rotation, the board must give notice to members of the same particulars of the recommended candidate as are required to be included in the register of directors (12.9 below) after his election. The purpose of this disclosure is to 'introduce' a new member of the board, including a director who has been co-opted and is now offering himself for election for the first time. The members will thus know a little more about him at the time of deciding whether to re-elect him.

The bias of the standard Table A system towards allowing the existing directors to select new recruits to the board is reflected in a rule which requires advance notice in writing to be given to the company 14–35 days before the meeting of the name of any person who is to be proposed for election as a director being neither recommended by the directors nor a retiring director seeking re-election: Art 76. This rule does not prevent an 'opposition candidate' from standing but alerts the existing directors to this intention so that they are not taken by surprise.

The minimum of 14 days' advance notice (it was only three days in the 1948 Table A) is imposed so that the directors will have time in which to inform members of the candidate before they vote, or appoint proxies to vote, at the general meeting.

At a general meeting of a public company resolutions for the election of directors must be put to the vote separately for each director unless the meeting has previously agreed, without any vote cast against it, to a procedural resolution permitting appointment of two or more directors by a single resolution: s 292. This is to restrict the device of linking in the election a well-supported and another weaker candidate in the same resolution so that votes for the former will assist the latter.

The articles may authorise a director to assign his appointment to a successor of his choice. But any such assignment is only effective if approved by special resolution: s 308. A more effective device is to provide in the articles that a named director may on or after retirement nominate some person to become a director: this appointment does not require approval by members though they can still remove the person nominated by an ordinary resolution under s 303 (12.7 below).

The 1985 Table A (Arts 65–69) now provides (the 1948 Table A did not) for the appointment by any director of an 'alternate director' to attend and vote for him at any meeting of the board at which the appointing director is not present. Under the Table A procedure the appointment of an alternate director requires the approval of the board by resolution unless he is already a member of the board to whom the absent director in effect gives the power to vote for him.

The Jenkins Report (para 83) concluded that an alternate director is 'in the eyes of the law in the same position as any other director', ie he attends board meetings as of right but only when his appointor is absent. Table A (Arts 66 and 69) provides that an alternate director is not entitled to directors' remuneration and is not an agent of his appointor, for whom the latter is answerable as principal. The alternate director should of course be entered in the register of directors or any other place where a list of the directors is required by law. He may, and often does, sign company documents as a director in the absence of his appointor.

12.3 Initial disqualification of directors

The principal statute is now the Company Directors Disqualification Act 1986, which consolidates provisions originally contained in the Companies and Insolvency Acts. If a person is disqualified by law he may not be appointed a director in the first place and must vacate office if, at the time when he is first disqualified, eg by court order, he holds a directorship. In addition the articles may impose additional non-statutory grounds of disqualification. These latter grounds usually require a director to vacate office, to which he has previously been validly appointed before the occasion of disqualification arose. Those topics are explained in subsequent sections of this chapter (12.4–12.6).

There is no legal objection to a company being a director of another company. In such cases it appoints an individual to represent it at board meetings.

An undischarged bankrupt may not, without the leave of the court by which he was made bankrupt, *act* as a director or be concerned directly or indirectly in the formation or management of a company: CDDA s 11. This statutory prohibition permits him to continue as a director provided that he does not act as such, eg by attending board meetings. But the articles (Table A Art 81) usually reinforce the statutory rule by providing that a director who is bankrupt or otherwise visibly insolvent shall vacate his office altogether (12.6).

The main effect of the Company Directors Disqualification Act 1986 is to empower the court in its discretion, but on specified grounds, to make orders for the disqualification of the person concerned from being (1) a director (2) a liquidator, administrator, receiver or manager of a company and (3) taking part or being concerned in the promotion, formation or management of any company except with the leave of the court: CDDA s 1. However in the context of company insolvency if the grounds for disqualification are found to exist the court must make an order: CDDA s 6.

The grounds for a disqualification order are:

(a) conviction of an indictable offence in connection with a company;
(b) persistent breaches of company law requirements in delivering accounts, returns etc to the registry as required by law;
(c) various forms of misconduct in company affairs as described below;
(d) the insolvency of a company in circumstances indicating that the director is unfit to be concerned in the management of any company.

The court is entitled to conclude that there has been 'persistent default' in the delivery of company documents (ground (b) above) if the person is found guilty, on the same or different occasions, of default three times in five years. However the maximum period of disqualification on this ground is five, not fifteen years: CDDA s 3.

Disqualification may be ordered if, in the course of liquidation of a company, it appears that a person has been guilty of fraudulent trading or other fraud as an officer etc of the company, or if he has been ordered to make a contribution to the company's assets on account of his responsibility for its wrongful trading (Chapter 20: 20.18 and 19). On receiving a report from its inspectors (Chapter 15: 15.9) the DTI may apply for a disqualification order against any person involved on grounds that 'it is expedient in the public interest that such an order should be made': CDDA ss 8 and 10.

New provisions on company insolvency, introduced by the Insolvency Act 1985 and consolidated in the Company Directors Disqualification Act 1986, are intended to cast the net wider than before so that the threat or actual penalty of disqualification may operate against directors who are irresponsible or incompetent rather than dishonest. In contrast to the other grounds of disqualification, which may apply to 'any person' concerned with the company in question, disqualification resulting from company insolvency is limited to the directors. In making out a case for disqualification it must be shown that:

(a) the person is or has been a director of a company which has become insolvent. A company is insolvent if it goes into liquidation and cannot pay its debts and liquidation expenses, or if an administration order is made (Chapter 10: 10.11) or an administrative receiver is appointed (Chapter 10: 10.3). Note that the order or appointment is itself treated as sufficient evidence of insolvency;

(b) the conduct of the director in connection with that company alone, or taken with his conduct as a director of other companies, makes him unfit to be concerned in the management of any company: CDDA s 6.

Application should be made to the court within two years from the commencement of the company insolvency, but the court may extend the period in a particular case: CDDA s 7.

In considering allegations of unfitness the court is required to have regard to a list of matters (CDDA Sch 1) in relation to the director's actual conduct. The list is in two parts – the first is a list of forms of misconduct or default in company administration, such as the maintenance of company registers and records and delivery of annual returns or accounts, as well as misapplication etc of company property. The second part of the list relates to company insolvency, beginning with the director's responsibility for its causes and continuing with various shortcomings of the director in connection with insolvency and insolvency procedures.

To ensure that the conduct of each director of an insolvent company is brought under review the Official Receiver, a liquidator, administrator or administrative receiver, has a duty to report on the conduct of directors to the DTI. The DTI may also take the initiative in calling for a report. Application to the court for a disqualification order is made by the DTI in appropriate cases. When the matter was before Parliament the DTI resisted demands that creditors should have the right to apply to the court. It was argued that some creditors might use such a right to bring improper pressure on directors to pay their debts in priority to others.

Even a magistrate's court has power to make disqualification orders in connection with indictable offences and persistent breaches in filing documents. But its power is limited to making orders for disqualification up to five years only.

Higher courts have power to disqualify for up to 15 years (except in respect of persistent default in filing documents). Where the ground is company insolvency the order must be for a minimum of at least two years.

To prevent evasion director includes 'shadow director' in the context of company insolvency; acting in breach of a disqualification order is a criminal offence and entails personal liability for the company's debts. A person who acts in the management of a company in accordance with the instructions of another person known to him to be disqualified or an undischarged bankrupt is also personally liable: CDDA s 15.

The articles may impose initial disqualification from being a director on persons who are e g aliens or minors.

If a company goes into insolvent liquidation, every director (or shadow director) within the previous year is prohibited automatically for a period of five years thereafter from being a director, or concerned in the management, of any other company which has the same or a similar name: IA s 216. The court, however, may grant exemption. The purpose is to prevent the 'phoenix syndrome' in which an insolvent company transfers its business to a new company under the same name and management.

12.4 Share qualification

There is no general legal requirement that directors shall also be shareholders of the company. The argument for such a requirement is that those who manage a company, more especially a public company, should have and be seen to have a stake in it. The argument against it is that if the minimum shareholding (called 'directors' share qualification') is set at a nominal level it is meaningless and if it is set higher it tends to exclude or discourage otherwise suitable candidates who lack capital.

Many companies do, however, include in their articles a special article requiring directors to 'hold' a specified number of shares. The effect of such a requirement is regulated by s 291. The 1985 Table A has nothing on this subject.

Section 291 provides that, on appointment, a director has a period of two months (or such shorter period as the articles may provide) in which to obtain his share qualification. If, however, he does not obtain it within the permitted period after appointment or if having obtained it he later ceases to hold it, he vacates office forthwith on the expiry of the initial period or on the subsequent disposal of the qualifying shares. The reacquisition of the required shareholding does not reinstate the director in office if he has vacated it. He should be reappointed. But, if having ceased to be a director under this rule, he nonetheless continues to act as such, the company may be bound by his transactions (Chapter 13: 13.6).

A director is not required to obtain his shares by allotment from the company (unless he agrees to do so) but may obtain existing issued shares by transfer from another person.

A director satisfies a qualification share requirement by becoming the registered holder of the required number of shares. But beneficial ownership of shares without entry in the register of members, e g purchase of shares not yet transferred to him in the register, or possession of a share warrant or letter of allotment, does not suffice. On the other hand a director who is the registered holder of his qualification shares is thereby qualified for office although he may not be the beneficial owner of the shares or may be registered only as joint holder with another person.

The articles may require that a director shall hold his share qualification 'in his own right'. This formula, however, does not require beneficial ownership but only that the director shall appear on the register as the holder.

At the time of his first appointment the director was already the registered holder of a sufficient share qualification but the shares were mortgaged. As a result of an unauthorised act of the mortgagee the company became formally aware of his interest in the shares. It was held that the director nonetheless held his shares 'in his own right' as the articles provided: *Pulbrook v Richmond Consolidated Mining Co* (1878) 9 Ch D 610.

In *Bainbridge v Smith* (1889) 41 Ch D 462 the court said 'the test is being on or not on the register as a member, i e with power to vote and with those rights which are incidental to full membership'.

However a liquidator who is registered as the holder of shares owned by the company in liquidation does not hold them 'in his own right' since he is on the register merely in a representative capacity: *Boschoek Pty Co Ltd v Fuke* [1906] 1 Ch 148. But he should not have been registered at all since the company was thereby accepting notice of a trust contrary to s 360 (Chapter 8: 8.11).

The period of two months available to a newly appointed director is strictly reckoned from the date of appointment (see *Holmes v Keyes* in Chapter 11: 11.11). But if the company introduces into its articles a new requirement of directors' qualification shares or if it increases the number of shares required, s 291 does not apply and the directors have an unspecified reasonable time in which to comply: this was so stated in *Molineaux v London, Birmingham and Manchester Insurance Co Ltd* [1902] 2 KB 589 where complicated facts raised a number of other issues as well.

12.5 Age qualification

Section 293, which is considered in this section, only applies to (i) public companies and (ii) private companies which are subsidiaries of public companies. Moreover even companies in this category can exclude s 293 by their articles. Hence s 293 has only limited scope.

Where s 293 is operative a director must retire at the AGM following his 70th birthday. However, even then he may be re-elected if special notice (Chapter 11: 11.5) is given and his age is disclosed. He is not automatically re-elected, without a vote, under the Table A provisions mentioned above (12.2). A director who retires at 70 does not retire by rotation and is disregarded for the purpose of the rotation system. If he, or someone in his place, is then elected, he or his successor are treated as continuing his term of office under the rotation rules. If, for example he were due to retire by rotation at the AGM of the next following year, he would do so – and special notice should again be given.

If a director fails to retire at 70, when he should do so, his acts thereafter are as valid as if he were entitled to be in office.

12.6 Other grounds of subsequent disqualification

The articles (Table A Art 81) usually summarise the statutory rules on disqualification and extend the effect of personal insolvency of a director by requiring that he vacates office altogether if he becomes bankrupt or makes an arrangement with his creditors.

A director admitted to hospital for treatment under the Mental Health Act 1983 also vacates office.

He may resign by notice in writing to the company.

Article 81 also provides that if a director is absent without leave from meetings of the board of directors for a period of six months, the directors may resolve that his office be vacated. Some of the case law is on articles which were differently worded. But it is considered that the Table A formula reckons the period of absence from the last meeting which the director attended and not from the first which he fails to attend. Secondly, it applies to involuntary absence e g on grounds of illness. But if it does apply the other directors may take account of the circumstances in deciding whether the absent director should vacate office.

The normal precaution is that a director who anticipates a period of absence applies for formal leave of absence at the last meeting which he attends. Leave is given and recorded in the minutes. There is then no problem.

12.7 Removal from office

Notwithstanding any provisions of the articles or of any agreement between the company and a director, such as a service agreement not yet expired which requires that he shall hold the office of director, any company in general meeting has overriding statutory power to remove a director from office by ordinary resolution (unless he is a director of a private company appointed for life before 1945). But special notice must be given of any resolution for removal or for the appointment at the same meeting of another director in his place: s 303.

On receipt of special notice from a member the directors will consider whether they have to include the resolution in the notice convening the general meeting. (See *Pedley's Case* in Chapter 11: 11.5).

If they agree or are obliged to include the resolution in the notice of the meeting, the company sends to the director concerned a copy of the member's special notice. The director may require the company to circulate to members a statement by him of reasonable length giving his defence. If the statement is received too late for issue in advance or if the company fails to circulate it as required, the director may have it read at the meeting. In addition the director has a right to address the meeting whether or not he is a member. But application may be made to the court by the company, or by any person aggrieved, for an order that the director's statement shall not be circulated or read on the grounds that it gives needless publicity for defamatory matter: s 304.

If the director is removed in this way the vacancy so created may be filled as a casual vacancy. But special notice must also be given of intention to propose the election of a person at that meeting to fill the vacancy and he succeeds (for purposes of retirement by rotation) to the unexpired term of office of the director whom he replaces.

In determining whether the ordinary resolution for removal has been carried by the required simple majority the provisions of the articles on voting must be observed even if they are designed to frustrate the general intention of s 303.

The three shareholders each held 100 shares but the articles provided that on any resolution for the removal of a director any shares held by that director should carry three votes per share instead of one. It was argued that this provision 'made a mockery of s 303' (and a similar device could make it impossible to alter the articles by special resolution contrary to s 9). But the Court of Appeal and the House of Lords both held that this factor does not invalidate weighted voting rights. It is simply a question whether or not the resolution is carried. In this case it would not be carried: *Bushell v Faith* [1970] 1 All ER 53.

In *Bushell's Case* each shareholder had a normal voting strength of one-third of the total and so could block any special resolution, requiring a three-quarters majority, to remove the weighted voting from the articles. But if a director's normal votes do not exceed one-quarter, it is normal practice to entrench the weighted voting system by providing that each shareholder shall have, say, 26 per cent of the votes against its removal. There is no reported decision on weighted voting as a device for preventing a company from exercising its statutory power (s 9) to alter its articles by special resolution. But it is difficult to see how a distinction could be made in such circumstances from the decision in *Bushell v Faith*, where the effect of the principle in frustrating an alteration of the articles was discussed, though it was unnecessary to take a decision on it.

The removal from office of a director who is also an employee of the company may entitle him to claim damages for breach of contract and/or statutory compensation for unfair dismissal. In giving the statutory power of removal of a director s 303(5) expressly reserves his entitlement (if any) to compensation or damages for breach of contract arising from the termination of his appointment as director or arising in any other capacity terminated by his ceasing to be a director, e g his salaried position as a managing director. But if he has no contract of employment the fact that he performs management functions does not automatically give him the status of an employee (see *Parsons Case* in 12.8 below).

The statutory power in no way prevents a company from having other powers in its articles to remove a director without resort to s 303. As the statutory procedure is cumbersome a company may, for example, have power under its articles to remove a director from office summarily by extraordinary resolution (or may even alter its articles to take such a power with a view to exercising it immediately afterwards).

12.8 Directors as officers and as employees

A director as such is not an employee of the company: he is one of its officers. The articles usually provide, however, that a director may be appointed 'to the office of managing director or to any other executive office under the company' (Table A Art 84). Many directors do work for their companies as managers. The essential distinction (12.20 below) is that a director is not required by his office to give more time to the business of the company than is made necessary by attending board meetings. If he does render other services he may do so without becoming an employee but he may alternatively become an employee even without a written service agreement relating to his functions as a manager. It depends on the facts whether he is then de facto an employee.

Three brothers were directors and equal shareholders. They all worked in the management of the company's business but were remunerated by voting agreed amounts at the end of the year. No PAYE income tax was deducted; they paid National Insurance contributions as self-employed: there were no service agreements. Two brothers used their votes to remove the third from office as director. He claimed compensation for unfair dismissal. He failed on the grounds that although a contract of employment may be made without formality the arrangements in this case did not constitute employment at all: *Albert J Parsons & Sons Ltd v Parsons* [1979] 1 RLR 117.

Company law draws a number of distinctions between the position of directors as such and any other functions which they may perform as managers or self-employed advisers, consultants, etc. A managing director (Chapter 13: 13.2) has a recognised special authority but he too is in other respects a senior employee, like a finance director, marketing director, etc, who combines the status of director with that of a manager or adviser. For convenience directors with this dual role are referred to below as 'working directors' and other directors who are merely directors and nothing more are called 'non-executive directors'. These terms are in common use.

Both types of director *as directors* are entitled only to such remuneration as the articles may provide. The articles may provide that this remuneration shall be determined in general meeting, ie voted as an annual allocation: eg Table A Art 82. It is common practice where the shareholders are also the directors of the company to distribute each year's profits as directors' remuneration approved in general meeting. The directors may have given only minimal services to the company but the payments are not generally open to challenge.

A husband and wife were the only shareholders and directors of the company which, for the last three years before it went into liquidation, had been trading at a loss. Although there were no profits, directors' remuneration was duly approved each year under the articles. The liquidator contended that these payments were recoverable. The wife, who had been ill, had performed no duties at all and the payments to the husband exceeded the market value of his services. The court held that if payments were made under a power in the articles and approved by shareholders, it was not material to enquire whether the company had obtained a benefit in the form of adequate consideration. However the payments to the wife were in reality a return of capital and not a payment for services at all. Those payments only were recoverable: *Re Halt Garage (1964) Ltd* [1982] 3 All ER 1016.

Alternatively the articles may provide for directors' fees either as fixed annual amounts or as a fee to be paid for attendance at each board meeting. A fixed annual fee is the most usual provision with entitlement to reimbursement of expenses incurred in the performance of their duties.

Remuneration which has become due is a debt owed by the company but the directors, since they are not employees, do not have any preferential claim to payment in a winding up (Chapter 20: 20.9). The directors may waive their entitlement to their fees but this waiver is only binding on them if they enter into a contract to that effect either between themselves or with the company.

The articles usually (Table A Art 82) provide that directors' fees 'shall be deemed to accrue from day to day'. If a director vacates office during a year he is then entitled to his fees up to that point. But he is not entitled to notice or to fees in lieu of notice. If the articles are altered so as to reduce the annual rate of directors' fees, the reduction cannot be made retrospective (see *Swabey's Case* in Chapter 4: 4.6).

A company may not undertake to pay directors' fees at a rate which is 'tax-free'; tax must be deducted: s 311.

The salaries and other conditions of service of working directors as managers are fixed by or under the authority of the board of directors. But information of these decisions is made available to members both in accounts (Chapter 14: 14.7) and by requiring a company to keep at its registered office (or other 'appropriate place' – see Chapter 3: 3.10) a copy of the service agreement of each director who has one with the company or any subsidiary (or if the contract of service itself is not in writing a written memorandum of its terms). A member has a statutory right to inspect any such agreement: s 318(7), but these rules on directors' service agreements do not apply if:

(a) the contract requires the director to work wholly or mainly outside the UK (but a note of its duration must be available); or
(b) the contract has an unexpired term of less than 12 months or can within that period be terminated by the company without payment of compensation.

If a company intends to enter into a long-term service contract, ie an agreement for more than five years, with a director, the contract must be approved by a resolution passed in general meeting: s 319. If the agreement is made with a subsidiary it must be approved at a general meeting of the holding company (and need not be approved by a general meeting of the subsidiary as well in the case of a wholly-owned subsidiary): s 319(4). The rule is intended to restrain certain abuses by which directors could claim substantial sums as damages for breach of a long-term service agreement if removed from office or otherwise dismissed.

In addition to a contract of service by which the director is to be an employee the requirement of approval under s 319 applies to a contract by which a director is to provide services, eg as a self-employed consultant. The rule is not restricted to contracts for the director's services in the capacity of director but applies to any form of service to any company of the group. It can even apply to a contract with a third party under which that party is to make available to the company the services of the director.

Approval is required under s 319 if (i) the agreement is for more than five years and (ii) the company cannot during the period of the agreement terminate it by notice (or only by notice given in specified and therefore restricted circumstances). There are rules which catch agreements for less than five years which may be extended or renewed.

In seeking approval the company must make available at its registered office for inspection by members a memorandum of the terms of the agreement. The memorandum is to be available for 15 days before the meeting and at the meeting itself. Only an ordinary resolution is required to approve the agreement. If an agreement which falls under s 319 is not approved, it remains in force but is deemed to contain a clause by which the company may terminate it on reasonable notice at any time. What is reasonable notice to terminate a director's employment depends on the circumstances but 12 months would usually suffice.

Although an agreement for director's services, eg as a consultant, is not open to inspection by members like a service agreement, it will usually be an arrangement with the company in which the director has a material interest, which must be disclosed in the annual accounts: Sch 5 para 1(c).

The payment of compensation to directors for loss of office also requires approval by the company in general meeting: ss 312–316. These rules on compensation for loss of office as director do not apply to payments made to working directors who may be dismissed in breach of their contracts of service, which are subject to general rules of liability to pay damages for breach of contract. The statutory code is confined to ex gratia payments. The new provisions on long-term service agreements are, of course, intended to narrow this loophole.

The code deals with payments to a director 'as consideration for or in connection with his retirement from office' in any of three circumstances:

(i) the payment may be made by the company to the director: s 312;
(ii) a purchaser of the whole or part of the company's undertaking or property may make a payment (or give other valuable consideration) to a director of the vendor company: s 313;
(iii) a person who makes an offer for shares of a company may make a payment or give valuable consideration to a director (such as a higher price for his shares than is offered to other shareholders). The rules in this case apply whenever a general offer is made to all shareholders, or another company makes an offer with a view to the company becoming its subsidiary or the subsidiary of its holding company, or an individual makes an offer to acquire control of at least one-third of the voting power in the company, or any offer is made for shares which is conditional on acceptance to a given extent: s 314.

In the cases of (ii) or (iii), ie payment to a director by a third party, the rules apply to any such payment made as part of an agreement for transfer of the business or within a period of three years beginning one year before and extending to two years after the making of the agreement or offer.

In any of these cases the proposed payment must be disclosed to members of the company and approved by them in general meetings. In the case of (i) the company itself may not make the payment to the director unless it has been so approved. In cases (ii) or (iii) the director who receives a payment without his shareholders' approval holds the sum in trust. In the case of a sale of the company's undertaking under (ii) he holds the unauthorised payment in trust for the company and in the case of an offer for shares under (iii) he holds the excess payment for his own shares or other sum received in trust for other vendors of shares (and must bear the expense of distributing it to them).

In the *Duomatic Case* (Chapter 11: 11.16) a compensation payment to a former director had been informally approved by the ordinary shareholders, who were also the directors at the time, but it had not been disclosed to the preference shareholders. Although they had no votes, and so could not have approved or disapproved it, the failure to disclose it to all 'members', as required by s 312, led to a successful demand by the liquidator that it be repaid.

12.9 Publicity about directors

The Companies Act regulates the acts and transactions of directors of companies in three ways:

(a) some transactions such as company loans to directors are prohibited (subject to limited exceptions) (12.11 below);
(b) some transactions are prohibited or declared invalid unless approved by members of the company in general meeting. The rules on directors' long-term service agreements, compensation for loss of office (above) and substantial transactions with the company (below) fall under this head;
(c) some transactions, interests and arrangements are not restricted but the company is required to make information available to members and, in some cases, to the public about such transactions, etc, relating to its directors.

This section and the next are concerned with the statutory rules enforcing publicity or at least availability of information about directors, their interests and their transactions with the company and other companies which are members of the same group.

Since a company is an abstract person its directing minds are, or at least should be, its directors. Those persons who invest in or deal with a company should know the identity at least of the otherwise 'faceless' collectivity, i e the board of directors of the company.

Accordingly a company is required to give notice to the registrar of the names and some other particulars of its directors (and also of its secretary), to provide similar information in its annual return and to enter it in a register of directors maintained by the company.

As explained above the documents delivered to the registrar to secure incorporation include a statement of the first directors (and also the secretary): s 10(2). The statement must give the same particulars as are required to be entered in the company's register of directors and secretary. Whenever there is a change of directors, or in the particulars in the register, the company must within 14 days give notice thereof to the registrar: s 288(2).

If this change is a notice of the appointment of a new director or secretary the notice to the registrar must include his signed consent to act in that capacity.

On receipt of a notice of change of directors the registrar is required to publish in the *London Gazette* notice of receipt: s 711(1)(c). If the company fails to give its notice and in consequence no notification of its receipt appears in the *Gazette* the company cannot rely on the change against any person who is unaware of it: s 42. If for example no notice has been given of the resignation of a director and he later signs a document as director of the company, the company could not assert that he was no longer a director against any person who accepted the document in the belief that he was still a director (Chapter 2: 2.14).

The company must keep at its registered office a register of directors and secretary which must be open for inspection by members and (on payment of a fee) by other persons: s 288. The register must include the following particulars of each director who is an individual:

(i) his present Christian names and surname and any former names (with some exceptions);
(ii) his usual residential address;
(iii) his nationality;
(iv) his business occupation and any other directorships which he holds or has held within the previous five years (with the exceptions mentioned below);
(v) his date of birth if the company is a public company or is a subsidiary of a .public company.

But if the company is a wholly-owned subsidiary in a group of companies it is unnecessary to show any directorship of the parent or other wholly-owned subsidiary companies incorporated in Great Britain.

If the director is itself a company the required particulars for entry in the register are its name and registered or principal office.

Similar particulars must be included in the annual return: Sch 15 para 6.

A company is no longer required to state the names of its directors on its letterheads, etc. It is still free to do so and in that case it is required to give a complete list, i e all the directors or none. Any such list must give the surname and Christian name or initials of each director (or its corporate name if the director is another company).

These disclosure requirements apply to shadow directors also but it is difficult to enforce compliance since neither the company nor the shadow director is likely to admit that he is a shadow director.

12.10 Directors' interests in shares or debentures

There is no objection in principle to the ownership of shares or debentures of the company by its directors. In many companies the roles of director/ manager and shareholder/proprietor are necessarily and advantageously combined.

For various reasons it is also desirable that information of a director's interest in the securities of his company should be readily available to other members and to outsiders. The present elaborate rules (Sch 13) have been in force, with slight modifications over the years, since 1967. They require disclosure of a director's 'interest' in shares or debentures, i e not merely those which are openly registered in his name in the register of members but those in which he has an indirect interest through nominees, trusts, other companies, close relatives and other specified connections. One of the purposes of the system is to make it more difficult for directors, if so inclined, to make use of information obtained in confidence, as directors, for their personal advantage (see Chapter 17 on insider dealing). A shadow director is required to comply with these rules.

The interest in shares or debentures of which a director must give notice to the company under the above rules is elaborately defined by Sch 13 to include:

(a) an interest as a beneficiary of a *trust* which holds relevant shares or debentures;
(b) an interest in shares or debentures in which *another company* is interested if the director has one-third or more of the voting power at any general meeting of the other company or that company or its directors are accustomed to act in accordance with his directions or instructions;
(c) an interest by reason of making a *contract* to purchase the shares or debentures or having a right (otherwise than under a trust) to have them delivered to him or to his order, whether it is a right exercisable immediately or in the future, or his being entitled (otherwise than as proxy appointed to represent the holder at a specific general meeting) to exercise rights incidental to the shares or debentures (of which he is not the registered holder);
(d) an interest as a *joint holder*;
(e) an interest as a trustee in shares held in the trust if the trustee has any powers of decision or management. A bare trustee, eg a nominee who holds shares entirely subject to the instructions of the beneficial owner, does not have an interest;
(f) an interest of a *spouse or child under 18* of a director is treated as an interest of the director: s 328.

On first appointment a director is required to give notice in writing to the company of his interests (if any) in the shares or debentures of the company, or of its subsidiary or holding company, or of another company which is a subsidiary of its holding company: s 324. Thereafter he must give similar notice if he becomes or ceases to be interested (or enters into a contract to sell, or obtains, exercises or assigns a right to subscribe for any such securities). The notice must specify the number of shares or debentures and be given within five days.

For the purpose of these disclosure requirements any person is a director if the acknowledged directors of the company are accustomed to act in accordance with his directions or instructions.

The company is required to maintain a register in which it enters the information given by directors and also the grant to a director of a right to subscribe for its shares or debentures and the exercise by him of any such right: s 325. The register is open to inspection by members and (on payment of a fee) by other persons (Chapter 3: 3.10).

If any shares or debentures of the company are listed on a recognised stock exchange the company must notify the stock exchange not later than the next working day of any transaction in the listed securities of which a director of the company has given it notice: s 329.

Particulars of the interests of each director in shares or debentures (as described above) must be disclosed in the directors' report issued to members with the annual accounts: Sch 7 para 2. The particulars to be given are the director's interests at the beginning of the year (or if he became a director during the year at the time of his appointment) and at the end of the year.

If the company's shares or debentures are listed on any stock exchange (whether in Great Britain or elsewhere) or the shares or debentures of its holding or subsidiary company or of the subsidiary of its holding company are thus listed it is a criminal offence for a director of the company to deal in 'options' over any such shares or debentures: s 323. An option in this context is the purchase of a right to buy or a right to sell or the right to do either as the purchaser may elect. The ban also applies to close relatives.

The DTI may appoint one or more competent inspectors to investigate any suspected contravention of the ban on options or of failure to make disclosure of directors' interests: s 446.

12.11 Directors' loans

As a general principle a company is prohibited from making a loan to any director of the company or of its holding company: s 330(2)(a). There are, however, some limited exceptions to the general rule. To prevent evasion the ban is extended to some other transactions by which a director might otherwise obtain a loan or credit under arrangements made by the company. The risk of abuse is greater where the company is or is associated with a public company; such companies (called 'relevant companies') are subject to additional restrictions. This section of the chapter deals in turn with the essential features of the basic legal rules on loans to directors. Following sections cover relevant companies and the disclosures to be made in the annual accounts of directors' loans (if any).

All companies are prohibited by s 330 (unless one of the exceptions applies) from:

(a) making a loan to a director of the company or of its holding company;

(b) entering into a guarantee (or indemnity) or providing security in connection with a loan by any person to such a director;
(c) arranging for the assignment to the company or the assumption by it of rights, obligations or liabilities under a transaction which the company itself could not enter into by reason of rules (a) or (b) above;
(d) taking part in any arrangement whereby another person enters into a transaction forbidden to the company under rules (a), (b) or (c) above if the other person has obtained or will obtain a benefit from the company (its holding or subsidiary company or fellow subsidiary).

Rule (c) is to prevent the company taking an assignment (for consideration) of a loan to a director (or guarantee of such a loan) provided initially by a third party.

Rule (d) is more particularly intended to prohibit mutual arrangements by which company A makes loans to directors of company B and company B makes loans to directors of company A and each company indemnifies the other against any loss arising from the loans. It also prohibits company A from conferring benefits, eg the award of profitable contracts, on company B as consideration for loans, etc, by company B to the directors of company A. But it probably does not prohibit a loan by company B merely because companies A and B have commercial dealings (eg if B is a bank and A is one of its customers) which yield some incidental advantage to company B. The rule is intended to catch specific and intentional benefits in return for loans.

These prohibitions apply to shadow directors throughout the whole system: s 330(5).

There are four exceptions to the general prohibition against loans etc to directors.

First, loans (but not other transactions) are permitted up to a maximum of £2,500: s 334. Among other minor instances, this exemption would cover the case of a director whose drawings during the year against his share of the profits (to be paid as directors' fees – see 12.8 above) were found at the end of the year to exceed by a small margin the amount which could be paid to him.

Secondly, a subsidiary may make loans (without limit) to its holding company even though the latter may be a director of the subsidiary: s 336. This exemption also applies to guarantees and giving security.

Thirdly, a company is permitted to enter into any form of loan transaction, as described in (a)–(d) above, to provide a director with funds to meet past or future expenditure in the performance of his duties of director or to enable him to avoid such expenditure: s 337. However it is a condition of this exemption that the transaction shall be approved by ordinary resolution at a general meeting of the company either beforehand or subsequently not later than the next AGM. In seeking approval the company must disclose to members the purpose and amount of the loan and the extent of any liability incurred by the company, eg in the guaranteeing of a loan to a director by a third party.

This exemption is of less practical importance than may at first sight appear. The articles always provide (Table A Art 83) for payment to directors of expenses of various kinds 'properly incurred in connection with the discharge of their duties'. Hence a director does not need to borrow money for this purpose; he is entitled to claim a refund of his expenses from the company. If he takes a round sum advance to meet future expenses, then in a proper case this may be regarded not as a loan but as an arrangement to place funds of the company in the hands of an agent for use in the company's affairs. But the amount of the advance should be reasonable and the director should account for his use of the money as soon as it is practicable to do so. A DTI investigation of the affairs of a public company once discovered that the managing director had obtained and retained for a long period very substantial sums without any accounting for them. That is a loan not an advance to an agent.

Finally, a company whose ordinary business includes the making of loans (and other credit business such as guarantees) may make a loan to a director in the ordinary course of that business: s 338. The loan must be not greater in amount and the terms, eg rate of interest and security required, must be no more favourable than would be offered by the company to an unconnected person of the same financial standing. But this condition is not to prevent a director from obtaining a house-purchase loan on the same terms as are available to employees of the company (if it has such a loan scheme at all).

A 'moneylending' company, to which this exemption is restricted, is one whose main business is the lending of money or supply of credit, such as a bank or a finance company. A company which in the course of some other business makes loans occasionally is not a 'moneylending' company to which this exemption applies.

12.12 Loans to directors of relevant companies

A relevant company is any public company and any private company which is the subsidiary or holding company of a public company or the subsidiary of a private company which itself has a public company subsidiary: s 331(6). Since the risk of abuse is greater in this context the basic rules, set out in the preceding section, are tightened and extended in various respects.

The exemptions for loans to meet business expenses and loans by moneylending companies are respectively limited in amount to £10,000 (expenses) and £50,000 (loan in the course of moneylending business): s 337(3) and s 338(4). However, the £50,000 limit does not apply to a moneylending company which is a recognised bank, except where the loan is made to a director under the terms of an employee house-purchase scheme: s 338(6). As so many moneylending companies are recognised banks, this is a considerable exception to the £50,000 normal limit.

Secondly, a relevant company is prohibited from providing credit (subject to some exceptions) by a 'quasi loan' or a 'credit transaction'. These types of transaction are elaborately defined by s 331(3) and (7). In essence a quasi loan is a tripartite transaction by which the company arranges with a third party, such as a person whose business is to issue credit cards, that the director may have credit facilities for which the company will make the payment in the first instance to the credit card company and recover the debt later from the director. However, there are two exceptions to the general ban on quasi loans by relevant companies. These are quasi loans in which the director is required to make payment within two months and quasi loans not exceeding in aggregate £1,000: s 332.

A credit transaction is a bilateral transaction between the company and the director for the supply of goods or services or the sale of land on hire-purchase or rental or other deferred payment terms. Again there are two excepted categories. First, a relevant company may enter into a credit transaction with a director if the aggregate amount does not exceed £5,000. Secondly, a relevant company whose ordinary business includes such transactions, eg a hire-purchase or rental company, may enter into a credit transaction with a director where the amount and the terms are the same as those which would be offered to a person of the same financial standing but unconnected with the company: s 335.

Finally, the basic rules against loan transactions of all kinds are extended, in the case of relevant companies, to transactions with any 'connected person' of the director. If there is a limited exemption, transactions with the director himself and any connected person are aggregated in applying the limit.

A person is a 'connected person' of a director if, but only if, he is:

(1) the director's spouse or minor child or stepchild; or
(2) a company with which the director is 'associated' (subject to exceptions); or
(3) a person acting as trustee of a trust (other than an employees' share scheme or a pension scheme) whose beneficiaries or objects (if it is discretionary) include the director or any person connected with him under rules (a) or (b) above;
(4) a person acting as partner of the director or any person connected with him under (1), (2) or (3) above: s 346(2).

A director is for the purposes of (2) above 'associated' with a company (or other body corporate) if he (and persons connected with him) are interested in at least one-fifth of the equity share capital of the company or are entitled to exercise or control more than one-fifth of the voting power at a general meeting of the company. A relevant company may however make a loan etc to a partly-owned subsidiary even if it is associated with a director of the lender by his interest as a minority shareholder in it: s 333.

12.13 Directors' substantial property transactions

A later section (12.18) of this chapter explains the general principle that a director may not have an interest in a contract made by his company unless this conflict of interest is sanctioned either by the articles of association or by a resolution of the members in general meeting. There is also a specific procedure applicable to transactions of a director (or a person connected with him) and the company when those transactions are 'substantial'. It is convenient to take that topic at this point since the penalties and disclosure requirements for directors' loans and substantial property transactions have much in common.

A director's property transaction is 'substantial' and subject to the following rules if it relates to a 'non-cash asset' which has a value ('the requisite value') in excess of either £50,000 *or* 10 per cent of the company's net assets (subject to a minimum in this case of £1,000). The value of the company's net assets is usually ascertained for this purpose from the latest annual accounts laid before a general meeting: s 320.

A company is prohibited from entering into an 'arrangement' (which includes but is wider than a contract) whereby either:

(a) a director of the company or of its holding company or a person connected with such a director is to acquire from the company one or more non-cash assets of the requisite value; or

(b)   the company is to acquire from any person described in (a) above one or
       more non-cash assets of the requisite value;

unless the arrangement is first approved by a resolution of the company in
general meeting. If the director or connected person is a director of the holding
company or a person connected with a director of the holding company, it
must be approved by resolution passed in general meeting of the holding
company. But it is unnecessary to obtain their approval in general meeting of
the company itself if the company is a wholly-owned subsidiary. In certain
narrowly defined cases the above rules do not apply: s 321.

12.14 Directors' loans and substantial property transactions: consequences of breaking the rules

There are similar basic consequences if either loans to directors or substantial
property transactions involving directors (as described in detail above) are
made in breach of the relevant statutory rules. In either case the company may
at its option avoid the loan or other transaction unless:

 (i)   restitution of the money or other subject matter is no longer possible or the
       company (or its nominee) has been indemnified for the loss or damage
       which it has suffered; or
(ii)   a third party who has acquired rights bona fide for value and without
       actual notice of the contravention (and who was not a party to the
       prohibited transaction) would be affected by avoidance of the transaction:
       s 341(1)(b) and s 322(2)(b).

In the case of a substantial property transaction (but not a prohibited loan) the
company loses its right to avoid the arrangement if within a reasonable period
it has affirmed the arrangement by resolution passed in general meeting.

   There are civil sanctions, for unlawful loans to directors and for unapproved
substantial property transactions with directors, against those responsible as
follows.

   The director and any person connected with him involved in the transaction
and also any other director of the company who authorised the arrangement or
transaction which contravened the relevant rule is liable:

(1)   to account to the company for any gain which he has secured directly or
       indirectly; and
(2)   to indemnify the company for any loss or damage which it has suffered as a
       result of the arrangement or transaction.

But there are specified circumstances in which a person otherwise liable may
escape liability by showing that he took all reasonable steps to secure compliance with the rules or (in the case of a director who merely authorised the
transaction or arrangement) that he was unaware of the relevant circumstances constituting the contravention: s 341(5) and (6): s 322(5) and (6).

   There are also criminal penalties, which may include imprisonment, for
infringement of the prohibitions against loans to directors by relevant
companies: s 342.

12.15 Disclosure in the accounts of directors' transactions

Elaborate rules in Sch 6 require every company to disclose in its accounts
prescribed information of:

(a) directors' loans and similar transactions, whether lawful or not. An independent private company, ie one which is not a relevant company, must give particulars of loan transactions which are lawful for that company though prohibited for a relevant company. What has to be disclosed is uniform for all companies;

(b) any agreement for such a transaction; and

(c) any other transaction or arrangement (for convenience referred to below as a 'contract' though arrangement is wider than that) in which a director had directly or indirectly a material interest.

Loan disclosures are required in respect of every individual who was a director at any time during the period covered by the accounts. If for example a company has made a loan to an employee who is not a director at the time but the loan is outstanding when he joins the board, it must be disclosed.

A director has an interest requiring disclosure in a transaction with a person connected with him. The other directors may decide whether or not a director's interest is material enough to require disclosure: Sch 6 para 3. There are special rules for directors of recognised banking companies to whom the normal disclosure rules do not apply.

There are two exemptions from the general disclosure requirements:

(a) credit transactions not exceeding £5,000 in aggregate: Sch 6 para 8; and

(b) a material interest in any contract where the value is less than £1,000 or 1 per cent of the value of the net assets of the company (subject in this case to a maximum of £5,000).

If the accounts do not make the required disclosures it is the duty of the auditors in their report to give the required information 'so far as they are reasonably able to do so': s 237(5).

12.16 Notice to be given by directors

A director is required to give notice of his interest, direct or indirect, in any contract or proposed contract with the company and to declare the nature of his interest. This rule applies to any contract in which he has an interest, whether or not it is material, and includes an interest in a loan or similar transaction regulated by the directors' loan rules: s 317.

The statutory rules are not clearly expressed. They require that a director shall give notice of his interest in a contract at the meeting of the directors at which the contract is first considered. This wording implies that if the contract is made by the company's management staff under delegated powers and is not submitted to the board at all there is no obligation on the director to give notice of it at all. If the director's interest arises after the board has begun to consider the contract he should give notice at the first board meeting thereafter.

It is also permissible for a director to give a general notice in advance that he is a member of a specified company or firm and so will have an interest in any contract which the company may afterwards make with that other company or firm. This implies that he is not required to give detailed information of his interest in any contract. It suffices to disclose that he is interested. For purposes of the new directors' loans code he may give notice that some specified person is connected with him.

There are several reasons why directors should be conscientious in complying with this statutory duty – a part from the risk of a fine, which is unlikely to be imposed. As explained in the next section any remission given by the articles (Table A Art 85) from the general prohibition against a director having such an interest at all is conditional upon his making a proper disclosure to the board. If he does so, he deals openly with his colleagues and enables them to discharge their duty of deciding whether his interest is so material that it should be disclosed to shareholders through the accounts.

12.17 Directors' duties

In company law 'directors' duties' means the obligations and standards of conduct and performance imposed on directors mainly by common law developed through cases, but in recent times augmented by statutory prescriptions.

The function of the directors is to manage the business of the company and for that purpose wide powers are delegated to them by the articles of association (Chapter 13: 13.4). To that extent the directors are collectively the agents of the company. In the exercise of their powers and in their control of the company's property they perform a function similar to that of trustees. But they are neither agents nor trustees in the ordinary sense of those terms.

An agent is required to comply with the instructions of his principal, ie he has a duty of obedience, but directors exercise the powers delegated to them in whatever way they consider to be in the interests of the company. The members cannot instruct them what to do. Moreover it is the board of directors collectively and not the directors as individuals to whom the powers are delegated by the articles. The directors are also not trustees since 'a trustee is . . . the owner of the property and deals with it as principal . . . subject only to an equitable obligation to account to [the beneficiaries]': *Smith v Anderson* (1880) 15 Ch D 247. In contrast to trustees the directors do not have the company's property vested in them as legal owners; they merely have control of it. If of course a director does improperly appropriate to himself company property he then holds it as a constructive trustee (12.19 below).

However the analogy with agents and trustees is relevant because both have a *fiduciary* duty to those for whom they act which requires them to act in an honest and disinterested fashion. The case law on the duties of directors has been developed by applying to the special circumstances of company directors, as 'officers' of their company, the same standards as mutatis mutandis apply to agents and to trustees.

Any codification by statute of directors' duties is beset by technical difficulties. If the code entirely replaces the case law much which is valuable and precise is lost. If on the other hand the code runs in parallel with the earlier case law, there is likely to be conflict and confusion between them. The underlying difficulty is that the circumstances of companies and of directors vary so much that no statement of general principles is likely to fit every case. While recognising these problems the Jenkins Report recommended (para 99(b)) that 'a general statement of basic principles' should be enacted. The Companies Bill 1979, which did not become law owing to the change of government in that year, did contain a passage based on the Jenkins Committee recommendation. Its essential points are worth considering as a guide to what still has to be extracted from the mass of case law:

215

(a) a general duty to observe the utmost good faith towards the company. From this it follows that a director should exercise his powers bona fide in the interests of the company, for a *proper purpose*, with *unfettered discretion* and without *conflict of interest*;
(b) a duty not to make use of the money or property of the company or information acquired as a director to gain directly or indirectly an *improper advantage* for himself at the expense of the company or otherwise. A director who is in breach of this duty is accountable to the company for his gains. He is also liable to make good any loss resulting from misapplication of company property;
(c) a duty to show proper *skill, diligence* and *care* in the performance of his duties.

The remainder of this chapter is a review of the elements of a director's duty (identified by the key phrases in italics above) with illustrations from the considerable number of cases on these issues.

The directors owe these duties to the company as individual directors and also in the collective exercise of their powers. They are now required by statute to have regard to the *interests of the company's employees* in general as well as to the interests of its members but only the company can call them to account for a breach of their duty in this respect: s 309 (12.21). They do not ordinarily owe a fiduciary duty to nor are they accountable to individual members.

Shareholders approached the company to find a buyer for their shares. The chairman and two other directors agreed to buy the shares for £12 10s each without disclosing to the vendors that negotiations, which in the end came to nothing, were in progress with a third party for the sale of the company's undertaking at a price which was equivalent to more than £12 10s per share. The vendors sought to have the sale set aside on the grounds that the directors owed them a duty to disclose everything which the directors knew, which might affect the value of the shares. The court rejected this claim and held that the directors owed no duty to *individual* members: *Percival v Wright* [1902] 2 Ch 421.

The decision in *Percival's Case* has been much criticised on grounds of principle. On its particular facts it was not unfair. The shareholders had made the first approach and they were offered the full price of £12 10s per share for which they asked. They knew that the buyers were directors, who might have inside information. The prospective sale at a higher value per share came to nothing. In any such case it is open to shareholders to constitute the directors their agents or trustees, in finding a buyer, and thereby impose on them a fiduciary obligation.

The directors obtained options from the shareholders with a view to selling the shares to another company. But they used the options to buy the shares themselves and then resold them at a profit. It was held that the directors were as agents accountable for their profit to the shareholders as principals: *Allen v Hyatt* (1914) 30 TLR 444.

Although the directors were held not accountable to shareholders in *Percival's Case*, the company might have called on them to account to it (under the principle of *Gulliver's Case* in 12.19 below). But that issue was not considered since it did not in the circumstances arise. Finally, this was insider dealing (inasmuch as the shares were listed securities) and directors who behaved in that way nowadays would be liable to criminal penalties (Chapter 17).

In most cases the company by its articles or by ordinary resolution passed in general meeting can relax or waive the obligations of directors or approve their actions which are otherwise a breach of duty. On the other hand, if the directors commit or intend to commit a breach of duty, the company (or sometimes an individual member on its behalf) may bring proceedings for a declaration or injunction to restrain them or to have their act declared void, or to recover damages for loss, or to compel them to account for an illicit gain or to rescind a contract. The availability of each remedy depends on its appropriateness to the circumstances of the case.

The large number of cases, some doubtful or conflicting in their effect, illustrate how the rules set out above are applied. A particular case may depend on more than one rule.

12.18 Directors' duties with respect to their powers

The directors' duty is to exercise their powers bona fide in the interests of the company. The test here is subjective, ie did the directors have in mind what they considered to be the interests of the company? If they did the court will not substitute its opinion, if it be so, that by an objective test the decision taken by the directors did not or was unlikely to benefit the company. In the *Smith and Fawcett Case* (Chapter 7: 7.16) the directors' decision to refuse to approve a transfer of shares in order to induce an offer of shares to one of the directors was upheld on the basis that the directors were concerned to preserve continuity of management of the company by obtaining a controlling shareholding for one of the directors. On the other hand a blatant instance of procuring a benefit for a third party is an invalid exercise of the directors' powers since it is a breach of their duty.

The managing director of two small companies was also the controlling shareholder. He was in poor health and wished to arrange that his wife should have a widow's pension from company funds after his death – but without bequeathing to her his shareholding. It was therefore arranged that he should enter into a quite unnecessary service agreement with one of the companies, by which a pension was to be paid to his widow if he died in service – as he did. To cover this transaction a suitable alteration was made to the objects clause to provide for pensions to widows of directors. It was held nonetheless that the decision to grant the pension was void because it was taken without any regard to the interests of the company: *Re W and M Roith Ltd* [1967] 1 All ER 427.

(In view of the decision in the *Rolled Steel Products Case* (Chapter 3: 3.11) it is now doubtful whether the grant of a pension under an express power was correctly treated as ultra vires the company in the *Roith Case* (see also *Horsley & Weight* in Chapter 3: 3.13) but it is still a clear example of the improper use of directors' powers).

However the directors now have a statutory duty in the exercise of their powers to have regard to the interests of the company's employees (12.20 below).

The interests of the company to which the directors must have regard means the interests of present and future members and, if there is more than one class, of all classes of members. If these interests conflict it is the directors' duty to hold a balance between them.

In the bona fide exercise of their powers the directors are also limited to the proper purposes of those powers. This issue most often arises when the directors allot shares for a questionable purpose. The power to allot shares is given to the directors primarily for the purpose of raising capital or acquiring assets which the company needs. But it may extend to other purposes which are beneficial to the company. The directors are, however, in breach of their duty if they allot shares (however honest and disinterested they may be) for the 'collateral purpose' of altering the balance of voting power within the company, eg in order to facilitate or to resist a take-over bid.

Two shareholders between them had 55 per cent of the issued shares and were opposed to a take-over bid which the directors and remaining shareholders wished to succeed. The directors allotted additional shares to the impending bidder solely to reduce the shareholding of their opponents to less than 50 per cent. The company did not need the additional capital raised by the issue of the shares. The Privy Council held that 'it must be unconstitutional for directors to use their fiduciary powers . . . purely for the purpose of destroying an existing majority, or creating a new majority which did not previously exist' even if the directors bona fide (ie without seeking to secure an advantage to themselves) believe that this exercise of their power to issue shares is in the interests of the company: *Howard Smith Ltd v Ampol Petroleum Ltd* [1974] AC 821, PC.

There is an important distinction between the directors' duty to act in the interests of the company, as they perceive them, and the directors' duty to exercise powers only for a proper purpose. In the latter case the members of the company in general meeting may approve and thereby validate the use of directors' powers for an irregular purpose.

The directors had allotted shares to create additional votes in order to resist a take-over bid. It was held that this exercise of their powers for an improper purpose could be ratified by ordinary resolution passed in general meeting: *Bamford v Bamford* [1969] 1 All ER 969. This decision followed an earlier one (*Hogg v Cramphorn Ltd* [1967] Ch 254) in which it was decided that, if the directors have already allotted the shares, the votes attached to the new shares may not be used at the meeting held to approve the directors' action retrospectively.

The other main duty of directors in the exercise of their powers is to preserve their capacity to reach entirely unbiased conclusions as to what is best for the company. They are in breach of this duty if they fetter their discretion or if they become involved in a conflict of interest. It would be wrong for the directors to enter into a contract with another person as to how they will vote at board meetings. If, for example, a director is appointed on the nomination of a debenture holder or a trade union representing employees he should not accept instructions as to how he will vote. But if the directors make a contract for the benefit of the company and on its behalf, they may as an incident of the contract agree to use their votes so as to secure the proper performance of the contract.

A director is also in breach of his duty of disinterested service to the company if he has personal or other interests which conflict with those of the company. It need not be shown that by reason of the conflict of interest the company has suffered loss. The director's duty is to give the company his undivided commitment to its interests and merely to have interests adverse to the company is a breach of that duty.

The company made a contract to purchase goods from a firm in which a director was a partner. The company was entitled to avoid the contract. 'No one having such duties to discharge shall be allowed to enter into engagements in which he has or can have a personal interest conflicting . . . with the interests of those whom he is bound to protect. . . . It may sometimes happen that the terms . . . are as good as could have been obtained from any other person: they may even at the time have been better. But . . . no enquiry on that subject is permitted' (Lord Cranworth LC): *Aberdeen Rly Co v Blaikie* (1854) 1 Macq 461.

The duty does not apparently prevent a director from holding directorships in two or more competing companies perhaps because each company gives implied consent to his holding office in the other. But it has been said that if the latent conflict of interest in such a situation becomes acute the director should resign from the board of one of the companies. (Dictum of Lord Denning in *SCWS v Meyer* – Chapter 15: 15.6).

The more usual conflict of interest situation results from a contract between the company and the director or some company or firm in which he is interested as a director or shareholder. As already explained, the director has a statutory duty to declare the nature of his interest to the board of the company: s 317 (12.15 above). But due compliance with the statutory rule of disclosure does not exempt him from the common law restriction against having such an interest at all.

This principle if it were applied without exception would be unworkable. It would for example prevent a director from entering into a contract of employment with the company to work as a manager in its business (12.8 above). The basic solution is provided by the articles which (Table A Art 85) permit directors to be employees of the company or interested in contracts with the company if, but only if, the director gives notice of his interest in compliance with s 317 (12.16 above). The same remission also permits the director to retain any profit, e g salary from employment, which he may obtain from his interest.

The other safeguard to the company, imposed as a condition of permitting directors to be interested in its contracts, is a rule (Table A Art 94) which prohibits a director from voting at a board meeting on any matter in which he has an interest, with certain exceptions. These exceptional cases, where the director may vote, relate to a guarantee, security, or indemnity of certain types, a director's subscription for shares or debentures of the company or as an underwriter of such an issue, and the approval of a company pension scheme. In these situations the conflict of interest is usually a technicality. If a director is not qualified to vote, he may not be counted among the directors 'present' for the purpose of establishing a quorum: Table A Art 95. This can give rise to problems as illustrated by the *Rolled Steel Products Case* (Chapter 3: 3.11).

There may be cases for which the articles do not provide a solution; e g all the directors may be disqualified from voting and so being counted in the quorum. In those situations the proper course is to convene a general meeting, at which full details must be disclosed, and invite the shareholders to approve the contract. In the absence of fraud a director may vote as shareholder to approve a contract in which he is interested. His duty to avoid a conflict of interest is limited to his role as director.

The company purchased a steamship which it needed (to replace another) from one of its directors at a reasonable price. A week later a general meeting approved the contract. The vendor who held one-third of the total votes voted in favour of the resolution to approve the contract. It was held that the contract was originally voidable but was effectually ratified at the general meeting and that the vendor director was fully entitled to cast his votes in what he deemed his personal interest. He had apparently purchased additional shares before the meeting to increase his votes: he was entitled to do so: *North-West Transportation Co Ltd v Beatty* (1887) 12 App Cas 589.

It may happen that a director fails to give notice of his interest as required by s 317, with the result that relieving provisions of the articles do not apply, or some other circumstance may lead to a contract made in breach of the basic prohibition. The contract is then not void but voidable at the option of the company. If the company does not elect to rescind the contract, it cannot both affirm the contract and recover from the director the profit which he has obtained from the contract between him and the company.

Burland was a shareholder and a creditor of an insolvent company in liquidation. He purchased plant from this company and resold it at a profit to another company of which he was a director. There was dispute as to how far the plaintiff (Earle) and other directors were aware of Burland's previous transactions. The claim made against Burland was to recover from him his profit on the basis that he had not made any adequate disclosure of his interest. The Privy Council found that Burland might have bought the plant with a view to its resale to the company of which he was a director but he had not acted in the purchase as the company's agent. He was in no way bound to resell it to the company. The claim to recover the profit failed. The company did not seek to rescind. 'To rescind the sale is one thing, but to force on the vendor a contract to sell at another price is a totally different thing' (Lord Davey): *Burland v Earle* [1902] AC 83.

If, however, the contract in which the director has an undisclosed interest is between the company and a third party, then the company may both rescind the contract and recover from the director his profit in it.

The plaintiff who was a director of the company entered into negotiations with the chairman of the company on behalf of another company without disclosing that he had an interest in the other company. Lord Denning said 'when a director fails to disclose his interest, the effect is the same as in contracts uberrimae fidei . . . non-disclosure does not render the contract void or a nullity. It renders the contract voidable at the instance of the company and makes the director accountable for any secret profit which he has made'. In this case the contract was between the company and a third party: *Hely-Hutchinson v Brayhead Ltd* [1967] 3 All ER 98.

As mentioned above (12.13) statute now requires that substantial property transactions, in which a director or a person connected with him is interested, shall be submitted to a general meeting for approval (regardless of any exempting provisions of the articles) and gives the company a right to avoid the contract if this is not done.

12.19 Directors' duties with respect to the company's property
In their dealings with the company's property the directors are in a position very like that of trustees (see 12.17 above). The practical application of that principle can be analysed into three more specific duties.

First, the directors have a duty to apply company property exclusively for company purposes.

In a complicated situation where company funds had been used illegally to assist a third party in the acquisition of shares of the company (see Chapter 5: 5.19) the court held the directors liable, saying that 'the property in their hand or under their control must be applied for the specified purpose of the company and to apply it otherwise is to misapply it in breach of the obligation to apply it for the purposes of the company'. *Selangor United Rubber Estates Ltd v Cradock (No 3)* [1968] 1 WLR 1555. This case contains the leading modern analysis of duties of directors in this respect.

If in breach of this duty the directors cause loss to the company, eg by paying a dividend out of capital, they are liable to make good the loss to the company (see Chapter 5: 5.25 *Flitcroft's Case*).

Secondly, if the directors appropriate to themselves property of the company, which for this purpose includes property or profits which it is their duty to obtain from a third party for the company, they are liable to account to the company for that property. The application of this rule is illustrated by the cases on 'fraud on a minority' such as *Menier v Hooper's Telegraph Works* and *Cook v Deeks* (Chapter 15: 15.3), where the directors at fault were also the controlling shareholders. Although directors may use their votes as shareholders as they see fit (*Beatty's Case* in 12.18 above) their votes will not be counted to effect approval of their own fraud on the company.

This principle is also put on a statutory basis in connection with improper loans to directors and property transactions not approved in general meeting as required (12.14 above).

Thirdly, a director is accountable to the company for any personal gain which he may obtain by the use of information or opportunity available to him in his capacity of director. This is the position even where the company itself could never have obtained the profit which accrued to the director and so has suffered no loss.

The managing director made contracts for the building of fishery vessels for the company and was paid a commission by those to whom the contracts were given. He also received payments from a supplier of ice to his company. It was held that he had been properly dismissed and must account for his receipts. 'If it is a profit which arises out of the transaction, it belongs to his master . . . unless his master knows of it' (Bowen LJ): *Boston Deep Sea Fishing and Ice Co v Ansell* (1888) 39 Ch D 339.

The company owned one cinema and had the opportunity of acquiring two more but could not finance the transaction. A second company was formed to acquire the two cinemas. The first company subscribed £2,000 in capital, which was all it could raise, and the directors and their associates subscribed £3,000 to make up the total price of £5,000. Later the share capital of both companies was sold and the shares of the second company were sold at a considerable profit. The new owner of the company caused it to claim the profit from the directors. It was held that they were accountable, although the effect was merely to reduce the agreed price paid for the two companies for the sole benefit of the purchaser. 'Those who by use of a fiduciary position make a profit [are] liable to account for that profit' (Lord Russell) regardless of whether the profit would otherwise have gone to the company, or whether the directors had a duty to obtain it for the company, or whether the company suffered any loss or whether the directors were doing for the company all they could and taking a risk with their own money: *Regal (Hastings) Ltd v Gulliver (1942)* [1942] 1 All ER 378.

The House of Lords noted in passing that if the directors had convened a general meeting to approve the transaction, they would have been relieved of their duty to account to the company. It would have been a mere formality since the directors were also the only shareholders.

A director cannot escape from his duty to account for his profit by resigning from his office of director in order to obtain the profit thereafter.

A managing director was unsuccessful in obtaining a profitable contract for the company but the other party intimated that it would give the work to the managing director personally. He then informed the board of the company that he wished to retire on health grounds and later took on the work on his own account. He was held accountable to the company for his profit: *Industrial Development Consultants Ltd v Cooley* [1972] 2 All ER 162.

In *Cooley's Case* the basic breach of duty was aggravated by the director's deliberate concealment from the company of the relevant facts. Complete openness is a positive obligation in any such circumstances.

In negotiations with the company for compensation for the premature ending of his contract of service the director did not adequately disclose his own past breaches of duty to the company. It was held that the company might on discovering these facts recover the compensation payment. *Horcal Ltd v Gatland* [1984] BCLC 549.

On the other hand, if the opportunity is fairly put to the board of the company, which decides that it will not take it up, and the director pursues it after a reasonable interval, there are Canadian and Australian decisions to the effect that the director is no longer accountable to the company for his profit since his duty to the company has expired: *Peso Silver Mines Ltd v Cropper* (1965) 58 DLR (2d) 1: *Queensland Mines Ltd v Hudson* (1978) 52 AJLR 399 (PC) (this was an Australian case but the final decision came on appeal to the Privy Council). Much will always depend on the facts of each case.

The safest course for a director in this situation is to invite the company to resolve in general meeting that he is released from duty and accountability to it. His position is then beyond doubt (on the authority of the dictum in *Gulliver's Case*).

12.20 Directors' duty of competent performance

The directors' duty of skill, diligence and care in the performance of their duties is a simpler matter since it is almost impossible to frame rules which will apply to the different circumstances of different companies. The leading case below formulated some now familiar principles but does not greatly help in applying them to specific instances.

The company had lost more than £1 m partly because of the frauds of its chairman, 'a daring and unprincipled scoundrel', who advanced large sums to the firm of stockbrokers (of which he was partner) who acted for the company in connection with its investments. The other directors made no enquiries concerning the abnormal amounts of money apparently in the hands of the brokers. The committee of the board responsible for deciding how surplus funds should be invested did not function. The directors were clearly in breach of duty but they escaped liability because under the articles officers were liable only for *wilful*, i e deliberate neglect or default, not present in this case: *Re City Equitable Fire Insurance Co Ltd* [1925] 1 Ch 407.

Although the device by which the directors escaped liability in the *City Equitable Case* is now void under s 310, the search for means of giving directors indemnity continues (3.22 below). Three propositions were laid down in the *City Equitable Case*:

(a) a director is expected to show no 'greater degree of skill than may reasonably be expected from a person of his knowledge and experience';
(b) 'a director is not bound to give continuous attention to the affairs of his company. His duties are of an intermittent nature to be performed at periodical board meetings';
(c) if normal business practice (and the articles) permit delegation to an employee 'a director is, in the absence of grounds for suspicion, justified in trusting that official to perform such duties honestly'.

Company practice has changed considerably over the half century since the principles were formulated. It is no longer common for a non-executive director to be asked to sign cheques drawn on the company bank account.

Signature of cheques is treated as a management function. But banks still insist that boards shall pass formal resolutions authorising named individuals, whether or not they are working directors, to draw cheques on important accounts. A different safeguard is provided by the establishment of an 'audit committee' of working and non-executive directors with whom the auditors can discuss their annual audit programme and their findings. It is doubtful whether a modern court would still consider that directors should only be liable for negligence which was 'in a business sense culpable or gross': *Lagunas Nitrate Co v Lagunas Syndicate* [1899] 2 Ch 392.

The standard set in (a) above is personal to the director. In recent years there has been much discussion of the possibility of setting an objective or general standard applicable to directors in every case. It is difficult to frame a standard which is precise enough to be effective and yet flexible enough to comprehend many different directors in many different situations. Moreover the law cannot really measure business efficiency. One quiet question at a board meeting can be far more effective than an hour's general but rambling discussion. Business entails taking risks and it is not reasonable to conclude that everything which goes wrong is the fault of a company management.

However the need to impose stricter responsibility on directors as a sanction against drifting into company insolvency has led to an innovation which may prove to be the beginning of a trend. When the court is considering the possibility of making directors personally liable for the company's debts on account of 'wrongful trading' (Chapter 20: 20.19) it must judge the actual conduct of each director by the standard of 'a reasonably diligent person having . . . the general knowledge, skill and experience that may reasonably be expected of a person carrying out the same functions as are carried out by that director in relation to the company': IA s 214(4).

There has been a similar trend in connection with the requirement at (b) above, ie attention to the company's business. If it is proposed that a director should be disqualified because the company has become insolvent (12.3 above) the court must have regard to the director's conduct in respect of a list of matters set out in a schedule: CDDA s 9 and Sch 1. The first part of the schedule is concerned with matters of company management and administration. This does not mean that a director is at fault if he personally has not attended to the company accounts, returns or registers. He may delegate these tasks but, if he does so, he is responsible nonetheless for their due performance.

When the Insolvency Bill 1985 was under discussion in Parliament it was proposed that mention should be made of the standard practice of submitting to directors, of large if not small companies, periodic management accounts to show the latest estimated financial position. However it was realised that it is difficult to prescribe what management accounts should contain. In any case it is not the accounts but the attention which the board gives to them which matters. Hence the proposal was dropped as impracticable. But it may reappear on some later occasion.

12.21 Directors' duties to employees

The common law doctrine is that in the exercise of their powers of management the directors should have regard only to the interests of the company as a whole, ie to the general body of shareholders (12.18 above). It is often in the interests of the company to behave as a good employer and to maintain good relations with its employees and with the trade unions which represent them. These factors permit and induce boards of directors to take account of the interests of employees in normal circumstances and so long as the business of the company is profitable.

A conflict of interest between shareholders and employees may nonetheless arise in an acute form if all or part of the business becomes unprofitable and the directors deem it necessary to close it down, sell it off, concentrate the company's activities on a limited number of sites or even install labour-saving plant. In any of these situations the interest of shareholders in profitability conflicts – or appears in the short term to conflict – with the interest of employees in preserving their jobs. To some extent the employment protection and industrial relations legislation preserves the balance by requiring the company as employer to consult with trade unions before declaring large-scale redundancies: Employment Protection Act 1975 s 99.

Since 1980 directors have been required 'to have regard in the performance of their functions [to] the interests of the company's employees in general, as well as the interests of its members': s 309. However s 309 goes on to stipulate that only the company, and not its employees, can enforce this duty which the directors owe to the company. This stipulation is included to prevent employees or their trade unions from suing the directors for breach of their obligations. The effect of s 309 is therefore mainly to provide directors with a justification if their dealings with employees are criticised by shareholders.

A company which sells or closes its business has statutory power to make redundancy payments (in excess of the prescribed scale) to its employees: s 719 (Chapter 3: 3.14). If the memorandum or articles so provide this power may be exercised by the directors: s 719(3)(b).

12.22 Insurance against directors' liability
Directors, especially of public companies, are now much more at risk in the performance of their duties. The standards are stricter and the possibility of legal proceedings begun by dissatisfied shareholders is greater than it was, owing to increased awareness of the general issue. A shareholder's action which fails may nonetheless entail heavy expense and much anxiety to the defendant director(s).

It is now quite common practice for a company to take out an insurance policy to cover liability to the company and to its directors arising from alleged negligence or breach of duty. There is no problem in the company insuring against its own liability. But it is believed that if the company insures its directors, at the company's expense, the arrangement is void under s 310 (referred to in connection with the *City Equitable Case* in 12.20 above). Section 310 makes void any contract for indemnifying any officer of the company in advance against liability for negligence, default, breach of duty or breach of trust. The directors sometimes pay a small part, typically one-tenth, of the premium on the company policy. But it is doubtful whether they are thereby insuring themselves, and so evading s 310.

Chapter 13

The management of the company

13.1 The proceedings of directors

Every company must have one or more directors. It is left to each company to determine what powers they shall have and how they shall exercise those powers. But the great majority of companies, large and small, have articles on the model of Table A to determine how the directors shall manage the business. References to Articles below are to Table A (1985) Arts 88–98 unless otherwise stated. Many companies continue to have articles based on the 1948 Table A, which are differently worded and, on some points, different in substance. Where necessary these differences are explained below.

Unless the articles otherwise provide the directors can only exercise their powers collectively. They usually hold board meetings at intervals so that they may review the situation and exchange views before reaching decisions. But there is generally provision for collective decision by signature of a resolution by all the directors (entitled to notice of a meeting of the board) as a substitute for a resolution passed at a meeting: Table A Art 93.

The directors may decide when and how often board meetings shall be held. Many boards, especially boards of large companies, have a regular practice of holding meetings at fixed dates such as the last Wednesday of each month. In smaller companies it may suffice to call meetings by special arrangement to deal with occasional business such as the consideration of the accounts or the convening of the AGM. It is usually provided that a meeting shall be called if any director requires it. There need be no prescribed period of notice. But notice should ordinarily be given to all directors. Article 88 provides, however, that notice need not be given to a director who is for the time absent from the UK and it must be long enough notice to give directors a reasonable opportunity of attending. The time and place fixed for the meeting must also be reasonable. If adequate notice is not given the proceedings are void (unless ratified at a later meeting).

The company which had five directors invited applications for 106,000 preference shares. All the directors attended a meeting at which it was resolved not to allot any shares until applications had been received for at least 14,000 shares. Applications were received for only 3,000 shares but two directors called a meeting at a few hours' notice only. Two other directors who received the notice did not attend; the fifth director who was abroad did not receive any notice. The two directors who had called the meeting formed the required quorum of two. In the absence of the other members of the board the directors present purported to rescind the resolution passed at the previous meeting and allotted the shares. These proceedings were held to be void: *Re Homer District Consolidated Gold Mines* (1888) 39 Ch D 546.

The company had two directors, Barron and Potter, but it proved impossible to hold board meetings, for which a quorum was two, since Barron refused to attend meetings. On 21 February 1914 Potter sent to Barron, a country clergyman, a notice of a board meeting to be held on 24 February. But Barron had not received the notice on 23 February when he arrived at Paddington Station for the purpose of attending the EGM which he himself had called for 24 February. Potter met Barron at Paddington and purported to hold a board meeting at which he proposed that three more directors be appointed. Barron demurred and Potter, as chairman, used his casting vote to carry his proposal. At the EGM on the following day Barron's resolution for the appointment of additional directors of his choice was carried. It was held that the encounter at Paddington Station was not a board meeting: one director could not convert a casual meeting into a board meeting, unless the other agreed: *Barron v Potter* [1914] 1 Ch 895.

But on a more suitable occasion even five minutes' notice has been held sufficient as the director did not object at the time: *Browne v La Trinidad* (1887) 37 Ch D 1.

The notice need not state the business which is to be transacted at the meeting (unless the articles so provide).

A meeting of the directors can only reach valid decisions if there is a quorum present. The quorum may be fixed by the articles, or if not in that way, then by express decision of the board itself or by inference from the practice of the board. If no quorum has been established in advance, a majority of the board forms a quorum.

In determining whether there is a quorum for each item of business, any director disqualified from voting on it must be excluded: Art 95. Failure to give notice of his interest will disqualify him (Chapter 12: 12.18 and the *Rolled Steel Products Case* in Chapter 3: 3.11). If the number of directors in office falls below the quorum level the remaining directors are usually authorised to act as a board solely for the purpose of appointing additional directors or of summoning a general meeting of the company: Art 90.

The standard articles authorise the board to elect a chairman to hold office for as long as the board may decide with power to appoint a temporary chairman to preside if the permanent chairman is absent: Art 91. The chairman usually has a casting vote: Art 88.

Unless the articles otherwise provide each director present has one vote and a resolution is carried only if a majority of the votes cast at the meeting is in favour of it. If there is an equality of votes (and the chairman has no casting vote) the resolution is lost. When there is provision in the articles for appointing alternate directors (Chapter 12: 12.2) a director may appoint another director to be his alternate (to cast his vote) or someone else. There is no statutory provision for proxy voting at board meetings.

The powers of the board are delegated to the directors by the articles. The directors cannot sub-delegate their powers to committees or to single directors unless the articles provide for this – as they usually do: Art 72. The power to appoint a managing director (13.2 below) is a different form of authorisation given for sub-delegation of powers by the board.

Minutes must be kept of the proceedings of meetings of the directors: s 382. Minutes when signed by the chairman of the meeting or by the chairman of the next succeeding meeting are evidence that the resolutions and other matters recorded in the minutes were passed. But other evidence may be given to rebut the evidence of the minutes. The minutes are usually a short formal record of documents produced and decisions taken; the discussion is not recorded though a director may insist that his dissent from some resolution shall be minuted.

It is not necessary or usual to read aloud the minutes of the previous meeting before the chairman signs them nor need he sign them at a meeting of the board. But it is common practice for the secretary to send a copy of the minutes to each member of the board before the next meeting. The chairman then opens the meeting by enquiring whether any director objects to the minutes before he signs them. The minutes of a previous meeting thus approved are merely approved as an accurate record. The directors have the right to inspect the minutes, and so have the auditors if they need to do so in the course of their audit work. Members have no right to inspect the minutes of board meetings.

13.2 Managing Director

A distinction is made (Chapter 12: 12.8) between the role of a director, who performs his duties by attendance at board meetings (Chapter 12: 12.20) and the management functions, which some directors may also perform, usually as employees of the company.

The articles (Table A Art 84) permit the board to appoint any director 'to the office of managing director or to any other executive office' in the company.

In making these appointments the board is exercising its power (Art 72) to 'delegate . . . such of their powers as they consider desirable' to each working director. It is not normal to define in detail the limits placed upon the delegated powers. It is understood that a director with a specified departmental role may do what is usual. However the board may restrict even a managing director to particular functions (as in *Caddies Case* in Chapter 1: 1.9). The extent of a working director's *actual* authority as agent of the company is implied by normal practice, if not otherwise defined.

In his dealings with outsiders on behalf of the company the director also has *apparent* authority implied by what is normal for such a departmental director to do.

Here, however, a managing director is in a special position since his apparent authority extends to making any contract of a commercial nature as agent of the company. This point is illustrated by *Freeman & Lockyer's Case* (in 13.10 below). Contrast this with the position of say a sales director, who has authority to make contracts for the sale of the company's goods – not so much because he is a director as because he is the departmental head of the sales department, with the personal status of director.

The 1985 Table A (unlike the 1948 Table A) put all directors who hold executive office on the same basis as regards retirement by rotation (Chapter 12: 12.2). All are excluded from retirement by rotation: Art 84.

The appointment of a managing director continues only so long as he is a director. If the company removes him from his directorship under s 303 (Chapter 12: 12.7) before the expiry of his agreed term as managing director he may recover damages for breach of contract (*Shirlaw's Case* in Chapter 4: 4.6).

13.3 Company Secretary

Every company must have a secretary (or joint secretaries): s 283. The same person may be both a director and the secretary. But the sole director of a private company may not also be its secretary. To prevent evasion of this rule a company may not have another company as its secretary if the sole director of that other company is also sole director of the first company nor have another company as its sole director if the sole director of that company is also secretary of the first company: s 283(4). If anything is to be done by a director and by the secretary the same person may not act in both capacities: s 284.

If the office of secretary is vacant or if he is unable to act his formal duties may be done by a deputy or assistant secretary or if there is none by any officer of the company authorised in that behalf by the directors: s 283(3). Unless named in the articles the secretary is appointed by the directors. Particulars of the secretary must be included in the statement of directors, secretary and registered office to be delivered to the registrar to secure the incorporation of a new company and the secretary must sign the statement to signify his consent to act: s 10(3). The particulars of the secretary to be supplied in this way are the same as those which must be entered in the company's register of directors and secretary, ie his present surname and Christian name (and any former name – subject to the same exceptions as apply to directors) and his usual residential address (or if the secretary is a company its name and the address of its registered or principal office): s 290. If there is a change of secretary notice (with the same particulars of the new secretary and his consent to act) must within 14 days be given to the registrar: s 288(2).

There is no statutory prescription nor any definition in Table A of the general duties and responsibilities of a company secretary. He is, however, an 'officer' of the company: s 744. A number of statutory rules of procedure require that documents shall be signed by a director and by the secretary; eg the annual return or an application for reregistration of an unlimited company as limited or vice versa.

The directors of a public company are required to take reasonable steps to ensure that the secretary is a person of the requisite knowledge and experience and has a professional qualification in law, accountancy or company administration (or other qualifications in lieu): s 286.

The duties of a company secretary vary a great deal according to the circumstances of the company. In a large company he is likely to be the principal or one of the principal administrative officers of the company (and there is now attributed to him a suitable degree of authority to make contracts for the company in this role (13.11 below)).

In the majority of companies the secretary has the duty of preparing the agenda and other papers for meetings of the board of directors, attending meetings and taking notes with a view to drafting the minutes and issuing instructions as required by decisions of the board. He has charge of the register of members (or deals with the professional registrars) and is concerned with the registration of share transfers and the issue of share certificates. He usually has custody of the statutory registers, records, and documents and the duty of keeping them complete and up-to-date. He also has charge of the company seal and records its use. He is one of the prescribed witnesses who sign documents to attest the due application of the seal: Art 101. Many of the company forms prescribed for use in supplying returns and notices to the registrar require that the completed documents shall be signed by the secretary who is therefore answerable for the accuracy of their contents.

13.4 Directors and shareholders in general meeting

The members as shareholders own the company, determine what its constitution shall be by their statutory power to alter the memorandum and articles and can remove its directors from office; in like manner they are usually vested with the power to appoint directors. But the directors while in office exercise powers collectively delegated to them by the articles. They are not controlled by the members in general meeting nor subject to instructions from that source as to how they should manage the company. The general meeting cannot therefore instruct the directors what to do nor restrain them in the exercise of their powers nor overrule them in their decisions.

The articles vested the general power of management of the company in the directors and provided that on certain property transactions no resolution of the board of directors should be valid if either of the two managing directors dissented from it. One of the managing directors did dissent from such a resolution and the company in general meeting then passed an ordinary resolution to 'ratify' the board resolution. An injunction was granted to restrain the company from acting on the resolution. 'In truth this is an attempt to alter the terms of the contract between the parties by a simple resolution instead of by a special resolution' (Farwell LJ): *Salmon v Quin & Axtens Ltd* [1909] 1 Ch 311.

The directors had in exercise of their powers of management begun legal proceedings against certain of the directors as individuals. The three defendants in their capacity of shareholders were able to carry an ordinary resolution in general meeting instructing the directors to discontinue the action. It was held that the resolution was invalid . . . 'the general body of shareholders . . . cannot themselves usurp the powers which are by the articles vested in the directors any more than the directors can usurp the powers vested by the articles in the general body of shareholders' (Green LJ): *John Shaw & Sons (Salford) Ltd v Shaw* [1935] 2 KB 113.

As the supervision of the day-to-day running of the company's business is necessarily entrusted to the directors by delegation to them of wide powers (13.5 below) a majority of the shareholders, if dissatisfied with the policy or performance of the directors have no immediate means of enforcing their views upon them. Apart from the upheaval of removing the directors from office, the articles may be altered to reserve to shareholders the decision on certain matters; in effect the directors' proposals must then be submitted to a general meeting before they may be implemented. Recent changes in the Companies Acts have added to the list of transactions which by law require shareholders' approval; one example is the approval of directors' substantial property transactions (Chapter 12: 12.13) introduced in 1980. As will be seen (13.5 below) the 1985 Table A contains a clearer definition than the 1948 version of a power to the company in general meeting to give instructions by special resolution to the directors. But for practical reasons any such instructions can only affect future transactions and cannot be retrospective (as illustrated by the attempt made in the *Shaw Case* above).

There is also a rather uncertain doctrine of 'concurrent powers' exercisable by the directors or by the company in general meeting. The case law suggests that this doctrine is limited to situations where (i) the directors are unable or unwilling to exercise their powers and (ii) action is required to protect the company's interests.

Three of the four directors had, as a majority of the board, prevented the company from commencing proceedings for infringement of its patent by another company in which they were interested. The fourth director had a controlling shareholding but he could not, as the law then stood, remove the other directors from office. He began proceedings on behalf of the company and it was held that as he represented the majority in general meeting he had the right to do so. In this case there was no deadlock on the board.

However, the court noted of the three directors that 'their duty and their interests are in direct conflict' and may have had in mind that they were thereby disabled from taking a decision in their own interests (unless approved in general meeting): *Marshall's Valve Gear Co Ltd v Manning, Wardle & Co Ltd* [1909] 1 Ch 267.

At a time when the company had no directors two individuals acting on its behalf but without authority from the company began legal proceedings to enforce its claim against debtors. Later when the company was in liquidation the liquidator purported to ratify what had been done. It was argued that ratification was not possible unless the company could have taken this action at the time and, having no directors in whom alone the power to institute proceedings was vested, it could not have done so. This argument was rejected by the House of Lords: 'the company could have done so either by appointing directors or as I think by authorising proceedings in general meeting, which in the absence of an effective board, has a residual authority to use the company's powers' (Lord Hailsham LC): *Alexander Ward & Co Ltd v Samyang Navigation Co Ltd* [1975] 2 All ER 424.

An instance of simple deadlock preventing effective action by the directors may be found in *Barron v Potter* (13.1 above). But the courts are not always ready to invoke this principle.

In *Re Argentum Reductions (UK) Ltd* [1975] 1 All ER 608 where there was 'an unhappy state of deadlock in the board of the company' the court declined to apply the doctrine of parallel or residual powers of the company in general meeting and commented that there are 'deep waters' here. Indeed there are.

Finally, it is worth noting the interaction between directors and members in situations where the directors have used or intend to use their powers for a purpose other than that for which the powers are given. A single member may apply to the court for an injunction or declaration that the directors have no power to act in this way. But the members collectively in general may authorise or ratify their action: *Bamford's Case* (Chapter 12: 12.18). In upholding the High Court decision in *Bamford's Case* the Court of Appeal expressly rejected the view that a general meeting has a 'residual power' to do what the directors cannot do. It is best to regard the decision as an instance of the members releasing the directors from a constraint on the powers given to the directors.

13.5 The directors' powers of management
The 1985 Table A Art 70 defines the directors' powers as follows:

'Subject to the provisions of the Act, the memorandum and the articles and to any directions given by special resolution, the business of the company shall be managed by the directors who may exercise all the powers of the company'.

This formula starts from the inherent limit that the company cannot authorise the directors to enter into ultra vires transactions which even the company in general meeting could not approve (the *Ashbury Rly Carriage Case* in Chapter 3: 3.15), and then confers on the directors the entire powers of the company subject only to three restrictions, ie the directors may not do things which either the Companies Act, or the memorandum and articles, reserve to the company in general meeting, and the company in general meeting may by special resolution give directions to the directors on matters within their competence.

This form of words differs from the 1948 Table A Art 80 phraseology but the general effect is the same. The most important difference is an express stipulation that a special resolution passed in general meeting is to be binding on the directors. By contrast the 1948 Table A referred vaguely to 'regulations' (made in general meeting): it was uncertain what that meant.

Article 70 also provides that if the company alters its memorandum or articles or gives directions, these shall not have retrospective effect to invalidate what the directors have already done.

As an example of the first restriction s 9 empowers a company to alter its articles by special resolution and s 121 permits a company to alter its authorised capital by ordinary resolution in general meeting. The directors therefore do not have power to do these things.

Among the restrictions which may be imposed by the articles the most important is a limit on the amount which the directors may borrow (Chapter 9: 9.2). The 1985 Table A however contains no such limit and so, if the company's power to borrow is unlimited in amount – as is usually the case, the directors have unlimited powers. Here is one of the major differences between the 1948 and 1985 versions of Table A. The 1948 Table A, which is still the model for the articles of many existing companies, has an Art 79 which limits the directors' borrowing powers to an amount equal to the nominal value of the issued share capital. However in reckoning how much has actually been borrowed Art 79 (1948) excludes 'temporary loans obtained from the company's bankers in the ordinary course of business'. This and some other elements of the wording of the 1948 Art 79 have caused much uncertainty and difficulty. That may be one of the reasons why the 1985 Table A simply omits the limit altogether.

Unless all shareholders are also directors, which is not uncommon in a small private company, the former may well wish to limit the amount which the latter may borrow without reference to them in general meeting. It is likely therefore that most companies will continue to place a limit on the maximum amount which the directors may borrow. It is always open to the directors to convene a general meeting to obtain a company decision to borrow a larger sum. But the current Table A offers no model and the wording of any limit found in the special articles of a company needs careful scrutiny, whenever it is material. This is especially important if the limit follows the wording of the 1948 Table A; it may do so, even if the amount fixed is different, e g a multiple of issued share capital *and reserves*, which is a common formula.

13.6 The contracts of a company
A company is subject to the same rules as any other person in the making of contracts. It must follow the correct procedure (Chapter 2: 2.5) and may only make binding contracts within the limits of its legal capacity (Chapter 3: 3.11). Since a company is an artificial person its contracts are made on its behalf by its agents. The risk, to which the other party to a contract with the company's agents is exposed, is that the agents may have no authority or be exceeding the limits of their authority. The remainder of this chapter deals with those problems and the various safeguards given to the other party.

It has been explained (13.5 above) that the principal agents of the company are its directors to whom wide powers of management are delegated, including the power to make contracts. Most of the case law is concerned with transactions effected by directors, real or apparent. But in a large company it is only the most important contracts which are negotiated or approved by directors individually or collectively. The bulk of a company's commercial contracts are made by its management staff whose authority is determined by normal principles of agency; their company 'principal' is the board of directors. In addition recent developments in company law have recognised that a company secretary may by virtue of his administrative responsibilities have apparent authority to make contracts of certain types for the company (13.11 below). Case law on this subject is not confined to directors and is partially based on common law agency principles.

There are three main problems to be considered. First, the persons who appear to be the board of directors may in fact not be directors at all. Secondly, the board of directors may enter into a contract without having authority to do so. Thirdly, an individual director, or the secretary or some other apparent agent of the company, may make an unauthorised contract. In all three situations it is possible nonetheless that the company will be bound by the contract made without actual authority. But the rules which may produce that result overlap and the resulting code is very confused – and confusing.

13.7 Irregularly appointed directors

It is provided by statute that the acts of a director or manager shall be valid notwithstanding any defect which may afterwards be discovered in his appointment or qualification: s 285. It is usual to reproduce this safeguard in the articles though it adds little: Art 92. Case law (the rule in *Turquand's Case*) adds that an outsider, dealing with those who could have been and appear to have been appointed directors and who act as such, is usually entitled to hold the company bound as if the apparent directors had been duly appointed. There are also rules on notices of the appointment, etc, of directors to be delivered to the registrar and the consequences of doing this or of failing to do so (Chapter 2: 2.14).

The limitations of s 285 were explored before the House of Lords in *Morris v Kanssen*. It only applies when a person has apparently been appointed a director and it is later discovered that by reason of a procedural slip, eg a meeting not properly convened, the appointment is a nullity. It does not apply if no appointment was made at all, nor usually if a director duly appointed ceases to be a director but continues to act as such. Section 285 does not cover an 'appointment' which is a complete nullity because it was made by persons who had no authority at all to make it, nor does it help a person who deals with an irregularly appointed 'director' if the former knew of or should previously have discovered the irregularity. Accordingly s 285 is not of much practical importance.

Differences arose between the first two directors of the company, K and C. C later forged an entry in the minute book to show the appointment of S as a third director. C and S illegally expelled K from his directorship. For two years there was no general meeting and in consequence the appointment of all directors expired under the provisions of the articles. At the end of this period C and S, purporting to act as directors, appointed M a director. M was aware that K disputed the legality of the board. As a board, C, S and M allotted shares to themselves. K brought an action for rectification of the register on the grounds that the allotment of shares was void since it had not been made by directors (duly appointed) as the articles required. His action succeeded.

In resisting K's claim M relied on s 285 but this argument failed. The House of Lords held that s 285 is limited to irregularities of appointment procedure. C had ceased to be a director (but see *Dawson's Case* below); S had never been appointed one. Hence neither was a director and their purported appointment of M as a director was void and so was the allotment of shares.

Before the House of Lords M also argued that under the rule in *Turquand's Case* (13.8 below) he was entitled to assume that C and S had been duly appointed. But he failed on this point also since he was a director himself with access to the records and he was aware that the legality of the board was disputed.

C had ceased to be a director by expiry of his term of office without reappointment and it was held that this situation was not covered by s 285: *Morris v Kanssen* [1946] 1 All ER 586. Article 92 now deals with this point but the 1948 Table A (Art 105) did not.

With reference to the final point in *Kanssen's Case* above it has been held that if a director ceases to hold office because he no longer has the required qualification shareholding (Chapter 12: 12.4) but reacquires the shares, he does not thereby become a director again but, in acting as a director, his acts are validated by s 285 – a most unsatisfactory distinction: *Dawson v African Consolidated Land and Trading Co* [1898] 1 Ch 6.

As already stated s 285 only helps a person who, in dealing with directors, is initially unaware of the true facts and the 'defect' is 'afterwards discovered'.

The articles required directors to acquire qualification shares within two months of appointment. The three original directors failed to comply with this condition. But as a board they appointed one of themselves (the plaintiff) to be managing director. In his claim for remuneration for his services the plaintiff could not rely on s 285 since his appointment was made by 'directors' who had ceased to hold that office, he was aware (or should have been) of the share qualification requirement, and even if the other 'directors' had still held office they could not have appointed as managing director a person who was no longer a director. But he recovered remuneration on a quantum meruit basis: *Craven-Ellis v Canons Ltd* [1936] 2 All ER 1066.

The outsider who deals with the company through officers who appear to him to be acting in their office as if duly appointed (provided always that under the articles their appointments could have been made) is more likely to find his safeguard in the rule in *Turquand's Case* (explained below), ie the company cannot deny that they are duly appointed.

A bank had honoured cheques drawn on a company bank account in reliance on a letter which purported to come from the company secretary and which enclosed a copy of what purported to be a board resolution (giving a mandate to honour cheques signed by any two directors and by the secretary). The 'directors' and 'secretary' acted in those capacities without ever having been properly appointed. It was held under the rule in *Turquand's Case* (13.8) below that, as the bank did not know or suspect or have the means of discovering that no appointments had been made, it was entitled to assume that the persons concerned had been duly appointed in accordance with the articles: *Mahony v East Holyford Mining Co* (1875) LR 7 HL 869.

The outsider may also find some safeguards in the rules which require a company to give notice to the registrar (and through him to the public) of changes among its directors. The persons named as the first directors (and who give their consent) in the papers delivered to the registrar to secure incorporation of the company become its first directors. Thereafter the termination of appointment of a director appointed at any time is not effective against an outsider, if unaware of it, unless notice is given to the registrar who gazettes receipt of that notice. These rules do not close every loophole but they narrow the risk to the outsider considerably: ss 42, 288(2) and 711(1)(c).

13.8 The rule in *Turquand's Case*
It is necessary to begin with the case itself.

Under the company's deed of settlement (corresponding with the modern articles) the directors had power to borrow only such sums as had been authorised by general resolution of the company. A debenture for £2,000 had been issued under the seal, signed by two directors and by the secretary. The resolution passed in general meeting to sanction this borrowing did not specify the amount which might be borrowed. It was therefore no authority to the directors to borrow anything. The bank had not seen the resolution and had no knowledge of its inadequacy. But it was held to be entitled to assume that the authority prescribed by the articles, of which requirement it had constructive notice, had been effectually given by ordinary resolution, ie by internal procedure of which the bank had neither actual nor constructive notice: *Royal British Bank v Turquand* (1856) 6 E & B 327.

The starting-point in an analysis of *Turquand's Case* is that, except where s 35 (13.9 below) applies, every person dealing with a company has constructive notice, if he does not have actual notice, of the contents of the memorandum and articles (and also of any special or extraordinary resolution or registered charge) because these documents are available for inspection on the company's file at the registry (Chapter 2: 2.12). Hence the bank was deemed to know, if it did not actually know, that the directors needed the authority of a suitable ordinary resolution for the issue of the debentures to cover the loan.

The second stage is that, being aware of the need for authorisation, the bank was entitled to assume, unless it knew or should have suspected the contrary, that the internal procedure for giving that authority had been adequately completed. It had no constructive notice of the contents of the ordinary resolution since a resolution of that category was not on file at the registry.

In the same way the bank in *Mahoney's Case* (13.6) was deemed to know that there was a procedure for appointing the directors and secretary of the company but entitled to assume that they had been appointed. In the *Rolled Steel Products Case* (Chapter 3: 3.11) the creditor was deemed to know that a quorum of two for board meetings had been fixed by the articles; it was not entitled to assume that a quorum was present, because it had obtained a copy of the minutes and knew that one of the two directors present was disqualified by failure to give notice of his interest.

The rule in *Turquand's Case* is also sometimes called 'the indoor management rule'. Within the limits set out above it covers all matters of internal procedure of a company. A person who relies on it has no duty to make enquiries as to whether the procedure has been carried out and does not lose his rights because he did not do so.

The rule is confined, however, to collective action by the board of directors. It does not extend so far as to give an individual director a presumed authority because under the articles the board might have delegated it to him.

A single director made a contract without having actual authority to do so. The secretary, also without authority, wrote a letter purporting to confirm what the director had done. The articles permitted the board to delegate its powers to single directors. It was not suggested (13.10 below) that the director who had made the contract was or had been held out to be a managing director. The Court of Appeal held that there was no presumption that there had been delegation of authority. It was said that . . . 'I know of no case in which any director, acting without authority in fact, has been held capable of binding a company by a contract with a third party, merely on the ground that that third party assumed that the director had been given authority by the board to make a contract . . .' The Court of Appeal was influenced by the fact that the transaction was of an unusual character and the circumstances put the plaintiff on enquiry (which he did not make): *Houghton & Co v Nothard Lowe and Wills Ltd* [1928] AC 1. (On the authority of the company secretary, see 13.11 below).

Secondly, the rule does not apply where the outsider knew of or should have known or suspected the irregularity. If he knew or had the means of discovering the irregularity he is not really an outsider to whom the internal procedure is a closed book as the principle requires. This is why Morris, as a purported director, could not invoke the rule in *Morris v Kanssen* (13.7 above).

But a member or even a director of the company if he deals with its directors in his personal capacity may be able to rely on the rule.

The plaintiff was a director of company A and negotiated a loan from company B to company A. While the negotiations were in progress he also became a director to company B. Following the first board meeting of company B which he attended the plaintiff agreed with the chairman of company B that the plaintiff would make a personal loan to company A if company B gave him an indemnity against loss. The relevant letters to the plaintiff were signed by the chairman of company B. It was held that as the plaintiff was involved in these negotiations only as a director of company A (and for himself) he could be an 'outsider' in relation to company B although he was one of its directors. Company B was held liable (see also Chapter 12: 12.18): *Hely-Hutchinson v Brayhead Ltd* [1967] 3 All ER 98.

If the procedure requires a special or extraordinary resolution, a copy of the resolution will be on the file at the registry. By constructive notice the person dealing with the company is deemed to know of the absence of such a resolution from the file, and its contents if it is defective.

Thirdly, the rule does not apply to a company document which is a forgery. The issue of a forged document is not the act of the company and there is no presumption that it is genuine: *Ruben's Case* (Chapter 7: 7.3).

Even a document bearing a genuine but unauthorised signature of an employee as representative of the company has been treated as a forgery. If the person who signs appears to have authority, ie it would be 'usual' for him to have it, the presumption of authority ought to apply, but is apparently excluded by the simple proposition that an unauthorised signature is in these circumstances a forgery.

A branch manager of a company drew bills of exchange in the name of the company to pay his personal debts. In the High Court the company was held liable on the ground that the bills had been signed by an employee of appropriate status. The Court of Appeal overruled this decision partly on the ground that it was not within the 'usual' authority of a branch manager to sign bills of exchange for the company and partly on the ground that a forged signature is a nullity: *Kreditbank Cassel GmbH v Schenkers Ltd* [1927] 1 KB 826.

Finally, the rule does not apply to an ultra vires transaction because a person dealing with a company is deemed, apart from where s 35 applies, to have constructive notice of the limits placed on the contractual capacity of a company by its objects clause.

13.9 Statutory protection of an outsider

The wording of s 35 has been quoted and analysed above (Chapter 3: 3.17) in connection with the ultra vires doctrine. Where it applies, a person dealing with the company may enforce his rights even though the directors were exceeding their delegated powers. He is unaffected by constructive notice of the memorandum and articles, has no duty to find out what they may contain, and is deemed to act in good faith until the contrary is established.

Where the transaction is intra vires the company there is an overlap between s 35 and the rule in *Turquand's Case*. The main additional safeguard given to a person dealing with a company is that s 35 may enable him to enforce an ultra vires transaction.

There are, of course, situations to which the rule in *Turquand's Case* applies and s 35 does not. If the 'directors' have not been appointed or if directors duly appointed reach a decision at a board meeting which has not been properly convened or at which no quorum is present, the former rule applies, since the outsider may deem that these internal matters are in order, but the latter does not since these are not 'transactions decided on by the directors'.

An outsider who deals with a company through a single director, acting as its agent but lacking actual authority from the board, cannot safely rely on either s 35 or *Turquand's Case*. This is because both rules relate to defective authority of a *board* of directors. *Marcus's Case* (13.10 below) is not really an exception. There is, however, a different legal principle on which the outsider may sometimes rely as explained below.

13.10 The liability of the company for acts of a single agent

Under normal principles of the law of agency a company may be bound by a contract made on its behalf by a single agent, if he appeared to have its authority to do so.

As explained above (13.2) the actual and also the apparent authority of an agent to act for a company is often determined by what is usual or normally done by a person in his position in the company management.

It follows that actual and apparent authority often coincide in their extent. But apparent authority may be wider if a person who is not an appointed agent at all is allowed by his principal to act as such, or when the principal has made positive representations ('holding out') that a person is his agent or has his authority. Any person dealing with a company through an agent can hold the company bound by a contract made within the agent's apparent authority unless the former is aware that the agent's actual authority (usually expressly given if any at all) is less than that.

Brewers appointed a manager of a public house with express instructions not to purchase cigars, tobacco, etc, as bar stocks for sale. It was held, however, that such purchases were usual (on the part of a manager or proprietor of a public house) and therefore within his apparent authority. Hence the brewers were bound by the contract made within his apparent but in excess of his actual authority: *Watteau v Fenwick* [1893] 1 QB 346.

See also *Hely-Hutchinson's Case* in 13.8 above where the chairman was permitted by the other members of the board to exercise the powers of a managing director although they had not been given to him by express delegation.

Company law is mainly concerned here with determining what is the apparent authority of officers of the company such as the chairman, managing director, other directors or the secretary. But the same principle is equally applicable to less senior employees such as a branch manager (as in *Schenkers Case* in 13.8 above).

The primary function of an *ordinary director* is to take part in collective decision making at board meetings. By reason of his position he has no usual nor apparent authority to act as an individual agent of the company in the making of contracts.

In the making of the contract Proved Tin was represented by a single ordinary director who acted without authority from his board. The articles of Proved Tin permitted the delegation of the board's powers to a single director (this is common form as in Table A Art 72) but Rama had not inspected the articles when the contract was made. It was held that a single director had no apparent authority (nor in this case any actual authority) to make a contract for the company. It was also held that Rama could not rely on the articles as a representation because Rama had not looked at them. Constructive notice of the articles is confined to the negative or restrictive terms which they may contain: *Rama Corp Ltd v Proved Tin and General Investments Ltd* [1952] 2 QB 147.

See also *Houghton & Co v Northard Lowe & Wills Ltd* (13.8 above) for another example of the lack of apparent authority of a single director to make contracts.

A *chairman* has no more authority to make contracts than an ordinary director. But he is more likely to usurp the functions of a managing director (or chief executive) and the court will more readily deduce that a company has held out its chairman as its managing director by allowing him to act as if he had been appointed to that office (*Hely-Hutchinson's Case*). The deduction is more easily made in cases where there is no other director who is the properly appointed managing director.

The usual powers of a *managing director* have been described above (13.2). The company is therefore generally bound by any commercial contract made on its behalf by a managing director duly appointed even if he exceeds his actual authority since he has usual and apparent authority to make contracts.

The company may also be bound by a contract made without authority by an ordinary director (or by the chairman) if he appears to have the required authority.

In the leading case below on this topic of apparent authority by holding out, Diplock LJ laid down four conditions to be satisfied if a company was to be bound by the contract made:

(a) there must have been a representation to the other party that the agent has authority to make a contract of this kind;
(b) the representation must have been made by a person or persons with actual authority to manage the business either generally or in respect of the matters to which the contract related;
(c) the other party must have relied on the representation and been induced by it to enter into the contract;
(d) there must be nothing in the memorandum or the articles to deprive the company of capacity to make the contract or prevent it from delegating to an agent authority to make it for the company.

A property development company was formed by K and H. H contributed half the capital but left the management in the hands of K. K and H were directors and each of them appointed his nominee as a director, i e a total of four. The quorum for board meetings was four. But H was often abroad. The articles provided for the appointment of a managing director but K had not been appointed to that office. To the knowledge of the board K acted as if he were a managing director and in that way he employed the plaintiffs, a firm of architects, to do work for the company. It was held that the company was liable to pay their fees since K had apparent authority to engage them: *Freeman & Lockyer v Buckhurst Park Properties (Mangal) Ltd* [1964] 1 All ER 630.

In considering whether it can be a case of agency by holding out it is necessary to ask:

(i)   is the contract intra vires the company (condition (d) above);
(ii) does the board of directors have the normal wide powers of management (condition (b) above); and
(iii) is there any provision of the articles which prohibits the delegation of these powers to a single director (condition (d) above)?

If these tests are satisfied then there are questions of fact, i e:

(iv) was a representation of authority made;
(v)   by the board;
(vi) to the other party;
(vii) which induced him to enter into the contract?

The representation need be no more than passive acquiescence by the board in the conduct of negotiations by the single director leading to the making of the contract. This is illustrated by what happened in *Hely-Hutchinson's Case* and in *Freeman & Lockyer's Case* above. The *Proved Tin Case* is distinguished from these cases by the fact that there was no evidence here that the other directors knew of, and therefore acquiesced in, what the active director was doing.

Whether passive acquiescence of the other directors renders the contract 'a transaction decided on by the directors', thus bringing s 35 into operation, is a debatable question. In *Marcus' Case* (Chapter 3: 3.17) the board had virtually abdicated in favour of one director, who thus was the board in fact, rather than its apparent agent.

13.11 The authority of the company secretary

The company secretary has a special position because he is recognised as an officer of the company but (unless he is also a director) he is not a party to the collective decisions of the board of directors.

He may, of course, have express authority from the board to make contracts. Has he any usual or apparent authority implied by holding the office of secretary? Until recently the courts have been inclined to treat a company secretary as a very minor figure without much authority of any kind. If, for example, he issued a forged share certificate the company was not liable: if he wrote a letter confirming what a director had done that was not a representation by the company (see *Ruben's Case* (Chapter 7: 7.3) and *Houghton's Case* (13.8 above) and the case below).

At the request of the secretary a director made a loan to the company. The board meeting which confirmed the loan was not properly constituted since it lacked a competent quorum of directors entitled to vote. It was held that the secretary had no authority to borrow for the company and the purported ratification was void: *Re Cleadon Trust Ltd* [1939] Ch 286.

In 1971, however, there was a sudden recognition of the reality, ie that a company secretary may have considerable administrative responsibilities and must make contracts for the company in the course of his duties.

A company secretary without authority hired cars ostensibly for the company but actually for his own use. His company was bound by these contracts since they were within his apparent authority. The Court of Appeal dismissed some earlier dicta ('a secretary is a mere servant: his position is that he is to do what he is told and no person can assume that he has any authority to represent anything at all': *Barnett, Hoares & Co v South London Tramways Co* (1887) 18 QBD 815 per Lord Esher) as out of date. The modern company secretary is 'the chief administrative officer of the company. As regards matters concerned with administration, in my judgment, the secretary has ostensible authority to sign contracts on behalf of the company'. But Salmon LJ went on to reserve his opinion as to whether a company secretary has apparent authority 'to sign a contract relating to the commercial management of the company, for example, a contract for the sale or purchase of goods in which the company deals'. No such contract had to be considered in this case: *Panorama Developments (Guildford) Ltd v Fidelis Funishing Fabrics Ltd* [1971] 3 All ER 16.

Apart from the nature of the contract, administrative or commercial (as in *Cleadon's Case* above), the court would also take account of the size of the company and the responsibilities of the company secretary in its management structure. Apparent authority is based on usual authority, except where it has been extended by 'holding out'. It is necessary therefore always to consider what in fact had become the routine work of the secretary in question.

Chapter 14

Accounts and audit

A ACCOUNTS

14.1 Introduction

A statutory duty is imposed on every company to keep accounting records: s 221. The directors are also required to lay before the company in general meeting annual accounts, with directors' and auditors' reports all containing prescribed information and also to deliver to the registrar (unless the company is unlimited) a copy of the accounts: s 241. A copy of the accounts, and of the reports of the directors and auditors, must be sent to every member and debenture holder of the company and to its auditors, at least 21 days before the meeting: s 240; s 387.

The general purpose of the system is to make available annually a complete and, so far as possible, informative and accurate summary of the net worth of the company and the results of the latest year's trading for the guidance of members and of creditors.

14.2 Accounting records

Every company must keep accounting records sufficient to show and explain the company's transactions and:

(a) to disclose with reasonable accuracy the company's financial position at any time; and
(b) to enable the directors to ensure that any balance sheet or profit and loss account gives a true and fair view of the state of the company's affairs and of the company's profit or loss respectively: s 221.

In particular the accounting records must contain:

(i) day-to-day entries of receipts and expenditure and of the matters in respect of which they were received and paid;
(ii) a record of the assets and liabilities of the company;
(iii) where the company deals in goods, statements of the stock held by the company at the end of each financial year, of the stocktakings on which the stock statements are based and (except in the case of retail trade) of sales and purchases of goods showing what was sold or bought and to whom or from whom.

The accounting records must be kept at the registered office or at such other place as the directors think fit. If they are kept at a place outside Great Britain accounts and returns in respect of the business to which they relate must be sent to and kept in Great Britain.

The accounting records must at all times be open to inspection by the officers of the company but only for the purpose of their duties.

There was a dispute between the plaintiff, C, and the controlling shareholder of the company. C, as director, demanded access to the accounts for the purpose of pursuing his dispute and (it was alleged) of passing information to competitors of the company. C relied on the statutory provision that 'the books of account . . . shall at all times be open to inspection by the directors': s 222(1). The court refused to order the company to produce its accounts to C as director since he did not require access to them for the performance of his duties. Moreover an EGM was shortly to be held to pass a resolution to remove C from his directorship. *Conway v Petronius Clothing Co Ltd* [1978] 1 All ER 185.

Every private company must preserve its accounting records for at least three years and every other company for at least six years: s 222(4).

Failure to comply with these rules is an offence punishable by fine or imprisonment unless the officer in default shows that he acted honestly and ought to be excused.

14.3 Balance sheet and profit and loss account

The statutory obligation to produce accounts is now related to the accounting reference periods of the company which are normally periods of a year.

The directors of every company must prepare a profit and loss account (or if the company is not trading for profit an income and expenditure account). The account must begin on the first day of the relevant accounting reference period and end either on the day on which the period ends or on some other day, to be selected by the directors, within seven days before or after the end of the accounting reference period: s 227(2). The latter alternative enables a company to make up its annual accounts for periods ending on, for example, the Friday nearest to the last day of each successive accounting reference period. A balance sheet must also be prepared as at the closing date to which the profit and loss account is made up.

A company selects an accounting reference *date* by notice given to the registrar within six months of its incorporation: s 224(2). If it fails to do this, 31 March becomes its accounting reference date. The accounting reference *period* ends on that date, and the next period begins on the following day. Normally therefore an accounting reference period is 12 months ending on the same date in each calendar year. The intention of this system is to restrain a company from juggling with its accounting periods to postpone the disclosure of bad results or to prevent exact comparison with earlier periods or otherwise to mislead.

A company may, however, alter its accounting reference date but not more often than once in five years and not so as to extend the current accounting reference period to more than 18 months: s 225. The notice given to the registrar of the new date should indicate whether the current period is to be extended or cut short.

To the above general restrictions on an alteration of accounting reference date there are three exceptions:

(a) a *first* alteration may be made within five years of the date originally fixed;

(b) a holding or subsidiary company may always alter its date to bring it into line with the other company's date;
(c) the DTI may grant remission from the five-year interval requirement: s 225(6) and (7).

In general notice of an altered accounting reference date must be given within the period which will be altered by it.

'Financial year' means the period which the accounts relate, whether or not it is a 12-month period: s 742.

A company's accounts for each financial year must comprise (i) its profit and loss account (ii) a balance sheet (iii) the directors' report (14.7 below) and (iv) the auditors' report (14.16 below). If the company has subsidiaries group accounts may also be required (14.5 below): s 239.

The balance sheet is signed by two directors after it has been approved by the board. The board must also approve the other documents annexed to the balance sheet: s 238.

The form and content of the accounts and of the notes to the accounts are prescribed by Sch 4 and Sch 5 respectively. Schedule 6 requires various 'particulars' of matters in which the directors are concerned (Chapter 12: 12.15 and 14.6 below). The overriding requirement is that the balance sheet and the profit and loss account shall give 'a true and fair view': s 228(2). A company which has a Stock Exchange listing may have to give additional information in its accounts. There is no objection to the inclusion of additional information, not required by law, and the accounts often include a large amount of extra information.

14.4 Time for laying and delivering accounts
It is the duty of the directors of a company within the period allowed:

(a) to lay before the company in general meeting accounts (with a copy of every document required to be comprised in the accounts) in respect of every accounting reference period (this term is explained in 14.3 above); and
(b) to deliver to the registrar a copy of those accounts (unless one of the exceptions mentioned below applies).

An unlimited company is, if it satisfies certain conditions (Chapter 1: 1.21), exempt from the obligation to deliver any accounts to the registrar: s 241(4).

A small or medium-sized company (as defined by s 248) is permitted, at its option, to deliver to the registrar 'modified accounts', which omit certain details (as provided by Sch 8). This remission is given so that companies up to a certain size may preserve greater secrecy about their affairs. They are still required to prepare the normal full accounts and lay them before the members in general meeting. It is likely that some further remissions on these lines will be granted shortly.

The period allowed for compliance with the duty is ten months from the end of the relevant accounting reference period for laying and delivering the accounts of a private company and 7 months in the case of any other company. But in either case if the company carries on business or has interests outside the UK, the Channel Islands and the Isle of Man the directors may by giving notice (with appropriate particulars) to the registrar, extend the period allowed by three months (ie to 13 months for a private and ten months for a public company: s 242.

These basic rules are modified if the company's first accounting reference period is more than 12 months from the date of incorporation, or if it has altered its accounting reference date. But there is always a permitted interval of at least three months between the close of the period to which the accounts relate and the prescribed date by which it must 'lay and deliver' its accounts as described above.

The rules do not require that the accounts shall be laid before the company at an AGM rather than an EGM but it is usual to deal with the accounts at the AGM for the year (Chapter 11: 11.1).

If the accounts are in a language other than English the copy delivered to the registrar (for filing and public inspection) must have a certified English translation annexed.

14.5 Group accounts

If a company has one or more subsidiaries, group accounts dealing with the state of affairs and profit or loss of the company and its subsidiaries must be prepared and laid before the company in general meeting and delivered to the registrar in compliance with the same rules as apply to the accounts of each company taken separately: s 229.

Group accounts are not, however, required in the following cases:

(a) when a holding company is itself the wholly-owned subsidiary of another body corporate incorporated in Great Britain: s 229(2). In effect an intermediate holding company is not required to produce consolidated accounts since the parent company of the group will do so. A company is deemed to be a wholly-owned subsidiary of another if its only members are the holding company and its subsidiaries, or their nominees: s 736(5)(b).
(b) when the directors consider that it is impracticable or uneconomic to produce group accounts; or that the result would be misleading or harmful to any member of the group; or that the relative businesses are so different as to preclude treating them as a single undertaking. In certain cases the directors must obtain the approval of the DTI for dispensing with group accounts: s 229(3).

Failure to produce proper group accounts is an offence for which a director may be fined.

The group accounts normally contain a consolidated balance sheet dealing with the state of affairs of the holding company and all its subsidiaries and a consolidated profit and loss account dealing with the profit or loss of the company and those subsidiaries. But group accounts may be prepared in some other form if in the opinion of the directors this would be a better way of presenting the same or equivalent information and also that the members of the company will more readily appreciate the information in that form. In particular the group accounts may take the form of consolidated accounts for the holding company and some only of its subsidiaries together with separate group accounts for other subsidiaries or separate accounts for those other subsidiaries. Alternatively the information may be given by expanding what is disclosed about them in the accounts of the holding company. These different methods may be combined and the group accounts may be wholly or partly incorporated in the accounts of the holding company: s 229(6).

The method of disclosure is thus very flexible. The general purpose and effect of the rules on group accounts is to disclose the real worth and profits of the parent company of the group.

Group accounts must give a true and fair view of the state of affairs and profit or loss of the holding company and the subsidiaries dealt with thereby as a whole, so far as concerns the members of the holding company: s 230(2).

To facilitate the preparation of group accounts the directors of a holding company must secure that the financial year of each subsidiary coincides with that of the holding company unless there are good reasons for not doing so: s 227. If the financial year of a subsidiary does not coincide with that of the holding company, the group accounts usually incorporate the results of the subsidiary as shown in its accounts ending in the course of the holding company's financial year.

A holding company is required to disclose in its accounts the name and country of incorporation of its subsidiaries, and the proportion of the shares (of each class) of the subsidiary which it holds.

If, however, a full list of subsidiaries would be excessive, the particulars may be confined to those which are significant. But it must then be disclosed that the list is not complete: Sch 5 paras 4 and 5. It is permissible however to omit, with the approval of the DTI, a subsidiary, incorporated or trading outside Great Britain, to avoid causing harm to any company of the group: Sch 5 para 3.

If a company has an interest of one-tenth or more, as defined, in another ('associate') company, similar disclosures may be required by Sch 5 Pt II.

A subsidiary (with certain exceptions for subsidiaries which trade outside Great Britain) is required to disclose in its annual accounts the name and country of incorporation of its ultimate holding company: Sch 5 paras 20–21.

14.6 Disclosure of emoluments of directors and employees

The annual accounts laid before the company in general meeting must give information of:

(a) the aggregate amount of the directors' emoluments:
(b) the aggregate amount of pensions paid to directors or former directors (but excluding pensions provided by schemes funded by the company's contributions);
(c) the aggregate amount of any compensation for loss of office paid to directors (Chapter 12: 12.8);
(d) any loans (made during, or outstanding at the end of, the year) to directors (Chapter 12: 12.11 and 12.12);
(e) any contract or transaction with the company or with a subsidiary in which a director had directly or indirectly a material interest (Chapter 12: 12.15).

Requirements of disclosure in respect of (d) and (e) above have already been considered (Chapter 12: 12.15).

In addition to the above information of the *aggregate* amounts paid to directors as emoluments, which includes both directors' fees and any management remuneration (to be shown separately), the accounts of a company may have to give information of the emoluments of individual directors. A company which is neither the holding company nor the subsidiary of another company need not make the disclosure if the aggregate emoluments of directors for the financial year do not exceed a specified level (currently £60,000): Sch 5 para 23. Where disclosure is required, the accounts must show:

(a) the emoluments of the chairman;
(b) the emoluments of the highest-paid director (unless he is also the chairman);
(c) the number of directors whose emoluments fall into each of a prescribed 'band' (at present 0–£5,000, £5,000–£10,000 and so on);
(d) the number of directors who receive no emoluments or who have waived their entitlement (and the amount so waived): Sch 5 paras 24–27.

However disclosure under (a) and (b) above is not required if the individual discharged his duties wholly or mainly outside the UK.

There are also disclosure requirements in respect of the higher-paid employees, if their emoluments exceed a certain level (at present £30,000 pa): Sch 5 Pt VI.

If proper disclosures are not made in the accounts it is the duty of the auditors, so far as they are reasonably able to do so, to give the required information in their report on the accounts: s 237(5). Payments made by subsidiaries to directors or employees of a company are included in their emoluments for the purpose of determining what has to be disclosed in the company's accounts.

14.7 Directors' report
The accounts must include a report by the directors which complies with the requirements of s 235 and Sch 7. The matters to be covered by the report are:

(a) a fair review of the development of the business of the company and its subsidiaries during the financial year and of their position at the end of it. In practice this 'review' may be very brief and general in its terms. But a public company usually provides a mass of detail in either or both of a 'chairman's statement' or a 'managers' review' or 'highlights of the year', and the like, which are issued with the annual accounts. Although these documents have no formal legal status, it is customary for the board to consider them in draft – and with much care, since it is this information which investment analysts, financial journalists and others draw on, in forming an opinion of the company's current and prospective situation. A private company of course may content itself with a simple 'fair review' stating that the position is 'satisfactory';

(b) the amount (if any) which the directors recommend should be paid as dividend and the amount (if any) which they propose to carry to reserves. The articles usually provide that the company in general meeting cannot declare a dividend in excess of the amount recommended by the directors (Chapter 5: 5.25 and Table A Art 102);

(c) the names of the persons who at any time during the year were directors;

(d) the principal activities of the company and of its subsidiaries and any change therein during the year;

(e)   particulars of any significant changes in the fixed assets of the company or its subsidiaries. If the market value of land differs significantly from its value as shown in the accounts the difference must be indicated 'with such degree of precision as is practicable';

(f)   the number of shares or debentures of the company (or another company of the group) in which a director had an interest, shown as at the beginning and end of the year (or at the date of the director's appointment to the board during the year instead of at the beginning of the year);

(g)   particulars of money given for political or charitable purposes in excess of £200 (but a wholly-owned subsidiary of a holding company incorporated in Great Britain need not make this disclosure since its ultimate holding company will disclose the aggregate gifts of the group);

(h)   any important events affecting the company or its subsidiaries which have occurred since the end of the financial year;

(i)   an indication of likely future developments in the business of the company and its subsidiaries;

(j)   an indication of the activities (if any) of the company and its subsidiaries in the field of research and development;

(k)   the number and nominal value of any shares of the company which have been purchased by the company, or by its nominee, or in circumstances where the company has a beneficial interest in its shares acquired by a third party, or where the company has a lien or charge on its own shares (and the amount secured by the charge);

(l)   the policy of the company on the employment of disabled persons (and their training, promotion etc), if the company has (on average) more than 250 employees;

(m)   such information as may be prescribed by regulation in relation to the company's arrangements for the health, safety and welfare at work of its employees;

(n)   the arrangements for providing information to employees and consulting and encouraging them to become involved in or aware of matters which concern them or relate to the performance of the company, if the company has (on average) more than 250 employees.

There are additional requirements for companies which produce 'special category accounts'; ie banking, insurance and shipping companies.

It is the duty of the auditors to consider whether anything in the directors' report is inconsistent with the accounts, and if there is any inconsistency to mention it in their auditors' report: s 237(6).

14.8   Failure to comply with legal requirements relating to the accounts

The main safeguard against defective or inaccurate accounts is the requirement that (with one limited exception) the annual accounts must be accompanied by the report of auditors, whose duties in this connection are considered later in this chapter. As mentioned above the auditors should, among other duties, disclose in their report anything wrongly omitted from the accounts, insofar as they are reasonably able to discover it.

The role of the auditor does not in any way relieve the directors of their primary duties in connection with the accounts. They must maintain proper accounting records, prepare proper accounts, and lay them before the company in general meeting. Within the same time limit they must also deliver a copy of the accounts (in full or modified form) to the registrar, who places them on the company's file at the registry for public inspection. A failure to perform any of these duties entails liability to a fine.

Default may also have longer lasting effects on the directors. One of the grounds upon which a court may by order disqualify a director from acting as director or being concerned in the management of a company, directly or indirectly (and certain other positions in connection with companies), is persistent default in complying with the requirements of company law in relation to the delivery of accounts (among other documents) to the registry: CDDA s 3. The maximum period of disqualification in this case is five years. It is of course a penalty additional to any fine which the director may have been required to pay for each default (Chapter 12: 12.3).

Failure to deliver the accounts to the registry within the prescribed time (14.4 above) is a default, for which the maximum fine increases according to the length of the delay: s 243. The court may also make an order requiring a director to deliver the accounts: s 244. In proceedings for the disqualification of a director a previous court order under s 244 is itself evidence of a default, which may count against him: CDDA s 3(b)(i).

These penalties may be imposed whether or not the company has become insolvent; the offence lies in failure to deliver the accounts.

If the company does become insolvent, this may lead (Chapter 12: 12.3) to an order for disqualification, for a minimum of 2 and a maximum of 15 years, on the grounds that the director is 'unfit to be concerned in the management of a company': CDDA s 6. In determining whether he is unfit the court is required to have regard to a number of specified matters (CDDA s 9) which include failure to keep accounting records and failure to prepare and sign annual accounts as required by law: CDDA Sch 1.

It is not of course required of a director that he shall personally perform the relevant obligations. It is a defence, in a prosecution for failure to lay accounts before the company in general meeting or to deliver the accounts to the registry, to show that the director 'took all reasonable steps for securing that those requirements would be complied with': s 243(3). What the law demands is that a director shall ensure, by his own efforts or the work of another person, that the legal requirements are met.

The law does not impose on a director any direct obligation to keep himself informed of the company's financial position. What he should do in that respect must depend in part on the circumstances of the company and his role, e g as a non-executive or a specialist working director. A general prescription is just not possible. But his failure to give company finances his attention is a fault.

In dealing with an application for a disqualification order the court is required to consider 'the extent of the director's responsibility for the causes of the company becoming insolvent'. That responsibility might – there is not yet any judicial decision on the point – be held to include gross failure to attend to the financial position of a company drifting towards insolvency: CDDA Sch 1 para 6. The tests of 'wrongful trading' (Chapter 20: 20.19) may have a rather similar effect.

B AUDITORS

14.9 Appointment and removal of auditor

Every company (unless it is a 'dormant company') is required to appoint an auditor or auditors for the purpose of reporting to members on the accounts examined by them on every balance sheet, profit and loss account and all group accounts laid before the company in general meeting: s 384 and s 236. The intention and effect of the audit system is that independent professional experts examine and report on the accounts presented to members, who themselves have no access to the accounting records and other sources of relevant information. The auditors report whether in their opinion the accounts give a true and fair view and if not in what respects the accounts fall short of that standard.

The first auditors of a company may be appointed by the directors at any time up to the first general meeting before which accounts are laid: s 384(2). Auditors so appointed hold office until the conclusion of that first meeting. They will, of course, audit the first accounts and report on them. If the directors make no appointment of first auditors the company in general meeting may do so.

The company is required to appoint auditors annually at the general meeting, usually the AGM, before which accounts are laid: s 384(1). In the ordinary course the meeting reappoints the same auditors as before to hold office until the next year's meeting convened to consider the accounts. As the date of that subsequent meeting approaches those auditors examine the next year's accounts and report on them.

If the company fails to appoint auditors for the ensuing year at the general meeting at which accounts are laid the company must give notice within one week of the DTI which has power to appoint an auditor to fill the vacancy: s 384(5).

If a casual vacancy occurs, eg by the death of the auditor, the directors or the company in general meeting may make an appointment to fill it. While there is a casual vacancy, the surviving or continuing auditors, if any, may act. If, for example, A and B have been appointed joint auditors but A is obliged by ill health to retire before completing his term, B may continue to act and A's place may be filled in the manner described.

The appointment of a new auditor at a general meeting or the removal of an auditor from office requires special notice (Chapter 11: 11.5). An auditor may be removed before the expiry of his term of office by ordinary resolution notwithstanding any agreement (such as a contract for his services for the full term): s 386. Special notice must be given to the company of intention to propose a resolution for his removal and he has the same rights as are given to a director in similar circumstances (Chapter 12: 12.7). If he is voted out the company must give notice of his removal to the registrar within 14 days.

It is also necessary to give special notice of a resolution to be passed at a general meeting to appoint as auditor anyone other than the auditor appointed at a previous general meeting, ie:

(a) to appoint as auditor a person other than a retiring auditor;
(b) to fill a casual vacancy in the office of auditor;
(c) to reappoint as auditor a retiring auditor who was appointed by the directors to fill a casual vacancy: s 388(1).

It is usual to appoint a firm by name as auditors and to treat this as the appointment of the partners of the firm for the time being so that special notice is not given merely because of a change in the partnership. References to auditors in this connection include firms holding auditorships.

In certain circumstances a company may by passing a special resolution exempt itself from the normal obligation to appoint auditors and to produce audited accounts to its members and to the registrar: ss 252–253. This exemption is only available to a company if:

(a) it is eligible to deliver modified accounts to the registrar as a *small company* in the defined sense (14.4 above) or if it would have been such a company, on account of its size, but is disqualified by reason of being a member of a group which includes a public (or 'special category') company; and

(b) it has been *dormant* throughout the period covered by the accounts, ie it has had no transaction (other than receiving payment for subscribers' shares) which it would be required to enter in its accounting records (see 14.2 above).

The practical effect of the rather involved language summarised in (a) above is that an inactive subsidiary of a public company, as well as an independent private company, may claim this exemption, provided of course that it is a 'small company' by size and also a 'dormant' company.

It might be thought that the audit of a small, inactive company is a mere formality. But this is not necessarily so, since the auditor has to satisfy himself by investigation that the company has in fact remained inactive. For this work he charges an appropriate fee. The 'dormant company' procedure of dispensing with an audit altogether does therefore avoid unnecessary work and expense.

14.10 Resignation of auditor

Auditors sometimes resign over disagreements with the directors or dissatisfaction with the company's accounting system (in so far as it affects their work as auditors). On the other hand, an auditor may resign without any controversy because he is retiring from practice or does not find the work sufficiently remunerative. But any resignation of an auditor is important and it is provided, therefore, that an auditor may only resign his office by depositing a notice in writing at the registered office specifying the date from which his resignation is to take effect and containing either:

(a) a statement that there are no circumstances connected with his resignation which he considers should be brought to the notice of members or creditors of the company; or

(b) a statement of any such circumstances: s 390(2).

A copy of every such notice of resignation must be sent within 14 days to the registrar and if it states the circumstances of the resignation, a copy must within the same period be sent to every person entitled to receive a copy of the annual accounts. But the company or any person aggrieved may within the same period apply to the court for an order that copies of the notice shall not be distributed on the grounds that it would give needless publicity to defamatory matter. Failure to take the required action on an auditor's notice of resignation is an offence punishable by fine.

An auditor who states the circumstances of his resignation in his notice may also deposit with it a requisition calling on the directors forthwith to convene an EGM to receive and consider his explanation of the circumstances. The auditor also has the right to put a written statement of reasonable length of the circumstances of his resignation before members of the company (but subject to the same safeguard against defamatory matter). He may exercise this right by requiring the company to circulate his statement before the general meeting at which his term of office would otherwise expire, or before any general meeting called to fill the vacancy caused by his resignation or called on his requisition. The notice of the meeting issued to members must (unless it is too late to do so) state that such a statement has been made: s 391(3). Finally the auditor may attend any such meeting and speak at it about his resignation. He is also entitled to receive the notice of the meeting and any circular issued to members in connection with it.

The indirect effect of these elaborate procedures is that the directors are less likely to press any disagreement to the point at which the auditor is impelled to resign.

14.11 Qualification for appointment as auditor
The qualification for appointment as auditor of a company is:

(a) membership of a recognised body of accountants; and
(b) independence of the company.

The recognised professional qualification is mainly membership of the Institute of Chartered Accountants (in England and Wales or of Scotland or in Ireland) or of the Association of Certified Accountants. Foreign qualifications may be recognised by order of the DTI and there are transitional provisions (closed to new entrants since 1968) for recognition of persons qualified by experience to act as company auditors: s 389.

The test of independence excludes the following categories from eligibility for appointment as auditors:

 (i) any person who is an officer or servant (ie employee) of the company;
 (ii) any person who is a partner or employee of an officer or servant of the company;
(iii) a body corporate;
(iv) any person disqualified for any of the above reasons from acting as auditor of the holding or subsidiary company of the relevant company or of another subsidiary of its holding company: s 389. ('Company' here includes a body corporate.)

There are guidelines as to the other services or connections with the client company and any of its associated companies which an auditor may properly combine with his audit function. These are matters mainly of professional ethics and not of company law.

14.12 Remuneration of auditor
In the ordinary course the remuneration of the auditor is either fixed by the company in general meeting or in such manner as the general meeting may determine. It is usually left to the directors to agree with the auditors the amount of their fees.

The remuneration of an auditor appointed by the directors or by the DTI may be fixed by the directors or by the Department as the case may be.

The amount of the auditors' remuneration (including any expenses reimbursed to him by the company) must be shown separately in the profit and loss account.

14.13 The role of the auditor

The primary function of the auditor is to report to members on the accounts examined by him: s 236. In that connection a number of rights and duties of auditors are defined by statute. The firms of accountants who ordinarily hold the appointment of company auditors enter into a contract (usually in the form of a letter of engagement) which may give them additional functions, such as dealing with the company's tax returns, as well as their primary role of auditing the accounts.

There is no comprehensive definition of the status of an auditor in relation to the company. In certain restricted contexts, such as a DTI investigation (s 434(4)) or assistance to a liquidator in criminal proceedings against delinquent officers or members of the company (IA s 219(3)) it is expressly stated that the 'agents' of the company include its auditors. The auditor is not generally regarded as an 'officer' of the company and the statutory definition of 'officer' (s 744) does not mention the auditor. However, in proceedings against 'officers' for what is still often called 'misfeasance' (Chapter 20: 20.20 – CA 1948 s 333 now replaced by IA s 212) it has been held that in that context an auditor may be liable as an 'officer' for dereliction of duty (see 14.17 below). It is fair to conclude therefore that the statutory office of auditor does impose on its holder certain obligations to the company in specific situations.

To sum up, an auditor holds a statutory office under the company with which he also has a contractual relationship. In that capacity his primary role is to report to members on the accounts which the company is required to send them each year.

14.14 The rights of the auditor

The auditor has a right of access at all times to the books and accounts and vouchers of the company and a right to require from the officers of the company such information and explanations as he thinks necessary for the performance of his duty: s 237(3). It is doubtful nonetheless whether the auditor can obtain a court order to enforce these rights. But the auditors are required to qualify their report if information has been withheld from them: s 237(4).

In a dispute between the directors and auditors over the auditors' performance of their duties, in which there was likely to be litigation, the court refused to make an order giving the auditors a right of access to the company records: *Cuff v London and County Land and Building Co Ltd* [1912] 1 Ch 440.

In the above case the court considered that the appropriate action for the auditors was to request a general meeting at which their differences with the directors could be ventilated. In modern practice the statutory resignation procedure (14.10 above) would enable the auditors to demand that a meeting be held.

If the company has a subsidiary incorporated in Great Britain the auditor may require from the subsidiary and its auditors such information and explanation as he requires. If it is incorporated elsewhere the holding company must take reasonable steps to obtain it for him: s 392.

It is an offence punishable by fine or imprisonment for an officer of a company knowingly or recklessly to provide false or misleading information to the auditor: s 393.

The auditor is entitled to attend any general meeting of the company and to receive a copy of all notices and other communications relating to meetings which members are entitled to receive. He is also entitled to be heard at any general meeting on any part of the business which concerns him as auditor: s 387.

14.15 The auditor's investigation

The statutory duty of the auditor, in preparing his report, is to investigate and form an opinion on the adequacy of the accounting records and the returns sent in from branches, as well as the accuracy of the accounts based on that material. If there are deficiencies, he will mention them in his report (see 14.16 below): s 237(1). It has also been said in the case below that:

'an auditor is not to be confined to the mechanics of checking vouchers and making arithmetical calculations . . . his vital task is to take care that errors are not made . . . to perform this task properly he must come to it with an enquiring mind – not suspicious of dishonesty, I agree – but suspecting that someone may have made a mistake somewhere and a check must be made to ensure that there has been none'.

Lord Denning was considering a case in which the auditor had queried whether a statement of patent royalties (which the auditor was required to sign) was based on a correct interpretation of the patent licensing agreement. It was held that the auditor was entitled to check the accuracy of the statement in its legal as well as arithmetical aspect and for that purpose to require his client to take legal advice: *Fomento (Sterling Area) Ltd v Selsdon Fountain Pen Co Ltd* [1958] 1 All ER 11.

In effect there are three stages or elements in the task of the auditor:

(i)   to verify the accuracy and completeness of the accounts by reference to the books of account;
(ii) to check whether they give a true and fair view; and
(iii) to report adequately to members of the company (14.16 below).

The nature and method of checking needed in the audit is a matter of professional practice on which the auditor has a steadily increasing volume of memoranda of guidance issued by professional bodies. He should in particular prepare an audit plan designed to cover systematically the whole of the accounts, using the correct methods of checking. He is concerned with such matters as the value of the company's stock of materials or finished goods at the close of the accounting period, the accuracy of its list of trade debtors (and the risk of bad debts), the possibility of latent liability arising from current or threatened litigation, etc. For all these elements in the accounts there is a suitable method of checking or investigation to be applied.

It is not the duty of the auditor to check every individual item in this fashion. If a random but adequate test check discloses no apparent irregularities or deficiencies, that may suffice to discharge the auditor's duty. If, however, he encounters something which is suspicious or even unusual, it then becomes his duty to investigate this area of the accounts more fully and to obtain satisfactory explanations, which he would ordinarily verify, at least on a sample basis.

The managing director had falsified the company's books in three ways. Two of them involved false dates on invoices for purchases and sale of goods. As regards purchase the falsification of the invoice dates was apparent because the managing director had crossed out the supplier's original dates, which fell just before the balance sheet date, and had written in later dates falling after the balance sheet dates (so that the cost of these purchases were excluded from the accounts of the period). The auditor in his routine examination noted these alterations and asked for an explanation. The managing director, confirmed by the secretary who was his brother-in-law, said that the dates were altered to conform to the actual dates of receipt. The auditor accepted this explanation without seeking to verify it, eg by enquiry addressed to some suppliers whose invoices had been altered. It was held that 'as a matter of business common sense he should where necessary have communicated with the suppliers'. This finding was based on the expert evidence of an accountant: *Re Thomas Gerrard & Son Ltd* [1967] 2 All ER 525.

In his enquiries the auditor may properly confine himself to matters which affect the accounts. It is not his duty to report on the efficiency with which the company conducts its business nor, except as an incidental consequence of his audit investigation, is he required to discover defalcation or other dishonesty of its staff. He is of course required to ensure that the accounts properly disclose the matters prescribed by statute such as any directors' loans and directors' emoluments.

There is a considerable volume of case law on the performance by auditors of their duty of investigation. It is doubtful, however, whether the majority of these decisions are any longer a reliable guide to the standard of performance required of an auditor. In the leading case below it was said that

it is the duty of an auditor to bring to bear on the work he has to perform that skill, care and caution which a reasonably competent, careful and cautious auditor would use. What is reasonable skill, care and caution must depend on the particular circumstances of each case. An auditor is not bound to be a detective . . . he is a watchdog not a bloodhound'.

Although this principle is still valid, ie the auditor is to be judged by the current standards of good professional practice applied to the particular audit task, it has been said (in 1967) that 'the standards of reasonable care and skill are upon expert evidence more exacting today than those which prevailed in 1896'. For example, it is still probably the law, as it was in 1896, that it is no part of the auditor's duty to take stock but, unlike 1896, he is expected at least to satisfy himself that the value of stock is based on proper stocktaking procedure.

The managing director, who had been with the company for many years, supplied false figures of the value of closing stocks at the year end. It was held that the auditor was not at fault in accepting these figures without checking them in any way. It would in any event have been very difficult to check either the quantity or the value of the stock of raw cotton since the market price fluctuated and there was substantial but variable waste of material in course of manufacture: *Re Kingston Cotton Mill Co (No 2)* [1896] 2 Ch 279.

After 90 years this is still the leading case with its celebrated remark ('watchdog not a bloodhound') but the observation that professional standards change over the years (quoted above) was made in the *Thomas Gerrard Case*.

14.16 The auditor's report

The auditor's report on the accounts is a formal document. It should state whether in the auditor's opinion the company's balance sheet and profit and loss account have been properly prepared in accordance with the provisions of the Companies Act and whether the balance sheet gives a true and fair view of the state of the company's affairs at the end of its financial year and whether the profit and loss account gives a true and fair view of the company's profit or loss for that year. There are suitable modifications of wording for a report on the consolidated accounts of a holding company relating to the group as a whole: s 236. Accounts are only 'properly prepared' (see Chapter 5: 5.24) if they deal correctly and completely with all the matters (so far as relevant) required to be disclosed by the statutory rules on the content of the accounts. 'True and fair view' is not a defined term but its significance has been developed in rules of professional practice.

In preparing their report the auditors are required to consider three other matters:

(a)   whether proper books of account have been kept;
(b)   whether the company's accounts are in agreement with those books of account; and
(c)   whether the auditors have obtained the information and explanations which, to the best of their knowledge and belief, are necessary for the purposes of their audit: s 237(2).

If the auditors are satisfied on these points they make no reference to them in their report on the accounts. But if they are not fully satisfied they must say so in their report.

The auditors may therefore be obliged to qualify their report in any of four respects ('true and fair view' and (a), (b) and (c) above). In addition the auditors may have, under rules of professional practice, to state in their report any departure in the accounts from recommended principles of accounting practice even if, as is usually the case, these are merely instances of preferring one optional method of accounting to another.

The auditors have a general duty to disclose their findings to the members by sufficiently explicit statements in their reports. If they reach a conclusion on some material point they must state it and not cover it up by oblique or vague language.

The auditor had reported by letter to the directors his doubts as to whether loans to associated companies shown as current assets in the balance sheet would be repaid. Hence it was doubtful whether a dividend could be paid. Under pressure from the directors the auditor's report said merely that 'the value of the assets shown on the balance sheet is dependent upon realisation'. The auditor was held liable for misfeasance because the ambiguous wording of his report 'gave weight' to the director's improper recommendation for the payment of a dividend: *Re London and General Bank (No 2)* [1895] 2 Ch 673.

It will be remembered that the auditor is now required to include in his report, if he is reasonably able to do so (ie if he discovers it), any information relating to the directors which the directors have improperly omitted from the accounts

(14.6 above) and to consider and, if necessary, disclose any inconsistency between the accounts and the directors' report (14.7 above).

The auditor's duty to report to members is discharged by delivering his report to the company which must annex it to the balance sheet laid before the company in general meeting: s 238(3). The report must be read aloud at the general meeting (not necessarily by or in the presence of the auditor) and must be available for inspection by members: s 241(2).

14.17 The liability of the auditor
If the auditor fails to perform his statutory duty and the company is in liquidation the court may order the auditor to pay compensation to the company, e g because it has paid a dividend out of capital (as in the *London and General Bank Case* in 14.16 above).

If he fails to show a reasonable standard of skill and care in the performance of his duties he may be liable to pay damages to the company for a breach of an implied term of his contract. But it is often not the company, but its members or creditors, who have suffered loss. The auditor is only liable to them for the tort of negligence if there is a special relationship between them and the auditor which imposes on him a duty of care in respect of the financial information provided by the accounts.

A bank had supplied information about a customer to a third party, which was expressed in misleading terms. It was held that the bank owed a duty of care (and had failed in that duty) to a person to whom it supplied information with sufficient awareness of the purpose for which the information was required. The bank however escaped liability because, in making its report, it had expressly disclaimed all liability for it: *Hedley Byrne & Co Ltd v Heller & Partners Ltd* [1964] AC 465.

In connection with the position of the company auditor, the significance of the *Hedley Byrne* decision is that the House of Lords reviewed the case below, which was concerned with the liability of an auditor, and held that the view expressed by Lord Denning was correct.

C was negotiating to take a financial interest in the company. At his request the company asked its auditors (the defendants) to prepare special accounts. In doing so, with full knowledge of the purpose for which the accounts were required, the auditors made errors. The Court of Appeal, by a majority, held that the auditors were not liable to C for the loss which he had incurred by relying on the inaccurate information in the accounts. This conclusion was reached on the ground that there was no contract between C and the auditors, who therefore owed him no duty of care. Lord Denning, in a minority judgment, argued that there is a 'special relationship', imposing a duty of care, in cases where a person in a professional capacity supplies information for a known purpose. As indicated above, the House of Lords later held that Lord Denning's view was correct: *Candler v Crane Christmas & Co* [1951] 2 KB 164.

For some years after the *Hedley Byrne* decision it was considered that the auditors did not stand in a 'special relationship' with members or creditors of the company, and so owed them no duty of care, since in auditing the accounts the auditors did not know for what purposes the members or creditors might make use of the information (if incorrect) contained in the accounts. However, as a result of the case below, it is now clear that auditors may owe a duty of care to persons whom they can reasonably foresee are likely to make use of the accounts for a particular purpose.

In their audit of the annual accounts the auditors failed to disclose certain matters by way of qualifying their report. In this they were guilty of want of care. Later the plaintiff made a take-over bid for the company and, to some extent, relied on the audited accounts. The court held that the auditors owed a duty of care, even in the absence of knowledge at the time of their audit, if the circumstances were such that it was reasonable to foresee that the information in the accounts might be used for a particular purpose. However it was shown that the plaintiff, in deciding to bid for the shares of the company, did not rely on the information in the accounts, but was mainly influenced by other factors. On those facts it could not be held that want of care on the part of the auditors was the cause of his loss. On that ground his claim against the auditors was dismissed: *JEB Fasteners Ltd v Marks, Bloom & Co* [1983] 1 All ER 583.

There are a number of criminal offences in connection with the publication of inaccurate company documents. They all require some degree of mens rea such as acting knowingly, wilfully, recklessly, etc.

Chapter 15

Protection of the minority

A SHAREHOLDERS' ACTION

15.1 Majority control

A company is a legal person separate from its members. It has its own property, rights and obligations. Although its members invest in the company, and so have a stake in it, the law does not recognise that they have even an insurable interest in its assets (*Macaura's Case* in Chapter 1: 1.3). If, therefore, the company's property is misappropriated or lost or if its affairs are mismanaged, the company alone is the person who should bring legal proceedings against those who have caused it damage. If an individual shareholder wishes to complain of any such matter he should bring his proposals before the company in general meeting and seek to persuade other members to his point of view over the course of action which the company should take. If, however, he fails to persuade a majority (which in this chapter means members who have the majority of votes) to approve his proposals he is usually bound by the majority decision. If he tries to bring legal proceedings on behalf of the company, his right to do so is likely to be challenged and his action dismissed. This is the principle of majority control which is often described as 'the rule in *Foss v Harbottle*'. Its essential points are that in proceedings to enforce or protect the rights of a company the company is the proper plaintiff and that a decision whether the company should sue at all is to be taken by voting in a general meeting (or by the directors if the power of decision has been delegated to them).

The Victoria Park Company was formed by special Act of Parliament in 1837 to acquire land near Manchester for development as a residential area. The action was brought by Foss and another shareholder on behalf of themselves and all other members except Harbottle and seven associates (mainly directors of the company) on the grounds that they had defrauded the company by selling land to it at much inflated prices thereby securing an undisclosed profit. It was strongly argued that the company was by then in such a state of disorganisation that no meeting of shareholders could be held to decide whether the company should sue. The court, however, held that it was possible to call a general meeting, that this was the proper course and that it was not competent to individual shareholders to bring an action on behalf of the company. The court added, however, 'the claims of justice would be found superior to any difficulties arising out of technical rules' (Wigram VC), ie the need to relax the principle on occasion was foreseen: *Foss v Harbottle* (1843) 2 Hare 461.

15.2 The limits or exceptions to the rule

In various circumstances the principle of majority control does not apply – usually but not always because the majority of members either cannot in law, or in fact have not taken, a decision binding on the company. In such case a minority may maintain legal proceedings either on behalf of the company or themselves. These instances of 'minority protection' are usually classified under the following main heads:

(a) illegal or ultra vires transactions cannot be sanctioned by a majority vote nor can such a vote relieve those responsible from their personal liability;
(b) an ordinary resolution passed by a simple majority of votes is not a valid decision in a case where the law or the memorandum or articles require that a special or extraordinary resolution be passed. No resolution is valid unless proper notice has been given to members of the meeting at which it is passed;
(c) if the majority defraud the company or a minority of its members they cannot by their voting control approve their own act nor prevent a minority from bringing an action in the courts against them;
(d) a member cannot be deprived of his personal rights arising under the constitution of the company.

It is, however, difficult to fit all the existing case law neatly into this classification for reasons which are explained below. In addition to these types of minority protection an individual member is also given a statutory right to petition the court for a remedy in certain cases.

As an example of illegality, a company may not pay a dividend out of capital since this is a return of capital without complying with the statutory conditions. In the leading case on this point (*Flitcroft's Case* in Chapter 5: 5.25) the court noted that the dividend in question had been approved in general meeting. But the judge commented:

'A limited company cannot in any other way make a return of capital, the sanction of a general meeting can give no validity to such a proceeding, and even the sanction of every shareholder cannot bring within the powers of the company an act which is not within its powers' (Jessel MR).

If a company decides in general meeting to act illegally or ultra vires, the majority decision does not prevent a shareholder from applying to the court for a declaration or injunction to restrain the company from acting on the majority decision (as in *Simpson's Case* in Chapter 3: 3.13).

A special resolution is required for an alteration of the articles of a company: s 9. An ordinary resolution is invalid insofar as it purports to alter the articles or to sanction an act which infringes or disregards the articles. This was the result in *Salmon's Case* (in Chapter 13: 13.4). The leading case on this point is set out below.

A trade union (to which company law principles applied on this point) by its constitution provided that any alteration in the rate of members' contributions should only be made if approved by a two-thirds majority obtained in a ballot of members. A delegate meeting, without taking a ballot, passed a resolution to increase the rate of contributions. The plaintiffs, who were members, successfully sued two members of the management committee and the union for a declaration that the resolution was invalid. The case is notable for the masterly judgment of Jenkins LJ on the exceptions to the rule in *Foss v Harbottle: Edwards v Halliwell* [1950] 2 All ER 1064.

A special resolution will normally suffice to override the articles, since it can be regarded as an alteration of the articles limited to the transaction in question. However, no resolution of any kind is valid if the notice convening the meeting is irregular; *Kaye's Case* and *Baillie's Case* (both in Chapter 11: 11.7) illustrate this point.

There is some conflicting case law on the question whether a simple majority decision can validate an irregularity of procedure at the meeting itself.

The articles provided that a poll (Chapter 11: 11.11) should be held if demanded by at least five members. The demand was properly made but the chairman refused to allow a poll to be held. A member applied to the court for a declaration that the resolution (carried on a show of hands) was invalid because there should have been a vote on a poll. In dismissing the application the court said that:

'if the thing complained of is a thing which in substance the majority of the company are entitled to do or if something is done irregularly which the majority of the company are entitled to do regularly, or if something is done illegally which the majority of the company are entitled to do legally, there can be no use in having litigation about it, the ultimate end of which is only that a meeting had to be called and then the majority gets its wishes':

MacDougall v Gardiner (1875) 1 Ch D 13.

This dictum is a restatement of the essential point of the rule in *Foss v Harbottle*. The decision has been much criticised on the grounds that it conflicts with the principle (Chapter 4: 4.4) that the articles are a contract which a member can enforce against the company and the other members: s 14. But the contract is limited to matters which affect the members in their rights as members. A distinction can be made between *individual* rights, to which the protection given by s 14 applies, and collective rights, to which perhaps it does not. So far, so good. But the decision in *MacDougall's Case* was a denial to members of their right to vote on a poll. There is another case (*Pender v Lushington*) considered later (15.4 below) in which the right to vote was treated as an individual right, enforceable against the company. Case law is not always consistent; it is simpler to recognise that *Pender* and *MacDougall* represent conflicting views of the law rather than make fine distinctions of fact in an attempt to reconcile them (but see 15.4).

Another area of doubt and difficulty is where directors use their powers in an irregular, and therefore invalid, fashion, eg by allotting shares to alter the balance of votes at a general meeting. Recent case law establishes that a majority voting in general meeting can authorise or ratify the directors' action (*Hogg v Cramphorn Ltd* and *Bamford v Bamford* both in Chapter 12: 12.18). The anomaly here is that an individual shareholder may challenge the directors' action in the courts but the company in general meeting may validate it. As already stated, the general rule is that where a minority has a right of challenge, the majority has no power to validate the act in question.

15.3 Fraud by a controlling majority
In the simplest type of case the members of a company who are the majority deprive the company of its property for their own gain and then use their votes to prevent the company taking any action against them. In these circumstances the minority of members who are the losers, through their indirect interest in the net value of the company, are allowed to bring proceedings against those who both control the company and have defrauded it. This is perhaps the most important of the exceptions to the rule in *Foss v*

Harbottle. But the exact scope of the exception is rather uncertain because the controlling majority are usually also directors and so the rules on directors' duties (Chapter 12: 12.19) may also apply.

The term fraud is used both to cover misappropriation of property and in some cases oppression of a minority. In the straightforward case of misappropriation it must be shown that what has been taken was the company's property. If, for example, the directors have obtained a personal advantage without depriving the company of anything which belongs to it, that is not 'fraud' in this sense and the company in general meeting may even approve what they have done or propose to do. In the *Regal Hastings Case* (Chapter 12: 12.19) the House of Lords observed that if the directors, who were also controlling shareholders, had convened a general meeting to approve their action they would have been entitled to retain their profit. They had not deprived the company of anything, since the company lacked the money required to subscribe for the shares taken by its directors.

But in applying this test it does not have to be shown that what was taken from the company was already its property in law. It is sufficient if what was taken was something which would otherwise have accrued to the company for its benefit such as the profit to be made from a contract diverted at the last moment from the company to the controlling majority.

The company sued one of its directors who had obtained a concession (to lay a submarine cable) for the company and had then transferred it to another company in which he was interested. The majority shareholder of the company halted the action and put the company into liquidation so that it should not pursue its claim. Menier, a minority shareholder, was held entitled to sue on the company's behalf: *Menier v Hooper's Telegraph Works* (1874) 9 Ch App 350.

The plaintiff sued for himself and other shareholders; the defendants were the controlling shareholders and directors of the company. They had negotiated a contract on behalf of the company, then made it for themselves, and passed a resolution in general meeting that the company had no interest in it. It was held that the contract belonged *in equity* to the company and that the plaintiffs could in these circumstances sue on behalf of the company: *Cook v Deeks* [1916] 1 AC 554.

If it was company property, then – to establish fraud – it must also be shown that what was the company's property did pass to the controlling shareholders. If by their incompetence the company's property passes to a third party, for example by sale at an undervalue, that may be negligence but it is not fraud.

The defendants were directors of Company A and also of its partly-owned subsidiary, B; the plaintiff was a minority shareholder of B. The defendants had sold the principal asset of B for £182,000 to another company in which A had a 25 per cent interest. The plaintiff sued for a declaration that the defendants had been negligent and should have obtained a price of at least £1 m. The action failed on the preliminary point that a shareholder has no right to sue on behalf of the company if he alleges only negligence and not fraud by those who control it: *Pavlides v Jensen* [1956] 2 All ER 518.

But if the result of the transaction is that the company's property does pass to the controlling shareholders who are also the directors, it need not be shown that there was actual dishonesty. It suffices in such cases if the directors have enriched themselves at the company's expense even if this was (or appears to be) the result of mere negligence on their part.

The company purchased land from a deceased person's estate at probate value, ie £4,250, and later resold it at the same price to one of the directors who, with her husband (also a director), were controlling shareholders. She later resold it for £120,000. In an action by minority shareholders in which fraud was not alleged a preliminary objection was raised that except in case of fraud the rule in *Foss v Harbottle* denied to the plaintiffs the right to sue on behalf of the company. The objection was dismissed on the grounds that (unlike *Pavlides Case* above) there was here a case of alleged negligence from which a director had obtained a *so far unexplained benefit*. Some authorities consider that this case turns more on breach of duty by directors than on the exceptions to the rule in *Foss v Harbottle: Daniels v Daniels* [1978] Ch 406.

To succeed in an action of this type the minority shareholder must establish three essential points:

(a) that property which *belonged* to the company has been taken from it (see *Menier's Case* and *Cook's Case* as to this test);

(b) that the property has passed to the *defendants* and not to a third party (see *Pavlides Case*); it is unnecessary to allege dishonesty (*Daniels' Case*);

(c) that the defendants have sufficient *control* of the company to prevent it from taking action to enforce its rights against them (as envisaged by the *Foss v Harbottle* principle).

The test required by (c) is satisfied if there has in fact been a resolution passed in general meeting (as in *Cook's Case*). It also suffices if the state of the share register shows that the defendants do possess or control a majority of votes available to be cast at a general meeting (as in *Pavlides Case* and *Daniels' Case*).

It is generally safe to assume that if those who defraud the company are a minority, no disinterested shareholder would vote to approve their action. But if the defendants, although a minority in terms of voting power, are also managers of the company, they may be able to secure sufficient support by presenting to the general meeting an incomplete or even misleading picture of the facts. If they secure majority approval by those means, should they be regarded as in 'de facto control' of the company? The case law, including the latest decision, raises some doubts on this issue.

The defendant formed a company and sold to it for £7,000 a mine which was worthless. Part of the price was satisfied by the allotment of shares. The true facts were not disclosed to the other directors and members who believed that £7,000 was a fair price. The sale was approved by 344 votes to 324: 106 votes of the majority which approved were cast by the defendant in right of his shares. The minority shareholders' action succeeded. This case also established that a minority may bring a representative action on behalf of themselves and other shareholders against the company and those who control it although the basis of the claim is derivative, ie on behalf of the company. An earlier action (*East Pant Du United Lead Mining Co Ltd v Merryweather* (1864) 2 H & M 254) was dismissed on the technical point that the minority were suing on behalf of the company without having its authority to do so (see 15.5 below): *Atwool v Merryweather* (1867) LR 5 Eq 464.

B and L were respectively chairman and vice-chairman of a public company (Newman), in which another company (TPG) had a 25½ per cent shareholding. B and L had outright control of a third company which held 35 per cent of the issued shares of TPG. B and L therefore had influence over a substantial minority shareholding of a public company (Newman) but they certainly did not have voting control of it, as is generally required when this exception to *Foss's Case* is used. TPG was in financial difficulties. B and L considered, with some commercial justification, that it would be in the interest of Newman to acquire most of TPG's assets at a price of £325,000. As B and

L had an interest in the transaction, it was submitted for approval to a general meeting of Newman – and was approved.

One of the directors of Newman had strongly opposed the transaction; he was later removed from the board. The auditor of Newman had at first valued the assets of TPG at £235,000 but B and L later persuaded him to support their valuation of £325,000.

The action was brought by a minority shareholder (Prudential) of Newman. The claim was (i) a personal claim for damages against B and L (ii) a representative claim on behalf of the shareholders of Newman and (iii) a derivative claim (see 15.5 below) on behalf of Newman. The basis of each claim was that Newman had been induced to pay an excessive price for the assets of TPG. It was alleged against B and L that they had conspired to defraud Newman and that for that purpose they had misled the board of Newman, its auditors and finally its shareholders. Although B and L were not controlling shareholders of Newman, it was argued that they had 'de facto control' since by the supply of inaccurate information they had been able to secure the decision which they wanted.

In a High Court action which lasted 40 days most of the allegations against B and L were upheld – and their 'de facto control' was accepted. The judge (Vinelott J) applied the phrase 'the claims of justice' (in the *Foss v Harbottle* judgment) as justification for permitting the action to proceed against defendants who were not in voting control of the company, and despite the fact that a general meeting had approved the transaction. His view was that such approval was invalid if obtained by 'unfair or improper means'.

The Court of Appeal (after a 30-day hearing) reversed the findings and conclusions of Vinelott J on most points. By this stage Newman had been joined as a plaintiff to the action and so it was no longer necessary to decide the case as a derivative action (see 15.5 below) brought by a minority on behalf of the company.

However, the Court of Appeal did find that B and L had deceived the board of Newman, and later its auditors and its shareholders, on one of the numerous points of the original allegations made against them. They had caused Newman to make advance payments of £216,000 to TPG before the purchase was approved at the general meeting. These payments were to some extent 'dishonestly concealed' from the board of Newman; they were not disclosed to the auditor; their 'origin and purpose' was not properly disclosed in a circular to shareholders, which was (in that respect only) 'tricky and misleading'. The parties reached an out-of-court settlement of the damages and costs.

The decision of the Court of Appeal is important for two main reasons. First, the court rejected the concept of 'de facto control' since it required the court to accept, before it had been proved, that misleading information had been supplied, as alleged. Without that unproven assumption, the case would have to be dismissed at the outset since, in a situation such as this, the defendants were not a controlling majority in any other sense. Secondly, the Court of Appeal disapproved of permitting a minority shareholder to combine in the same action a direct claim on his own behalf with a derivative claim on behalf of the company (this is considered further in 15.5 below): *Prudential Assurance Co Ltd v Newman Industries Ltd (No 2)* [1982] Ch 204.

The protection given to a minority in cases of fraud by a majority is part of a wider, but rather disjointed and uncertain, system of preventing a majority from misuse of their votes. It is perhaps useful to review this topic from the wider standpoint.

The general principle is that at a general meeting a member may cast his votes as he sees fit. Even if he is a director voting on a matter in which he has a personal interest (as in *Beatty's Case* in Chapter 12: 12.18) he may vote and his votes will be counted. If, however, he votes to approve his own fraud against the company, his votes will be disregarded in determining the result (*Cook's Case* above). By statute the votes of a shareholder, to approve a sale, by off-market purchase, of his own shares, are also disregarded: s 164(5) (Chapter 5: 5.17).

A different safeguard, but to the same effect, is a court order by which a shareholder is forbidden to vote at all. By statute (ss 216 and 454) the court may make such an order as a sanction against non-disclosure of ownership etc of shares. In different circumstances, the court may direct that in voting on a resolution to authorise the allotment of shares by directors for an irregular purpose, the votes attached to shares already allotted shall not be used (*Bamford's Case* in Chapter 12: 12.18).

Again, there are situations in which a majority vote, eg to alter the articles (Chapter 4: 4.7) or to vary class rights (Chapter 7: 7.13), is declared invalid because the majority did not vote bona fide in the interests of the company, or of the class, as the case may be.

In the case below the court declared that it could always intervene 'to subject the exercise of legal rights to equitable considerations'. It is uncertain however how far that doctrine will be taken. In *Foss v Harbottle* the court declined to arbitrate on disputes within a company – and that is the more general judicial approach (see also *Greenhalgh's Case* in Chapter 4: 4.7).

The plaintiff held 45 per cent of the ordinary shares and her aunt, the second defendant, held 55 per cent. The articles provided that if any shareholder wished to dispose of her shares she must offer them to the other; the aunt wished to remove this from the articles but could not carry a special resolution to do so. The aunt voted in favour of ordinary resolutions to increase the share capital and to issue new shares to working directors and to trustees for employees on such a scale that the plaintiff's shareholding would be reduced to 24½ per cent of the increased issued capital. The court held that it was equitable to restrain the aunt from exercising her majority control for this purpose since it was directed mainly to depriving the plaintiff of her 'negative control' of the existing articles. In its decision the court applied a dictum of the House of Lords in *Ebrahimi v Westbourne Galleries Ltd* (Chapter 18: 18.4) that the exercise of legal rights by a majority might be restrained if the majority acted unfairly: *Clemens v Clemens Bros Ltd* [1976] 2 All ER 268.

Now that there is a simpler statutory procedure by which a minority may apply to the court for a remedy against 'unfair prejudice' (15.6 below) it seems likely that the common law remedy, which is so uncertain in its scope, will lose much of its importance.

15.4 The shareholder's personal rights

In the circumstances described above the minority shareholder brings his action ostensibly to enforce the rights of the company against those who have mismanaged or defrauded the company. He has a personal interest in the matter but he is not protecting personal rights. There can be cases, however, where his complaint is that the company itself, controlled by the majority, is denying to him rights which belong to him individually. Here he is suing to protect his own immediate interests against the company rather than to protect the interests of the company (and indirectly his own) against other shareholders.

The exact dividing line between the two categories is never easy to draw. It is clear that the individual shareholder cannot say that because he has an interest in having the company properly managed he has, on that account only, a *personal* right to assert against any who mismanage it or defraud it. The action to protect a shareholder's personal rights is confined to cases such as the exercise of voting rights or the receipt of a dividend where the member lays claim to something of the nature of property such as the right to vote or to receive a dividend.

In breach of the articles the chairman at a general meeting rejected certain votes cast by the plaintiff. In the action the company contended that any irregularity was a matter for the company to complain of. The plaintiff succeeded in his argument that he was entitled to sue since *his* votes had been improperly rejected: *Pender v Lushington* (1877) 6 Ch D 70.

The articles provided that dividends should be 'paid'. The company proposed to distribute a dividend in the form of debentures. The plaintiff, a member, obtained an injunction preventing the company from distributing a dividend otherwise than in cash as the word 'paid' required: *Wood v Odessa Watermarks Co* (1889) 42 Ch D 636.

As indicated above (15.2) it is very difficult to reconcile the decision in *Pender's Case* with that in *MacDougall's Case*, also concerned with a denial of voting rights. But there is a distinction. Pender was complaining that his individual votes had been improperly rejected; MacDougall however was seeking to assert a claim (of a collective nature) that all members should be allowed to vote on a poll instead of a show of hands.

15.5 Procedural aspects of minority shareholders' actions

When a member sues on behalf of the company he is said to bring a derivative action since he is enforcing rights derived from the company. But he is also bringing an action on behalf of shareholders (other than the defendant majority) and so it is a representative action. It is usual to make the company a defendant so that any judgment obtained will be binding on the company. If this were not done, the majority would be free to use their control of the company to ensure that matters went on as before. As the action is brought by the minority member in his own name he is liable to pay the legal costs; as he is protecting the interests of the company, any financial benefit of the action will, however, accrue to the company. For this reason the Court of Appeal in the *Newman Industries Case* (15.3 above) held that a shareholder might not sue both in a representative capacity for the benefit of the company and to assert a personal claim against the company, with the right to retain any damages awarded to him on that claim.

It would be unfair that a minority shareholder should bear the risk of paying the legal costs of his action, insofar as he did not recover them from the defendants, since he sues to obtain a remedy for the company not himself. Under a ruling of the Court of Appeal (*Wallersteiner v Moir (No 2)* [1975] 1 All ER 849) he may apply before the case comes to trial for an order that, whatever the outcome, the company shall indemnify him against his costs (in full). However the order will only be made if it appears to the court that the plaintiff is acting reasonably and in good faith in bringing his action.

15.6 Statutory remedies

A dissatisfied minority shareholder has three general statutory remedies against mismanagement or unfairness on the part of those who control the company:

(a) he may petition the court for an order for the compulsory winding up of the company on the 'just and equitable ground' under IA s 122(1)(g);

(b) he may apply to the DTI for the appointment of inspectors to investigate the affairs of the company (15.7 below);
(c) he may petition the court for suitable relief on the ground of 'unfair prejudice' to the interests of members under s 459 as described below.

He may not wish to have the company wound up under (a); under either (a) or (b) he may have difficulty in making out a sufficient case.

The Cohen Report on company law in 1945 (paras 58–59) and the Jenkins Report of 1962 (para 205) recognised that a minority shareholder, especially in a private company with only a handful of members, may be vulnerable to unfair treatment on the part of those who manage and control the company. The latter may take all the available trade profits as working directors' remuneration, or allot additional shares to themselves or their associates or refuse to pass a transfer of shares of a deceased member in order to compel his personal representatives to sell the shares to themselves. If colourable commercial reasons can be adduced the courts cannot or will not interfere in the ordinary way. The philosophy of *Foss v Harbottle* dies hard.

The first attempt (CA 1948 s 210) to provide relief at the discretion of the court did not work well. It was replaced in 1980 (now ss 459–461) but some of the earlier case law is a useful guide to the current law.

A petition to the court for relief under s 459 may be presented by a member of the company, or by a person to whom shares have been transferred (although his transfer has not yet been registered) or by a personal representative of a deceased member or by a trustee in bankruptcy of a bankrupt member. The DTI also may present a petition, on the same grounds, following the receipt of a report of its inspectors (15.7 below).

The petition should specify the relief requested and must be based on the grounds that either:

(a) the affairs of the company are being or have been conducted in a manner unfairly prejudicial to some part of the members, including at least the petitioner; or
(b) an actual or proposed act or omission of the company (or on its behalf) is or would be prejudicial as in (a) above.

These grounds differ from the pre 1980 law in prescribing 'unfair prejudice' (instead of 'oppression') and in permitting a petition based on a single act or omission.

In deciding whether there has been 'unfair prejudice' to members the court will take account of all the relevant circumstances. In the *Noble Case* (below) the court said that action which 'seriously diminished' (or jeopardised) the value of the petitioner's shareholding would be prejudicial to him in this sense. But prejudice might also be found in the exclusion of a 'partner' director from his established position (as in *Ebrahimi's Case* in Chapter 18: 18.4) or in denial to a member of his rights, eg to information of the financial position which ought to be found in the accounts.

The directors proposed to use the company's available cash to expand and diversify its business. The executors of a deceased shareholder petitioned on the grounds that the directors' refusal to promote a scheme for the purchase of their shares or for a reconstruction by which cash would be returned to shareholders was 'prejudicial' to them (they urgently needed the cash for family maintenance). The court dismissed the petition; the grounds adduced did not amount to 'prejudice' and the directors were under a duty to use the company's cash in what they deemed its best advantage: *Re A Company* [1983] 2 All ER 36.

The petition was presented by the executors of a deceased shareholder, who at the time of his death had been a guarantor of the company's bank overdraft. At that time the company was in a poor financial condition. But the controlling shareholder had restored its finances and had paid off the overdraft. She had also allotted more shares to herself and taken most of the profits as management commission (under a pre agreed formula) so that no dividends were paid. Under the pre 1980 law the petitioners alleged 'oppression'. The petition was dismissed (and would have been under the 'unfair prejudice' test) since on balance the position of the petitioners had not been prejudiced: *Re Jermyn Street Turkish Baths Ltd* [1971] 3 All ER 184.

B and N were the two directors. B had provided the capital but he left the management in the hands of N on the understanding that N would consult him on all major matters of company policy. N did not do so; B did no more than make enquiries of N on social occasions and he accepted N's vague assurances that all was well. The two men quarrelled and B petitioned on the grounds that his exclusion from consultation, as agreed, was 'prejudicial'. The court dismissed his petition, pointing out that his position was largely the result of his previous indifference: *Re RA Noble & Sons (Clothing) Ltd* [1983] BCLC 273.

SCWS set up a company jointly with M and another man because at the time M could obtain for the company government licences which it needed. Later, when the licences were no longer needed, SCWS used its control of the joint company to run down its business, which was thereby diverted to SCWS itself. M petitioned on the grounds of 'oppression' and the court ordered that SCWS should buy his shares at a valuation related to the company's situation before SCWS destroyed its business: *Scottish Co-op Wholesale Society v Meyer* [1958] 3 All ER 66.

Relief will only be given if the prejudice is deemed 'unfair'. This will generally be established by showing that there has been a breach of previous understandings or deliberate discrimination (as in *Meyer's Case* above). It need not be shown, however, that there has been bad faith nor even an intention to cause prejudice; the test is whether in the opinion of 'a reasonable bystander' what has occurred is unfair prejudice: *Noble's Case* above. The petitioner does not lose his remedy because he too has behaved badly – though this may be taken into account.

The petitioner had accused the other shareholders of diverting the business of the company to themselves. They removed him from his directorship. He then set up a rival business and used his connection to secure for it part of the company's clientele. He did not forfeit his right to relief because he did not have 'clean hands': *Re London School of Electronics Ltd* [1985] BCLC 273.

The unfair prejudice, which is the basis of the petition, must relate to the petitioner's position as a member of the company. If he is dismissed from his job by the company, that is prejudice to his position as an employee not as a shareholder, if he is both: *Elder v Elder and Watson Ltd* 1952 SC 49.

The petitioner was one of three directors and shareholders. His real grievance was that the other shareholders would not arrange for the company to pay a debt which it owed to another company in which he was interested. The petition, which alleged other grievances such as his exclusion from the management, was dismissed: *Re Bellador Silk Ltd* [1965] 1 All ER 667.

The petitioner must show that there is unfair prejudice 'to the interests of some part of the members (including at least himself)': s 459(1). In spite of the words 'some part' it is considered that it suffices to show general prejudice to all members, as will often be the case when it is a public company. But it must always be *'unfair* prejudice'; a complaint of inefficient management, by which all shareholders suffer loss, is not enough: *Re Five Minute Car Wash Service Ltd* [1966] 1 All ER 242.

The court has general power to 'make such order as it thinks fit for giving relief'. But a number of powers are specified, which include power to order purchase of the petitioner's shares (by the company or by other shareholders), to alter the memorandum of articles, and, perhaps most significant as an alternative to common law remedies, to authorise the petitioner to institute civil proceedings in the name or on behalf of the company: s 461(2)(c). The company is, of course, automatically liable for the costs of an action of this kind.

In ordering the purchase of the petitioner's shares, the court will give directions as to the basis of valuation (as in *Meyer's Case* above). It has recently been held that no 'discount' is normally required because the petitioner has only a minority shareholding (in conventional share valuation allowance is often made for this factor). In ordering the purchase of shares of a 'quasi-partnership' company, the court would normally direct that the shares should be valued simply as a proportion of the issued capital. But if the circumstances, including the petitioner's conduct, made it appropriate, the court in its discretion may order some other basis: *Re Bird Precision Bellows Ltd* [1985] 3 All ER 523.

If, of course, the petitioner wishes to remain as a shareholder, other relief may be appropriate.

The founder of a valuable business transferred it to a company in which he was a minority shareholder but he (and his wife) held all the voting shares. He was chairman and life director. The two sons held the non-voting shares and were the other directors. The father treated the business as if it were still his own and disregarded the decisions of the board. An order was made to remove him from his office of director: *Re H R Harmer Ltd* [1959] 1 WLR 62.

If the court orders an alteration of the memorandum or articles, the alteration takes effect at once as a consequence of the court order. A copy of the memorandum or articles, as altered, must be delivered to the registrar within 14 days. Thereafter the company cannot, under its normal powers, make alterations to the provisions ordered by the court, unless the court gives leave: s 461(3).

B DTI INVESTIGATIONS

15.7 Grounds for DTI investigation

The DTI *must* appoint one or more competent inspectors to investigate the *affairs* of a company, ie how it has been managed, if the court so orders: s 432(1). In practice, however, the court does not make such orders.

The DTI *may* in its discretion appoint inspectors to investigate the affairs of a company in either of the following situations:

(a) if (in the case of a company with a share capital) not less than 200 members or members who hold at least one-tenth of the issued shares apply for an investigation; or (in the case of a company with no share capital) if at least one-fifth in number of the members apply to the DTI: s 431(2). The applicants must produce evidence of the reasons for their application sufficient to satisfy the DTI;

(b) if it appears to the DTI that there are circumstances suggesting any of the following;

    (i) that the affairs of the company are being or have been conducted with intent to defraud creditors or otherwise for a fraudulent or unlawful purpose or in a manner unfairly prejudicial to some part of its members or that any actual or proposed act of omission is or would be so prejudicial or that the company was formed for any fraudulent or unlawful purpose; or

    (ii) that persons concerned with the formation or the management of the affairs of the company have been guilty of fraud, misfeasance or other misconduct towards the company or towards the members (or persons to whom shares have been transferred or transmitted by operation of law); or

    (iii) that its members have not been given all the information with respect to its affairs which they might reasonably expect.

If any of the grounds in (b) above exists, the DTI may appoint inspectors even though the company is in liquidation.

In practice the sequence of events leading up to an investigation is likely to be a dispute between members or between members and directors of the company in which malpractice is alleged; the complainants may bring their allegations before a general meeting and/or the court but without success; finally application is made to the DTI and if the Department is satisfied that any of the grounds specified in s 432(2) may exist it appoints inspectors under its powers under that subsection.

15.8 DTI investigation procedure

Investigation of the affairs of a company is a cumbersome method, which is slow and expensive, and may do serious damage to the interests of the company. The DTI usually conducts a preliminary investigation before reaching a decision whether to appoint inspectors. For this purpose the Department has statutory powers to require the company or any other person to produce books and papers in its or his possession and to provide an explanation of them: s 447. There are penalties and additional powers to prevent evasion: ss 448–452.

The normal practice is to appoint a barrister and an accountant to act as joint inspectors, with powers to question officers and agents of the company, its holding, subsidiary or associate companies: ss 433–436. When the inspectors have completed their investigation they make a written report to the DTI, which usually publishes it: s 437.

15.9 Subsequent proceedings

The DTI pays the initial cost of the investigation but may recover it from those at fault in the course of legal proceedings against them: s 439. The Department may also present a petition to the court for an order for the compulsory liquidation of the company or for statutory protection of a minority: ss 440 and 460. In practice, however, the Department, after exposing malpractice (if any), prefers to leave it to members of the company or other interested parties, such as the regulatory bodies in the City of London, to pursue such further action as they see fit.

Formal investigation by inspectors is a slow process. The inspectors, who have professional work to do, may be unable to give more than, say, one day a week to their investigation. As a result the investigation may take years to complete and the report comes too late for any effective action to be taken. The inspectors' work may be frustrated if suspect transactions have been effected in foreign countries. Yet the inspectors' report may be gravely damaging to company directors and others, who have no opportunity of public rebuttal if they are not charged with any liability or offence, resulting in legal proceedings.

These investigations may also be very expensive to the Department. A single investigation can cost as much as £250,000.

It was decided in 1980 that the Department would usually confine itself to the use of its own powers of investigation under s 447. A dissatisfied shareholder is unlikely therefore to secure the appointment of inspectors, unless the matter has become a public scandal, causing concern to the Department or to the City of London in its wider implications.

15.10 Other investigations

The DTI may appoint an inspector or inspectors to investigate and report on the membership of a company and otherwise to determine who is really financially interested in or able to influence the company. The DTI *must* make such an investigation on the application of the same number of members as may apply for an investigation under s 431: s 442. Alternatively the Department may conduct its own investigations. If there is difficulty in obtaining the required information in either type of investigation the Department may by order restrict the transfer of the shares in question, the exercise of the voting rights attached to them, or the payment of dividends on them: s 445; s 454.

If the DTI has reason to suspect contraventions of the rules which prohibit directors from dealing in certain options and which require them to give notice to the company of their interest in its shares or debentures (Chapter 12: 12.10) the Department may appoint inspectors to investigate and report whether there have in fact been such contraventions: s 448.

Chapter 16

Amalgamation and reconstruction schemes

16.1 Amalgamation and reconstruction

These are not defined terms and their meaning is important only in the context of certain reliefs from stamp duty and capital duty granted in connection with schemes of amalgamation and reconstruction. Broadly an amalgamation is, in company law, the merger of two or more companies and reconstruction is either a transfer of a company's undertaking to another company owned by substantially the same shareholders or an alteration of the capital structure of a single company or of the group structure of a group of companies. The general result of any change of this kind is that an individual shareholder's rights are in some way altered. It is not always possible, especially where a large number of persons is affected, to obtain the consent of all those whose rights are to be altered. Company law, therefore, provides three statutory schemes by which a non-assenting minority may be compelled to accept alterations approved by a large majority; but the minority is also given appropriate safeguards.

16.2 Reconstruction under ss 110–111 of the Insolvency Act

The essential features of a reconstruction of this type are that a company ('the transferor company') which is or is about to go into voluntary liquidation transfers the whole or part of its undertaking to another company ('the transferee company') in exchange, wholly or in part, for shares of the transferee company to be distributed among the members of the transferor company. If such a scheme is approved by special resolution of the transferor company the members of the transferor company are bound by it except that a member who did not vote in favour of the special resolution may by notice in writing to the liquidator given within seven days after the passing of the special resolution (and left at the registered office) require the liquidator either to abstain from carrying the resolution into effect or to purchase the dissenting member's interest for cash. Under this procedure a dissenting member can thus obtain money instead of accepting shares of the transferee company: IA s 111.

The interest of creditors are also protected. Firstly, if the company is in creditors' voluntary liquidation, the liquidator may not carry out the scheme unless it is approved either by the court or by the liquidation committee: IA s 110(3)(b). Secondly, if within a year of the passing of a resolution for winding up voluntarily an order is made for the compulsory winding up of the company, the special resolution to approve the scheme is invalid unless approved by the court: s 110(6). The effect of this provision is that a dissatisfied creditor can challenge the scheme by presenting a petition for compulsory winding up. To avoid difficulties with creditors, which may wreck the scheme, the liquidator is likely either to arrange for the payment of all the company's debts at the outset or negotiate with the creditors for their acceptance of the transferee company as their new debtor, and a release of their claim on the transferor company.

The option of a dissenting member to receive the value of his shareholding in cash cannot be nullified by effecting a sale of assets for shares, under a power in the objects clause, and then going into liquidation. Any such power is applicable to cases where, after the sale, the transferor company is to continue in business. The justification for this is that in liquidation a member has a normal right to a cash distribution.

The transferor company in general meeting approved a scheme whereby holders of its £1 shares (fully paid) would receive £1 shares (17s 6d paid) of the transferee company (under the scheme). The shares of the transferee company to which dissenting members would become entitled were to be sold and the proceeds of sale distributed among them. These arrangements were sanctioned by provisions of the memorandum and articles. It was held that the scheme was void since by statute a member was entitled to require the liquidator to purchase his interest at its value: *Bisgood v Henderson's Transvaal Estates Ltd* [1908] 1 Ch 743.

The usual procedure is to convene an EGM at which two special resolutions are proposed, ie:

(a) to approve a scheme for the sale of the undertaking in exchange for shares of the transferee company; and

(b) to put the company into members' voluntary liquidation.

If resolution (a) is not carried, resolution (b) may then be withdrawn. The notice must specify that a sale under IA s 110 is proposed and also disclose any benefit which the directors are to receive. Resolution (a) usually approves a draft sale agreement which the liquidator is authorised to enter into. The liquidator is required to give notice to members of the transferor company of their respective entitlements to the consideration shares of the transferee company. He may be authorised to sell their shares if they do not give notice of dissent and fail within a specified time to apply for the shares; the proceeds can then be distributed between them.

Dissenting shareholders should, therefore, give notice to the liquidator within seven days of the passing of the resolution and thus require him to purchase their interest at a price which in default of agreement is to be determined by arbitration. They cannot be deprived of their right to that price by any provision of the articles (see *Bisgood's Case* above). If they do not give the statutory notice of dissent and also fail to comply with any prescribed requirements for applying for shares, they may only get what the shares realise on a forced sale. In any hearing before an arbitrator the dissenting shareholder bears the burden of proving the value of his interest; he is not allowed to put questions to the directors to elicit the information which he needs.

Unless the transferor company has sufficient cash in hand the sale agreement should provide for part payment of the consideration in cash so that the liquidator can purchase the interest of dissenting shareholders. Otherwise the scheme may have to be abandoned.

There can be considerable difficulties in apportioning the sale consideration between preference and ordinary shares according to their respective entitlements. These problems, when added to those presented by a dissenting minority and the possible objections of creditors, make this procedure cumbersome and uncertain. It is often possible to achieve the desired result by different means under a scheme of arrangement (16.3 below). But there is some doubt as to whether this is permissible if the transaction falls within the limits of ss 110–111. Obviously it is prudent to effect the sale first and put the transferor company into liquidation after a sufficient interval, so that the sale and the liquidation are not stages of the same transaction, planned and executed at the same time.

16.3 Scheme of arrangement under ss 425–427

A company may, with the approval of the court, make a compromise or arrangement with the creditors or any class of them, such as debenture holders, or with the members or any class of them such as the preference shareholders. In approving the scheme the court may order that transactions such as a transfer of assets or an allotment of shares shall take immediate effect. A scheme of arrangement is therefore a very flexible and effective method of reconstruction (and may save large sums in stamp duty by avoiding altogether the issue of written instruments of transfer). The drawback of a scheme of arrangement is that it requires application to be made to the court at two stages and the documentation, including an explanatory circular, may be expensive. At the second stage of court approval the objections of any dissenting minority are considered and the court may make any appropriate order for them as it sees fit.

The first stage of a scheme of arrangement is to prepare a memorandum setting out the details of the scheme and also an explanatory statement explaining adequately how the scheme affects those concerned. In particular any material interest of the directors must be disclosed. The explanatory statement is issued to members (or to creditors as the case may be) with the notice convening the meetings ordered by the court.

The explanatory statement sent out with the memorandum of the scheme disclosed that the assets of the company had been revalued but not the amount of the new valuation. It was held that this was insufficient information. The court commented that only a small minority of members is likely to attend a meeting to vote in person and that the majority vote by proxy (if at all) and must reach a decision on the documents issued with the notice of the meeting. 'It is for that reason that the court takes the view that it is essential to see that the explanatory circulars ... are perfectly fair and, as far as possible, give all the information reasonably necessary to enable the recipients to determine how to vote.' But information which a banking company is permitted by special dispensation to omit from its annual accounts need not be given (*National Bank Case* below): *Re Dorman Long & Co Ltd* [1934] Ch 635.

The second step is to apply to the court for an order to convene the requisite meeting or meetings. The memorandum of the scheme and the explanatory statement are produced to the court with this application. The court will consider whether the scheme appears to be a compromise or arrangement with creditors or members within the limits set by s 425. But the court is not at this stage concerned with the merits or fairness of the scheme or any possible objections to it.

It is the responsibility of the company, or other applicant to the court, to decide what separate class meetings (if any) should be held. If members of the same class of shareholders have conflicting or different interests in the scheme separate meetings should be called of each group which has a distinct common interest. If this is not done the court may at the second stage decline to sanction the scheme.

H, through its wholly-owned subsidiary (MIT), owned 53 per cent of the ordinary shares of Hellenic & General Trust Ltd ('the company'). On application to the court a single meeting was ordered of all members of the company to approve a scheme by which H would acquire the issued shares of the company for a cash price which was a fair one. Over 80 per cent of the votes (including those of MIT) were cast in favour of the scheme but the National Bank of Greece ('the bank') which held 14 per cent of the shares of the company voted against the resolution as under Greek law the bank would have to pay heavy taxes on the sale. But the resolution had been carried at the meeting by the required three-quarters majority. However, when the scheme came before the court for approval, the bank objected on two grounds; first the interest of MIT, as the wholly-owned subsidiary of H, was so much identified with that of H as purchaser, rather than with the other members of the company, that MIT and the other members were not a single class. A *separate* meeting of the other members should have been ordered and if it had been held the resolution would not have been carried by a three-quarters majority (since the bank held 14 out of the 47 per cent of shares not owned by MIT). Secondly, it was argued that acquisition of shares in this way should have been effected under s 428 which requires acceptance by holders of 90 per cent of the shares and again the bank with its 14 per cent could have blocked the acquisition. On both points the court upheld the bank's objections: *Re Hellenic & General Trust Ltd* [1976] 1 WLR 123.

The decision in the *Hellenic Case* on the second point is in conflict with the decision in *Re National Bank Ltd* [1966] 1 WLR 819. Moreover it is common practice to resort to schemes of arrangement in take-over operations. This point is further considered below.

If the court orders that a meeting or meetings shall be held it will fix a substantial quorum such as members, present in person or by proxy, who have or represent at least one-third of the total votes which can be cast at the meeting. At each meeting the scheme must be approved by a majority in number who also represent three-quarters in value of the creditors or members present in person or by proxy.

If that approval is obtained, the scheme goes to its third stage, ie the result of the meetings is reported to the court which is asked to make an order to sanction the scheme. At this stage a dissenting minority may put its objections before the court. The court is concerned with two main issues. First, whether the statutory requirements have been satisfied as to the nature of the scheme, the holding of separate meetings (if necessary to obtain the approval of creditors or members in their different interest groups) and the passing of resolutions by the required majority at each meeting. Secondly, the court must be satisfied that the majority which approved the scheme reached its decision bona fide in the interests of the class and on a reasonable view of its effect on their interests.

This was a scheme for converting part of each debenture into a deferred income bond on which interest was payable out of profits. The Court expressed its attitude as follows:

'The court must look at the scheme, and see whether the Act has been complied with, whether the majority are acting bona fide, and whether they are coercing the minority in order to promote interests adverse to those of the class whom they purport to represent; and then see whether the scheme is a reasonable one or whether there is any reasonable objection to it, or such an objection that any reasonable man might say that he could not approve it' (Lindley LJ).

Re Alabama, New Orleans, Texas and Pacific Junction Rly Co [1891] 1 Ch 213.

The fourth stage is that the court makes an order to approve the scheme and a copy of that order (and of any ancillary order to implement the scheme) is delivered to the registrar. The scheme is then binding on all members of the class of members or creditors and any transactions specified in the order take effect. If, for example, the scheme provides for the cancellation of minority shareholdings of a partly-owned subsidiary and the issue of shares of the holding company to the former minority shareholders of the subsidiary, those transactions take effect immediately the court order is delivered to the registrar.

The scope of 'schemes of arrangement' is very wide. But there are certain limits placed upon it. Section 425 refers to a 'compromise or arrangement' with members or creditors. It has been used to effect an alteration in the rights of debenture holders or of shareholders in a winding up, since it can be used even if the company ·is by then in liquidation. It can also be used for a reorganisation of the capital structure of a company, including the substitution of securities of another company for those held in the company itself. However there must be some element of 'give and take' on both sides. A simple surrender of rights, without obtaining anything in return, is neither a 'compromise' nor even an 'arrangement'.

Although s 425 does not expressly exclude its application to changes, such as a variation of class rights or a reduction of share capital, for which there is another, specific procedure, the court would probably decline to approve a scheme of arrangement as an alternative. Although the case law is conflicting, it is generally accepted that a scheme of arrangement is an available alternative in the types of transaction described in 16.2 above and 16.4 below. As mentioned above (the *Hellenic Case*) it is doubtful whether a scheme of arrangement ought to be used as an alternative to the specific procedure for acquisition of shares, in a take-over situation, to 'mop up' the non-accepting minority holdings under s 428. However there are two advantages in using a scheme of arrangement for this purpose. First, it is only necessary to secure the consent of three-quarters (in votes) of those who attend the meeting held to consider the scheme; s 428 procedure on the other hand requires 90 per cent acceptance (in shares) from the shareholders to whom the offer is made. Secondly, under a scheme of arrangement the procedure for implementing the approved scheme is simpler than the corresponding stage of s 428 procedure.

On the other hand a scheme of arrangement must always come before the court for final approval – and the court will then listen to objections. Under s 428 there is a right of appeal to the court, but in practice it is rarely exercised and even more rarely does it succeed, since different criteria are applied. This factor, ie the need to apply to the court in a scheme of arrangement, makes it more expensive than the other. Hence it is usually only economic to use a scheme of arrangement if the transaction involves very large values in cash or other assets.

16.4 Acquisition of shares under ss 428–430A–F

This is the procedure, standard in take-over bids, by which a person, usually a company ('the transferee'), whose offer for shares of another company ('the transferor company') has been accepted by the holders of at least 90 per cent of those shares, may compel the holders of the remaining 10 per cent (or less) to transfer their shares on the same terms. Again the non-accepting minority is given safeguards.

The long-standing statutory rules on this subject were replaced in 1986 (Financial Services Act 1986 Sch 10) by a revised version. The purpose of the revision was to eliminate a number of defects and to elaborate the code to bring it into line with modern take-over bid practice. The remainder of this section is a summary of the revised rules now in force.

Any person, including an individual or two or more persons acting jointly, may make a 'take-over offer' to acquire *all* the shares, or all the shares of a class, of a company, which it does not already hold. For this purpose there is excluded from the offer and the statutory procedure, any shares which the offeror, or his associates (as suitably defined) hold or have contracted to acquire. The offer may by its terms include new shares (if any) allotted after the offer is made. Any shares acquired by the offeror, or his associates, by other means, such as market purchase, during the period of the offer are excluded in reckoning the total for purposes of the 90 per cent acceptance requirement.

Any variation of the offer, such as an increase in price, is treated merely as a variation of the original offer and not as a new offer to which new time limits apply. The offer may comprise alternatives, such as securities of the offeror or cash, or a mixture (possibly with the option to the offeree to select his own 'mix') or both.

The *same terms* must be offered to holders of all shares of the same class. An offer for two classes of share, such as preference and ordinary shares, is treated as two separate offers. By way of exception if some shareholders reside in a country whose law prohibits or constrains them from accepting the offer made to UK shareholders, the offer to them may be of some different consideration of equivalent value.

To bring into play the provisions summarised below the offeror must obtain, within four months from the date of his offer, acceptance by holders of at least 90 per cent of the shares for which he makes his offer. As soon as that level of acceptances is reached, the offeror may, if he wishes, without waiting for the four-month period to expire, serve notice on the shareholders who have not accepted his offer that he intends to acquire their shares on the terms of the offer.

If the original offer comprised alternatives, such as an option to sell consideration shares of the offeror to a third party for cash, the same substantial alternative (perhaps by different means) must be made available to those whose shares are to be acquired compulsorily. This principle was first established in *Re Carlton Holdings Ltd* [1971] 2 All ER 1082. It is now imposed by statute because it is only fair that the same inducements which led holders of 90 per cent of the shares to accept should be part of the compulsory acquisition process. The shareholder has six weeks in which to select the alternative which he prefers.

Within the same period of six weeks from receiving the offeror's notice the shareholder may apply to the court seeking either a cancellation of the acquisition of his shares or a variation of the terms. His prospects of success in such an application are poor.

The non-accepting shareholder did not assert that the offer was unfair or the price inadequate. He based his objection on the allegation that at the time when he received the offer he lacked information upon which to decide whether or not it was fair. The court expressed some sympathy but held that as the holders of 699/700ths of the shares had accepted, his objection could not be upheld as sufficient: *Re Evertite Locknuts Ltd* [1945] Ch 220.

The issued capital of Bugle Press Ltd was £10,000 of which the directors, J and S, held £4,500 each (in £1 shares) and the applicant held £1,000. J and S formed another company of which they were the only members and it offered to acquire all the shares of Bugle Press Ltd. J and S accepted the offer in respect of their shares, thereby effecting 90 per cent acceptance of the offer; the new company then sought to acquire the 1,000 shares of the applicant compulsorily, but Harman LJ described this as 'a barefaced attempt' to evade a fundamental rule of company law and upheld the applicant's objection: *Re Bugle Press Ltd* [1960] 3 All ER 791.

Broadly, an objection to the financial terms of the offer is likely to fail, since the court will not set aside the view of the large majority that the terms are fair. But if there is some other factor (as in the *Bugle Press* and *Hellenic Trust Cases* (16.3 above)) the court may have regard to the equity of the matter.

If no objection is made or upheld, the offeror is entitled and bound to proceed with the acquisition on the expiry of six weeks from giving his notice. He sends to the transferor company (i) a second copy of his notice of intention to acquire the shares of each shareholder (ii) a transfer of the shares executed by his representative and (iii) the consideration in cash or shares etc. The transferor company then registers the transfer of the shares to the offeror and holds the consideration in trust for the former shareholder. Any money must be held in a separate trust bank account. Any consideration shares which are not claimed within two years may be sold. Any cash unclaimed after 12 years reverts to the offeror as his property.

Finally, the shareholder who does not accept the offer when it is first made is given a second chance to do so, so that he may escape from the disadvantages of becoming a small minority holder of shares in a company now dominated by a single holder of 90 per cent or more of the issued shares. If the offeror does not elect to acquire the outstanding shares when acceptances reach the 90 per cent level, he must within one month of getting the 90 per cent, give notice to shareholders who have not accepted that this level of acceptances has been reached. The shareholders may then within the next three months require the offeror to acquire their shares on the terms of the offer.

Section 428 procedure is particularly useful in take-over bids for shares of public companies, which have a large number of shareholders. Apart from dissentients, some shareholders will fail to respond or prove untraceable. The offeror can give notice to acquire their shares and then carry it out without need of any response on their part. But, as illustrated by the *Bugle Press Case*, the procedure is also available where the number of shareholders is small and the 'target' is a private company.

Chapter 17

Insider dealing, Stock Exchange regulations and the City Code

(In this chapter citations refer to sections of the Company Securities (Insider Dealing) Act 1985, unless otherwise stated)

17.1 The scope of the insider dealing legislation

In *Percival v Wright* (Chapter 12: 12.17) the vendor shareholders knew that they were selling to directors, who might have inside information. The principle established in that case still stands, ie directors do not 'hold a fiduciary position as trustees for the individual shareholders', though they do stand in that position in relation to the company itself (the *Regal Hastings Case* in Chapter 12: 12.19).

The legislation with which this chapter is concerned approaches the problem of insider dealing from a rather different standpoint. It does not impose on directors any obligation, and therefore liability, towards individual shareholders. It makes insider dealing a criminal offence. The definition of the offence goes wider than a prohibition against dealing by directors. It aims to catch everyone whose connection with a company may give him inside information, which he could use to secure an unfair advantage to himself. On the other hand, it is restricted to dealings 'on a recognised stock exchange' (and some similar market situations). The essential feature of such dealings is that buyer and seller do not know each other's identity. Indeed, the system of pooling (Chapter 7: 7.17) makes it impossible to identify the shares which pass from a particular buyer to a particular seller.

The directors in *Percival's Case* could not have been prosecuted under the legislation now in force since they purchased the shares by private treaty. No offence is committed by insider dealing in the shares of a private company since these shares are never dealt in on a stock exchange.

17.2 Insider dealing

An individual who is or at any time in the preceding six months has been knowingly connected with a company may not deal on a recognised stock exchange in securities of that company if he has information which:

(a) he holds by virtue of being connected with that company; and
(b) it would be reasonable to expect a person so connected (and in the position by which he is so connected) not to disclose the information except for the proper performance of the functions attaching to his position; and
(c) he knows that it is unpublished price sensitive information in relation to those securities: CSIDA s 1.

The scope of these basic provisions is further extended to other individuals and situations as will be explained below.

An individual is connected with a company if he is a director of that company or of a 'related company', ie of its subsidiary or holding company or of a fellow subsidiary in the same group: CSIDA s 9. He is also connected if he is an officer or employee of the company or of a related company or if he (or his employer or a company of which he is director) holds a position involving a professional or business relationship which may reasonably be expected to give him access to unpublished price sensitive information which he should keep confidential unless the proper performance of his duties requires its disclosure.

The individuals primarily concerned are, of course, the directors of a public company. But the definition of 'connected' would include, for example, a clerk employed by a firm of stockbrokers through whose hands passes a confidential draft of a company announcement sent to the firm for submission to the Stock Exchange.

The definition of 'connected' requires that the individual concerned shall be 'knowingly' connected, ie shall have actual knowledge of his connection. If he obtains the relevant information directly from the company his knowledge of his connection should be a reasonable inference. But if he obtains it in some indirect fashion (and is not knowingly a 'tippee') he may well plead that he was not knowingly connected.

The other key term is 'unpublished price sensitive information'. This is defined as information relating to specific matters (ie not of a general nature) relating or of concern directly or indirectly to the company which is not generally known to persons who are accustomed to deal or would be likely to deal in the securities and which, if generally known, would be likely materially to affect the price of the securities: CSIDA s 10.

Information of an impending announcement of much increased or reduced profits for the year, or even the securing of a very large contract likely to yield large future profits, might fall within the definition of price sensitive information. A general impression in the mind of, for example, an employee that the company is doing well or badly probably does not. The directors of a public company are likely at most times to be in possession of price sensitive information, eg from figures based on management accounts submitted to a monthly board meeting, and it is difficult for them to buy or sell shares of the company while holding the office of director.

The Stock Exchange model code for listed companies requires that directors of listed companies should not buy its securities within the period of two months preceding the announcement of the company's financial results for the year or half year (nor sell them in that period save in exceptional circumstances). When a director deals in the securities of his company he is required by the model code first to notify the chairman (or other director appointed to receive such notification); the chairman must notify the board (or other directors appointed for the purpose). A written record is to be kept of notices given and written confirmation is required to be given to the director that his notice has been received. The model code also specifies a number of announcements which are likely to affect the market price of the company's securities. These include announcements of proposed dividends, profits or losses, major disposals or acquisitions of assets, changes in the nature of the business and information required to be given under the City Code (17.5

278

below). It must be emphasised that the model code is not statutory (though obviously it is binding on those to whom it applies). Observance of the code (or of company rules derived from it) would not automatically relieve a director of liability for a breach of the statutory rules.

The basic rules set out above prohibit an individual who is connected with a company from dealing (in the circumstances described) in the securities of that company. The rules are extended to other companies and to other individuals as described below.

If two listed companies, company A and company B, are both involved in an actual or contemplated transaction, the price of the securities of either company may be affected by the publication of information about the transaction (or about the abandonment of a transaction of which information has previously been disclosed). For example, company A may be about to award a contract worth a very large sum to company B. As another example, company A may have begun legal proceedings against company B for very substantial damages or to obtain an injunction to restrain company B from alleged infringement of company A's patents and company A then decides to abandon its claim. Persons connected with company A are then likely to be in possession of as yet unpublished price sensitive information relating to the securities of company B. In such a case any person who is (or has been within the previous six months) knowingly connected with company A is prohibited from dealing on a recognised stock exchange in the securities of company B. The ban ends, of course, on publication of the previously 'unpublished' sensitive information.

The ban also extends to dealings in securities of a company at a time when there is a take-over bid (see 17.5 below also). An individual who contemplates or no longer contemplates making a take-over bid (whether alone or with another person such as a company) for shares of a company in a particular capacity is prohibited from dealing on a recognised stock exchange in the securities of the other company, if he knows that the information of the impending or abandoned bid is unpublished price sensitive information: CSIDA s 1(5).

The reader will readily discern that the language of s 1(5) is far from clear. Its general intention is presumably to prohibit anyone who, in his job or in a professional or agency capacity, has confidential information about a take-over bid, from using that information in dealings in the shares of the 'target company'. It rarely happens that an individual is directly involved in making a take-over bid.

The other major extension of the rules is the prohibition against giving or using a 'tip'. First, an individual ('the tipper'), if he is for the time being prohibited from dealing on his own account, is also forbidden to communicate the relevant information to any other person (not merely to another individual) if he knows or has reasonable cause to believe that the person to whom the communication is made, or even some other person, will make use of the information for the purpose of dealing or of counselling or procuring any other person to deal in the relevant securities on a recognised stock exchange: s 1(8). As an example, this prohibition would apply to a director of a company who passed unpublished price sensitive information about his company to a merchant bank (a person, not an individual, in its collective entity) with a view to the bank advising its corporate clients (persons not individuals) on dealing in the securities of the company. A simpler example is the 'tip' given by a senior executive of the company to his wife's brother.

The tipper may also commit an offence in these circumstances if he merely 'counsels' another person to deal in the securities. This catches the giving of advice, ie to buy or sell securities, without disclosing the price sensitive information which underlies the advice: s 1(7).

Secondly, any individual ('the tippee') who has information which he knows to be confidential and price sensitive in relation to securities and which he has knowingly obtained, directly or indirectly, from another individual who is or was within the previous six months connected with a company and who held the information (to the knowledge or reasonable belief of the tippee) by virtue of the tipper's connection with the company, is prohibited from dealing in securities in any circumstances in which the tipper is so prohibited. There is a similar prohibition against the use by the tippee of information relating to a take-over bid: s 1(3).

To become a 'tippee' subject to this prohibition it is essential that confidential price sensitive information shall be received. An individual who is advised (without reasons given) by a person connected with a company that it would be advantageous to him to buy or sell its shares is not a tippee (unless the specific advice of an insider is regarded as price sensitive information in itself, ie likely to influence the judgment of market dealers, even without any supporting reasons).

The legislation as originally enacted in 1980 imposed restrictions on 'Crown servants', typically civil servants who might come into possession of confidential information in the course of their duties. The scope of these provisions was widened in 1986 (Financial Services Act 1986) to comprehend 'public servants', who are more widely defined. Moreover the DTI may by regulation add new categories. The basic prohibitions, as described above, apply to a public servant. He does not of course have to be 'connected' with a company in order to bring him under the code. As there is no 'connection' a public servant is simply prohibited from dealing in the securities so long as he has price sensitive confidential information about them. A period of 'connection' plus six months is not appropriate in his case.

17.3 Insider dealing: the exceptions

It is recognised that in a number of occupations, situations or offices an individual may properly deal in securities and yet be at risk if he can be regarded as having unpublished price sensitive information. The more important exceptions or relieving provisions of CSIDA s 3 relate to:

(a) a person who acts without intending to secure a profit (or avoid a loss) for himself or another person, eg (perhaps) a forced sale to raise cash to pay a debt;

(b) a liquidator, receiver, or trustee in bankruptcy who exercises his functions in good faith;

(c) a 'market maker' (ie a professional intermediary buyer and seller in stock exchange dealings formerly called a 'stockjobber') so far as he acts in good faith in his business and only has information which he obtained (and was likely to obtain) in the course of that business;

(d) an individual who carries through to completion a transaction and has information of it. For example, an individual who plans and then carries through a take-over bid by making a published offer for shares is dealing in securities at a time when he had (in the previous six months) been in possession of information which was likely to result in a rise in price;

(c) a trustee or personal representative (or an individual acting for a corporate trustee or personal representative) who acts on advice from an appropriate person who does not himself appear to be subject to any prohibition. Thus a trustee, who happens to have inside information, may deal in the securities for the trust, if he is advised by a stockbroker acting in a normal professional capacity: CSIDA s 7.

These formal, defined exceptions, do not provide for the problems which may arise within a large institution or firm, such as a merchant bank or accountants, which have large company clients. It is left to them to make suitable internal arrangements to prevent confidential price sensitive information obtained by one department from 'seeping' into another, where the individuals concerned are not 'connected' through their own duties with the company whose securities are in question.

The legislation applies to dealings on a recognised investment exchange, ie the Stock Exchange and its junior league – the Unlisted Securities Market. There are also licensed 'off-market dealers' dealing in 'advertised securities'; the same prohibitions extend to dealings through this market.

In enforcing the legislation, some difficulty has arisen from the possibility of dealing in foreign countries which have stock exchanges on which UK securities may be listed. There is however a prohibition against counselling, procuring or communicating information with a view to dealings of that kind: s 5.

'Market Stabilisation' is subject to its own regime (s 6), since the general rules would impede the operations of a specialised London market in securities.

The penalties for infringement of the legislation are a sentence of imprisonment for a maximum of two years or a fine, or both: s 8. Since the legislation was first enacted in 1980 there have been a few successful prosecutions. No one can know how far the risk of these penalties has acted as a disincentive against abuses. It is believed that those who break the law usually resort to transactions outside the UK, so that the risk of detection and prosecution is much less.

Until 1986 it was left to the DTI, acting on information obtained from regulatory bodies and other private sources, to enforce the rules by bringing prosecutions in appropriate cases. However in 1986 power was given to the Department to appoint inspectors, with statutory powers: FSA 1986 s 177. But experience of investigation by inspectors (Chapter 15: 15.9) indicates that it is usually slow and extremely expensive, since the inspectors are highly-paid professional men (barristers and accountants) working on a part-time basis. They too are sometimes frustrated by the veil which is too often thrown over transactions in foreign countries.

17.4 Stock Exchange regulations

A company which wishes to obtain and retain a Stock Exchange listing for its shares is required to conform to Stock Exchange requirements. Essentially this is a condition of listing and not part of the body of company law. Its main requirements may be summarised as follows:

(a)   to provide immediate information to the Stock Exchange of a number of specified events to enable the shareholders and the public to 'appraise the position of the company and to avoid the establishment of a false market in its listed securities';

(b)   to forward to the Stock Exchange through the company's brokers copies of proof documents for approval and of circulars, reports, etc as finally issued to members;

(c)   to issue the annual report and accounts within six months of the end of the financial year and also to issue a half-yearly report within four months after the date of the notice convening the annual general meeting;

(d)   to include information on numerous specified matters in the report and accounts;

(e)   to disclose the unexpired period of any service agreement made between any director and the company in proposing his re-election by the company in general meeting and to make available for inspection copies of all directors' service agreements in the three weeks up to the AGM;

(f)   to issue 'two-way' proxies to members entitled to vote at general meetings;

(g)   to issue equity shares for cash only on a 'rights issue' basis to existing members;

(h)   to issue to all members a copy of any circular issued to holders of any particular class of security;

(i)   to certify share transfers and return them on the day of receipt or the next following day;

(j)   not to demand a fee for the registration of share transfers;

(k)   to issue new share certificates without charge within 14 days of receipt of the relevant transfer (or within one month in the case of new issues of shares);

(l)   to split shareholdings into 'designated accounts' if requested;

(m) to issue share certificates in exchange for share warrants and vice versa within 14 days;

(n)   to adopt rules relating to directors' dealings in listed securities in terms no less exacting than those of the model code.

Some of these requirements overlap with statutory rules. Requirement (b), ie that documents to be issued to the public shall be submitted for approval before issue, is the most effective and pervasive control exercised by the Stock Exchange over listed companies. The company is often obliged, by this means, to amplify the information which it proposes to give. Moreover a special transaction may require the issue of a circular to members and the submission of a draft circular enables the Stock Exchange to exert influence over the substance of a company transaction while it is still at the preparatory stage.

It is too early yet to estimate the likely effects of the new regime introduced by the Financial Services Act 1986, and the major changes of Stock Exchange organisation. But the many incidental references in companies legislation to 'listed' shares and a 'recognised stock exchange' indicate the wide range of interaction between financial markets in London and the regulatory legal system. The Council of the Stock Exchange is the designated competent authority to apply and administer certain EC directives: The Stock Exchange (Listing) Regulations 1984 SI 1984/716 (to be replaced by listing rules made under FSA).

17.5 The City Code on Take-overs and Mergers

This too is a system of non-statutory 'self-regulation' which is likely to be developed and adapted under the new regime established under the Financial Services Act 1986.

Take-over bids, ie offers to acquire the issued shares of companies, are subject to statutory regulation under the Prevention of Fraud (Investments) Act 1958 (to be replaced by FSA). The main effect of these statutory rules is to ensure that a take-over bid document shall contain minimum prescribed information. It was recognised in 1967 that this system had failed to check abuses in take-over bids for public companies. Accordingly a Panel on Take-Overs and Mergers ('the Panel') was established in September 1967 by City institutions under the initiative of the Bank of England. The Panel, which is an authoritative supervisory body has a small working staff (the Panel Executive) to which doubtful or disputed points of practice can be submitted for immediate decision (with a right of appeal to the Full Panel). A City Code on Take-Overs and Mergers ('the City Code') has been issued (and is revised from time to time) as a method of affording guidance. The Code contains three main elements, ie General Principles, Rules and Practice Notes (dealing in detail with particular situations).

Like the Stock Exchange Listing Agreement, the City Code is not a statutory code. The sanction for its enforcement is that the institutions represented on the Panel can in the last resort expel from their ranks a member who is guilty of flagrant breach of the Code and the Stock Exchange can suspend the listing of shares of a company which refuses to comply with decisions of the Panel as to the proper conduct of a take-over bid. These sanctions are not entirely effective but open breach of the Code is rare. The City of London takes some pride in this system of 'self-regulation', ie the enforcement of rules which are not rules of law.

The City Code is not part of the body of company law and a summary of the main points suffices here. The main object, expressed in the General Rules, is to procure fair and equal treatment of all shareholders of a company based on disclosure of information and equal opportunity for all. Directors and their advisers are required to assume responsibility for the documents which they issue on the same basis as is applied to a prospectus (Chapter 6).

The Rules prescribe procedure for the various stages of a take-over bid and safeguards against manoeuvres and devices which may be unfair or misleading. As one example, if a take-over bid by a company offers shares of the bidder in exchange for the shares which it wishes to acquire, or if the directors of a company seek to dissuade shareholders from accepting an offer for their shares, a potent argument is the level of profits which the relevant company is likely to achieve in its current or later years. There are stringent rules (but not always effective) designed to ensure that a published forecast of profits is prepared on a realistic basis and that the company's advisers as well as its directors should review the basis of the forecast and state whether they find it reasonable.

Another fertile source of abuse is the purchase in the market of shares of a company before or during a take-over bid. The Rules require full disclosure of these purchases. The price which the take-over bidder offers for the outstanding shares must usually not be less than the highest price which he has paid to acquire shares in the market.

In a public company with a large number of shareholders, it is always to be expected that a considerable proportion of them will not vote in person or by proxy at a normal general meeting. The proportion of votes actually used can be increased by vigorous canvassing, through circulars and newspaper advertisements, in the context of a battle for control of the company. However 30 per cent of total votes may be a majority of the votes actually cast at a general meeting. For this reason a person who acquires 30 per cent or more of the total issued capital is then required, since he may have de facto control, to make an offer to the holders of the remaining shares to acquire their shares.

Chapter 18

Compulsory liquidation

18.1 The dissolution of a company

Just as a company is created by registration under the Companies Act, its existence ends, i e it is dissolved, when its name is removed from the register. In most cases dissolution is effected by liquidation (also called winding up). A liquidator is appointed with the tasks of realising the company's assets, paying its debts and distributing any surplus to members (in liquidation called contributories). A company may go into compulsory liquidation (which is the subject of this chapter) by order of the court. Alternatively, the members may agree to put the company into voluntary liquidation (Chapter 19) by passing a resolution in general meeting.

The registrar has a statutory power to strike off the register, without any liquidation, a company which he has reasonable cause to believe is not carrying on business or in operation: s 652. This power is used to clear off the register defunct companies for which no one will answer. A wholly-owned subsidiary, if it has no assets or liabilities other than a balance owing to or by its holding company, may also by arrangement with the registrar be dissolved in this way without the expense of a liquidation.

The Insolvency Act 1985 made considerable, but piecemeal, changes in the statutory provisions for the liquidation of companies. This new material and the existing provisions of the Companies Act 1985 on liquidation have been consolidated in the Insolvency Act 1986. In this, and the next two, chapters 'IA' before a section number indicates that the reference is to a section of the Insolvency Act 1986. If there is no prefix, the reference is, as elsewhere in this book, to a section of the Companies Act 1985.

18.2 Grounds for compulsory liquidation

The first step towards compulsory liquidation is to present a petition to the court (the Chancery Division of the High Court or, if the authorised capital does not exceed £120,000, the county court for the district in which the registered office is situated). The petition must specify, with supporting particulars, one of the recognised grounds. After hearing the petitioner, and the company or other interested parties if they wish to be heard, the court may in its discretion make an order for the compulsory liquidation of the company.

The grounds upon which a petition may be based are any of the following (contained in IA s 122):

(a) the company has by special resolution resolved to seek compulsory liquidation. This is uncommon since the company may more conveniently resolve to go into voluntary liquidation (Chapter 19);

(b) a public company, incorporated as such, has failed within the ensuing year to obtain a s 117 certificate permitting it to commence business. This also is uncommon since it is usual to form a company as a private company and then convert it to a public company, partly to circumvent the s 117 procedure (Chapter 1: 1.17);

(c) a public company, existing on 22 December 1980, has failed to reregister under the relevant procedure of the Companies Act 1980. This is no longer of any practical importance;

(d) the company has not commenced business within a year of incorporation or has suspended business for a whole year. This is a remedy of last resort for a shareholder who seeks to recover his money from a defunct company;

(e) the number of members is reduced to below two (so that the one remaining member may become liable for its debts). It is much simpler for the one member to arrange for shares to be registered in the name of a new member, making up the minimum of two again (Chapter 1: 1.5). There is no recorded case of a petition presented on this ground;

(f) the company is unable to pay its debts;

(g) the court is of the opinion that it is just and equitable that the company should be wound up.

In practice almost all petitions are presented either by a creditor, alleging inability to pay debts, or by a member, asserting the 'just and equitable' ground. The DTI (in addition to its right to petition on grounds (b) or (c) above) may present a petition following a report of inspectors: s 440 (Chapter 15: 15.9). However the Department usually leaves it to members to pursue this remedy if they wish to do so.

18.3 Insolvency as a ground for compulsory liquidation

A creditor has to satisfy the court that the debtor company is *unable* to pay its debts. As he usually is not in a position to produce details of its financial position the law (IA s 123) presumes in his favour that the company is unable to pay its debts if he can show any of the following signs of insolvency:

(a) he may serve on the company at its registered office a written demand in the prescribed form demanding payment of a debt of more than £750 owing to him. If within the ensuing three weeks (21 clear days) the company 'neglects' to pay the debt or to provide reasonable security for it, that will be taken as evidence that it cannot pay its debts;

(b) he may obtain judgment against the company for debt and then seek enforcement of the judgment by court procedure (execution). Insolvency is presumed if the execution is 'returned unsatisfied', i e if the court officer is unable to find assets of sufficient value to meet the debt;

(c) the creditor may also rely on other sufficient evidence of the company's inability to pay its debts, such as its ceasing to pay its trade debts as they fall due, or a statement of the company's assets and liabilities, which may include its contingent and prospective liabilities.

Although no minimum debt is specified in (b) or (c) the court does in practice require a debt in excess of £750 in each case. It suffices, however, if other creditors support the petition, making an aggregate claim for more than £750, even if the petitioner himself claims less.

The word 'neglect' in (a) denotes a refusal to pay where the company has no reasonable grounds for denying liability. If it does argue that it has credible grounds for denying the claim, the court will dismiss the petition. If of course the creditor has obtained a court judgment, under alternative (b), the company's denial will have been tested and rejected in the appropriate proceedings.

The claim must be for a definite (liquidated) sum. A claim for 'damages', not yet quantified, or for a specific sum less an uncertain deduction, is not sufficient for this purpose.

If the company asserts that it can in fact pay its debts, it must show that it can pay them as they fall due. It is not sufficient to show that it has assets which, if realised, might be sufficient.

The creditor usually relies on a debt, e g for the supply of goods, which has been incurred in direct dealings between him and the company. But it is expressly provided that a petition may be presented by a creditor who is entitled to the debt by assignment; e g a debt collector who has taken over the recovery of a debt may present a petition.

In exceptional circumstances, where the company is acting dishonestly, the minimum of £750 may be waived:

Despite its high-flown name the issued capital of the company was £1,007 and the paid-up capital was 1s per £1 share. It had no assets left and the directors refused to make calls on shareholders. A judgment creditor for £35 was allowed to petition for compulsory winding up as this was the only means of calling up the unpaid capital and so producing cash to pay his debt: *Re World Industrial Bank Ltd* [1909] WN 148.

18.4 The just and equitable ground
This ground, which comes at the end of a list of relatively specific grounds, is not to be construed eiusdem generis with them nor is it confined to those situations on which earlier decisions have been based: 'general words should remain general and not be reduced to the sum of particular instances' (*Ebrahimi's Case* below).

In its earlier applications the just and equitable ground was used in certain specific situations which are still relevant as illustrations. If they recur they are likely to result in an order for winding up on the just and equitable ground. Winding up may be ordered if the company is never able, or ceases to be able, to carry on the business for which it was formed. It is said that the substratum, i e the underlying purpose of the company, has gone. It is necessary, however, to consider the objects clause as a whole. If it permits several alternative activities, the inability of the company to pursue one of them is not grounds for liquidation since it may properly pursue an alternative main object (though the mere exercise of an ancillary power is not enough).

The first four paragraphs of the objects clause related to the acquisition of a particular German patent and the manufacture of products covered by it. The company was unable to acquire the patent, since the German government refused to grant it. The company then acquired a Swedish patent and also sold its products (produced in Germany without patent protection) in Germany as it had always intended. But the court held that 'it was not a general partnership to make a substitute for coffee from dates but to work a particular patent'. A shareholder's petition for a winding-up order was granted: *Re German Date Coffee Co* (1882) 20 Ch D 169.

287

The company was formed in 1899 with the declared objects of:

(a) acquiring the existing engineering business of Kitson & Co; and
(b) carrying on the business of general engineering.

In 1945 the company sold the business of Kitson & Co but planned to carry on other types of engineering business. It was held that the company was not confined by its objects clause to carrying on the business of Kitson & Co which in any case would change considerably over the years. The business of general engineering was the 'paramount object'. A petition for an order to wind up the company failed: *Re Kitson & Co Ltd* [1946] 1 All ER 435.

The most common occasion for a petition on the just and equitable ground is a bitter dispute between shareholders, leading to deadlock in the management of the company's affairs or a claim by a minority that the majority is acting in breach of long-established understandings between them. In many of these cases there is a very small group of shareholders and directors, between whom there has been a close personal relationship which has broken down. Companies of this type are sometimes referred to as 'quasi partnerships' to express the idea of partnership obligations of good faith etc. In *Ebrahimi's Case* below the House of Lords said that the courts may

'subject the exercise of legal rights to equitable considerations ... of a personal character arising between one individual and another which make it unjust or inequitable to insist on legal rights, or to exercise them in a particular way'.

The cases below sufficiently illustrate this kind of situation.

Two sole traders combined their businesses in a company of which they became the sole shareholders and directors. There was provision in the articles for the submission of disputes to arbitration and one dispute between the two men was decided in that way. Personal relations between them became so embittered that they only communicated by passing notes through the company secretary. One sued the other for fraudulent misrepresentation and the latter responded by presenting a petition for an order to wind up the company on the grounds of deadlock. The court noted that 'in substance these two people are really partners' and that if it had been a partnership in form also there were ample grounds for dissolution because the 'partners' could no longer work together. It was not practicable to resolve every dispute arising in the running of the business by resort to arbitration. An order for compulsory liquidation was made: *Re Yenidje Tobacco Co Ltd* [1916] 2 Ch 426.

Ebrahimi (the plaintiff) and Nazar carried on business as dealers in oriental carpets. From 1945 to 1958 they traded as partners, sharing equally in the management and in the profits. N, who regarded himself as very much the senior partner, bought carpets in the Middle East and E managed the retail shop in Kensington. In 1958 the business was transferred to a company in which N and E took 500 shares each and they were its only directors. Shortly after this George Nazar (GN), son of Nazar senior, became a shareholder and a director. N and E each transferred 100 shares to GN so that N had 400, E had 400 and GN had 200 shares. All three were directors and they shared the profits as directors' remuneration. In 1969, following disputes between E and the two Nazars over financial matters, the latter used their majority of the votes to remove E from his directorship under s 303, thereby depriving him of his share of the profits. E petitioned for statutory relief on grounds of oppression of himself as a minority (Chapter 15; 15.6) but this claim failed as he could not make out a sufficient case. His alternative claim for winding up on the just and equitable ground was successful: *Ebrahimi v Westbourne Galleries Ltd* [1973] AC 360.

Ebrahimi's Case was ultimately decided by the House of Lords. The principle that the courts will intervene to give equitable relief against unfair use of legal powers has been followed in *Clemens Case* (Chapter 15: 15.3) though it is unlikely that the courts, always reluctant to arbitrate on disputes between shareholders, will apply it generally.

As guidelines to its approach to problems of this kind the House of Lords said that relief might be given, against the exercise of rights given by the articles or by company law, where:

(a)   there was an association of a personal nature between the members of a company; and

(b)   there was an agreement (possibly implied by conduct as in *Ebrahimi's Case*) that they should all share in the management of the company. In *Re A & B C Chewing Gum Ltd* [1975] 1 All ER 1017 similar relief was given when two out of three shareholders refused to implement in favour of the third an express shareholders' agreement (not in the articles) that each should have the right to nominate one director; and

(c)   the aggrieved minority shareholder has no easy means of selling his shares at a fair price. That is often the position in a small private company whose articles impose a restriction on transfer of the shares.

The third point underlies the decision in a more recent case.

The essential facts were similar, in their origin, to those of *Ebrahimi's Case*. However there were negotiations between the majority and the petitioner for the sale of his shares to them. There was disagreement over the price and the majority offered to submit the matter to decision by an independent expert. The petitioner, however, sought an order for compulsory liquidation. The majority replied that under what is now IA s 125(2) an order may only be made 'in the absence of any other remedy'. The court held that the offer to buy the shares at a fair price did constitute an alternative and so the petition was dismissed: *Re A Company* [1983] 2 All ER 854.

In addition to ruling that relief might be granted without restriction by precedent or by the context of previous specific grounds in IA s 122(1), the House of Lords, in *Ebrahimi's Case*, held that relief could be granted without proof that the majority were acting in bad faith, ie not in the interests of the company.

The earlier case law suggests that a company may be wound up if it was formed for a fraudulent purpose. But there are other remedies by way of minority protection if it is managed fraudulently (Chapter 15: 15.3) or by way of rescission if the shareholder has been induced by fraud to invest in it. The mere fact that the company is not prosperous or is likely to fail is not of itself grounds for compulsory liquidation. The shareholder who contends that the directors have improperly refused to register his transfer of shares may apply under s 359 for an order for rectification of the register (Chapter 7: 7.16). In modern practice the remedy is most likely to be given in cases of deadlock in the management, or of unfair use of majority control, of a company.

18.5   Who may petition?

The petition may be presented by the company itself, or by its directors (or in the appropriate cases by its receiver or liquidator), or by creditor or creditors or by a member or members, who in the context of liquidation are referred to as 'contributories': IA s 124(1). In special circumstances a petition may also be presented by the DTI, the Official Receiver or the Attorney General.

If a majority of members of the company wish to put it into liquidation, their normal course of action is to pass an appropriate resolution (Chapter 19: 19.1) to commence a *voluntary* winding up. But there may be circumstances in which a compulsory liquidation is preferred. A company which is already in voluntary liquidation may, on its own initiative, or that of some other competent petitioner, apply for an order for compulsory liquidation (see the *Southard Case* in 18.6 below). The compulsory liquidation order then has effect from the date of the resolution by which the previous voluntary liquidation began.

Although the law was altered in 1985 to provide expressly that the directors may present a petition for compulsory liquidation, that was probably to clarify a matter of procedure. The general powers of management of the business delegated to the directors (Chapter 13: 13.5) do not include the power to end the existence of the company (*Re Emmadart Ltd* [1979] 1 All ER 599). On that view they would still need to obtain sanction from members in general meeting before presenting their petition.

A creditor is entitled to present a petition for the compulsory liquidation of a debtor company, provided that the amount owed to him (and any creditors who support him) exceeds £750 and that he can demonstrate the company's inability to pay its debts, as explained in 18.3 above.

He may be a secured or an unsecured creditor, an original creditor or an assignee (even by an equitable assignment). A creditor whose debt is payable at a future date or on the happening of a contingency may petition (since s 123(e) permits the court to take account of the liability to him) but he must as a preliminary to the hearing in court make out a prima facie case and give security for the company's costs. But to found a creditor's petition there must in every case be a liability of the company, existing or prospective, of an ascertained amount. A surety for the company who has not yet paid under his guarantee or a person whose claim is for unliquidated damages cannot therefore petition on those grounds.

A member's right to present a petition is defined indirectly by reference to his status as a 'contributory', ie a past or present member of the company: IA s 74(1). But even if he has nothing to contribute, eg because he holds fully paid shares, he has a right to petition for compulsory liquidation. Some persons who are not members, such as allottees of shares which have not yet been registered (Chapter 8: 8.1) nor paid for, become contributories because they are liable to contribute to the assets of the company: IA s 79(1).

The petitioner admitted that she had not been entered in the register of members, but claimed to be an allottee of shares. The sole director of the company contended that her name had been included in the return of allotments by mistake and that she was not even an allottee (Chapter 5: 5.13). The court held that an allottee was a contributory since there was a liability to pay for the shares. As, however, there was a dispute as to whether the petitioner was an allottee, the petition must be dismissed, leaving the petitioner to establish her claim (to be an allottee) in other proceedings: *Re JNZ Ltd* [1977] 3 All ER 1104.

A contributory is only entitled to present a petition if he satisfies two conditions.

First, he must show that he has an interest in the winding up. For this purpose he must generally show in his petition that the company's assets will suffice to discharge its debts in full so that there is likely to be a surplus to be distributed to members in which he will therefore participate. But if he alleges that the company refuses to supply him with accounts or other information of its assets and liabilities he is not required to demonstrate the prospect of a surplus for return to members. If the petitioner himself owes money to the company in arrears of calls due on his shares he is usually required to pay the amount of his unpaid calls into court.

The second qualifying condition is that the petitioner shall have been the holder of his shares for at least six months out of the 18 months up to the date of his petition. But he need not satisfy that condition if:

(a) he acquired his shares by direct allotment from the company; or
(b) he acquired them by devolution on the death of the previous holder; or
(c) the ground for his petition is that the number of members has fallen below two (when delay over a six months' qualifying period would make him liable for the company's debts): IA s 124(2).

The purpose of the second condition is to prevent persons from purchasing shares with a view to the immediate harassment of the company by petitioning for its compulsory liquidation.

The personal representative of a deceased member (or creditor) may petition (or continue proceedings begun by the deceased). But an executor who petitions before probate has been granted must be able to produce the grant by the time of the hearing. The trustee in bankruptcy of a member must first have the shares registered in his name (Chapter 8: 8.5) before he can petition. A member cannot be deprived of his statutory right to petition by any provision of the articles.

18.6 Procedure before and at the hearing

The general rules of procedure are contained in the Insolvency Rules 1986 SI 1986/1925. The petition (of prescribed form and content) is presented in triplicate at the office of the registrar of the court which has jurisdiction to wind up the company (18.2 above). In the presentation of the petition an affidavit, ie a sworn statement that the petition is true, must be made by the petitioner (or by an individual on its behalf if it is a corporation). The petition must also be advertised in the *London Gazette* or in either a London or a local newspaper (according to the situation of the registered office). A copy of the petition is served on the company at its registered office unless the company itself is the petitioner. The company or any other person who wishes to oppose the petition may give notice to that effect to the petitioner who reports to the court. The registrar of the court must be satisfied that there has been proper compliance with these rules of procedure before a date for hearing will be fixed. The petition must be advertised at least seven clear days before the hearing.

After the presentation of the petition there may be an interval of weeks or months before the hearing. To safeguard the property of the company, or for other sufficient cause, the court may be asked to appoint a provisional liquidator to take control until the hearing. If the court does this, it usually appoints the Official Receiver (a senior official of the DTI whose staff are primarily concerned with bankruptcy matters) to act as provisional liquidator for specific purposes only. The appointment may deprive the directors of all or some of their management functions but they still have power to oppose the petition: IA s 135.

Even if their management powers are not ousted by the appointment of a provisional liquidator, the directors should keep in view that an order for compulsory winding up, if made later by the court, will have retrospective effect to the date of presentation of the petition (or if the company was previously in voluntary liquidation to the date of commencement of that liquidation): IA s 129. Any disposition of property of the company from the relevant date of commencement of liquidation will be void unless the court orders otherwise: IA s 127. Assets and liabilities existing at this point must in effect be frozen pending the decision of the court on the petition since payment of existing debts out of these assets would give the creditors concerned an unfair advantage. If the company wishes to carry on its business, using current receipts to meet new liabilities, application should be made to the court, which is sympathetically disposed towards validating bona fide transactions in the ordinary course of business provided that continued trading is likely to be beneficial to creditors and to the company.

The petition was presented on 3 August and advertised on 10 August 1972. Over the period from 3 August to 9 October 1972, when an order for winding up was made, £25,313 was paid in to the company's bank account and £24,129 was paid out in normal settlement of trade debts owing to creditors. The court validated payments made up to 9 August but ordered that payments after that date should be recovered, if possible, from the creditors to whom they had been made. In so far as these sums could not be recovered the bank must make good the deficiency. The court held that it was not proper to validate payments which resulted in some creditors being paid in full out of assets which should have been retained to meet claims of all creditors unless this would benefit creditors as a whole. The proper course in such circumstances was to freeze the bank account at the date when the presentation of the petition became known (ie 10 August 1972 here) and to apply for leave to continue trading, using a new bank account for subsequent receipts and payments. In this case the company by its continued trading had increased its deficit by some £5,000 overall and so continued trading was not beneficial to creditors: *Re Grays Inn Construction Co Ltd* [1980] 1 All ER 814.

When the petition is before the court the petitioner and other parties who oppose or support the petition may be heard. The court has discretion as to whether it will make an order or dismiss the petition or adjourn or make an interim or other special order as it sees fit. A creditor whose debt is unpaid and who establishes that the company is unable to pay its debts (alleging one of the three grounds specified in 18.3 above) will usually be granted an order for compulsory winding up since it is recognised that only in this way can he ensure that any remaining assets are applied in payment of debts. His petition will thus succeed even though it is argued that there are no assets or that the claims of secured creditors will exhaust whatever assets remain: IA s 125.

The company owed the petitioner an undisputed debt of sufficient amount for goods supplied and clearly the company was insolvent. Neither the company nor any other unsecured creditor opposed the petition. But the holders of secured debentures opposed it on the grounds that satisfaction of their claims would leave nothing for the unsecured creditors and that if the company went into compulsory liquidation the lessor of premises occupied by the company as lessee would then terminate the lease and so reduce the assets available to them. The court held that the petitioner was in the circumstances entitled to the order as a matter of justice: *Re Crigglestone Coal Co Ltd* [1906] 2 Ch 327.

But if the company has reasonable grounds for disputing its liability no order will be made, even if it appears that the company is in fact unable to pay its debts. For in this case the petitioner fails to show that he is a creditor entitled to present a petition. The Companies Court will not determine disputes over company liabilities.

A, B and C were equal shareholders of two small private companies. In the course of a complicated dispute A presented a petition for the compulsory winding up of one company and B of the other. Each then applied for an injunction to restrain the other from proceeding with his petition since the debt on which each petition was based was disputed. The injunctions were granted. It was held that a creditor might present a petition based on an undisputed debt even though his motive was to obtain some different and indirect advantage. But if his claim was disputed on some substantial ground his petition must fail . . . 'a creditor's petition can only be presented by a creditor': *Mann v Goldstein* [1968] 2 All ER 769.

A creditor who presents a petition is treated as a representative of the class of creditors to which he belongs. Other creditors of the same class may appear to oppose the petition. In such circumstances the court will usually pay regard to the wishes of those creditors to whom the larger aggregate amount is owing. But the court will also consider what is the reason for the conflict between creditors and may prefer the arguments of the minority if they are more meritorious.

The holding company used its control of the subsidiary to put the latter company into creditors' voluntary liquidation. Later on, however, the holding company and an associate company which were the largest creditors of the subsidiary presented a petition for its compulsory winding up arguing that this alternative would be quicker and cheaper. Seven trade creditors of the subsidiary to whom the subsidiary owed smaller sums (in total) opposed the petition on the grounds that they preferred that the voluntary liquidation should continue under the direction of the liquidators appointed for that purpose. These liquidators were apparently raising questions which might prejudice the interests of the holding company. The court held that its duty was to consider the amount owing to each creditor and also the reasons given by the minority for its opposition. In the circumstances the court would permit the voluntary liquidation to continue: *Re Southard & Co Ltd* [1979] 3 All ER 556.

Other contributories may oppose a contributory's petition, eg on the ground that liquidation involving a forced sale of the company's assets is not the best course. Here too the court will generally respond to the wishes of the majority, unless it appears that their motives are improper or that they are seeking to avoid a necessary investigation of the company's affairs.

Essentially the outcome is at the court's discretion. It may adjourn the hearing so that some other necessary step may be taken, such as holding a meeting of creditors or of contributories. It also has discretion as to the award of costs.

If the court does order compulsory liquidation it is deemed to commence from the date of presenting the petition. A copy of the court order is sent to the registrar who then gives notice of its receipt in the *London Gazette*: IA s 129: s 711.

18.7 Investigation of the company's affairs
The Official Receiver, unless he has already been appointed provisional liquidator at an earlier stage (18.6 above), automatically becomes provisional

liquidator on the making of the court order for winding up: IA s 136(2). But he may later be replaced by another liquidator (18.8 below).

The Official Receiver has a duty to investigate the causes of the company's failure (if it has failed) and generally the history, business and affairs of the company: IA s 132. For this purpose he may require a 'statement of affairs' from persons connected with the company. The persons who may be required to submit the statement are past and present 'officers' (including the directors and secretary), any person(s) who formed the company within the previous year, employees of the company or of another company which is an 'officer' of the company in liquidation (or were so connected within the previous year): IA s 131(3). The persons upon whom the Official Receiver calls for a statement of affairs have 21 days within which to submit a statement in the prescribed form, showing particulars of assets, liabilities, creditors and their securities (if any) and such other information as may be demanded. The statement must be verified by affidavit (sworn declaration): IA s 131(2). On the basis of information obtained by his enquiries the Official Receiver reports to the court.

The Official Receiver may at any time before the company is dissolved apply to the court for the public examination of officers, or former officers of the company, and various other persons connected with the company: IA s 133. At the public examination questions may be put by the Official Receiver, the liquidator, a creditor, if he has submitted a formal claim for his debt, and a contributory. Public examination is reserved for cases of suspected fraud or other serious misconduct. It is a much feared sanction of compulsory liquidation. For that reason, directors who have uneasy consciences will often prefer to institute a voluntary winding up.

18.8   Appointment of a liquidator

The Official Receiver becomes the provisional liquidator at the start of the liquidation. He may continue in that position to the end and he takes over if the position becomes vacant after the appointment of another liquidator.

He is required to decide 'as soon as practicable', and in any event within 12 weeks from the making of the order for compulsory liquidation, whether to convene meetings of creditors and of contributories to choose a liquidator to take over from the Official Receiver. The creditors may however request him to call such meetings; he must comply if the request is made by one-quarter, in value, of the creditors: IA s 136. He is given discretion over calling meetings (in contrast to the pre 1986 procedure) because it may become evident to him that the company's assets are insufficient to pay the fees of a liquidator and that no creditor is willing to guarantee the payment of the fees. If that is so, it is a useless expense to convene meetings which can produce no result.

If the Official Receiver decides not to convene meetings, and is not required by creditors to do so, he gives notice to the court, to the creditors and to the contributories of his decision. He then continues as liquidator though he may apply to the DTI to appoint a liquidator in his place. The DTI however is not required to comply with his request: IA s 137.

If the Official Receiver does convene separate meetings of creditors and of contributories, each meeting may nominate a liquidator. The person (if any) nominated by the creditors' meeting automatically becomes liquidator, though the contributories have a right, within seven days, to apply to the court to appoint a different person or a person to act jointly with the creditors' nominee. If the creditors do not nominate a liquidator, any person nominated by the contributories' meeting becomes liquidator: IA s 139.

No one may be appointed liquidator unless he is an individual (ie not a corporate body) and is qualified to act as an insolvency practitioner. At this point, please refer back to Chapter 10: 10.4, where the rules on eligibility to be an insolvency practitioner are explained; the rules are found in IA ss 388–398 and supporting regulations.

If compulsory liquidation follows after a voluntary arrangement (Chapter 10: 10.12) or an administration order (Chapter 10: 10.11) the court has power to appoint as liquidator the previous supervisor or administrator as the case may be. There are obvious advantages in continuity of management of an insolvent company: IA s 140.

The position and powers of a liquidator and the related topic of a 'liquidation committee' (if any) of creditors and contributories, to work with the liquidator, are explained later (Chapter 20: 20.1 and 2).

18.9 The effects of an order for compulsory winding up

The main legal effects of an order for compulsory winding up are as follows (references are to sections of the Insolvency Act 1986):

(a) winding up is deemed to have commenced at the time of presenting the petition or if the company was already in voluntary liquidation at the time of passing the resolution for voluntary winding up: s 129;

(b) any disposition of property of the company after the commencement of the winding up is void unless the court otherwise orders. See 18.6 above on the purpose and effects of this rule: s 127;

(c) any transfer of shares or alteration of the status of a member made after the commencement of winding up is also void unless the court otherwise orders. The members of the company at the date of commencement are contributories and if they hold partly paid shares they may in fact have to contribute: s 127;

(d) any attachment, distress, execution, etc, in force against the assets of the company after the commencement of winding up is void. But the court may direct that it shall continue in force: s 128;

(e) no legal proceedings may be begun or continued against the company after the making of the winding-up order unless the court gives leave. This (like (d) above) is to prevent one creditor obtaining an unfair advantage over others: s 130;

(f) the liquidator, ie the Official Receiver or any person appointed liquidator in succession to him, is vested with wide powers of management: Sch 4 (Chapter 20: 20.3). A consequence of this regime is the automatic dismissal of the directors;

(g) the employees of the company are also dismissed and they may claim damages for breach of contract. But the liquidator may, by mutual agreement, retain them in the service of the company. He may need to do so if he carries on the business (see (i) below);

(h) the assets of the company remain its property but under the control of the liquidator, who has power to sell them: Sch 4 para 6 and s 144. The liquidator may, if need arises, apply to the court for an order vesting all or any part of the company's property in him: s 145;

(i) the liquidator may carry on the business of the company so far as may be necessary for its beneficial winding up: Sch 4 para 5 (Chapter 20: 20.3);

(j) charges over the company's property and certain of its transactions, if effected within certain specified periods before liquidation, may become void (Chapter 20 Part C).

The dismissal of directors and of employees is not mentioned in the Insolvency Act 1986 but is established by case law. The effect of an order for compulsory liquidation is to terminate the company's power to manage its own affairs as an autonomous entity. Those who manage or work for the company are therefore dismissed.

18.10 Final stages of compulsory liquidation

Unless the affairs of the company are very straightforward the liquidation may take months or years to complete. The liquidator is required, on completion of his task, to convene a 'final meeting' of the creditors to receive his report: IA s 146. He may, while the liquidation is in progress, summon meetings of creditors and of contributories, and he must do so at the request of one-tenth in value of the creditors or the contributories, as the case may be: IA s 168(2).

When the company's affairs have been completely wound up, the court on the application of the liquidator, may make an order for the dissolution of the company from the date of the order: s 568. Within 14 days of the making of the order the liquidator sends to the registrar a copy of the court order. The registrar then removes the name of the company from the register of existing companies. The registrar also gives notice in the *London Gazette* of the receipt of the order: s 711(1)(q).

The liquidator or any other interested person may, however, within two years of the dissolution, apply to the court for an order declaring the dissolution void: s 651. An order would only be made to enable the company to assert a claim to property which belonged to it at the date of dissolution or to enable some person to enforce such a claim against the company. But an order will not be made to enable a company to claim benefit under the will of a person who was living at the time when the company was dissolved: *Re Servers of the Blind League* [1960] 1 WLR 564.

On giving notice to the court and to the registrar of the final meeting, the liquidator vacates office and is released from his responsibilities. While the liquidation is in progress only the court or a general meeting of creditors may remove a liquidator from office. He may in certain circumstances resign by giving notice to the court: IA s 172.

18.11 Early dissolution

If a company's assets do not suffice even to pay the costs of liquidation, the creditors are unlikely to appoint a liquidator, so that the Official Receiver continues in that capacity (18.8 above). In these circumstances, unless the Official Receiver considers that further investigation is required, e g because of suspected malpractice, he may apply to the court for an order to halt the liquidation so that the company may be dissolved without more ado. He must however give a 28-day notice to creditors, contributories and any administrative receiver, before applying to the court: IA s 202.

Chapter 19

Voluntary liquidation

19.1 Types of resolution

The essential feature of voluntary winding up is that the decision to wind up is taken by the members of the company who pass a resolution to that effect in general meeting. But, as in any type of winding up, the creditors have the first claim on the company's assets for the payment of their debts. Unless the directors make a statutory declaration of solvency (19.2 below) the creditors have a decisive influence on the conduct of the liquidation since it must be assumed that all the remaining assets will be paid to them in settlement, wholly or in part, of the company's debts owing to them. This is the basis of the differences between members' and creditors' voluntary winding up.

A company may be wound up voluntarily under IA s 84:

(a) by passing an ordinary resolution when the period (if any) fixed by the articles for the duration of the company has expired or the event (if any) specified in the articles as the occasion for dissolution of the company has occurred; or
(b) by passing a special resolution; or
(c) by passing an extraordinary resolution to the effect that the company cannot by reason of its liabilities continue its business and that it is advisable to wind up.

The resolution of any type is expressed as a decision to wind up. If it is an ordinary resolution it should also refer to the relevant provisions of the articles; if it is an extraordinary resolution it should include the statutory reason given in (c) above, i e actual or prospective insolvency. A special resolution need give no reasons. The resolution to wind up, or another resolution passed at the same or a later meeting, appoints a liquidator.

An ordinary resolution to wind up is very uncommon since few companies have articles which include provision for dissolution at a time or by reference to an event specified in advance. But in such a case a resolution passed by a simple majority of votes suffices to implement a decision already expressed in the constitution of the company. In a situation of insolvency the company's position may be deteriorating rapidly; an extraordinary resolution requires only 14 days' notice in contrast to a special resolution for which 21 days' notice is required.

The members may exercise their normal right to waive the period of 14 or 21 days' notice required for a general meeting (Chapter 11: 11.4). However, unless a declaration of solvency is made, the company must also convene a meeting of its creditors. This requirement imposes certain constraints on the timetable of events, as explained later (19.3 below). Subject to that, the attendance of all members at a meeting or their unanimous consent may serve to validate the proceedings of a meeting which has irregularly convened (see the *Shanley* and *Bailey Hay Cases* in Chapter 11: 11.16). An irregularity in voting at a meeting (as in the *Caratal Case* in Chapter 11: 11.16 will invalidate the decision to wind up.

After passing a resolution to wind up, the company must within 14 days advertise the fact in the *London Gazette*: IA s 85. A copy of the resolution must within 15 days be delivered to the registrar: s 380. Finally, as in compulsory liquidation, every invoice, order for goods or business letter of the company, on which the name of the company appears (Chapter 3: 3.7), must state that the company is being wound up, eg 'XYZ Ltd in liquidation' on a printed letterhead: IA s 188.

19.2 Members' voluntary winding up

If a statutory declaration of solvency is made in accordance with IA s 89 there is a members' voluntary liquidation. But if the directors are not sufficiently confident of the outcome to make such a declaration there is a creditors' voluntary winding up.

The statutory declaration must be made at a meeting of the directors and must be to the effect that the directors who make it have made full inquiry into the affairs of the company and have formed the opinion that the company will be able to pay its debts in full with interest within a specified period (from the commencement of winding up) which may not be more than 12 months. The declaration must embody a statement of the company's assets and liabilities as at the latest practicable date before making the declaration. This last-mentioned requirement obliges the directors to consider the current financial situation and to put on record the figures on which they rely in making their sworn declaration. The declaration must be made by all the directors of the company or if there are more than two directors by a majority of the directors.

The interest to be paid is at the higher of the agreed rate and the rate fixed for judgment debts: IA s 189(4).

The declaration must be reasonably up-to-date, and so it is provided that it must be made within the five weeks before the passing of the resolution to wind up, or on the day of the meeting but before the resolution is passed. The declaration must be delivered to the registrar within 15 days of the passing of the resolution.

If the company nonetheless proves unable to pay its debts in full within the period specified in the directors' declaration (having gone into voluntary liquidation within five weeks after it was made) there are two consequences. First, the directors are presumed, until the contrary is shown, to have no reasonable grounds for the opinion expressed in the declaration. It is up to the directors to justify their error by adducing reasonable grounds for making their declaration. If they cannot do so they are guilty of an offence punishable by a fine or by imprisonment. Secondly, it is the duty of the liquidator, when he forms the opinion that a company in members' voluntary winding up will not after all be able to pay its debts in full within the period specified in the directors' declaration, to summon a meeting of creditors and to lay before that meeting a statement of assets and liabilities of the company. This must be done within 28 days from the time when the liquidator realises that the company is after all insolvent: IA s 95. Thereafter the liquidation proceeds as a creditors' voluntary liquidation, as if no declaration of solvency had been made: IA s 96.

It is normal practice to appoint the liquidator at the meeting which resolves to wind up. For technical reasons it is permissible at the meeting to propose an amendment to the special resolution, to nominate a different person (from the one named in the resolution in the notice of the meeting) to be liquidator: *Re Trench Tubeless Tyre Co* [1900] 1 Ch 408. But in any event the choice of liquidator rests with the members, and the creditors, who may expect to be paid in full, have no say in the matter.

If the members' voluntary winding up continues for more than one year the liquidator must summon a general meeting of the company within three months (or such longer time as the DTI may allow) after each anniversary of the commencement of the winding up. He lays before the meeting an account of his acts and dealings and of the conduct of the winding up within the preceding year: IA s 93.

As soon as the affairs of the company are fully wound up the liquidator makes up a full account of the entire liquidation and calls a final general meeting before which he lays this account: IA s 94. This final meeting must be advertised in the *London Gazette* at least one month in advance. Within one week after the meeting the liquidator sends to the registrar a copy of the accounts and a return that the final meeting has been held (or alternatively that it was convened but not held due to lack of a quorum if that was the case). Within three months of the receipt of the return by the registrar the company is dissolved, ie removed from the register. But the liquidator or any other interested person may apply to the court for an order to defer dissolution to some later time: IA s 201.

19.3 Creditors' voluntary winding up

If no statutory declaration is made and filed, the liquidation must proceed as a creditors' voluntary winding up, even if the company has reasonable prospects of paying and/or does actually pay, its debts in full within a year: IA s 90. The assumption which underlies the procedure of a creditors' voluntary winding up is that the remaining assets will all be applied in payment of debts and so the creditors should have paramount influence on every stage of the liquidation. But the liquidator has a duty to contributories as well as to creditors to discharge his task in a proper manner.

At the general meeting of the company, which is held first, three matters are considered, ie a resolution for winding up (usually an extraordinary resolution referring to the company's inability to pay its debts – see 19.1 above) and the nomination of a liquidator and of not more than five persons to be members of a liquidation committee. The decision whether to have such a committee is taken by the creditors. (On this committee's duties, see Chapter 20: 20.2).

The company is also required to convene a meeting of its creditors to be held not later than the 14th day after the general meeting of the company at which a resolution to wind up is to be passed: IA s 98. Notices of the creditors' meeting must be posted not less than seven days before the date of the meeting. In addition the meeting must be advertised by notice in the *London Gazette* and in two local newspapers circulating in the area where the company has its principal place of business ('the relevant locality').

The notice must either give the name and address of an insolvency practitioner who will in the interval before the meeting supply information to creditors concerning the company, or a place in the relevant locality where, on the two days before the meeting, a list of the company's creditors may be inspected. No charge is to be made for either service.

At the meeting of creditors there are also three matters for consideration. First, the directors are required to appoint one of themselves to preside at the meeting and must prepare a full statement of the position of the company's affairs (with a list of creditors and an estimate of their claims) to be laid before the creditors' meeting: IA s 99.

Secondly, the creditors' meeting may nominate a liquidator. If the creditors' nominee is a different person from the members' nominee for liquidator the former becomes liquidator unless the court (on application made within the ensuing seven days) orders that the members' nominee shall be liquidator alone or jointly with the creditors' nominee. The court may alternatively appoint some other person altogether to be liquidator: IA s 100.

Finally, the creditors at their first or any subsequent meeting resolve whether to appoint a liquidation committee. They may nominate up to five members of such a committee; they also have power to veto the persons nominated to represent the company but this is subject to a right of appeal to the court: IA s 101.

There are provisions for adjournment of meetings and appointments to be made at adjourned or subsequent meetings.

If the creditors' voluntary winding up continues for more than a year the liquidator is required to call annual meetings and eventually final meetings both of the company and of creditors. These rules are similar to those prescribed in a members' voluntary winding up except that they require two separate meetings, ie of members and of creditors to be held at each stage. There are similar provisions for the dissolution of the company: IA ss 105, 106 and 201.

19.4 The conduct of a voluntary liquidation

The essential difference between a voluntary and a compulsory liquidation is that, although there are various occasions for making an application to the court in a voluntary liquidation, it is in its normal course conducted 'out of court'. Secondly, the Official Receiver has no part to play in the early stages; the liquidator is appointed by members or by creditors and is not an officer of the court.

Partly because there are no regular reports or applications to the court a voluntary liquidation is usually simpler and less costly than a compulsory liquidation. The creditors of an insolvent company will often press the directors to initiate a voluntary winding up before they resort to a petition for compulsory liquidation, if their pressure fails. The directors prefer voluntary liquidation because of the provisions for public examination in open court in a compulsory liquidation (Chapter 18: 18.7). Although public examination is rare, it is a risk which it is better to avoid. On the other hand the creditors may opt for compulsory liquidation because, if no other liquidator is appointed, the Official Receiver conducts the liquidation at public expense (insofar as the company's assets do not suffice to meet the costs) and he can more readily bring the directors to account.

In a voluntary liquidation of either type only an insolvency practitioner, who must be an individual, may be appointed as liquidator: IA ss 388–389. In the parliamentary debates in 1985 it was suggested that in a members' voluntary winding up, where the company is presumed to be solvent, this requirement was unnecessary. But it was decided nonetheless that it should apply, so as to close a possible loophole against abuse.

A liquidator in either type of liquidation, compulsory or voluntary, has available a standard list of statutory powers, e g to carry on the business temporarily or to sell property of the company: IA Sch 4. But the powers are grouped into two categories. The first category comprises actions, such as making compromises between the company and its creditors or contributories, for which the liquidator must obtain sanction. The other category of powers is exercisable without sanction. The source of the sanction may be the liquidation committee, the court, or a meeting of creditors or contributories, according to the circumstances of the case. Certain powers require sanction in a compulsory but not in a voluntary liquidation; certain powers of the court in a compulsory liquidation are given to the liquidator in a voluntary liquidation: IA s 165(4) (in a compulsory liquidation the court may delegate them to the liquidator): IA s 160.

The general effect of these complicated provisions is that a liquidator does not generally lack legal powers to carry out his task. If he is in doubt as to what he should do, he may in a voluntary liquidation apply to the court for directions, like a liquidator in a compulsory liquidation: IA s 112.

If a company is insolvent, the creditors have the right to appoint the liquidator of their choice. But they are not obliged to appoint a liquidator at all. If, for example, the company's remaining assets are insufficient to meet the costs of liquidation, there is no advantage to the creditors in pursuing the matter. Indeed they would probably have to guarantee to a liquidator that they would pay his fees if the company was unable to do so.

Yet, in order to attain an orderly settlement of its affairs, the company and its directors may wish to proceed with the liquidation. In such cases a liquidator appointed by the company may hold office until such time, if ever, as the creditors make another appointment. In these circumstances there is scope for abuses which in the past have been known as 'centrebinding' (*Re Centrebind Ltd* [1966] 3 All ER 889 first established that the practice was legal at the time) and the 'phoenix syndrome'. In outline, the directors of a company, which did have substantial assets but even larger debts, deliberately postponed the calling of a creditors' meeting so that their nominee would take office as liquidator for the time being. The liquidator arranged a rapid sale of the assets at an undervalue to another company, owned and managed by the same directors and with a similar name. The new company, like the mythical phoenix, rose from the ashes of the insolvent company, to continue a dishonest course of trading behind the shield of limited liability. When the creditors' nominee took over as liquidator the 'cupboard was bare'.

Changes in the law made in 1985 are intended to prevent the continuation of this malpractice. Until a meeting of creditors has been held (in an insolvent liquidation) the powers of a liquidator (appointed by the company) are limited to safeguarding the remaining assets. Except for perishables etc he has no power to sell assets of the company: IA s 166. It is, however, possible to apply to the court, in a deserving case, for a remission of this restriction.

It is no longer possible to appoint as liquidator anyone but a professional insolvency practitioner, who must be a 'fit and proper person' (Chapter 10: 10.4). The liquidator of an insolvent company is required as a matter of course to report on the conduct of the directors (Chapter 12: 12.3). Among specific points for consideration, in an application to the court for disqualification of a director for up to 15 years, is any failure on his part to convene a meeting of creditors at the start of a creditors' voluntary winding up: IA Sch 4 para 9.

To suppress the 'phoenix syndrome' it is provided that, if a company goes into insolvent liquidation, every person who was a director within the previous 12 months is prohibited, except by leave of the court, from being a director or otherwise concerned in the management of another company which has the same or a similar name. This prohibition lasts for five years: IA s 216.

19.5 The effect of voluntary winding up
To facilitate comparison the summary below follows the same sequence of topics as Chapter 18: 18.9 (effects of compulsory winding up). References are to sections of the Insolvency Act 1986:

(a) the decision to wind up, taken by passing a resolution in general meeting, has no retrospective effect. Winding up is deemed to commence at the passing of the resolution: s 86;

(b) the company's property must be applied first in payment of its debts and any surplus may then be distributed to members: s 107;

(c) a transfer of shares or an alteration of the status of members is void unless sanctioned by the liquidator: s 88;

(d) there is no automatic restraint on seizure of company assets or taking legal proceedings against the company. But the liquidator may apply to the court under s 112 to obtain an order to that effect against a creditor;

(e) on the appointment of the liquidator and his powers see 19.4 above. The directors remain in office but their powers cease except insofar as the liquidator or the company in general meeting (in a members' voluntary liquidation) or the liquidation committee (if any) or the creditors (in a creditors' voluntary liquidation) may sanction the continuance of their powers: s 91(2) and s 103;

(f) the employees' contracts of employment continue unless and until determined by the liquidator. A sale of the business may result in the automatic transfer of the employees to the service of the purchaser: Transfer of Undertakings (Protection of Employment) Regulations 1982;

(g) the position over the company's property is the same as in compulsory liquidation;

(h) the company only has power to carry on its business for purposes of beneficial winding up: s 87. The liquidator has an express power to that end: Sch 4 para 5;

(i) the effect on charges and previous transactions is the same as in compulsory liquidation (Chapter 20 Part C).

In any type of liquidation commercial contracts of the company may become terminable at the option of the other party if the contract so provides, as it sometimes does.

To summarise the main points of difference, a voluntary, unlike a compulsory liquidation, does not have retrospective effect, does not bring the company under the supervision of the court and of the Official Receiver, does not result in the automatic dismissal of employees and does not automatically stay action against the company and its property by creditors. In other respects the situation is broadly the same in either type of liquidation.

19.6 Compulsory after voluntary winding up
Either a creditor or a contributory may present a petition for compulsory liquidation of a company notwithstanding the fact that it is already in voluntary liquidation: IA s 116.

A creditor has merely to demonstrate the normal grounds (Chapter 18: 18.3). When, however, the court hears his petition there is often opposition to it from other creditors (as in the *Southard Case* in Chapter 18: 18.6). Although the court may begin by considering which creditors have the largest claim on the company, it will readily take account of their motives and other factors.

The petition was presented by a creditor who had obtained judgment against the company for £50,000. The managing director and controlling shareholder then put the company into voluntary liquidation, with a liquidator appointed by him as representative of various creditor companies under his control. The petitioner's proxy, who arrived late, had been excluded from the creditor's meeting. In support of his petition, which was opposed by some other creditors, the petitioner explained that he wished to have the management of the company investigated by the Official Receiver. In granting the petition the court said that it was bound to have regard to 'fairness and commercial morality': *Re Palmer Marine Surveys Ltd* [1986] 1 WLR 573.

Although the petitioner for compulsory liquidation often wishes to have an investigation of what has been done so far, it is expressly provided that, except on proof of fraud or mistake, action taken in the voluntary liquidation is valid: IA s 129(1). The burden of proof of irregularity rests ultimately on those who allege it.

19.7 Winding up subject to the supervision of the court
This obsolete procedure was abolished in 1985. A creditors' voluntary winding up, introduced by the Companies Act 1929, has proved a much more convenient alternative.

Chapter 20

Conduct of a liquidation

A THE LIQUIDATOR AND THE LIQUIDATION COMMITTEE

20.1 The position of the liquidator

The two previous chapters have described how a compulsory and a voluntary liquidation respectively are initiated and what is their particular legal effect. In either case a liquidator is appointed with the general tasks of taking control of the company's property and turning it into money from which to pay its debts and then distribute any surplus remaining to its members. This chapter first describes the personal position, powers and duties of the liquidator and then the procedures and legal issues which may affect the conduct of the liquidation.

The liquidator replaces the directors in the general management of the company's affairs but with the task of closing down the business (or selling it) instead of carrying it on. In dealings with other persons on the company's behalf he is its agent (even though appointed by the court or by the creditors) but has no personal liability for the contracts which he makes. In his control and disposal of the company's assets he has the responsibilities of a trustee for creditors and contributories collectively but he does not have legal title to the assets (unless the court by order under IA s 145 vests them in him). If he misapplies property of the company or becomes accountable for it or is guilty of misfeasance (see 20: 20.20 below) or breach of fiduciary or other duty civil proceedings may be instituted to bring him to account or to compel him to make a contribution to the company's assets: IA s 212.

After the company has been dissolved an individual creditor or contributory may sue the former liquidator to recover damages for loss caused by his failure to perform his duties properly.

The liquidator had overlooked a debt owed by the company to a creditor and recorded in the books. He had distributed all the assets without making payment to this creditor, who was unaware of the liquidation. It was held that the liquidator had a duty to invite creditors, of whose claims he was aware, to prove their debts and the mere publication of a general advertisement for claims was not enough. The creditor recovered from the liquidator damages for his loss: *Pulsford v Devenish* [1903] 2 Ch 625.

As the liquidator occupies a fiduciary position he must not secure secret profit from it. He has a right of indemnity out of the company's assets for expenses incurred in performing his duties as liquidator. A person to whom the liquidator becomes indebted for these expenses, eg a solicitor employed in legal matters, is entitled to be subrogated to his right of indemnity.

A liquidator is required to keep proper books of account and minute books of proceedings at meetings. A creditor or contributory may, subject to control by the court, inspect these records:

In a compulsory liquidation the liquidator must pay money received into the Insolvency Services Account at the Bank of England (where it earns interest at very low rates). However, the DTI may, at the request of the committee of inspection, permit the liquidator to use a special bank account for the purposes of receipts and payments in the course of carrying on the business. In a voluntary liquidation the liquidator may use whatever account he chooses except that assets which are unclaimed or undistributed after six months must be paid into the Insolvency Services Account. The sanction of the DTI is required for investment of surplus funds.

There are procedures for fixing the amount of the liquidator's remuneration (sometimes as a percentage of amounts realised and money distributed).

The court may remove from office a liquidator appointed in a compulsory liquidation: IA s 172. In voluntary liquidation the power of removal rests with a general meeting of members or of creditors according to the type of liquidation: IA s 171. As the position of liquidator may only be held by an insolvency practitioner, the liquidator automatically vacates office if he ceases to be authorised to act in that capacity. He may resign under various prescribed procedures, which require the consent of those who appointed him.

20.2 The liquidation committee

In compulsory or creditors' voluntary liquidation there may be a liquidation committee (formerly called 'a committee of inspection'): IA ss 141 and 101. The decision whether there should be such a committee rests with the creditors alone in a creditors' voluntary liquidation (though it may include up to five members chosen by a company general meeting). In a compulsory liquidation either creditors or contributories may insist, against the wishes of the other, on having such a committee appointed, unless the court orders otherwise. If there is no committee the court, or the DTI, or a meeting of creditors or of contributories may have to be asked to exercise its functions or give a consent instead of it.

In a members' voluntary liquidation there is never a liquidation committee. The liquidator refers to a general meeting of members, when it is required or appropriate to do so.

The function of the committee is to work with the liquidator and to keep itself informed of his progress. The liquidator, at his discretion or at the request of any member of the committee, may call a meeting as and when considered necessary. A quorum for meetings is two members.

Apart from its general functions, the liquidation committee has some specific duties. It fixes the amount of the liquidator's remuneration. He requires its sanction for the exercise of certain of his statutory powers (20.3 below).

The members of a liquidation committee like the liquidator are in a fiduciary position and may not secure any profit from the liquidation, purchase any of the company's assets or receive remuneration except with the leave of the court.

A member may resign and a meeting of creditors or of contributories may remove any member appointed to represent them. A member is disqualified if he becomes bankrupt, compounds with his creditors or is absent from three consecutive meetings of the committee without the leave of the members who with him represent creditors or contributories as the case may be. If a vacancy occurs the liquidator may call a meeting of creditors or of contributories to fill it. But the committee may continue to act so long as it has at least two members.

20.3 The powers of the liquidator

It has been explained (Chapter 19: 19.4) that Sch 4 of the Insolvency Act 1986 (following the provisions of earlier company legislation) contains a standard list of legal powers which a liquidator, with the appropriate sanction in certain instances, may exercise. A brief summary will incidentally illustrate the kind of practical problems and transactions of a liquidator in the course of his work. (References are to paragraphs of Sch 4).

The different stages of the liquidator's work overlap in time. The logical first stage is to get control (he does not usually need to ask the court to vest him with legal title under IA s 145) of the company's property. He may bring legal proceedings (para 4) or negotiate with contributories (para 3) or make claims against the estates of deceased or bankrupt contributories (paras 8 and 11). He can carry on the business, with a view to selling it as a going concern (para 5). He will have financial transactions which may include dealings with bills of exchange (para 9) borrowing money on security of the company's assets (para 10) and employing agents such as banks or stockbrokers (para 12).

His power of sale (para 6) enables him to 'realise', ie turn into money, the assets of the company.

He has then to pay the company's debts, either by paying the full amount due (para 1) or by negotiating a compromise with creditors (para 2). 'Winding up the company's affairs' (para 13) may include terminating its commercial and employment contracts. If a surplus remains, after all liabilities have been settled, it is distributed to members according to their entitlement (para 13).

Apart from these general business activities the liquidator is subject to various prescribed procedures for dealing with specific problems, as described in the latter part of this chapter.

B CONTRIBUTORIES AND CREDITORS

20.4 Calls on contributories

At the commencement of winding up every present and past member of the company, plus the personal representatives of deceased members and the trustee in bankruptcy of a bankrupt member, are theoretically liable to contribute to the company's assets, and rank as contributories, even if they have no actual liability: IA ss 74–82. References below to 'members' as contributories include those who represent them as explained above.

A member is liable to contribute if the company is unlimited or is limited by guarantee (Chapter 1: 1.20 and 21) or if he holds partly paid shares or shares which have been issued for an inadequate consideration (Chapter 5 Part A).

In a normal case, however, a member holds fully paid shares of a limited company and is a contributory with no actual liability to contribute (Chapter 18: 18.5).

Those who are members of the company at the commencement of winding up are 'A List contributories' since they have primary liability (if any at all).

Those who are no longer members but have been previously are 'B List contributories'. For them liability arises only if the A List contributory who now holds their shares is liable to contribute but cannot pay and they were members within the year before winding up commenced. Their liability is limited also to contributing to pay debts of the company incurred while they were members and still unpaid: IA s 74.

There are special rules where the company was originally unlimited but was reregistered as limited before the winding up (Chapter 1: 1.23). In this case any person who was a member at the time of reregistration is liable if winding up commences within the ensuing three years. But he is liable to contribute only if there are debts incurred before reregistration and still outstanding: IA s 77. A second rule brings into the net of liability those persons who were members within a year of commencement of winding up, even though the present holders of their shares have discharged their own liability (if any) on the shares. But this rule applies only if none of the members at the time of reregistration is still a member at the time of liquidation.

If the company has made a payment out of capital for the redemption or purchase of its own shares (Chapter 5: 5.18) and goes into insolvent liquidation within the year following the payment, the persons to whom the payment was made and the directors who made the declaration of solvency under s 173(3) are liable to contribute the lesser of the capital payment and the amount required to discharge the company's unpaid debts: IA s 76.

In practice no A or B List of contributories is prepared unless actual liability falls on persons who are to be included in the list.

The power to make calls on contributories is vested in the liquidator (in compulsory liquidation the court delegates to him its statutory power under IA s 150). Those concerned are given a right to state their objections (if any) to being included in the list. The call when made is a speciality debt for which the liquidator may sue within the subsequent 12-year limitation period: IA s 80.

In making his calls on contributories the liquidator estimates the company's deficiency and allows for the possibility of default by some contributories. A contributory to whom the company owes a debt may only set off that debt against his liability on the call if all creditors of the company have been paid in full: IA s 149(3). A liquidator may, with the appropriate sanction (20.2 above), make compromises with contributories over the calls made on them.

A liquidator must make a call on the A List contributory, and await his default, before he may make a call on the relevant B List contributory. Although the B List contributory's liability is limited to the amount required to pay debts outstanding from the time of his membership, what he contributes goes into the general fund for payment of all outstanding debts, whenever incurred.

20.5 Recovery of assets
If the company is insolvent it is likely that creditors will have begun to enforce their claims for payment. All proceedings and seizure of assets is stayed automatically in compulsory liquidation and by the liquidator's application to

the court for an order under IA s 112 in voluntary liquidation. He has also to recover from creditors and others any property of the company which they are not – by reason of the liquidation – entitled to retain.

Any seizure of assets by a creditor in execution of a judgment for debt or by a landlord who levies distress, if made after commencement of liquidation, is or may by court order be void under IA ss 128 and 112. The court would also refuse to make any necessary order, eg a charging order on land or a garnishee order in respect of debts owing to the company, for which a judgment creditor might apply *after* commencement of winding up. If the creditor has at the commencement of winding up issued but not completed execution against goods or land or attachment of debts, he is not entitled to retain the benefit of it against the liquidator IA s 183. This rule deprives the creditor of his rights by way of charge over assets against which execution has issued. But if he has already received payment either by sale of goods seized in execution or by voluntary payment made by the company he does not lose the right to it because he obtained it as a consequence of issuing execution.

A judgment creditor had 'issued execution' to enforce payment of a debt owing by the company. To avoid sale of its goods seized by the sheriff, the company paid the amount to him and the money was in his hands at the commencement of liquidation. It was held that the creditor was entitled to claim the money from the sheriff since it was not 'the benefit of execution' (ie not the proceeds of sale of the goods in execution of the judgment): *Re Walkden Sheet Metal Co Ltd* [1960] Ch 170.

A judgment creditor had obtained a garnishee order, whereby a debt owing to the debtor company by a third party was 'frozen'. The third party then paid the money over to the creditor. It was held that this was 'the benefit of execution' and so the creditor must account for the money to the liquidator: *Re Caribbean Products (Yam Importers) Ltd* [1966] Ch 331.

Case law of this kind incidentally shows how many technical and subtle distinctions exist in this branch of the law.

Normally the commencement of liquidation is the critical date. But if a creditor receives notice of the calling of a meeting at which the company will go into voluntary liquidation (14 or 21 days later) the date of the notice is substituted for the date of passing the resolution: IA s 183(2).

A judgment for debt against a company may be followed by 'execution', ie the sheriff of the county court seizes goods of the company with a view to selling them. (There are modified procedures for seizure of land and recovery of debts owing by third parties to the company). If the judgment creditor receives payment of his debt, and expenses, out of the proceeds of sale by the sheriff, before the creditor and the sheriff have notice of winding-up proceedings, the creditor is entitled to retain the money.

If however the sheriff has the goods in his possession pending sale, or has the proceeds of sale in his hands, at the time when notice is given to him of the appointment of a provisional liquidator, or the making of a compulsory liquidation order, or the passing of a resolution for voluntary winding up, then he must hand over the goods or money to the liquidator. The sheriff may however recover his own costs before he does so, and may sell the goods for that purpose and account for the net balance remaining: IA s 184. If the company pays the debt to the sheriff to prevent a sale, he accounts for it to the creditor, since it is not proceeds of execution by sale (the *Walkden Case* above).

If, however, the judgment debt exceeds £250 and the sheriff has proceeds of sale, or money paid by the company in his possession, he must wait 14 days before paying money over to the creditor. If meanwhile the sheriff receives notice of the appointment of a provisional liquidator, or of the presentation of a petition for winding up or of the convening of a meeting for voluntary liquidation, he must account to the liquidator for the net sum after recovery of his own expenses: IA s 184.

In this case, and in the case of a landlord who has seized goods of the company in levying distress for unpaid rent (for which no preliminary court judgment is required) the court may in its discretion permit the creditor or landlord to recover his debt from the proceeds of sale of the goods. A landlord who has seized goods but has not yet sold them at the commencement of liquidation has no title to them. They are still the company's goods and a sale would be void unless sanctioned by the court under IA s 127. However the court would permit a landlord to recover his arrears of rent by sale of seized goods in a proper case.

The commencement of liquidation causes a floating charge to crystallize. The holder of the charge may then appoint a receiver to take control of the property subject to the charge. If, as is common, the charge comprises the entire undertaking and assets of the company, the receiver's rights prevail over those of the liquidator, who must in general respect the rights of secured creditors of the company. If necessary the receiver may apply to the court for an order requiring the liquidator to hand the property over to him.

If of course a receiver is appointed before liquidation commences, then he will already have taken control of the property and retains it despite the liquidation.

These are the respective positions of liquidator and receiver in a situation in which the liquidation does not render the charge, under which the receiver is appointed, invalid.

The effect of liquidation may be that the charge becomes void (Chapter 9: 9.19 (unregistered charge) or in the circumstances described in 20.14–17 below). In that case the receiver vacates office and accounts to the liquidator for his past transactions and the company property still in his hands.

There is no legal impediment to the same insolvency practitioner combining the positions of receiver and liquidator. But his responsibilities in the two positions are different and so professional opinion is now against such an arrangement.

20.6 Disclaimer

The liquidator has power to disclaim property of the company which is 'onerous', ie an unprofitable contract or property which is difficult to sell or which has liabilities attached to it: IA s 178.

In order to disclaim the liquidator must give notice in the prescribed form. The effect is to terminate from the date of the disclaimer all rights and liabilities of the company (but not of anyone else) in the property disclaimed.

Disclaimer will often cause loss or damage to another person, such as the other party to an unprofitable contract or the landlord of leasehold property disclaimed for the company as lessee. Any person so affected becomes a creditor of the company for the amount of his loss.

Any person who has an interest in property of the company may also:

(a) serve on the liquidator a notice requiring him to decide within 28 days whether he will disclaim or not. If he does not disclaim within that period (or any extension granted by the court) his power of disclaimer terminates;

(b) apply to the court for an order vesting in the applicant the disclaimed property. Its value is then set against his claim as creditor of the company: IA s 181.

There are special provisions (IA ss 179–180) applicable to disclaimer of leaseholds and of land subject to a rentcharge. A copy of the notice of disclaimer must be served on any person who is interested in a leasehold as underlessee (tenant of the company) or as mortgagee. The disclaimer does not take effect if within the next 14 days the interested party applies to the court for suitable relief: IA s 179. The likely consequence is a transfer of the property to the applicant. Except in these circumstances a liquidator may disclaim property without obtaining leave of the court, which up until 1985 he required.

20.7 Debts of the company

In dealing with the creditors of the company the liquidator's duty is to establish that they have valid debts owing to them, and to determine the amount of those debts, and then to pay the debts in due order of priority, so far as the available assets suffice. He is not, however, generally required to pay secured creditors, as they will recover their debts by realisation of their securities (see 20.8 below). But the liquidator may opt to redeem the security, which entails payment of the debt charged on the property.

It is normal practice for a liquidator to write to all known creditors of the company and invite them to submit a formal notice of their claims. He may also advertise, but this is not sufficient notice to a creditor whose debt is recorded in the company's books (*Pulsford's Case* in 20.1 above).

The creditors 'prove' their debts by submitting such particulars and evidence as the liquidator may require. There is a formal procedure for 'proof of debts', with a right of application to the court in some cases of dispute.

The employees of the company may make a single collective claim for their arrears of wages. A secured creditor, if he opts to prove his debt, or such part of it as is not in his estimation recoverable from his security, must disclose his security.

It is the duty of the liquidator to obtain proper evidence of an enforceable debt owed by the company before admitting and paying it.

The liquidator of an insurance company accepted as adequate proof of reinsurance contracts the 'slips' which are usually issued in such transactions. He later paid sums in settlement of these debts. But there were technical defects in these documents and the company had no legal liability to pay these debts. If these proofs had been rejected the company could have paid its other debts in full. The liquidator had to pay to the company a sum sufficient to enable it to discharge its other debts in full with interest: *Re Home and Colonial Insurance Co Ltd* [1930] 1 Ch 102.

It is for this reason that so many of the cases on ultra vires contracts (eg the *Introductions Case* in Chapter 3: 3.13) are challenged by liquidators against claims by creditors. If he suspects that the contract is void, he refuses to admit the claim and leaves the creditor to sue for it.

Claims against the company must be valued at the commencement of winding up, with an estimate of the amount of a future or contingent liability. However a landlord may claim for the whole estimated amount of his loss likely to arise during the remaining period of the lease. A surety for a debt of the company may make a claim before he has actually been called upon to pay the debt to the third party.

The liquidator may negotiate with creditors to obtain a compromise of their claims. The new procedure for 'voluntary arrangement' introduced in 1986 (Chapter 10: 10.12) may be useful in this context. It is available to a company already in liquidation.

The rules on 'set off' are not, as such, part of company law. But they may present difficult and uncertain issues to a liquidator.

The company's bank overdraft exceeded the agreed limit but the company wished to pay a dividend. It therefore borrowed a sufficient sum to provide the dividend from a third party (Quistclose) and paid this amount into a special dividend account at the bank. The bank was aware that the loan had been paid into the account for that specific purpose. When the company went into liquidation the bank claimed (against Quistclose) to be entitled to retain the loan money by way of set off against the overdraft. It was held that the loan money was held by the bank on trust to pay the dividend and for no other purpose. It could not, therefore, set off its obligation as constructive trustee against the company's ordinary indebtedness to the bank: *Barclays Bank Ltd v Quistclose Investments Ltd* [1970] AC 567.

The company had a fixed loan from its bank and also a normal trading account. It was agreed that any credit balance on the trading account, such as existed at the commencement of insolvent liquidation, should not be used to repay the fixed loan. On liquidation, however, the bank was entitled to merge the two accounts instead of repaying the credit balance to the liquidator. The distinction between this case and the previous one is between an agreement not to set off debts and a payment made for one purpose only: *National Westminster Bank Ltd v Halesowen Presswork & Assemblies Ltd* [1972] 1 All ER 641.

A liquidator has the same protection from undue pressure by unpaid utility suppliers as is given to a receiver (Chapter 10: 10.13).

20.8 Secured creditors
A secured creditor is one who by reason of a mortgage, charge or lien, can resort to all or some property of the company for the payment of his debt. Any surplus obtained from the property after the debt and the creditor's proper expenses have been paid is available to the liquidator for the payment of unsecured debts.

In the case of an insolvent company a secured creditor has the choice of four alternatives:

(a) he may realise the security and prove his claim as an unsecured creditor for any balance of his debt; or
(b) he may value the security and prove for the balance (if any); or
(c) he may rely on his security and not prove at all; or
(d) he may surrender his security and prove for the whole of his debt.

If the secured creditor adopts alternative (b) the liquidator may either redeem the security on payment of an amount equal to the creditor's valuation or he may require the security to be sold so that the proceeds may be applied towards payment of the debt. The creditor on his side may, by notice in writing to the liquidator, require him to elect whether to redeem. If the liquidator fails within six months to give notice to the creditor of his election, the liquidator loses the right to redeem the security at the creditor's valuation.

If the creditor adopts alternative (c) the liquidator may redeem the security by paying the debt in full.

A secured creditor must disclose his security in proving his debt and he votes (by reference to the amount of his debt) at creditors' meetings only in respect of the unsecured balance of the debt (if any). If he votes in respect of the debt he is deemed to have surrendered his security.

20.9 Preferential debts

Certain unsecured debts of a company are given priority in payment over the other unsecured debts. If the available assets suffice, the preferential debts are paid in full and only the balance is shared by other unsecured creditors. If the available assets do not suffice to pay preferential debts in full they are paid rateably. Unless the preferential debts can be paid in full from other assets, property subject to a floating charge must be applied first in the payment of preferential debts and the holder of the charge is entitled only to the balance. Similarly in a compulsory liquidation, preferential debts must be paid out of goods (or the proceeds of sale) taken by a landlord who distrains for rent within the three months before the date of the winding-up order. But in this case the landlord becomes a preferential creditor for the amount taken from him in this way: IA ss 175–176.

It is the debt rather than the creditor which is preferential, ie part of a debt owing to a creditor may be preferential, but the balance is recoverable only as a non-preferential debt. This situation may arise, for example, if the unpaid wages or salary of a company employee exceed the £800 limit, as explained in (c) below.

In determining how much may be claimed as a preferential debt, it is necessary to reckon back from the relevant date. In normal circumstances the relevant date in compulsory liquidation is the date of the making of the court order (not the date of the petition). But if the company was previously in voluntary liquidation the relevant date is the date on which the resolution to wind up was passed. If the company was previously subject to an administration order, which has now been discharged (Chapter 10: 10.11), the date of the order is the relevant date.

In a voluntary winding up the relevant date is the date of passing the resolution to wind up.

In a receivership the relevant date is the date of appointment of the receiver, unless the company is then in liquidation, when the liquidation 'relevant date' is maintained: IA s 387.

When the insolvency code was extensively revised by Parliament in 1985 unpaid rates and taxes were largely, but not entirely, eliminated from the category of preferential debts. Preferential debts are now defined by IA Sch 6 as follows:

(a) income tax deducted from the pay of company employees under PAYE rules in the 12 months before the relevant date (para 1). Deductions from payments to sub-contractors in the construction industry are similarly treated (para 2);
(b) VAT owed by the company and referable to the period of six months before the relevant date (para 3). For some other excise duties the period is 12 months (para 5). There is also a 12-month period for certain social security contributions (paras 6 and 7);

(c) wages and salaries of employees of the company in respect of the period of four months up to the relevant date, limited to £800 (or such other sum as may be prescribed) for each employee (para 9). Holiday pay and contributions to occupational pension schemes (paras 8 and 10) are also preferential.

Loans to a company which it uses in paying wages, etc, are preferential to the extent that the wages, if not paid with this money, would have been preferential (para 11). This provision is of great importance to banks, who are often creditors of insolvent companies for sums advanced through a 'Wages Account'. Sums paid by the Department of Employment to employees of insolvent companies in respect of various payments due to them also become preferential debts.

Directors as such are not employees and so unpaid directors' fees are not preferential debts. But a director may also be a salaried employee with a preferential claim for arrears of salary. A company secretary is usually an employee. An independent contractor, who renders services to a company, is not an employee.

The company secretary claimed that his arrears of remuneration were a preferential debt. It was held that a company secretary, if employed full-time, may be a 'servant'. The plaintiff failed in this case because he delegated his routine tasks to subordinate staff and only attended at the company's office occasionally. It was a contract for services not a contract of service: *Cairney v Black* [1906] 2 KB 746.

The company had two accounts at its bank, i e a general account and a wages account. Money was transferred from the general to the wages account and both were in debit at the commencement of liquidation. It was held that the debits in the general account caused by transfers to wages account were just as much loans for the payment of wages as the debit balance on wages account. In deciding how much of the transfers remained outstanding the court applied the rule in *Clayton's Case*, i e credits were set against the earliest then outstanding debit entries in that account. The test is simply whether money was advanced for the purpose of paying wages and whether it was used for that purpose: *Re James R Rutherford & Sons Ltd* [1964] 3 All ER 137.

A creditor who has security for sums owing to him by the company, some being preferential debts and others not, may apply the proceeds of realising his security to the discharge of the non-preferential debts so that he preserves the maximum amount of preferential debt in the net balance of his outstanding claims: *Re William Hall (Contractors) Ltd* [1967] 2 All ER 1150.

The effects of preferential debts on the assets available to the holder of a floating charge and a landlord who has levied distress have been described. The liquidator may, if necessary, recover from them assets which he needs to discharge preferential debts. The company may set off sums owing to it by a creditor to whom it owes a preferential debt; he is then only entitled to priority in respect of the net amount owing after set off.

20.10 Deferred debts
A debt owed to a member in his character of member is a deferred debt which may only be paid after all ordinary debts of the company have been paid in full: IA s 74(2)(f).

This category includes dividends declared before the commencement of liquidation and still unpaid. If there is a surplus the liquidator need not reserve money from it to pay dividends which are so far unclaimed. It is up to the shareholders to prove their deferred debt (see Chapter 5: 5.25 – the *Compania Electricidad Case*).

Ordinary unsecured debts, which are not preferential, such as sums owing to trade creditors, are of course paid after preferential debts have been paid in full and *before* any payment of deferred debts. The payment of any class of creditors in full requires sanction (20.3 above).

20.11 Distributions to members and employees

If the company's debts and liabilities have been fully discharged, the liquidator may then distribute the remaining assets among the members according to their rights and interests in the company: IA s 107. In a compulsory winding up the sanction of the court is required: IA s 154. The liquidator will be guided by the articles as to the rights of members (and classes of members) and as to the method of distribution in cash or kind (e g Table A Art 117). In particular if there are preference shares the articles may provide for repayment of paid-up capital in priority to distribution to ordinary shareholders (with or without arrears of preference dividend). If different amounts have been paid on shares of the same class the liquidator should equalise the position between them by making calls on those members who have paid least or repaying those who have paid most. Nothing extra is due, however, to holders of shares for which any premium was received at the time of issue. Capital is repaid to the persons who are registered holders of shares at the time of repayment.

The memorandum or articles may provide that assets remaining after payment of debts and costs of liquidation shall be applied to some other purpose, e g to a charity or to another institution with similar objects. It is also possible for the company to decide either by resolution passed in general meeting or by the exercise of a power conferred on the directors by the memorandum of articles, that provision shall be made out of its assets for the benefit of employees: s 719 (Chapter 3: 3.14). The decision is most likely to be taken after sale of the company's business and with a view to making voluntary payments to redundant employees. The task will then probably devolve on the liquidator who has statutory power (after discharge of liabilities and providing for liquidation costs – which must take priority) to give effect to any decision taken in the appropriate way before liquidation commences. He himself has no discretionary power to make such payments, at the expense of members, unless a previous decision has been validly taken: IA s 187.

C LEGAL PROCEEDINGS AND PROBLEMS INCIDENTAL TO LIQUIDATION

20.12 Irregularities in the conduct of the company's business

The liquidator may well find that there have been irregularities in the conduct of the company's business before liquidation began. To counter these abuses certain transactions which occurred shortly before liquidation are by statute made void with the result that the liquidator may thereby augment the company's assets available to its unsecured creditors. In other cases the appropriate remedy is to bring proceedings before the court so that those at fault may be brought to account. The remainder of this section is concerned with the revised rules which came into force in 1986.

20.13 Avoidance of floating charges under IA s 245

If a company goes into liquidation or if it becomes subject to an administration order (Chapter 10: 10.11) any floating charge which has been created within a specified period ('the relevant time') before the liquidation commenced or the petition for the administration order was presented, automatically becomes invalid in certain circumstances, as described below.

To bring the charge within the scope of IA s 245 it must have been created within the period of 12 months before liquidation commenced (or the administration order petition was presented). But the period is extended from 12 months to two years if the charge was created in favour of a person connected with the company. Moreover in the case of an administration order, the period is in every instance extended forward from the date of the petition for the order to the making of the order, so that a charge created while the proceedings are pending may be brought within the net.

It is not every charge however which, if made at the relevant time, becomes invalid in the circumstances of a liquidation or an administration order. Normally IA s 245 does not affect the charge unless at the time of creating the charge the company was unable to pay its debts. This may be demonstrated in the same way as in a creditor's petition for compulsory liquidation (Chapter 18: 18.3). But when a charge is created in favour of a person who is connected with the company, its validity may be affected by s 245 without proving that the company was at the time insolvent.

To recapitulate, it is first necessary to consider (at the beginning of liquidation or making of an administration order) (i) whether the charge was created at a relevant time and (ii) whether the company was then insolvent or the charge was given to a connected person. If by those tests the charge falls under s 245, then it is invalid except insofar as consideration for it was given at or after (but not before) the creation of the charge. Consideration which suffices and is secured by the charge is:

(a) money paid or goods or services supplied to the company; *or*
(b) discharge or reduction of the company's debts; *and*
(c) interest (if any) at the agreed rate on either the amount or value of (a) or (b).

Section 245 is aimed at charges created to secure existing indebtedness of the company without financial improvement of its position. It does not invalidate a floating charge created in order to obtain new consideration (or the reduction of its liabilities).

Although the details differ slightly from the pre 1986 rules (CA 1985 s 617 now repealed) the earlier cases are still a guide as to how the principles are to be applied.

The sequence of relevant events was:

(a) an arrangement to create a floating charge as security for advances;
(b) advances made over a period of almost eight weeks;

(c) the creation of the charge; and

(d) five days later voluntary liquidation.

It was held that as the lender had not encouraged any postponement and the money had been lent in reliance on the company's undertaking to create a charge the charge was not invalid: *Re F and E Stanton Ltd* [1929] 1 Ch 180.

Difficult questions of interpretation of the rules can arise when the charge is given to a person who is already a creditor of the company but who continues to do business with it and thereby to give it support in continuing its operations. If, for example, a floating charge is created in favour of a creditor and he then makes a new loan expressly to enable the company to repay the debt existing when the charge was created, the new loan will not be treated as consideration sufficient to support the charge: *Re Destone Fabrics Ltd* [1941] Ch 319. The case below fell on the other side of the line.

The company went into liquidation within a year of giving a floating charge to its bank to secure an overdraft on current account. When the charge was created the overdraft stood at £68,000. Before it went into liquidation the company had drawn cheques to a total of £110,000 and paid in to the credit of the account a total of £111,000 so that the overdraft stood at £67,000 at the commencement of liquidation. It was held that the debt existing when the charge was created had been fully repaid by the subsequent credits (the rule in *Clayton's Case, Devaynes v Noble* (1816) 1 Mer 572 was applied, i e unless otherwise agreed a credit is set against the earliest outstanding debit). The debit balance of £67,000 at the time of liquidation was to be treated as new lending in consideration of the charge, which was therefore a valid security for it: *Re Yeovil Glove Co Ltd* [1965] Ch 148.

20.14 Transactions at an undervalue

A transaction is at an undervalue if the company receives no consideration at all or consideration which is significantly less in value than the consideration given by the company in that transaction: IA s 238(4).

If a company goes into liquidation or becomes subject to an administration order, the liquidator or administrator may, if certain conditions are satisfied, apply to the court for an order to restore the position to what it would have been if the company had not entered into the transaction. 'Transaction' is defined to include a gift, agreement or arrangement: IA s 436. It might be, for example, a charge, fixed or floating, which the court could cancel, a transfer of property which the court could order to be returned to the company, or a contract which might be cancelled.

As with the avoidance of floating charges (20.13 above), a transaction at an undervalue only falls under the avoidance provisions if the transaction occurred at a 'relevant time'. If that, and the other conditions, are satisfied, the court is required to make an order.

The standard 'relevant time' is two years before liquidation or petition for an administration order (plus the interval between petition and order): IA s 240.

The court's power to counteract transactions at an undervalue is restricted to artificial dealings. The court may not make an order to nullify a genuine commercial decision, for which the following justifications exist:

(a) the company entered into the transaction in good faith and for the purpose of carrying on its business, *and*

(b) there were at the time reasonable grounds for believing that the transaction would benefit the company: IA s 238(5).

In effect s 238 is aimed mainly at gifts of the company's property for purposes quite unconnected with its business. Taking examples from the case law in Chapter 3: 3.13, s 238 would probably not be applicable in a *Charterbridge Case* situation but it would in a *Lee Behrens Case* situation (pension to the widow of a deceased director out of sympathy for her needs as the sole motive). The courts will have to decide whether a *Brunner Mond Case* situation is or is not a transaction at an undervalue for the benefit of the company. It should be remembered of course that s 238 only applies if there is a liquidation or an administration order within a limited time of the relevant transaction.

20.15 Voidable preferences

'Preference' is closely related to 'transaction at an undervalue' since each is designed to replace part of what in the pre 1986 law was called 'fraudulent preference' (CA 1985 s 615 now repealed). To some extent they overlap but there can be a preference which is not a transaction at an undervalue (as illustrated by the *Kushler Case* below).

A company gives a preference, which falls under IA s 239, if in favour of a creditor or guarantor it does or permits something which puts that person in a better position in an insolvent liquidation of the company than he would have been if that thing had not been done. There are additional conditions to be satisfied however before the court, on the application of a liquidator or administrator, must make an order to restore the position to what it would have been if no preference had been given.

There are in this case also time limits related to the commencement of liquidation or to the administration order, as the case may be. In addition to the interval between petition and administration order, the 'relevant time' comprises a standard period of six months back from the commencement of liquidation or the petition for the administration order. But this period is extended to two years when preference is given to a person who is connected with the company otherwise than by reason only of being its employee.

The other condition for the application of s 239 is that in giving the preference the company 'was influenced in deciding to give it by a desire' to give preference. But, where the person preferred is connected with the company, otherwise than by reason only of being its employee, it is presumed that the company was so influenced unless the contrary is shown.

It is reasonable to assume that some of the case law on fraudulent preference is still a reliable guide to the application of the reformulated principle of 'preference'.

Shortly before the company went into insolvent liquidation the directors stopped paying trade creditors so that the bank overdraft, which they had guaranteed, was paid off. It was held that this was a fraudulent preference of the bank which must account for the money: *Re M Kushler Ltd* [1943] 2 All ER 22.

The company discharged its liability to a contractor by payment to him of a large sum. This was done so that the company might then purchase its requirements from a cheaper source of supply. As there were reasonable commercial reasons for the transaction it was not a fraudulent preference. In terms of s 239 there was no evidence that the company was 'influenced by a desire' to prefer the payee over its other creditors: *Re Paraguassu Steam Tramway Co, Adamson's Case* (1874) LR 18 EQ 670.

20.16 Voidable transactions: incidental points
The rules on floating charges (20.13), transactions at an undervalue (20.14) and preferences (20.15) are more extensive or more stringent if the person who benefits is 'connected' with the company. A person is 'connected' if he is:

(a) a director or shadow director of the company, or
(b) an 'associate' of such a director or of the company: IA s 249.

The definition of 'associate' (IA s 435) runs to a page and a half of print. Briefly this category comprises a wide range of relatives of an individual; persons connected through employment or trusts; and links through companies under the control of the person in question or his control shared with associates.

There is also a list of the powers of the court when it seeks to restore the position to what it would have been without the transaction or preference which has been made void. Apart from the return of property and the cancellation of charges on company property, the court may order that a guarantee shall be revived and/or security given in support of a liability: IA s 241. In a situation such as the *Kushler Case* the court, in ordering the bank to repay the money, could reinstate the director's guarantee and also any security which he might have given to support it.

20.17 Provisions against debt avoidance
This is a new element in company law, though it is modelled on a long-standing sanction against debt avoidance by individual debtors (Law of Property Act 1925 s 172 now repealed). It differs from the rules described above in two respects i e (i) there is no time limits on its retrospective effect and (ii) it can be applied against a debtor company without proof of its insolvency. It must be a transaction at an undervalue.

To bring these provisions into operation it has to be shown to the court's satisfaction that the transaction was entered into *for the purpose* of putting assets beyond the reach of a person making a claim against the company, or for the purpose of prejudicing his interests in relation to such a claim: IA s 423(3). The same rules may be invoked against a transaction of an individual. Under the old law, the most usual instance of such a transaction was a transfer of property by the debtor or some dealing with it by which his creditors would be impeded.

M had given a legal charge over his land to his bank as security for a loan. The bank began proceedings to enforce its security. M then granted a lease of the land to his wife at its full economic rent, so that the family could remain in occupation even if the bank as mortgagee obtained an order for possession or sale. The effect of granting the lease, even at a full rent, was to reduce the market value of the land, as tenanted property is less readily saleable than vacant property. Under the law then in force (s 172 of the 1925 Act above) the court held that M had acted with intent to defraud creditors and set aside the lease: *Lloyds Bank Ltd v Marcan* [1973] 3 All ER 754.

It remains to be seen whether a court would hold that these facts amounted to a 'transaction at an undervalue' as required by IA s 423. But at least the case illustrates the kind of motive which may inspire such a transaction.

20.18 Fraudulent trading
If in the course of winding up a company it appears that any business of the company has been carried on with intent to defraud creditors of the company,

or creditors of any other person, or for any fraudulent purpose, the court may, on the application of the liquidator, declare that any persons who were knowingly parties to the carrying on of the business in this manner shall be liable to make such contributions (if any) to the company's assets as the court thinks proper: IA s 213. This wording differs from that used in earlier legislation (CA 1948 s 332) in two respects. First, only the liquidator can apply for such a declaration and in consequence a creditor cannot intervene in order to secure a payment direct to himself, as happened in *Re Cyona Distributors Ltd* [1967] Ch 889. Secondly, the declaration requires the persons at fault to make a *contribution* to the company's assets available to pay its debts. This change too emphasises that an individual creditor, although he in particular may have suffered loss, is not entitled to direct compensation.

Fraudulent trading is also a criminal offence punishable by fine or imprisonment. Criminal proceedings may be instituted even though the company is not in liquidation: s 458.

The combined effect of these provisions is that 'intent to defraud', ie 'real dishonesty . . . involving moral blame' (*Re Patrick and Lyon Ltd* [1933] All ER Rep 590) has to be proved by evidence which satisfies the burden of proof in criminal cases, even though only civil proceedings are brought. Guilt must be proved beyond reasonable doubt and not by the civil standard of the balance of probability. The Cork Report (para 1776) noted grimly 'that the difficulty of establishing dishonesty has deterred the issue of proceedings in many cases where a strong case has existed for recovering compensation from the directors or others involved'.

The facts of the leading case below sufficiently illustrate the main issue which is likely to arise.

Although there was no visible prospect that the company's trading prospects would improve, the directors on the advice of the managing director ordered further supplies which he, at least, knew could not be paid for. In holding the managing director liable the court said that it was 'a proper inference' on facts such as these that there was an intent to defraud: *Re William C Leitch Bros Ltd (No 1)* [1932] 2 Ch 71.

However it was the same judge (later to become Lord Chancellor) who shortly afterwards in another case said that there must be evidence of 'real dishonesty'. It rarely happens that there is evidence, apart from mere probability, that the directors both knew that the debts would not be paid, as they fell due, and yet quite deliberately caused the company to incur those debts.

In other cases it has been established that:

(a) a single transaction can constitute 'carrying on business': *Re Gerald Cooper Chemicals Ltd* [1978] 2 All ER 49; and

(b) payment of creditors can be 'carrying on business' but failure to pay one creditor, whose claim was disputed, does not show an 'intention to defraud' him even though no assets remain to pay his debt: *Re Sarflax Ltd* [1979] 1 All ER 529;

(c) only the directors are likely to be held liable since the company officers, such as the secretary, even if aware of the relevant facts, do not take the decision to carry on the business: *Re Maidstone Building Provisions Ltd* [1971] 3 All ER 363.

The Cork Report therefore recommended that, in addition to the existing law on fraudulent trading, there should be a new form of civil liability only for 'wrongful trading' as a deterrent against irresponsibility, not amounting to dishonesty, on the part of directors.

20.19 Wrongful trading

If a company is in insolvent liquidation, the liquidator may apply to the court for a declaration that a present or past director shall be liable to contribute to the company's assets: IA s 214.

It must be shown that the defendant was a director of the company at the material time. In deciding whether to make a declaration of his liability the court is required to consider two issues:

(a) did he know or ought he to have concluded at some time before the commencement of the winding up that 'there was no reasonable prospect that the company would avoid going into insolvent liquidation'?; and

(b) did he take 'every step with a view to minimising the potential loss to the company's creditors', which he ought in these circumstances to have taken?

In judging the director under (a) and (b) the court is required to consider what 'a reasonably diligent person' would have known and done if he had had 'the general knowledge, skill and experience' (i) to be expected of a person in that position and (ii) actually possessed by the defendant director.

This formula goes considerably further than the recommendation of the Cork Report (para 1806), which proposed merely that there should be liability if the company was permitted to incur debts at a time when it was insolvent and when there was no reasonable prospect that the debts would be paid.

There has been much criticism of IA s 214 by bodies such as the Confederation of British Industry and the Institute of Directors. There is likely to be much litigation before it is clear what s 214 means in practice. The critics are particularly dissatisfied with imposing on a director, with the benefit of hindsight, knowledge which he did not at the time possess ('ought to have concluded') and courses of action ('every step') which may not be obvious at the time.

The DTI, however, argued that (i) directors should have an obligation to keep themselves informed of the financial position of the company, eg by consideration of management accounts and (ii) they should be expected to consider possible remedial action, such as retrenchment, in addition to avoiding running up debts which the company could not pay.

The broad conclusions to be drawn are that a director will not escape liability merely by saying that he was ignorant of the company's financial position; secondly, unless there are substantial reasons for expecting a recovery, the directors should, as soon as they become aware that the company can no longer pay its debts as they fall due, either cease trading or take steps to deal with its insolvency in one or other of the ways described in Chapter 10.

20.20 Misfeasance

This topic too is an existing element of company law which has been recast in the overhaul of insolvency law in 1985. The current law is found in IA s 212.

Section 212 may be invoked against a past or present 'officer' of the company, such as a director or the secretary, a liquidator (see 20.1 above), administrator or administrative receiver (Chapter 10), and any other person who has been concerned in the promotion, formation or management of a company, provided that the company is now in course of liquidation.

The basis of liability is that the defendant (in civil not criminal proceedings) has either:

(a) misapplied, retained or become accountable for money or other property of the company; or
(b) has been guilty of misfeasance or breach of any fiduciary or other duty in relation to the company.

In any such case the court may order him to repay, etc, company money or to make a contribution to the company's assets.

Application to the court for such an order may be made by the Official Receiver, the liquidator, or a creditor or contributory.

It is not entirely clear what is to be treated as 'misfeasance or breach of fiduciary or other duty'. In the *Home and Colonial Insurance Case* (20.7 above) a liquidator, and in the *London and General Bank Case* (Chapter 14: 14.16) an auditor (treated as an 'officer' in this context), were held liable for acts of negligence. But other cases have placed more emphasis on the concept of 'breach of duty', which is rather more than negligence. The central concept of misfeasance is perhaps that someone who has accepted a responsibility in relation to the company has failed to show a proper standard of care or integrity in the discharge of that responsibility.

20.21 Criminal and other proceedings

As mentioned above (Chapter 18: 18.7) the Official Receiver may, in a compulsory liquidation, apply to the court for the public examination of officers of the company: IA s 133. There is also a procedure for the private examination of officers and others before the court registrar, ie not in open court.

The DTI has power to appoint inspectors to investigate the affairs of companies, including companies which are in liquidation: s 432(3) (Chapter 15 Part B).

It is one of the duties of the liquidator to conduct a thorough general examination of the past history of the company, to ensure that he traces and recovers all its assets, including sums recoverable from officers of the company as compensation etc. If he discovers evidence of a criminal offence by a past or present officer, it is the liquidator's duty to report the matter to the Director of Public Prosecutions: IA s 218. If the company is insolvent, the liquidator has a duty (Chapter 12: 12.3) to consider whether the conduct of any director justifies an application to the court (by the DTI) for his disqualification. He must in any case review the record of every director and report his conclusions to the DTI.

The effectiveness of these sanctions against misconduct depend on the integrity and skill of the liquidator. The main reason for introducing (in the Insolvency Act 1985) a requirement that a liquidator, and also an administrative receiver, shall always be an authorised insolvency practitioner (Chapter 10: 10.4) is to prevent the appointment to these offices of persons who may be willing to act in collusion with the directors and to turn a 'blind eye' to their past misdemeanours. The liquidator's performance of his duties must affect his prospects of obtaining a renewal of his authorisation to continue to act as an insolvency practitioner. He cannot afford to be lax.

Any past or present officer of a company in liquidation is guilty of an offence if, within the period of 12 months before the commencement of liquidation, he has concealed or removed property of the company (of a value of £120 or more), falsified its records or altered or destroyed them, omitted information fraudulently from the records or pledged its property, which has not yet been paid for, otherwise than in the ordinary course of business: IA s 206.

20.22 Dissolution

Dissolution is effected by the removal of the company from the list of active companies at the registry. The registrar dissolves a company in this way after an interval of three months from receiving notice of the holding of a final meeting (Chapter 18: 18.10 and Chapter 19: 19.3): IA s 205. As explained above, the Official Receiver may cut short a pointless compulsory liquidation and obtain an early dissolution (Chapter 18: 18.11).

It is open to the Official Receiver or any person who has an interest in the company to apply to the DTI for a postponement of the dissolution of the company: IA s 205(3). There is a right of appeal to the court against a decision on such an application. In the same way, if the Official Receiver applies for early dissolution, a right is given to apply to the DTI (with an appeal to the court) against the Official Receiver's application.

If the registrar intends to strike a company off the register without any liquidation at all (Chapter 18: 18.1) he must first follow a procedure which includes formal notice to the company and a notice in the *London Gazette*: s 652. But in this case the company itself, or a member or creditor who 'feels aggrieved' by the summary dissolution may within the ensuing 20 years apply to the court under s 653. In a proper case the court may then order that the name of the company be restored to the register.

These are 'fall back' procedures to deal with the case of a company which is dissolved at a time when it has assets which have not been disposed of or liabilities which could have been discharged in the course of liquidation. It is unlikely that problems of this kind will arise in a properly conducted liquidation. However, some third party may, unknown to the liquidator, hold property in trust for the company or have a claim against it, eg under a guarantee.

Unless claimed through a revival of the company any assets of a dissolved company pass to the Crown as bona vacantia: s 654. Property of this kind is not always worth having and so the Crown, through the Treasury Solicitor, may disclaim it within 12 months of discovering that it is Crown property. In that event any person who is interested in it may apply to the court for the property disclaimed by the Crown to be transferred to him upon such terms as may seem just to the court: s 657(5). As an example, the Crown might disclaim a small strip of land giving access to a house and the houseowner could ask for it to be added to his property, instead of merely having a right of way over it.

Index